The WAR *on* POWDER RIVER

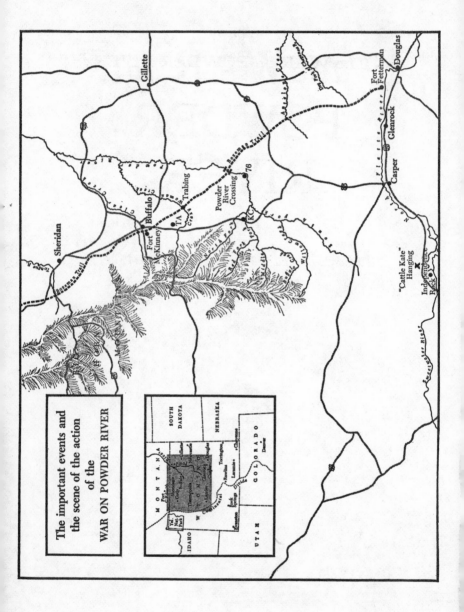

The important events and
the scene of the action
of the
WAR ON POWDER RIVER

The WAR on POWDER RIVER

Helena Huntington Smith

UNIVERSITY OF NEBRASKA PRESS · LINCOLN

First Bison Book printing October, 1967

Most recent printing shown by first digit below:

2   3   4   5   6   7   8   9   10

Bison Book edition reproduced from the first edition by arrangement with McGraw-Hill Book Company.

CONTENTS

PART FOUR: 1891: THE STORY OF A YEAR

PART FIVE: "AN INSURRECTION IN WYOMING"
1892

PART SIX: AFTERMATH

The Johnson County war might have been only a footnote on history's page were it not for two writers who, in reporting history, became part of it themselves. One was Sam T. Clover of the Chicago *Herald*. He was there at the ten-hundred-times-told KC fight, and he set the story down in five newspaper columns, every detail repeated so often since; the siege, the firing of the cabin, Jack Flagg's miraculous escape, and Nate Champion's bloodstained diary.

Sam Clover was a horseback correspondent of the kind brought forth by the Indian wars. He was also the kind of smart reporter who always manages to be there when the story breaks. Some people found his smartness objectionable, but he achieved one of the great eyewitness triumphs of nineteenth-century reporting. Behind it lay two years of covering assignments for the *Herald* in the West. He had reported some troubles between Indians and whites on the Cheyenne reservation in Montana, and at the end of 1890 he was sent to Fort Yates, North Dakota, where the ghost-dance excitement was in full swing on the Standing Rock reservation, where Sitting Bull was interned and a mortal feud was in progress between Agent McLoughin and the old Sioux leader. That story has been told by Stanley Vestal.

At Fort Yates Clover struck up a great friendship with Captain Edmond G. Fechet of the 8th Cavalry, later Major Fechet of the Sixth; and he was riding with Captain Fechet at the head of the column when the final fight transpired and Sitting Bull was killed.

After a year back in Chicago—it was shortly after Christmas, 1891— Clover went down to the stockyards to look for possible feature stories on cattle shippers from the West. There he ran into an acquaintance from Montana who tipped him off on a coming expedition against Wyoming cattle thieves. Clover and his editor decided that the tip might be worth investigating. It was.

The second scribe who both reported history and made it was Asa Shinn Mercer, publisher of the *Northwestern Livestock Journal* in Cheyenne. For eight years the paper had been a mouthpiece for the cattlemen, but a few months after the invasion Mercer turned and denounced them in violent terms, not without suspicion of political motives. He was boycotted, sued, and beaten; his printing plant was seized. Two years later, in 1894, he published a little book resoundingly entitled *The Banditti of the Plains, or the Cattlemen's Invasion of Wyoming in 1892. The Crowning Infamy of the Ages.* The cattlemen managed to seize and destroy most of the copies that came off the press. Such tactics have made lesser books famous; they made Mercer's immortal. The book is long since back in print and available on every library shelf, but on the rare occasions one of the original edition comes onto the market—not oftener than once every few years—it sells in three figures.

Two other chroniclers of the Johnson County incident and its preceding events dwelt at the hurricane's eye of their own story. John Clay, Jr., the bullet-headed Scottish businessman who came out to Wyoming in the early eighties as a promoter of cattle companies, was not directly involved in the fracas, but he is the historian *par excellence* of that superb folly, the great beef bonanza on the western plains. Call it the cattle craze, the beef bubble, or what you will, he was in the thick of it from start to finish and was one of the few who came out still wearing his shirt. But while he writes freely enough on the financial excesses of the time, he is silent on the errors of policy committed by the Wyoming Stock Growers' Association in those years; not surprisingly, since he himself was one of the chief authors of the policy and the errors. He omits all mention, for instance, of the violently unpopular maverick laws, or the secret employment blacklist, or the reckless use of the roundup boycott against small independent ranchmen on the increasingly general assumption that they were probably thieves, or potential thieves, or "sympathizers with thieves"—an assumption not only general but dangerous as well.

The fourth author on the they-were-there list was one of the rustlers. The controversy over what the term meant and who was or was not one will doubtless go on until doomsday. Jack Flagg was called a cow thief. He was, in any event, a rebel who twisted the tails of the big outfits by all means—fair or foul. At any rate he was a highly intelligent man, a cowboy, schoolteacher, editor, author, and politician of exceptional ability.

"A Review of the Cattle Business in Johnson County, Wyoming, Since 1882, and the Causes That Led to the Recent Invasion" by Oscar H. Flagg has been ignored by every historian of the period until now with the exception of one who borrowed extensively from it without acknowledgment. Never yet between covers, it ran serially in the weekly Buffalo (Wyoming) *Bulletin* for eleven installments in 1892, the first appearing

when Nate Champion was scarcely three weeks in his grave. The book
is biased where its author's personal conflicts are involved but is largely
accurate in regard to general facts, as revealed by crosschecking with
other sources. It gives the best close-up picture in existence of the
feuds on Powder River, and it is a remarkable piece of work in view
of its author's lack of training.

Jack Flagg was born in West Virginia in 1861 and left home as a
lad to go to Texas at the height of the cow-trail fever. He came up to
Wyoming with a herd in 1882 and thereafter punched cows in Johnson
County, working at least three years for the English-owned Bar C
outfit on Powder River. Then he was blackballed by the all-powerful
Stock Growers' Association, which amounted to declaring him an outlaw. In return he declared war on the big outfits. From their own point
of view they were quite right in calling him a dangerous man.

A C K N O W L E D G M E N T S

I will begin this list where so many others have begun, with thanks to that
great mother of research, the Library of Congress; especially to the staff of
the newspaper room, who toted huge musty volumes and threaded microfilms
—I never could learn to thread them myself—with inexhaustible patience for
several years. To Dr. J. R. K. Kantor, at the time reference librarian of the
Bancroft Library, who answered an interminable flow of inquiries and supplied
material; and to Miss Margaret Digby, director of the Plunkett Foundation
for Co-Operative Studies in London, who put me on the track of the microfilmed Horace Plunkett diaries.

Great thanks to Dr. Gene M. Gressley, archivist of the University of
Wyoming at Laramie, and to Professor T. A. Larson, head of the history department, who not only placed all their historical materials at my disposal but
showed kindness above and beyond the call of duty, since I landed by air
in Laramie for my second visit at a moment when the town's only taxi company
had gone out of business, so they ferried me about in their own cars when-
ever I needed a lift, which was oftener than daily. Thanks to Lola Homsher,
director of the state historical library in Cheyenne; and to Russell Thorp, old
friend, all-round Wyoming expert and for many years secretary of the Wyoming
Stock Growers' Association, who disagreed with practically every word he
knew I was going to write, yet gave unstinted help in obtaining the information wherewith to write it.

And thanks to the friends of an unforgettable summer in Buffalo, all of
them steeped in memories of the conflict on one side or the other; to Thelma
Gatchell Condit, Powder River historian; to Anita Webb Deininger, descended
doubly from the "rustler" side in the war, being the daughter of Lou Webb of
the "Hat" outfit and granddaughter of A. S. Mercer, the controversial historian;

to Fred W. Hesse, one generation removed from the cattlemen's side, and to his wife Edith who listened patiently to our interminable discussions; to the late Johnny Tisdale; to Burton S. Hill, history-collecting lawyer; and to Margaret Reinbold, chauffeur extraordinary, who drove our party of history-seekers from Powder River Crossing to the head of Red Fork and the head of Middle Fork and the red sandstone walls and secret places of the Hole in the Wall, on down to the canyons and carved abutments of the creeks on the western slope, over roads some of which would make even a mule stop and think twice. To Frank Hicks of the *Buffalo Bulletin,* who furnished office space in which I pored for weeks over the ancient files of his paper, hitting a jackpot almost every day. To Mrs. J. Elmer Brock, who made available some of her late husband's papers. To Oliver Gray Norval, whose unique contribution to the solution of the George Dunning mystery will be cited in its place.

To the late Ralph Mercer and his wife Jennie, who entertained me at their ranch above the Big Horn Basin one afternoon and showed me an album of precious unpublished photographs, some of which appear in this book. To Lamar Moore of Winslow, Arizona, whose apparently inexhaustible collection of Western items culled from obscure local newspapers rescued more than one chapter from a bog of inconclusiveness, into which it was falling when my research leads ran out.

To Lewis L. Gould of Yale University, who is completing his doctoral dissertation on "Willis Van Devanter in Wyoming Politics: 1884–1897," based on a study of the Van Devanter papers and those of Francis E. Warren. Beside supplying me with a number of valuable leads, he let me read the manuscript of "Lawyer for the Cattlemen: the Unpublished Papers of Willis Van Devanter on the Johnson County War," an article which will appear in an early issue of *Montana.* He directed me to the papers of United States Marshal Joseph P. Rankin in the National Archives, which solved the problems of two near-final chapters—the Wellman murder and the martial-law conspiracy—on which I had reached a dead end and my wits' end simultaneously.

To any number of lawyers and scholars and government experts who supplied information and advice, often on the spur of the moment; and, on the local scene, one more amateur of history, Johnson County Sheriff B. H. Turk, whose collection furnished two priceless remembrances of the old days in two unique and never before published photographs.

H.H.S.

Alexandria, Virginia

"Cattle Thieves, Beware!"

On the blizzardy morning of April 9, 1892, fifty armed men surrounded a cabin on Powder River in which two alleged cattle rustlers had been spending the night. The first rustler was shot as he came down the path for the morning bucket of water; he was dragged over the doorstep by his companion to die inside. The second man held out until afternoon, when the besiegers fired the house. Driven out by the flames, he went down with a dozen bullets in him. In the purple prose of an eyewitness writing a few days later:

Nate Champion, the king of the cattle thieves and the bravest man in Johnson County, was dead. Prone upon his back, with his teeth clinched and a look of mingled defiance and determination on his face to the last, the intrepid rustler met his fate without a groan and paid the penalty of his crimes with his life.

A card bearing the significant legend, "Cattle Thieves, Beware" was pinned to his blood-soaked vest, and there in the dawn, with his red sash tied around him and his half-closed eyes raised toward the blue sky, this brave but misguided man was left to lie by the band of regulators who ... rapidly withdrew from the scene of the double tragedy.

In fact, the time of day was not dawn but late afternoon, the former being a bit of poetic license on the part of the Chicago *Herald's* Sam Clover, the only newspaperman ever known to have been invited by lynchers to witness a lynching.

Was this just another shoot-'em-up from the gory annals of the West, in which fiction and fact have become so intermingled that the former often obscures the latter? Who were the "regulators?" Rude men on a far frontier, taking the law into their own hands for the protection of society (which of course would approve, just as it did in *The Virginian*)?

Hardly. In the first place Wyoming, in its second year of statehood, was scarcely a frontier any longer. In the second place the "regulators" were men of wealth and education and prominence not only in Wyoming but also in the East, so much so that when they fell into serious trouble the President of the United States sent troops to bail them out.

Two of the leaders were Harvard graduates; one a well-born Bostonian, the other the scion of a Wall Street banking family. One was from Pennsylvania, one was English, and one had been a Union officer from Kentucky in the Civil War. Five members of the party were livestock detectives in the pay of the cattlemen, two of them being under indictment in Wyoming, one for assault and the other for murder. Twenty-five of the group consisted of young professional gunmen from Texas, hired for the occasion, few of whom, it was said, had any idea of what they were getting into.

The leaders had thought of themselves as righteous men going forth to erase a gang of thieves; and they had the wherewithal, for by the time their expedition was finished, including a little matter of trouble with the courts, it had cost them more than $100,000. They had expected the people to rise in their support; the people rose, but in such a wave of fury as the West has never seen before or since. Thirty hours after their grisly victory on Powder River, the invaders were besieged in their turn by an army of several hundred hornet-mad cowboys and small-ranchmen, who would have meted out to them the same fate they had dealt their victims if the two United States senators from Wyoming had not been feverishly busy in Washington on their behalf. These gentlemen persuaded President Benjamin Harrison to order out the troops from nearby Fort McKinney, and the cattlemen's surrender was accepted in a somewhat ignominious mixture of rescue and arrest. So ended the Johnson County "invasion." Tragic and bizarre, it split the young state from scalp to toenails. The scars still show.

The fatal mistake made by the invaders lay in supposing that they had a crime wave on their hands in Johnson County when what they had was a war of rebellion.

It was not a war in the sense of pitched battles between masses of men. The invasion was the culmination of another kind of conflict, economic and savagely personal, between the few who had and were determined to keep and the many who wanted their share, a conflict which had been going on with mounting ugliness for six years. It was a war of the shot in the back from ambush on a lonely road under a pitiless sky, of the sudden descent by a little party of armed men and a body left dangling from a tree; a war in which the other side fought back with the rustler's weapons, the rope and the running iron, and the snarling dispute over who began it will never be settled.

Nor did it end with the capture of the misguided invaders. Its aftermath of more killing and bitter feuding went on for another two years before hostilities finally ceased.

The bitterly opposed measures which built up to the trouble applied to the whole Territory, yet they did not involve all of it. On the western slope of the mighty rampart of the Rockies which divides Wyoming in two there were happy counties which had no history, so far as the conflict of the eighties and early nineties was concerned.

Why? Who knows. Except that this was not a war of faceless men dropping bombs on other faceless men they never see except in their nightmares of hell. In the daily intimacy of range and campfire it was as personal as love, and twice as long-lasting. Before that bloody April morning on the Middle Fork of Powder River Mike Shonsey had been mixed up in an earlier attempt to kill Nate Champion, and in return Champion had twice humiliated him.

For some reason the personal feuds and the economic conflicts became concentrated in the northeastern quarter of Wyoming, on the eastern slope of the Big Horns, where the multiple headwaters of Powder River attracted adventurers and investors and the green grass grew and the cattle waxed fat. Until.

The Powder River
Country

POWDER RIVER is a very special stream with a special trick of nomenclature. Never under any circumstances are you to refer to it as "the Powder," or even as "the Powder River." The only people who didn't know this then and don't today are Army officers and highbrows. The Army referred to it as "the Powder," but the Army also brought infantry to fight mounted Indians, and imported hay into a country covered with the best grass in the world.

Only a few of the world's rivers have this peculiarity. Send your mind traveling to the Congo, the Nile, the Zambesi, the Yellow River, the Ganges, the Volga, the Don, the Danube, the Rhine, the Seine, the Thames; then to the Connecticut, the Hudson, the Ohio, the Mississippi, the Missouri, the Yellowstone, the Big Horn, the Snake, the Columbia, the Mackenzie, the Colorado, and the Rio Grande; yes, and the Nueces, the Colorado—the Texas Colorado, that is—the Trinity, the Canadian, the Cimarron, the Arkansas, and the Platte—merely to recite the names is like chanting a litany burdened with a people's past. They are all *the* rivers, with this handful of exceptions.

Green River may be "the Green" to modern topographers, but it was Green River to the fur traders; and when the trail drivers started pointing their herds on the long drive north, they crossed the northern boundary of Texas at Red River. If you said they crossed the herd over "the Red," the old-timers with the longhorned mustaches would roll over in their graves. If you talked about "the Wind" instead of Wind River you would sound mighty silly; the same applies to Tongue River. Powder River has always been Powder River in contemporary letters and newspapers and old roundup circulars and in the unrecorded talk of thousands

1

who didn't have any education, they only lived there. Nobody calls it "the Powder" except outlanders and people with no ear for speech.

Powder River starts down out of the Big Horns eastward in a series of sparkling, branching tributaries: Piney Creek and Clear Creek and Crazy Woman, and the North Fork and the Middle Fork and the South Fork, which is a long finger reaching southward to the central Wyoming plateau, and if you drive across it there after meeting it in central Montana it gives you a startled feeling—"What is Powder River doing here?" But it's a long river, 486 miles.

The three main forks come together near the place where Moreton Frewen was to establish his headquarters.

At this point Powder River makes a right-angle turn to the north. Before many miles its character changes and so do its memories. The sagebrush is drier and flatter. The Big Horns to the west are a blue ghost now glimpsed, now forgotten. By the time it reaches the Montana line on its way to join the Yellowstone, Powder River has acquired other characteristics entirely, the sparkle forgotten; the rustlers and the English forgotten. By this time it has become the river of the big Texas outfits that grazed their steers on Montana grass, the XIT and the Hash Knife and the Mill Iron; the river of great roundups with their memory unscarred by the bitter feuds of Wyoming; the river of the photographer Huffman and his immortal roundup pictures; it has become this other Powder River that was "a mile wide and an inch deep; too thick to drink, too thin to plough." Here at the Montana line the tales are of horses and men drowned swimming the Yellowstone. You're on another range now, in another world—and Powder River still has half Montana to cross.

In 1875, one year Before Custer, Wyoming's fourth legislative assembly drew some lines on a map and "created" a county to be called Pease (after a civic nonentity long forgotten), ordaining with frontier optimism that when the voters therein reached the number of five hundred the county might be organized. Four years later another legislature changed its name to Johnson in honor of another civic nonentity and reduced the number of electors necessary for organization to three hundred. At the time of its creation the so-called county with the Big Horn mountains running down its center had twelve thousand square miles of peaks and canyons and forests and buffalo and waving blond grass in which dwelt scarcely a score of white men, not even a white prostitute, and it still belonged to Red Cloud and his allies regardless of what the fourth Legislative Assembly had to say about it. So far as civilized institutions were concerned, the earth was without form and void.[1]

In the beginning the United States government created Fort Mc-
Kinney.

In 1876, after the annihilation of Custer's command on the Little
Big Horn, the Army chased Cheyenne Chief Dull Knife and his forlorn-
hope band of warriors up into the Big Horns and defeated them in an
engagement which ended Indian domination of the northern plains.
Lieutenant John A. McKinney of the 4th Cavalry was killed; the next
year an Army post was established far up on Clear Creek near where
it issues from the mountains and was named Fort McKinney in his
memory.

An Army post was the nucleus of a frontier economy. It had three
immediate needs, which it filled by letting contracts to the bearded en-
trepreneurs who invariably turned up: contract for hay, contract for
cordwood, contract for meat. Sale of such durable vegetables as cab-
bages, potatoes, and turnips was a natural corollary. A fourth need was
civilian freighting of supplies from the nearest main artery of transportation, in this case the Union Pacific at Rock Creek station, two hundred
and fifty miles to the south. There was also the need of a post trader. A
soldier named Elias U. Snider decided to stay around after his enlistment
expired and became sutler to the fort. He is called the first permanent settler of Johnson County.

The year 1878 finished out the first chapter of Genesis on Powder
River.

First came the post and its needs; then came those who would supply
its needs; then those who would supply the needs of the suppliers; and so
the economy grew.

In 1879, a few early comers decided to build a town, so they picked
a site six miles down Clear Creek from the military reservation. The first
hotel, soon to be named the Occidental, consisted of tepee poles and a
wagon sheet thrown together by a man named Buell. One day a party
of prospectors rode in from the Big Horns and asked if they might cache
a few pouches of gold dust with him for a few days. He offered them a
hole dug in the ground under his cot, and so the first bank came into
being coincidentally with the first hotel.

The town was named Buffalo, but not, as might be supposed, for the
monarch of the prairie. The first comers drew lots to see who should
have the honor of naming it, and the choice fell to a man from Buffalo,
New York. Not least among its immediate needs was whiskey. Buffalo
had seventeen saloons by the time the county was organized. At that
time the entire population numbered 637.

The 1884 legislature appropriated money for a courthouse for Johnson County. Soon its two tall red-brick stories were looming up like the pyramid of Ghizeh above the naked plain. Civic pride planted a row of saplings not as thick as a lady's wrist in front of the bare-boned structure. Today the towering cottonwoods which were those saplings cast their deep shade over the ivy-mantled courthouse and its lawn and the library and new museum in the rear.

1

Cheer Up, Boys
1879-1887

There is not the slightest amount of uncertainty in
cattle raising.
—BARON WALTER VON RICHTHOFEN, *in Cattle-Raising*
on the Plains of North America (1885)

ONE

The Beef Bonanza

In 1879 the West was growing old, though it was not yet aware of it. The buffalo were almost gone, and so for practical purposes were the Indians. The Union Pacific had been finished for ten years. One West after another had had its short and crowded day before vanishing over the horizon; the West of the explorers—the Verendryes and Lewis and Clark; the West of the fur trappers and traders; the West of the missionary pioneers—Marcus and Narcissa Whitman and Father De Smet; the West of the Mormon handcarts; the West of the covered wagons crawling overland to Oregon and California; the West of the short-lived Pony Express and of the first transcontinental telegraph and of the UP railroad-builders; the West of "Pikes Peak or Bust" and Last Chance Gulch and the Bloody Bozeman and Deadwood; the West of the sod-house frontier shoving the cattlemen out of Kansas and Nebraska; all these Wests had come and gone, or had stayed and consolidated into something resembling civilization.

The time was now ripe for the West of the cattle baron—of the great beef bonanza on the northern plains. The final flare of the long sunset had begun.[1]

Eighteen seventy-nine was the year of its beginning, but 1878, before the start of the bovine gold rush, saw several harbingers of things to come. In that year Cheyenne was just a raw young city of two or three thousand sprawled along one side of the UP tracks, but its fame was already attracting the adventurous. Far to the north of the territorial capital the magnificent reaches of not-yet-organized Johnson County were an empty paradise of waving grass; a cowman's paradise, with the Indians out but the cowmen not yet in. Nobody had come in except two

7

or three hundred assorted frontier types and the lonely little Army post, Fort McKinney.

But in 1878, the year after the post was established, a trader and freighter named Gus Trabing built a road ranch and station at the Crazy Woman crossing of the old Bozeman road, where he yoked up fresh bull teams for the last pull to the fort. At the end of December 1878, a young English swell named Moreton Frewen turned up at Trabing's. Only the clipped accents of Cambridge and Melton Mowbray distinguished him from other bearded, greasy travelers in that arctic waste, and the story he told was so incredible as to invite disbelief from the winterbound idlers in the store, who were finding it a hard day's work merely to keep warm. Some six weeks earlier a party consisting of Moreton and his brother Dick—now lying ill in a deserted log cabin—and two packer guides had set out from Fort Washakie on the western side of the Big Horns. They had crossed the mountain range in the dead of winter, a feat never before attempted and probably not duplicated until after the age of machines. They had followed up No Wood creek on the western slope, crossed the main range, and come down onto the headwaters of Powder River. Approaching the top of the divide they had found their worst fears realized—gulches filled and landmarks obliterated by drifted snow.

It was then that their chief guide, the superb Jack Hargreaves—who sounds quite the equal of Parkman's Henry Chatillon—came up with a stroke of frontier genius; he forced a herd of buffalo to break trail for them. Having sighted the herd on a snowy slope, he rode round the cluster of black bovine shapes and started them up into their rocking gallop, knowing they would head for the pass. They did, showing the way to the four men and packing the snow down hard with their thousand hooves so that the party could come through.

The audience of half a dozen at Trabing's, Frewen wrote, "not only thought we were phenomenal liars, but that ... an alibi so reckless went a long way to prove that we were 'wanted' somewhere and that the mere 'mad English' explanation of things was inadequate." [2]

Moreton went east to make a splash in New York society, but before he left the brothers had picked the site of their future ranch house, a few miles below the point where the three forks of Powder River come together. The less effervescent Dick Frewen remained in Wyoming—where, in that snowbound waste, one wonders? When Moreton Frewen returned from his social conquests the following spring, the great squared pine logs for the house were being fitted into place. Lumber, shingles, and furniture were on their way from Chicago to complete the two-story mansion which the awed yokels named "Frewen's Castle."

That summer, 1879, Frewen bought out the 76 brand from a ranchman on the Sweetwater named Tim Foley, and the first big herd of cattle was driven onto Powder River. In his memoirs he indignantly denies the story that the crafty Mr. Foley drove the cattle around and around a hill and that he, Frewen, bought the same herd twice. Next year he marketed eight hundred head of three-year-old steers, and the price paid off half his original investment. Northward the glorious land stretched to the Arctic Circle without a fence and with scarcely a habitation, almost as innocent of the white man and his works as it had been the day after Creation. Southward it was two hundred miles to the nearest rail point, Rock Creek station on the Union Pacific. Small wonder that when Frewen decided to set up his headquarters in central Wyoming he reasoned that he would have ten years, perhaps twenty, in which to build a fortune before being overwhelmed by the influx of men and beasts. Sadly he wrote forty years later: "Little we dreamed how immense was to be the pressure of settlement, in the years at hand, into that vast wilderness—a pressure which in four years would overfill the ranges the whole five hundred miles up to Alberta, and would a little later engulf us all in a common disaster."

Eighteen seventy-nine was a year of small runnels presaging a mighty flood. The Anglo-American Cattle Company, first of the big overseas corporations, was organized in London with American Harry Oelrichs as manager. The Honorable Horace Curzon Plunkett, third son of the sixteenth Baron Dunsany of Ireland, came to Wyoming for his health—which proved robust enough in the strenuous years to come—and established a "ranche," as the British spelled it, where one of the little branching tributaries of Powder River flowed out of the mountains.

A young Bostonian named Hubert E. Teschemacher had graduated from Harvard in 1878. Returning from a trip around the world, he was visiting his parents' home in Paris when he picked up an English-language newspaper and read an account of the wonders of the great West. He was seized with the desire to see more of the plains and mountains he had recently viewed fleetingly from a train window, and in the fall he and a classmate, Frederic O. de Billier, came to Wyoming to go big-game hunting. They remained to launch a half-million-dollar ranching enterprise on the North Platte.

And now all of a sudden everybody who was anybody on either side of the Atlantic was talking about the fortunes to be made by raising cattle in the West. Free grass, by courtesy of Uncle Sam! No costs beyond the paltry wages of a handful of cowboys! No capital investment worth mentioning—a few rude log buildings thrown up on the public domain. No risks—simply buy a herd and nature would do the rest.

To be sure the winters were severe, but the eastern press rang the changes on that story about the winterbound freighter and his team of oxen; his grief at turning them out, as he thought, to perish; his joy at finding them alive and fat the next spring. As a matter of record, at least one such episode had actually occurred, and probably more. Cattle could and did survive the winters on the plains—given grass and a sheltering coulee, provisos which were promptly forgotten.[3]

Much was heard about the wonders of "natural increase" and the prolific Texas cow, who would make a man rich without his lifting a finger. According to one statement: "If $200,000 were invested in Texas cattle it would double itself in four years and pay a semi-annual dividend of eight per cent." Another fellow who had started more modestly with $7875 stated: "In five years my annual income ($9070) is greater than my original investment." You could figure it all out on the back of an envelope, deduct two per cent for annual losses, and go out through the swinging doors a millionaire.

Three little books, one after the other, fanned the flames of speculation. In 1877, well before the influx of foreign money had started, a local publicity man, Robert E. Strahorn, published a booklet entitled "Handbook of Wyoming and Guide to the Black Hills and Big Horn Regions." Strahorn was even conservative by later standards. To be sure, he wrote "A steady profit of twenty-five percent per annum [on investments in cattle] is really a common result" and mentioned "one gentleman in southern Wyoming who for five years has made forty percent per annum," adding, however, "He has been especially judicious in his purchases and sales. . . . Constant supervision and study on the part of the *owner* of the stock is a grand point." * But when figures like twenty-five and forty per cent were mentioned, words of caution went whistling down the wind.

The Beef Bonanza, or How to Get Rich on the Plains, by General James S. Brisbin, USA, appeared in 1881; 1885 saw the publication of *Cattle Raising on the Plains of North America,* by Baron Walter von Richthofen, the handsome red-bearded Prussian who was cutting a swath in Denver with his real-estate schemes and his blonde English baroness. None of the authors was a soulless promoter out to fleece the unwary; none was even trying to float a cattle company. They were simply honest boosters carried away by the euphoria of the great West.

Phrase after phrase in their guileless little books, reread, wakes echoes of hollow laughter:

* Strahorn was undoubtedly speaking of Judge, later U.S. Senator, Joseph M. Carey, a lawyer from Philadelphia who was appointed U.S. Attorney for Wyoming when the Territory was organized in 1869. Two years later he brought in one of the first Texas trail herds and built an immense cattle enterprise.

"...the lightness of the snowfalls...climate mild and genial... supply of grazing...unlimited; an annual dividend of at least twenty-five percent" from Brisbin; and from Richthofen: "...no risks beyond losses arising from natural causes...and none arising from speculation. ... There is not the slightest amount of uncertainty in cattle raising."

Best of all was the delicious notion that no special knowledge or experience was required to make a go of the business. Wasn't it merely a form of outdoor sport that paid dividends?

"I don't see much to learn in handling cattle," said the managing director of a large overseas company. "Our young Englishmen would make capital cowboys. They are excellent horsemen; good riders; all they need is a little practice in throwing a rope." [4]

One gigantic cattle corporation followed another on the scene from 1880 through 1884; most of the big ones were organized abroad, and this dominance by foreign capital created some resentful undercurrents in the West during the mad decade. Strange to say it was the canny Scots who plunged the hardest, with the English a close second. In January 1881, the Prairie Cattle Company was launched in Edinburgh with a capital of half a million pounds. Throwing Scottish caution to the winds, its prospectus had virtually promised investors "not less than from twenty-five to forty per cent per annum" (those magic figures again) and dangled the possibility of even fifty per cent. By 1883 an American, Alexander H. Swan, had talked another group of Scottish tycoons into floating the three-and-a-half-million-dollar Swan Land and Cattle Company.

Meanwhile a vast proliferation of lesser companies—such only by comparison with these giants—was loosing upon the West a deluge of haughty young men, speaking with English accents and riding flat saddles, who managed at once to amuse and to irritate the natives. To the cowboys, oblivious to distinctions of rank, the importations were all "lords." Somehow the expression "cow servant" gained circulation; it was quoted gleefully all over the West, even to being fathered onto Moreton Frewen, among other things he did not deserve. It appears to have originated with a Briton, newly arrived in New Mexico, who objected to eating with the "cow servants"; in other versions he ordered them to handle his luggage or shine his shoes or throw water on his tent to cool it on a hot day.

And there was that other Englishman, newly arrived in Wyoming, who hired a horse at the livery stable and set out to find a fellow countryman's ranch. On the faint wheel track which passed for a road he encountered a lone rider, who turned out to be his friend's foreman. After assuring himself that he was on the right road he pursued in all innocence: "Is your mahster at home?" Came the level reply: "The son of a bitch hasn't been born yet." [5]

A process of mutual education went on. The more flexible of the "lords" caught on to the facts of social equality in the West; some of them even showed the local boys a thing or two. A cowboy ballad tells of a dudish-looking stranger who arrived at a roundup camp on the Cimarron—of all things—on foot! They invited him to dinner, of course, and after coffee and biscuits and beans he started to talk.

> *Such an educated feller, his thoughts just come in herds.*
> *He astonished all them cowboys with his long jaw-breaking words.*
> *He just kept on a-talking till he made the boys all sick,*
> *And they begun to look around for how to play a trick.*

The stranger himself offered them the opportunity; he asked if he might borrow a horse. Gleefully they led up the most notorious outlaw of their remuda, the Zebra Dun:

> *When the stranger hit the saddle, Dunny left the earth*
> *And traveled right straight up for all that he was worth,*
> *A-pitching and a-squealing and a-having wall-eyed fits,*
> *His hind feet in the stirrups, his front feet in the bits.*

> *We could see the tops of mountains under Dunny every jump,*
> *But the stranger he was growed there just like the camel's hump.*
> *The stranger sat upon him and curled his black mustache,*
> *Just like a summer boarder a-waiting for his hash.*

The boss offered the stranger a job, and the narrator concluded penitently: "There's one thing and a shore thing I've learned since I was born, That every educated feller ain't a plumb greenhorn." It was not, after all, so hard to get along with cowboys.

Witness the Scottish duke who jumped on the cowcatcher of a locomotive and took a ride, not for any particular purpose except as a gesture to demonstrate his want of "side." The gesture was a huge success and so was the duke.

And so the education went on. The cowboys for their part picked up the word *dude.*

The "lords" and the lordlings from London, Boston, New York, and Philadelphia met at that wonderful institution, the Cheyenne Club. No other cow-country capital had anything like it. It boasted of having the best steward and the best chef of any club in the United States, a wine cellar second to none—though Horace Plunkett grumbled that Americans did not know how to serve wine—and servants imported from Ottawa where, under the British flag, men were taught to be

servants instead of retorting curtly: "Do it yourself!" when requested
to shine a pair of shoes.*

On the club roster names out of Burke's *Peerage* appeared side by
side with names familiar to the highest financial circles of Wall Street.
The heady mixture of youth, money, and optimism bubbled in the high
air of the plains like the champagne the members consumed in record
quantities. According to John Clay, it was champagne for breakfast,
lunch, and dinner. There were gala evenings to which members came in
white tie and tails, which they facetiously dubbed their "Herefords,"
in reference to the popular breed of beef cattle which had a dark coat
and a white chest. There was the dinner given in August 1883 by the
British members for the Americans; the forty-one who sat down consumed sixty-six bottles of champagne and twenty bottles of red wine,
with the preprandial whiskey unaccounted for.[6]

Along with the social hydeho went the financial. To survivors of the
1929 bull market the whole thing must have a sadly familiar ring. There
were the same inflated prospectuses, the same milking of capital assets
to pay dividends, the same inverted pyramids of frantic extravagance
and debt. The western version of paying dividends out of capital was
to strip the herds of their immature beeves and thus to relieve them
this year of next year's marketable animals.

Another feature peculiar to frenzied finance on the plains was the
practice of buying herds by "book count." Instead of going to the expense of rounding up and counting the herd on an unfenced range, the
prospective buyer looked over the company's books, paying particular
attention to the size of the calf brand (which alone was tallied) and
which when multiplied by five, or by four if you were awfully conservative, was supposed to give the total. A liberal allowance was made for
"natural increase," a very modest deduction taken for annual losses,
and the deal was made. When the day of reckoning came, according
to John Clay, "it is safe to say that in many cases not half the number
of cattle represented on the books were in actual existence."[7]

The day of reckoning started to move in early. Losses turned out
to be much heavier than anticipated, in part—but only in part—because
some of the missing cattle had never existed at all. Dividends turned
out to be lower. The great Prairie Cattle Company created a sensation
by declaring a dividend of twenty and a half per cent for 1883, an-

---

* It would appear that some western ways rubbed off on the hoped-for docile
Canadians, for we learn in Lewis Atherton's *The Cattle Kings* of an occasion when
member Harry Oelrichs had to be disciplined for kicking a club servant down the
stairs when the latter refused to hold his horse (p. 66). What a pity the kicking
was not on the other foot!

nounced early in 1884, but it had to stretch and strain to make it. Where was that twenty-five to forty per cent? It never showed on any company's returns. Moreton Frewen's Powder River Cattle Company managed a dividend of a mere ten per cent in the same peak year of 1883, did no better the following year, and only after squeezing some juice out of capital at that.

The Cattle Ranche and Land Company of London, with which Clay was involved, was so badly managed that it even passed its dividend for the boom year of 1884. After a roundup and count in the fall of 1885, it was found that the 31,762 cattle on the books as of a year ago had shrunk to 13,500. Book count was coming home to roost.

But the buzzards flapped in heavily one at a time, not in flocks. Only a few of the astute smelled the omens and got out, while lordlings with more money than sense continued to buy herds by book count and throw them out on the overloaded ranges. One day while a blizzard was raging a row of gloomy faces lined the bar of Luke Murrin's popular saloon across the street from the Cheyenne Club. Losses were the painful topic of conversation, and that was when the saloon man pronounced his deathless epigram.

"Cheer up, boys," he quipped as he filled the glasses. "The books won't freeze."

TWO

The Castle Built on Sand

I will let loose against you the fleet-footed vines—
I will call in the Jungle to stamp out your lines!
The roofs shall fade before it,
The house-beams shall fall,
And the Karela, *the bitter* Karela,
Shall cover it all.
    —MOWGLI'S SONG *from* KIPLING, *Letting in the Jungle*

DURING THE early bonanza years Moreton Frewen was flitting ceaselessly from Powder River to Cheyenne to New York to London and back
again, dreaming up one wild scheme after another for making yet more
money out of his cattle. He was also taking time out to court the lovely
Clara Jerome, daughter of New York financier Leonard Jerome and
sister of Jennie Jerome, who married Lord Randolph Churchill. New
York was a hotbed of international matchmaking, but Moreton was
known as "fast." What with a scandalous episode or two and all his
race-track plunging, he was scarcely the type to appeal to a conservative
family. For a time his engagement to Clara was kept secret, but per-
severance won, and in 1881 they were married. He took his bride at
once to the log mansion on Powder River.[1]

And what a house it was! The great hall running up to the roof had
a fireplace at each end and was hung all around with Indian trophies,
buffalo robes, and the antlered heads of elk and deer. A solid-walnut
staircase ran up to the second floor where the sleeping quarters were,
but midway there was a sort of a mezzanine—the "musicians' gallery,"
Frewen called it—with potted plants and vines twining up from the
floor below. Downstairs there was a dining room, a library and office,
and the central hall-living room, forty by forty feet, besides the kitchen
and pantry. "Twenty of us," Frewen wrote his fiancée the year before
their marriage, "could dine in the hall comfortably, and then move out
to the piazza and watch the sunset." [2]

Throughout the summer and fall life at this wilderness mansion
was one long houseparty. Horses were kept at relay points between
Sussex—named in honor of the county in which Frewen had been born

—and Rock Creek station on the Union Pacific, two hundred miles to the south. Thus arriving guests could be bowled along to the ranch without slackening speed. A telephone line—one of the first in the West—connected the house with the 76 store and post office twenty-four miles downriver.

Early in 1881, a few months before his marriage, Moreton wrote his future sister-in-law Lady Randolph Churchill: "Last night there were a lot of redskins—more naked than ashamed—talking to each other through it. I never saw such ludicrous astonishment, and I improved the occasion to persuade them that our rifles shot on that principle!" [3]

The Frewens kept a visitors' book, its entries made up largely of notable names. Moreton was smitten with titles; he undoubtedly suffered because he himself was not born the son of a duke; and rarely does he mention in his memoirs anyone who was not at least the brother-in-law of an earl. His guest list for 1881 is worth quoting: "Sir Samuel and Lady Baker, Lord Mayo and T. Porter Porter, Horace Flower, Lord Granville Gordon, Louise Frewen, Henry and Mrs. Gaskell, G. C. Leigh, Lords Manners and Donoughmore." On October 5, we learn, "Manners and M. F. killed 95 wild duck, mallards, shovellers, widgeon and teal, within a mile of the house." Game was plentiful and slaughter the fashion.

With all the brilliant connections of which he was so vain, the one he never mentions in his memoir (published in 1924) is the one which outshines all the rest of them put together. He was the uncle by marriage of a young man named Winston Churchill.

In 1882 Frewen, then twenty-nine, went to London and with the flick of a wrist raised a million and a half dollars to extend his holdings on Powder River. Cattle prices reached their peak that year; they would never go so high again, but nobody knew it. "I had fallen into line with the company-mongering craze," he wrote ruefully years later, and the result was the organization of the Powder River Cattle Company, Ltd., with the Duke of Manchester as chairman of the board. [4] The enlarged 76 outfit bought out local smaller owners, and the next year trailed in additional great herds from Nebraska and Oregon.

The range claimed by the company ran from the headwaters of Powder River, with a piece of Tongue River thrown in, southward through central Wyoming to the Teapot Rock divide—some ninety miles north and south—by thirty miles eastward from the Big Horns. Only a small fraction of this great stretch was patented. In addition to the home ranch dominated by the "Castle," there was a second ranch north on

Crazy Woman creek and a third still farther north on Tongue River; there were a supply depot, store, and post office at the stage crossing on Powder River, and an unknown number of line camps. Estimates differ wildly as to the number of cattle carrying the 76 or its affiliated brands during the peak years 1883 and 1884; they range from Frewen's own estimate of 45,000, made many years later, to 59,000 and even 80,000 made by others. Nobody really knew; and what mattered a few tens of thousands one way or the other in the euphoric haze of the cattle boom?

The great roundups of 1883 and 1884 were like nothing ever seen again. Fifty years afterwards Ad Spaugh, trail driver and cowman, described the Cheyenne River roundup of 1884, of which he was one foreman and Lee Moore was the other. Twenty different cow outfits took part, with 200 cowboys and 2000 horses, and the roundup gathered and worked 400,000 head of cattle in six weeks. In the Powder River country, on May 20, 1883, twenty-seven roundup wagons and 400 cowboys met at the mouth of Crazy Woman creek. Fred G. S. Hesse, hard, English-born range foreman of the 76, was also foreman of the roundup, and the 76 alone had six wagons. Ten mounts to a man was the general roundup rule, and the wagons were strung along the river for two miles to allow the different saddle-horse herds room to graze without getting mixed up.

While dawn was still only a hint of things to come, the wranglers were bringing in the horses and penning them in a rope corral, and in a minute or two the boys were roping their mounts out of the remuda and saddling up in the half-light. While the first pink-and-gold clouds tinted the sky, impromptu rodeos broke out as half-wild horses took to bucking with their riders.

"Shouts of laughter would be heard," Flagg wrote, "as some tenderfoot would be thrown from his horse, and such exclamations as 'Stay with him!' 'Jump off!' 'Spur him in the eye!' would be yelled at some other poor fellow who would be striving with tooth and nail to stay on his unmanageable steed."

The cowboys all vied with each other in the splendor of their regalia; silver-mounted bridles and spurs, handmade boots with devices of scrolls, butterflies, or the Texas star worked into tops of colored leather; gaily colored scarves; and the finest hats that money could buy. By the time the sun appeared the men had been told off in small groups to drive every creek and watershed within half a day's riding and bring in the cattle. By nine o'clock the sun was high and the day was half over as the drives began coming in from all directions, each under its little cloud of dust. Soon as many as seven thousand cattle would be gathered on the roundup ground. Every day or two the camp would move to a new location and the process would be repeated over many weeks, until the whole vast area of the roundup district had been worked.

Eighteen eighty-four was the same picture all over again. Flagg estimated that 181,000 head of cattle were represented on that year's roundup on Powder River, fully two thirds of them British-owned. His total may have been exaggerated, but Frewen states that he branded nine thousand calves that year. Three or four years later the tally was down to three thousand.

Yet beneath all the glorious horseback pageantry nearly everything was amiss. A horrid little word, a new word, was being mentioned in company offices: *overstocking*. In the midst of the 1884 crescendo, while all the talk was still of twenty per cent dividends, the Prairie Cattle Company's officials were preparing their report which, issued early in 1885, was to admit that suddenly its great ranges appeared to be overstocked. Frewen meanwhile was discovering the same unpleasant fact with regard to his own Powder River ranges; moreover the dividend was off, the low return being attributed by the directors to their manager's Oriental expenditures, concerning which he had neglected to advise them.

The very personification of absentee ownership, Frewen never planned to spend more than a few cool fall weeks each year in his new empire—when the aspens lit their burning gold against the green-black of the pines, and the red-leaved wild plum bushes bore their Christmas-tree fruit, and the wild clematis draped its white froth over trees and brush to brush the shoulders of passing riders where the trail dipped to cross a runlet. And when the hunting was at its best.

Not for him or his kind was the hot, dusty grind of the roundup in July, nor the long, shut-in, blind-white winter months when the mercury ranged to ten, twenty, thirty below; when a blizzard howled one day but the next day the sun came out, and the snow flew up in a shower of diamonds under a horse's hoofs and the river bottom was rimmed by cake-frosting hills; when the arrival of a red-nosed neighbor bundled up to twice his natural size and kicking off his overshoes in the entry was a major social event. This sort of thing did not appeal to the owning class, British or American; they spent their winters in town or much farther away.

As early as the end of 1884 Frewen was considering yet another scheme, this one to evade the advancing menace of overstocking. He would remove the 76 herds all the way across Montana and into Alberta. There is even some suggestion that he may have taken immense leases between Fort McLeod and Edmonton without consulting his board.

At any rate the spring meeting in 1885 found his directors in London in an angry mood. By the time the meeting was over and before the "deflation" —another unpleasant little word—of 1885 was well under way, Frewen was out as manager. He was the first of the "lords" to come, and the first to go.

The almost-peak year of 1884 was Moreton Frewen's last season in Wyoming, although he did not know it at the time. It was marred by the accidental death of his old friend and companion in many a western adventure, Gilbert Leigh.

Soon after his arrival Leigh went on a hunting trip by himself. One evening he left his campfire and walked toward a low fringe of green some yards distant, which he must have mistaken in the dusk—so his friends reasoned—for the line of brush which marks all small water-courses in the West. But the fringe was not brush; it was the tops of pine trees growing at the bottom of a sheer-walled canyon a hundred feet below. His body was found a day or two later.[5] Johnson County still remembers Gilly Leigh, and it still points out to visitors the cliff where he fell to his death.

The Powder River Cattle Company went through successive travails of reorganization in the deflation of 1885, the depression of 1886, and the disaster of 1887. Frewen made one more trip to the house on Powder River to wind up his affairs. On June 23, 1885, he made a last entry in the visitors' book. Thirty-five years later he wrote: "It was a perfect sunny morning when I left, and with quite a lump in my throat I halted my horses on the ridge, and before passing forever out of sight took a long last look at the good black and white house which the river folk called 'the Castle.' It had proved the centre for a very short-lived social system, and now

> " 'Westward by northward loomed sadly my track
> And I must ride forward and still I look back,—
> Look back—ah how vainly!
> For while I see plainly
> My hands on the reins lie uncertain and slack.' "

He never came back. He was a man to go forward to fresh enthu-siasms and fresh failures, not linger over those which were dead and gone. During the successive reorganizations of his cattle company, with in-numerable wrangles inside the board of directors and a violent quarrel with Horace Plunkett, who succeeded him as manager over his strenu-ous and decidedly bad-tempered protests, Frewen remained his com-pany's largest stockholder, and even after it folded completely he still had plenty of money with which to support a magnificent load of debt and a scale of living to match. He spent the rest of his life promoting a succession of rather incongruous causes, ranging from free silver to protectionism, and keeping up an enormous correspondence with prominent people.

"The good black and white house which the river folk called 'the Castle'" in a few years simply ceased to be. There is some difference of opinion as to just when it disappeared and by what means. A local historian says that it was demolished in 1912, which seems too late in view of Frewen's own recollections, and that a neighboring ranchman bought the walnut staircase and used it in his home for many years.[6] According to another version, it was acquired by a local entrepreneur who cut it up into ash trays and bookends for sale as souvenirs. A real connoisseur, that one—knew a fine thing when he saw it. Conceivably the staircase met with first one fate and then the other.

In any case, whatever remained was dismantled and carried away piece by piece; every useful thing whether movable or no—and what isn't useful on a semi-frontier?—until nothing was left. Not a fencepost; not a half-rotted beam; not a strand of wire; nothing; until the site of Frewen's short-lived adventure was as flat as the palm of his hand.

And the sage came back, as it came back all over the West, onto the sites of forgotten homesteads, crumbling forts and abandoned Army posts, with of course the assistance of new homesteaders who carted away every log, fencepost, window frame, and door latch. The sage and the bluestem moved back, everywhere that the white man in his shifting track of empire had been and gone, obliterating every trace of soldiers and freighters, of lords and ladies; of tired horses and frontier riffraff and whores; you can visit these places today and find nothing but the hot smell of sage and the whispering of cottonwood leaves; sun and silence. Some buried foundation stones, a dimple or two of excavation, and the signs of sheep. If you look hard among the grass stems you may find an old nail and a fragment of sun-purpled glass.

There is something eerie about such totality of obliteration in so short a time, and the rest of the story is even eerier. Twenty years after Frewen's last long look at his house, which would make it around 1905, a friend of his revisited the spot. In 1884, during his final visit to Wyoming, his wife had written from England asking him to bring her back a good buffalo head. This presented problems. The buffalo were all wiped out excepting a few forlorn remnants, and it might not be easy to find one left to kill. He postponed the expedition. "... when one morning I was dressing in my bedroom on the ground-floor, and there within a hundred yards staring stupidly at the house was a big old lone buffalo bull. I ran into the hall, not even half dressed, picked an

Express rifle out of the rack and broke the poor brute's shoulder, killing him ten minutes later on the flat a quarter of a mile away."

What had led the miserable animal, one of the last survivors of the millions which once blackened the prairie, into the very dooryard of his enemy and his master? Was there some question haunting the depths of his dim brute brain, some sense of lack? "Where have *they* all gone?" The old bull hadn't a chance of living out his last lonely years in peace, for if Frewen hadn't finished him, some other slaughter-mad denizen of the West would have done the same.

The strangest part of the story is that the friend, writing Frewen, reported that the house was "clean gone." There was not a trace to show where it had once stood except that, a short distance away, the decapitated skeleton of the old buffalo bull was bleaching in the sun. And so an old buffalo, one of the last of his race, was all that was left to mark, however briefly, the site of a vanity more transient and less important than his old noble, shaggy, stupid self.

Frewen with his name-dropping and his grandiose ways had a knack for irritating the natives which was exceptional even in a "Lord." Two years after his departure the Cheyenne *Sun* was moved to publish its harsh epitaph: "Of all the English snobs of great pretensions who flew so high and sunk so low, probably the Frewens are the chiefs." [7] The editorial has been quoted so often that it has come to sound like an American verdict of posterity on Frewen, to whom Wyoming was only one episode in an excessively disorganized career.

But the editorial is not a fair judgment. Frewen was a colonialist, and his aims were simple to the point of naïveté. He wanted to snatch all the money he could out of a new country in the shortest possible time and take it home to spend.

Seeds of Trouble

I

WYOMING IN 1880 had a population of just under 21,000, exclusive of Indians, in an area of 98,000 square miles. As of the same census, population was approaching half a million in Nebraska and a million in Kansas, both of less area than Wyoming, while Nebraska had 63,387 farms and Kansas 138,561. In the same year the productive entities describable as farms in Wyoming numbered 457. The most enthusiastic agrarian could hardly have promoted a war between the farmer and the cowman in Wyoming in 1880, because the few so-called farmers—most of whom raised only hay—were farming as a side issue to stock-raising or trade, and they were not mad at anybody.

In the middle of the decade a railroad arrived in east-central Wyoming—the Fremont, Elkhorn and Missouri Valley Railroad, later the Chicago and Northwestern—which crossed the line in 1886 and reached Douglas, on the Platte, in 1887. This line brought farmers and would-be farmers, even some European immigrants of the type later dubbed by Montanans, without affection, "honyockers." They settled in considerable numbers along the eastern edge of the Territory, where an irrigation project, significantly named Wheatland, stabilized some of them.[1] But soon they began drifting into central Wyoming, where the cowboys called them "push roots" and "punkin rollers" and told how they were so green that some of them couldn't even read the brands of their own few cows, much less throw a rope. The same cowboys helped them out with good-natured disdain and courted their daughters. Environment won out, and before long the new arrivals' sons were roping mavericks and busting broncs with the best. In a word, they were absorbed into the prevailing cattle economy, and there went your noble sodbuster.

Despite heroic overestimates of population growth by Governors

Warren and Moonlight in the middle of the decade, the Wyoming population at the 1890 census had just passed 60,000, a density of .62 persons per square mile. In Montana the density was .91 per square mile. The boosters never understood that many persons in both territories preferred this blissful state of affairs. They disliked feeling crowded.

By 1890 the number of farms in Wyoming had risen to 3125, while in Kansas there were 166,000 farms and even Colorado, another state of mountains and plains, had more than 16,000 farms—five times as many as Wyoming.[2]

Thus we can forget the poor but noble farmer so far as Wyoming is concerned. Her "grangers" and "nesters" (terms borrowed from an agrarian economy and loaded with the passions prevailing at the time) were in reality stock-raising settlers.

Absentee ownership worked out no better in Wyoming than it ever has anywhere else, and Wyoming for a few short dizzy years had more than its share. And many of the foreign owners built up so much local hostility by a series of foolish and tactless acts that rustling took on aspects of retribution.

"The relations between the employees and the owners in the Big Horn Basin are most unsatisfactory owing to the absence of the majority of the former [*sic*] from the ranges," Horace Plunkett wrote Secretary Sturgis of the Wyoming Stock Growers' Association on June 27, 1886. "Sympathy is with stealing and much of it goes on unpunished."

The "cattle barons," as the press was beginning to call them, were not the only people in Wyoming, though it was sometimes thought necessary to remind them of the fact. There were also the settlers. They were anybody from everywhere; migrants from the East; mustered-out soldiers; freighters, prospectors, railroad-builders, townmen—all the drifters of a frontier economy who were filing on homesteads and turning their little bunches of cattle out on the open range to mingle with the big herds.

Finally there were the cowboys. To a lesser extent they too were everybody from everywhere: Texans who had come north with the longhorned herds; west-coast men who had come eastward over the mountains with the heavier, better-bred Oregon cattle; and all the assortment of tenderfeet who had fallen in love with the cowboy life—farm boys from Iowa and Missouri, college-bred easterners, penniless younger sons from England and Scotland determined that cowboys they would be, and some of them lasted out the initial period of hazing and hard falls until they became so adept at their new calling that only an expert could tell which was which. But, it was the Texans who set their stamp on the cowpunching profession from border to border.

Johnny Jones—a name and an individual we have invented—was a Texan, which he pronounced "Texian" who "come up the trail" in the early eighties with a big herd and elected to stay in Wyoming because of the higher wages, despite the cold climate which gave him untold misery until he got used to it. It was not all he had to get used to. There were men and equipment and ways from places foreign to Texas, especially the west-coast men who made out to know something about cattle themselves; but they "dally-welted"—used a long rope with several turns wrapped around the saddle horn instead of the short Texas rope tied hard and fast. These Oregonians called him a "rawhide," because of the Texas habit of mending anything that broke down or fell apart on the trail with strips of rawhide. But he "give" as good as he got, calling them in return "Goddam knockkneed Oregonians." Everybody knew that nobody but a Texian "knowed" anything about cows or had sat in the saddle long enough to acquire a decent pair of bow legs.

There was some of them kids that come up with the trail outfits, their first time no'th of Red River, and they was green sure enough. I remember one kid (he said), and when they passed him the sugar he says: "No thanks, I don't take salt in my coffee," because he hadn't never seen sugar before, only sorghum syrup. But Johnny was a top hand and no greenhorn. He possessed a highly specialized form of ignorance. There was the day the boss' sister came out to ride on the roundup, and as Johnny gave her a hand up to her seat on the neat little horse that had been specially broke to a sidesaddle, he said in the mellow voice of his kind, "Yes, ma'am. Cow and horse is all we know."

But what he knew he knew. He was quick with a rope and a gun—too quick, some people thought.

While the good times lasted Johnny and his kind were content to work for wages—as long as the wages kept coming. They were so young, hardly older than schoolboys, many of them; but they led men's lives, and because they sat so tall against the sunset most people forgot how young they were. They spent their money on gambling and whiskey and girls. The only possessions they had or wanted were their fancy boots and Stetson hats and silver-mounted horse finery. "I had plenty of good horses to ride, and the girls said I was the best-looking cowboy on Powder River," said one of them years after. What more could a cowboy ask?

But now came the tightening belt and the tougher times. Johnny Jones, a skilled hand and a steady one, had always been one of those kept on into the winter months and perhaps all winter. But now when fall came he was laid off. His mind turned to other prospects.

He had a girl in town; a redheaded hash-slinger at the depot restaurant. Her record was not one-hundred-per-cent stainless, but what the hell, Johnny figured; his own wasn't either. He was twenty-eight years old, and he was tired of raising hell and beginning to think about raising a family. He had his eye on a little spot at the bend of a creek which never ran dry; and the creek like an encircling arm enfolded a piece of bottomland where you could cut wild hay in a wet year—the rest of the time it would be a cinch to irrigate.

So Johnny and the redheaded ex-hash-slinger stood up before a justice of the peace and she became Mrs. Johnny Jones. He filed on the homestead. Naturally he planned to raise cattle. No farmer, he.

There were thousands of Johnnys, and as the tough times went on and grew tougher their number increased. And so did the homesteads on choice spots along the streams, where a sweet-faced missus in a calico dress herded a growing flock of tow-headed kids, and the fellow who headed up the outfit hadn't forgotten a single trick he brought with him from Texas. None of this was regarded with favor by the big owner. Often he professed his good will toward the small farming settlers— perhaps because the latter were so few as to be almost nonexistent. But these cowpunching settlers were another matter. Nobody had to teach those boys how to throw a rope; they knew. And they were not welcomed as rivals on the range.

Regardless of the settler's origin he and the cattle baron came into head-on collision over the maverick question, the most confused, embittered, explosive question ever to bedevil the cattle range. Despite the miles of newsprint expended during the eighties on such questions as illegal fencing by cattlemen on the public domain, it was not these land tangles which led to war in Wyoming. Trouble, like any sly quarry, is seldom where the pack is in full cry after it. Trouble in Wyoming lurked in the innocent shape of the maverick, the orphaned calf, the unbranded animal of uncertain and unprovable ownership. Whose maverick?

Wyoming—this is worth repeating—was a cowboy state, and the war in Wyoming was a cowboy war.

Seeds of Trouble

II

In 1879, that year of milestones, another milestone was passed when a little organization calling itself the Laramie County Stock Association changed its name to the Wyoming Stock Growers' Association, to become one of the greatest forces for good and ill in the history of the western cattle business. The idea of organization germinated in 1871 and came to fruition in 1873, when the designation "Laramie County" was adopted. Wyoming in those early days consisted for white men's purposes of a little area hugging the line of the Union Pacific in the southeast portion of the Territory. The rest of it still belonged to the Indians. But by 1879, three years after the Custer massacre, herds were moving north to the Cheyenne River, Moreton Frewen was established on Powder River, and this is where we came in. The name "Laramie County" was no longer adequate to cover the burgeoning stock business of the territory, so the original group became the Wyoming Stock Growers' Association.[1]

The men who built this engine of influence and stayed with it to the end were the sooners—the early birds who captured the one and only financial worm. They were on hand well ahead of the beef extravaganza of the eighties; they were still there when it had run its course. They made huge fortunes in the upswing of the seventies out of a combination of booming business, rising markets, and lots of grass with no overcrowding; and they did it on local capital or at most only as far away as Kansas City and Omaha. Very striking was the preponderance of eastern origins in this early group, especially New York and Pennsylvania.

Nine men who came to Wyoming in or before 1879 were active in planning the invasion, and five took personal part.

Throughout these years the policy of the Wyoming Stock Growers' Association, which was synonymous with that of the Territory and state of Wyoming, was dictated by what modern diplomacy calls the hard line. The dominant hard-liner was Thomas Sturgis, secretary of the Association from 1876 through 1887. Member of a well-to-do New York importing family, he had come west in 1873 at the age of twenty-seven. John Clay heaped praises on him—"the leading man in Wyoming . . . the real leader of the Association." [2]

But those who praised his intellectual grasp and his gracious manner failed to remark on his autocratic disposition. His "wonderful influence" —to quote John Clay again—may be summed up in two statements: He was the father of the employment blacklist, and he was the father of that instrument of calamity, the maverick law of 1884. He was the prime architect of disaster in Wyoming.

Secretary Sturgis imposed on all members of the Wyoming Stock Growers' Association a rule forbidding them to employ any man who owned a brand or cattle. As early as 1883, he discovered a special menace to the property of cattle owners; he warned of "a class of theft practised with apparent impunity by men . . . in the employ of well-known ranchmen. I mean the starting of a brand by men who have no cattle nor any means to buy any." At a later meeting he put through a resolution forbidding any member of the Association to employ cattle-owning cowboys. All such cowboys were to be placed on the blacklist and denied employment permanently. No proof or even charge of wrong-doing was involved; simple ownership was regarded as presumptive evidence of guilt or at least of the intention to become guilty. [3]

Just how Mr. Sturgis obtained his inside information as to the personal financial status of every cowpuncher on the range was never explained. Some of these men were foremen, on three times the pay of the average cowhand and endowed with extra energy and ability. It was easy for them to obtain backing from the local bankers and businessmen in the towns, just as easy as it was for the big operators to obtain it in New York or London. And they were the most independent class of men on earth. They would not take peonage lying down. Even some ordinary cowpokes were saving their tiny wages and buying the drag ends of trail herds that had gone lame or were too weak or poor for the general market. It was contended, to be sure, that some of these scratch-penny herds increased at a rate faster than normal; but to say, as the big owners habitually did, that of course So-and-So must be a thief— "because where would *he* get the money to buy cattle?"—was a piece of infuriating insolence which did nothing to cool the rising temperature.

Some cowmen had always allowed their trusted hands to run cattle on the range. A former cowboy of Charles Goodnight's recalled one of his precepts: "Never hire a man for a steady hand unless he's tried to save and do something for himself." Goodnight encouraged his men to save by running their first fifty head of cattle for nothing, after which he agreed with them on a fair charge.[4]

An old-timer who arrived in Johnson County in 1882 reported finding a large number of single men working for big and middle-sized outfits, who owned small bunches of cattle and were paying the company so much a head grazing fee. At the time, no one appeared to think that this practice would ruin the industry. Over in the Big Horn Basin, that immense central valley lying between the western slope of the Big Horns and the blue serrated ridges of the Rocky Mountains, their splendid isolation fostered in owners the old western notion that a man was a free agent and no s.o.b. in Cheyenne or anywhere else could dictate to him; and for a time they went on allowing their trusted punchers to run cattle.[5]

But in Wyoming the Association threatened that the owner was no longer free to use his own judgment as to the character of a trusted hand, but must absolutely refuse to keep on his payroll any employee who owned cattle. During 1884 and 1885 there were frequent threats of the blacklist for owners, with notice of second warnings to deviationist members who dragged their feet when ordered to fire a good hand for owning a few cows or some similar crime. For an owner to be blacklisted meant that he could no longer take part in the roundups or enjoy any other privileges. It was tantamount to reading him out of the stock business in Wyoming Territory.

The rule against allowing cowboys to buy mavericks or own cattle; the blacklist; the growing tendency on the part of the more injudicious and short-tempered of the big stockmen to equate all small independent ranchers with thieves—all this kindled a slow burn that smoldered along in the sagebrush roots for years. The no-owning rule hit everybody, the righteous and the unrighteous and the borderline cases who were merely a little human.

Montana at one point came close to following Wyoming's unfortunate example. At a meeting of the Montana Stockgrowers Association in Miles City in 1885 a similar resolution was introduced, to be binding on all members, forbidding them to employ any cowboy who had cattle on the range. It was adopted over the strenuous opposition of many members present, including Granville Stuart. In the words of his son-in-law, "Teddy Blue" Abbott, "he made quite a speech, in which he tried very hard to get all the members to allow their cowpunchers to own cattle. He said that ninety-nine per cent of them were honest men, that if they were allowed to buy mavericks and own cattle it would give them a chance to get ahead and give them an interest in the range, that this would do more than anything else to stop rustling, as the boys were on the range all the time."

At the next meeting of the Association six months later Montana's no-owning rule was rescinded and was never heard of again.[6]

Funny how much less trouble with rustling they had in Montana.

FIVE

Hard Times
and Hard Feelings

OLD MAN winter of 1886–1887 had a great deal to answer for on the northern plains, but he has been blamed for more than his just deserts. It has been stated in any number of casual histories that the winter broke the back of the beef bonanza, finished the eastern and foreign cattle companies, and put an end to the romance of the open range. It has even been said that there were no more cowboys after 1887. The truth of the matter is that the inflated cattle corporations had finished themselves by mismanagement and were going downhill before ever the winter set in. The handwriting was appearing on the wall as early as 1885.

It was faint at first. Momentum was carrying the cattle boom along, and when the roundups started in May they were almost as big and just as spectacular as ever. At the forks of Powder River there was another great array of roundup wagons; the same dashing, picturesque cowboys, the same merriment and displays of horsemanship, the same big herds; only not quite. There was a perceptible diminution in the number of cattle brought in daily to the roundup grounds, and a corresponding drop in the calf crop. The talk now was of the hard winter just past, the "climate mild and genial" evidently not living up to expectations. Could it be that, for hungry cattle on overstocked terrain, even a normal winter could be "hard"?

The summer of 1885 was dry in comparison with the exceptionally wet years which preceded it, though as nothing compared to 1886. The shortage of feed was so bad that the cowboys had a hard time holding the bands of roundup horses from their determined roving in search of feed and water, and before the summer was over the hungry cattle were browsing on such poor nutrients as sagebrush and greasewood—anything they could reach.[1] The result was that in the fall they went to market in poor condition and prices went down some more; mature steers which in 1883 had brought six dollars or more a hundredweight were now down to $4.25 and in the case of one unlucky shipper brought only $3.30.* [2] The next spring, 1886, the cattlemen were complaining of another "hard winter." They had not seen anything yet.

"The fall of 1886," wrote Ernest S. Osgood in *The Day of the Cattleman*, "found the cattlemen of Wyoming in a panicky condition. They were in the grip of a depression that would have caused a crash even if the winters had continued mild.... Cattle were selling for a lower figure than ever before in the history of the range, ten to fifteen dollars a head cheaper than in the preceding fall, with an overabundance of poorer grades, the result of the heavy turnoff of the weaker stock." [3] The handwriting was unmistakable by this time, but only to those who could read. A few could, and got out, but the majority went careening on in their crazy spiraling dance like insects on a midsummer evening. Yet the companies were feeling the pinch, so much so that the Wyoming Stock Growers' Association was forced to make the most painful of economies; it let at least six of its stock inspectors go and asked others to take a cut.

In the throes of the economy drive, in the spring of '86, a number of spokesmen for the cattle companies got together and agreed to cut cowboys' wages by at least five dollars from the prevailing pay of thirty-five or forty dollars a month. This was a seasonal wage, since the majority had only seven or eight months' work a year.

Horace Plunkett was to dedicate his later life to improving the lot of the Irish peasant, whom he understood, but he was a prime energizer of two moves at this time to depress the lot of the "intractable" American cowboy, whom he did not understand. "Wages must come down very much lower," he had frowned a year earlier. And he had attended a special stock meeting in Cheyenne "to establish a fair but reduced scale of wages for cowhands and to abolish free board at ranch houses" [4]—a reference to the old law of hospitality on the western frontier. On the cattle range it meant that the latchstring was on the outside for casual visitors; but it also meant a means of subsistence for unemployed cowboys during the winter months. By "riding the grubline" from one ranch to another they got by until work started next spring. When the Wyoming cattle companies elected to cut wages and eliminate the "grubline" at one

---

* A mature steer marketed at four years old in those days when in average to good condition weighed around 1100 pounds. Thus $6 a hundredweight meant a price of $66 a head, while $4 a hundredweight meant only $44.

stroke, many cowhands who would just as soon have remained honest were virtually driven into killing cattle and selling the beef in order to get through the winter.

And the "fair but reduced scale of wages" for cowhands resulted in the only cowboy strike in the history of the northern range. It is no surprise to learn that Jack Flagg was one of the leaders.

The Knights of Labor, at this time the most powerful and fast-growing labor organization in the country, had recently won a strike against the Union Pacific and had gained many recruits among discontented cowboys in Texas and Wyoming, although cowboys as a class were too individualistic to be organized easily. The Knights probably precipitated the 1886 strike, though there is no proof.[5] It is apparent that while some Wyoming outfits had gone along with the wage cut, others had refused or had yielded promptly to the cowboys' demands for restoration. What happened next is described by the May 27, 1886, *Rocky Mountain Husbandman*, a Montana newspaper:

When roundup No. 23 met on the south fork of Powder River on the 10th inst., the boys concluded to strike for $40 a month all around. This was done by the men who were already receiving $40 who disapproved of the idea of men working by their side for $35 and as low as $30 per month. Not a wheel moved until the foremen submitted to the terms made by a committee from among the cowboys, to the effect that no man should work on roundup 23 for less than $40 a month.

What made the strike a territorial affair was the system whereby outfits of adjoining roundups exchanged representatives—the cowboys called them reps—to claim any strayed cattle. The strike committee decided that no reps might work on Roundup 23 for less than $40 either, so they were all sent home to their respective headquarters to ask for the raise, "and the boys worked their cattle while they were gone."

They all came back with the raise with the exception of Judge Carey's representatives, the CY men, who had been turned down. There ensued a typical cowboy dispute, noisy but essentially harmless, in which the CY reps were ordered, "with threats of violence and bodily harm," said Cheyenne severely, to cut out their horses and leave the roundup. They did so perforce, and a local correspondent reported gleefully that "the other boys refusing to work any cattle of that outfit, CY cows with maverick calves are now running around here as thick as 'the flowers that bloom in the spring, Tra-la.'" Truly the big outfits of that era had achieved a miracle of unpopularity.[6]

Meanwhile the strike had spread to two other roundup districts in the Sweetwater–Platte area, and the effect in Cheyenne was explosive enough in any case. Was not Judge Carey, owner of the CY, president of the Wyoming Stock Growers' Association and the richest and most powerful man in Wyoming? This was worse than insubordination, it was lèse majesté, and Secretary Sturgis determined to punish the "mutineers." His first thought was to prosecute the strike committee for committing a breach of the peace. Would the CY men go before a justice and swear out a complaint? Thirteen years in Wyoming had taught the secretary very little about cowboys.[7]

When the prosecution idea fell through, Sturgis turned to the black-list, but here he encountered unexpected opposition within his own executive committee. T. W. Peters, English half-owner of the Bar C outfit, was in favor of letting the matter drop. Peters fought hard for the culprits, arguing that it would be poor policy to make martyrs of them and even threatening to resign over the issue. At first he refused to fire his own employee, Jack Flagg, who had been active on the strike committee as a representative with one of the more southerly roundups. Peters had to be rapped on the knuckles and reminded that if he persisted in his course he would be faced with expulsion from the association.[8]

The debate seesawed on into midsummer, when the record fades. But the iron hand of Secretary Sturgis evidently prevailed, for at the end of 1886 Jack Flagg had been blackballed and was unable henceforth to get a job with a cow outfit. Thereupon he took up a homestead on the Red Fork of Powder River and bought a brand and a little bunch of cattle and went into cattle-raising for himself; from this ensued an awesome train of consequences. The brand was called the Hat.

And so departed the drouthy and dismal summer which preceded the worst winter in range history, and the romance of the range went with it.

The *what?* True it is that the open range inspired a flood of nostalgic reminiscence such as no other phase of American life except the Confederate side in the Civil War has ever inspired, to say nothing of a flood of rather drippy popular songs. But with all that the open range system was impractical, it was doomed, and as far as the cattle were concerned it was brutal.

For one thing the huge roundups, like the dinosaurs, were too big to survive. Some owners complained that those dashing magnificos, the foremen—who were no more above showing off than was anybody who ever wore cowboys clothes—were in too much of a hurry; they seemed more interested in demonstrating how fast they could work through the country than they were in getting all the cattle. Haste made mavericks; the more cattle missed by the roundup, the more calves would grow up unbranded to be a loss to their owners and a temptation to thieves.

Careful cowmen knew too that big roundups killed calves, since the bigger the roundup, the more little ones would lose their mothers in the bawling melee, never to find them again. But if there were any careful cowmen around in the roaring early eighties they went unheard. There wasn't even a pretense of feeding the weaker cattle in winter or of herding them into areas where they could find shelter; instead they were loosed onto open plains where the icy blasts roared down from the North Pole, and the wretched cattle turned tail and drifted before the blasts until they piled up against one of those newfangled obstructions, a barbed-wire fence, and died. Due to lack of herd management the bulls were turned out on the range at haphazard; the calves came as nature willed instead of during mild spring weather, and countless numbers of them, born into winter storms, were frozen to death. Such monstrous waste would have doomed the open range even if the winter of 1886–1887 had not cut the jugular. Meanwhile there was the folly, the greed, the crime of overstocking.

Overstocking simply meant that there were more cattle than there was grass for them to eat. They grazed the ground bare and hence they reached the market in poor condition, which lowered prices; then distress selling lowered prices some more. Now if a hard winter should happen to come along——

It did.

The Winter of Death

A business that had been fascinating to me before suddenly became distasteful. I never again wanted to own an animal that I could not feed and shelter.

—GRANVILLE STUART

NO AMOUNT of retelling ever seems to wear out the story of a great disaster. It is so with that of the winter of 1886–1887, when the weather gods wrote *finis* to the cattle boom in a crashing climax which all but obliterates the fact that the boom was finished anyway. John Clay's oft-quoted words still stand as its epitaph:

"Three great streams of ill-luck, mismanagement and greed met together.... From the inception of the open range business in the West and Northwest, from say 1870 to 1888, it is doubtful if a single cent was made if you average up the business as a whole. Some of course sold out, taking with them their money, and lived happily ever afterwards, but when you bundle up, strike an average...the story with its flavor of romance ends in hollow failure."

The winter was no local affair. It held the entire northern grazing region in its grip. "From southern Colorado to the Canadian line, from the 100th meridian almost to the Pacific slope," Clay wrote in the early twenties, "it was a catastrophe which the cowmen of today who did not go through it can never understand."

The story of the winter begins with the preceding summer. It was dry, 1886 being the one year of severe drought which broke the exceptionally wet decade of the eighties. Wyoming was a parched desert from the Little Missouri, the Belle Fourche, and the Cheyenne River on its eastern border to the continental divide and beyond. John Clay, on an inspection trip to visit some of his company properties, saw "scarce a spear of grass"; at a roundup on Wind River the cattle came in exhausted for want of water.[1]

It was the same everywhere, and the shortage of feed was com-

35

pounded by the fact that more cattle than ever before had been piled onto the range to eat it; throughout all the comments on that year of disaster the word *overstocking* clangs like a leaden bell. In Montana, according to the local press, the forage was in the worst state known since the coming of the white man. The range was half bare from over-stocking; the earth in every direction had been trampled into powder, and every gust of wind was laden with dust and sand. The cowpunchers tied their neckerchiefs over their noses and mouths to keep out the chok-ing dust, but their eyes were gummed and blackened with it. Streams as large as the Rosebud ceased to flow; springs and creeks never before dry in the recollection of the oldest settlers were nothing but beds of sun-baked mud. Where a few puddles still stood in the stream beds the water was so alkaline that the men could not drink the coffee brewed from it, and even the tired and thirsty horses refused to drink. Poisonous weeds, normally choked out by healthy grass stems, sprang up on the half-bare ground and cattle ate them and died.

The summer saw misery piled on misery before ever the winter set in. Many Montana cattlemen were getting out, driving their herds to Alberta in a vain hope of escaping the oncoming wrath, but Granville Stuart, after weighing all the factors, decided against Canada but did decide to move his herd to the north side of the Missouri, where the range was somewhat less crowded. As they approached the river the wind was from the north, and when the thirst-crazed cattle smelled the water they broke into a run and plunged down the bank, bellowing pitifully. The desperate efforts of the cowboys failed to hold them, and a large number were engulfed in the quicksands beside the ford. Luckily, Stuart wrote, a steamboat was tied at the landing with a donkey engine on its deck, and the sinking animals were roped around the horns and the donkey engine pulled them out one at a time. Despite all efforts seventy were lost.

Everywhere grasshoppers, spawn of drought, were holding their maddening, clicking carnival and eating a considerable proportion of the feed before the cattle could get to it. Prairie fires added to the grief in Wyoming, Montana, and Dakota.[2]

In the face of these conditions, which were known to all, fools who had not yet learned that a cow cannot eat gravel kept bringing in more cattle and piling them onto the bone-dry range. One company with no former holdings in Wyoming brought in 5000 head, another turned loose 6000. The gigantic interstate Continental Cattle Company drove up 32,000 head of unacclimated southern steers and dumped them out to "rustle" for themselves on a northern range, with no grass to rustle, and winter coming on. It was herds like these which showed up next spring with losses of ninety per cent or more, virtually every animal dead.

"Even with the best of winters it would have been a case of suicide," Clay wrote. "As things turned out it was simple murder, at least for the Texas cattle." [3]

It was not to be the best of winters but the worst. Even while disgusted cowboys were turning out the fresh, trail-weary herds upon plains already eaten bare, lordlings with more money than brains were having their last rounds at the Cheyenne Club, preparatory to departing for Paris, London, the Riviera, and the brownstone mansions of Manhattan. They never came back to the same Wyoming. Most of them never came back at all.

An eerie silence blankets that Wyoming winter with a pall almost as deep as the snow. Except for a few lines in Jack Flagg there is virtually no firsthand account of what it was like. Montana and northern Dakota produced personal reminiscences and vivid, fully researched accounts of that terrible season which are classics to be found on every library shelf. Montana correspondents in Butte, Livingston, Fort Assiniboine, Fort Keogh, Fort Benton, and other points filled the New York *World,* the Chicago *Tribune,* and other eastern papers with hair-raising dispatches which appeared under such headlines as WHOLE HERDS LYING DEAD, yet not a syllable about the winter's disaster ever appeared under a Wyoming dateline, so far as this writer has been able to discover.

Aside from John Clay there is one major source and one only on the winter in Wyoming—an article by Professor T. A. Larson of the University of Wyoming which appeared in the Wyoming *Annals* for January 1942. It is based on a study of the two Laramie newspapers of the time, the *Boomerang* and the *Sentinel.* While maintaining their editorial position that everything was rosy, both papers printed news items on the weather, many of them exchanges from country weeklies, these country cousins generally showing a greater readiness to face up to the facts.

Wyoming's professional optimists worked hard at creating the impression that nothing was amiss; that the inclement weather had paused at the imaginary line which divided Wyoming from her less fortunate neighbor to the north. In fact, the available data indicate that the weather in both territories followed a nearly parallel course; although Wyoming was farther south, its altitude was greater. On the 7000-foot-high Laramie plains the mercury even today hits fifty below every few winters.

The wolf-pack blizzards which howled over Montana in December spared southeastern Wyoming for the moment, and on January 6 the editor of the Laramie *Weekly Boomerang* pronounced: "The winter bids fair to be one of the most favorable ever bestowed on Wyoming.... The great annual scare is over, and the alarmists of 1886 are now at liberty to perfect themselves as the liars of 1887." That was the day the storms began.

The first storm lasted without a break for ten days. Reports from scattered points told of snow four feet deep on the level and bottomless drifts. Douglas, on the nineteenth, had not seen a train for two weeks; one finally arrived, but on the twenty-fourth was "reported to have gone into winter quarters, as it can get neither backwards nor forwards." A stage between Sheridan and Buffalo took thirty-six hours to make the thirty-six miles. All through December and January a violent windstorm raged without ceasing along the line of the Union Pacific in Nebraska and all across southern Wyoming, and doctors in Cheyenne and Laramie had many cases of nerves and sleeplessness due to the wind. Trains were blown off the tracks in Colorado by a sixty-mile gale, and two men were badly injured in Wyoming when the wind blew them off a railroad hand-car.

Then, late in January, came a treacherous little thaw. Described as "a brief respite" and "a let-up," it seems to have affected all of Montana and Wyoming, where it lasted a day or two, just long enough to melt the snow on top, forming pools of water. Jack Flagg reported it. "Teddy Blue" reported it—and these two cowboys out on the range were the ones who saw its fatal import the most clearly, for it was followed by another freeze which bound the entire region in a glittering, deadly sheath. The crust covered everything from the Missouri River down into southern Wyoming; on February 10, the *Daily Boomerang* noted: "The snow on the Lost Soldier division of the Lander and Rawlins stage route is four feet deep, and frozen so hard that the stages drive over it like a turnpike."

It lasted all the rest of the winter. For the cattle it was death piled on death. Many slipped and fell on the icy surface and, too weak to regain their feet, died where they lay. In places where the crust was thinner they broke through with each lurching step, until their legs were scraped bare of hide and they left bloody tracks on the snow. Worst of all, it robbed them of their last hope that the wind might blow a few patches bare and expose a mouthful or two of grass.[4]

The "three great streams of ill-luck, mismanagement and greed" now culminated in the most appalling mass slaughter of animals the West had ever seen or would see again, second only to the slaughter of the buffalo.

All witnesses agree that the horses with their far greater intelligence came through very well. They would paw through the crust to find a few blades of grass; defying normal animal instincts, they would head into a blizzard if necessary and fight their way to the south side of a mountain where they could find some shelter from the blasts. But cattle drifted before the gales, following the course of least resistance, until they came to a fence where they piled up and died, or they gravitated downhill into hollows and railroad cuts where the snow was certain to be deepest, and there crowded together helplessly to await death. Nothing got fat that winter except the wolves.

All over the winterbound area the starving, moaning animals invaded the streets of towns or hung around ranch houses, forgetting their wild instincts in the dim hope that the human gods who had gotten them into this fix would somehow get them out of it. The newspapers reported these visitations, and Osgood wrote: "One morning the inhabitants on the outskirts of Great Falls looked out through the swirl of snow to see the gaunt, reeling figures of the leaders of a herd of five thousand that had drifted down to the frozen Missouri from the north. Inhabitants of ranch houses tried not to hear the noises that came from beyond the corrals. The longing for another chinook that never arrived became the yearning for a miracle."

There were dozens of such incidents. In Medora the cattle ate frozen garbage from the cans outside stores and houses and gnawed at tarpaper on the sides of shacks. The humped-up skeletons, nothing but skin and bones, collected around manure piles, nibbling at bits of straw which had passed through the digestive tracts of horses.[5]

The Wyoming data as usual are skimpier, but Larson, harking back to the winter of 1880–1881, which was bad enough, relates that the Laramie city clerk complained to the Association about cattle invading the city during storms. The wretched creatures, their eyes rolling in terror of man, overcame their terror and annoyed the citizens by browsing on shade trees, knocking down gates and, as a final act of effrontery, lying down and dying in the streets. A rancher somewhere, searching desperately for something to feed a starving cow who had strayed into his dooryard, fed her a pot of spoiled beans. She literally exploded in death all over his corral.

The opinion prevailed that as many cattle were lost from thirst as from starvation. There was no water. All small streams were frozen solid, and far in the future was the happier day which would see overshoed cowboys with their ear flaps pulled down chopping holes in the ice of tanks and streams so the cattle could drink. In many areas gravitational pull sent them drifting down onto the big rivers, where they would walk out on the ice to the air holes; this happened on the Missouri and the

Yellowstone in Montana and on Wind River in Wyoming. As the leaders tried to drink the crowding of the herd behind them would push them in, and they were swept out of sight and life.

The relatively few cowboys who were kept on during the winters worked themselves to the bone trying to herd the cattle away from these death traps and back into the hills, but it was a losing game. "You'd get one bunch of cattle up the hill and another one would be coming down behind you," "Teddy Blue" wrote, "and it was all so slow, plunging after them through the deep snow that way; you'd have to fight every step of the way. The horses' feet were cut and bleeding from the heavy crust, and the cattle had the hair and hide wore off their legs to the knees and hocks." The cowboys were proud that they had saved thousands of cattle, but there were too many they could not save.[6]

The cowboys piled on such quantities of clothing that it was a wonder they could get on a horse. When an ironic sun shone on the arctic expanse they tried to ward off snow blindness by blacking their eye sockets with the black deposit from a kerosene-lamp chimney and by cutting eyeholes in the same black neckerchiefs with which they had tried to protect themselves from the dust and ashes of the preceding fall. The subzero air knifed into their lungs; exertion in such air can cause death, and the bodies of cowboys who died were tied onto their horses for transportation back to the ranch, where they were deposited in a snowdrift to await burial when the ground softened next spring.

"For all this," Howard wrote, "they got no medals, nor expected any. A cowboy's job was to look after the herd; he was being paid for it— $40 a month. But hundreds of ranchers and riders underwent such hardships in that dreadful winter that they forsook the range forever, crippled in body and spirit."

There is no reason to think that the Wyoming cowboys were any less heroic than the Montana cowboys, wherever they were on the range; it is just that the record maintains its eerie silence concerning them. Where an individual owner like Granville Stuart, cowman to the bone, kept "plenty of men on the range to look after the cattle," saving all they could, it is likely that Wyoming's absentee corporate "cattle barons," ignorant of range conditions, had pursued their pennywise policy of turning off all hands during the winter in the face of the worst winter in history; hence there were no men left on their ranges to put up a gallant if largely useless fight. The many small and medium-sized-ranch owners of Wyoming took their experiences of that dread winter to the grave with them, but they were probably no different from the ones we have told.

Mention has been made of the way cattle drifted down onto railroad tracks and into the cuts, seeking shelter and a place cleared of snow.

Because of this fact the passengers on a Union Pacific train had an experience they would remember all their lives. Rotary snowplows had cleared the track, and the trains ran between canyon walls of white. A year later "one of the most prominent stockmen of the territory" described his journey homeward from Chicago to a reporter for the *Weekly Boomerang*. It was in the middle of February; for fifty-four days one snowstorm had succeeded another; from Omaha to Ogden the carcasses of dead cattle could be counted by the hundred at every stage of the journey. Near Ogalalla, Nebraska, was a place where the starving, freezing animals had drifted by thousands to the railroad track, where they lay down on the rails, too weak to stand, and finding between the embankments thrown up by the snowplows some shelter from the wind. The line of them stretched out for miles; every train for weeks had been delayed three to six hours here, and when the train stopped, the *Boomerang* recalled a year later, "the beef blockade formed a sight that made the stockman sick and terrified the tenderfoot."

It was impossible to drive the herds off the sides of the track as they could not climb the snowbanks; some were driven down at places where a creek ran under the roadbed, but more thousands ran wildly along in front of the engine, too crazy to seek safety by leaving the rails even where they could. Male passengers and trainmen, armed with sticks and chunks of coal, drove the herd ahead of them, the train slowly following, until finally a woodyard was reached and the track was cleared.

"Those who were on the train that day will never forget their strange western experience as long as they live; two hundred well-dressed gentlemen driving 50,000 head of dying cattle seven miles to lift the beef blockade." [7]

While all this was going on the katydid booster kept sawing away at his familiar tune. "The beef market is rising," chirped the editor of the *Boomerang* on January 10, squarely in the teeth of the facts, "and in the spring no finer beeves will put money in their owners' pockets than those from this section of Wyoming." In his enthusiasm he forgot that beeves were shipped in the fall, not in the spring. Soon the whole country with the exception of Wyoming newspaper readers knew about the cattle catastrophe in the West; it was being headlined in Boston, New York, Pittsburgh, Chicago, St. Paul, and Denver among other places. In Chicago, city editors were sending their reporters to watch hotel registers for the names of eastern cattle capitalists who might be journeying west to check into the state of affairs, and a *Tribune* reporter cornered the son of a Boston tycoon in his hotel room. The young man had had a ghastly trip; he had been half frozen, hazed by the cowboys, and bucked off a horse. He could barely move and could not even sit except on a pillow. Nevertheless, the interview proceeded reasonably well until the reporter pursued: "Well, but the percentage of loss. You've forgotten to—" At this point the Bostonian rose wrathfully though painfully to his feet and terminated the interview.[8]

During most of this time a deafening silence issued from Cheyenne. Apart from a few patronizing references to Montana's troubles, there was virtually no mention of the weather until February 10, when the *Weekly Leader* came out with a record-breaking whopper. "The range cattle business in Wyoming has suffered no unusual loss during the present season. Should the spring be as favorable as the winter has been, the season will close with a remarkably small loss."

Three weeks passed and then the editor of the *Boomerang* achieved the climax of idiocy by writing: "Range cattle have been shipped to eastern markets in such good condition in the past two years that easterners have become jealous." In view of the notoriously bad condition in which they had been shipped, the remark was clear proof that Wyoming was suffering from a neurosis.

Montana too had her quota of katydids—"the cold snaps never last long enough to be unpleasant" chirped one of them from Helena in February 1887—but Montana also abounded in very bright, very vocal young men who knew how to pick up a penny by sending correspondence to the big-city papers; their "exaggerations" and "inventions" were roundly condemned. The worst offender was the Ananias whose dispatches to the New York *World* from Fort Keogh told of dead cattle, sixty-below temperatures, snow eight to fifty feet deep and the like. He was finally identified as a Lieutenant J. M. T. Partello. Demands were heard that he be disciplined by the War Department, but nothing came of it.[9]

The lieutenant, if it were he, really did tell some tall ones—snowflakes the size of milk cans and cattle frozen to death standing up, only their horns showing above the snow! But while there can be no justification for the Brobdingnagian snowflakes, cattle were in fact frozen in a standing position, for if a weak cow floundered into a snowdrift she could not get out, and as more snow fell around her there she stood; or she might stand helpless in a coulee, imprisoned by the accumulation of ice about her feet until she too was literally snowed under. Gulches, unused railroad cuts and the like, fifty feet or more deep, would be drifted full to the brim, and temperatures touching sixty below were confirmed. A good citizen in Miles City, who said he had lived in Montana for twenty years, was outraged by the stories of cattle drowned in the rivers; how, he asked, would they get through ice three feet thick? Nothing could better illustrate the mental gulf between the rangeman and the city man; the good citizen might just as well have been living in New Orleans, or he would have known that big, swift-running rivers develop air holes no matter how thick the ice.

By March nightmarish talk of fifty and sixty per cent losses was being heard. It *couldn't* be—— Didn't those pesky correspondents know that a Montana cow could stand anything a buffalo could?

In the middle of the agitation over eastern press reports and the flurries of denial, a roundup captain from Custer County walked into the office of the *Yellowstone Journal* in Miles City with a signed statement describing the conditions he had observed on the range. The editor refused to print it. But it got on the wires anyway, from Fort Keogh.

Spring came at last. When it did, the tallest and worst tales proved to be true.

The April stock meetings were scantily attended and gloomy; in Montana openly so but in Cheyenne, where the members of the Association were still suffering from a case of Cheyenne-Clubitis compounded by wishful thinking, a glaze of optimism was still spread over foreboding. In an interview Secretary Adams spoke of mavericks and maverick sales, but not of conditions on the range. At the meeting he spoke hopefully about "exaggerated reports of the winter's losses," and those present appeared satisfied with his view. Said Clay tersely: "The members did not realize their situation."

The chinook, the real one, had come around the first of March, behind schedule, on the heels of a last blizzard which had stalled trains and frozen the ears of trainmen on the Northern Pacific and other roads all over the Middle West and West. Now, however, reports from scattered Montana points brought the wonderful news of temperatures up to forty and fifty degrees with a warm wind from the southwest, and on March 5 the *Yellowstone Journal* exulted: "All day Sunday and yesterday the glorious chinook with unabated vigor has been undoing the work of the ice king...the snow has disappeared as if by magic. Dripping eaves and slushy streets give evidence of the good work performed and the hill tops loom up black and rugged.... At the risk of a setback we cannot refrain from a third call, springtime has surely come, gentle Annie."

On the same date the *Dickinson Press* hailed the wondrous arrival in North Dakota in almost the same words. Only Cheyenne, as usual, was silent, for having never officially admitted the existence of the winter, how could it welcome the chinook? But even as winterbound women looked out of the windows of ranch houses at the warm sun and the first patches of bare ground with tears of thankfulness in their eyes, they could not know, nor could their men, that a worse hell than all they had been through awaited them when the roundups began.

The rivers broke up a few days later, when the sun softened the ice and loosened it along the riverbanks, and the raging current did the rest; soon three-foot-thick cakes, veritable ice floes, were grinding and tossing on their way downstream. "The ice is going out on the Missouri," the papers reported; or "The Rosebud has broken up, and the ice reached this point [Miles City] on Wednesday under the Yellowstone ice." By now they were all breaking up, the Yellowstone and the Missouri and Tongue River and Powder River and the Big Horn and the Cheyenne River and the Little Missouri over in frozen Medora, in a terrifying demonstration of the powers of spring. A cowboy in camp on a river bend would be awakened by a noise of crunching and crashing as the river piled a load of mammoth ice cakes into his dooryard; he got out with all speed and made it to the top of the bluff just in time. Gentle Annie! People in Miles City still talked of the time Tongue River had overflowed and sent massive chunks of ice slithering into the downtown streets, but that was nothing. No one before or after ever saw a spring breakup like the one in '87.

Lincoln Lang, Roosevelt's ranching neighbor, told the story. As the snow melted, every dry gulch, where last summer the earth was a burning powder and even the sagebrush seemed to give up in the heat, every such gulley became a torrent—the air was filled with the steady roar of running water—the creeks were out of bounds. "A few days later such a grim freshet was pouring down the river valley as no man had ever seen before or ever would again . . . one day we heard a roar above that of the rushing water, coming from the direction of the Little Missouri. The river was out of its banks clear up to the cottonwoods, going down in a raging muddy torrent—huge grinding ice-cakes up-ending and rolling over each other, tearing down trees in their path. Countless carcasses of cattle were going down with the ice, rolling over and over as they went, sometimes with all four stiffened legs pointed skyward. For days on end, tearing down with the grinding ice cakes, went Death's cattle roundup of the upper Little Missouri country. In countless valleys, gulches, washouts and coulees the animals had vainly sought shelter. . . . Now their carcasses were being spewed forth in untold thousands by the rushing waters, to be carried away on the crest of the foaming, turgid flood. . . .

"With them went our hopes. One had only to stand by the river bank a few minutes and watch the grim procession going ceaselessly by . . . our tally sheet, succeeding the spring roundup, showed a loss of about eighty per cent." [10]

The men who rode the range were not given to literary self-expression, and of all those who experienced the spring roundups of 1887 few told what they were like. In Wyoming the Upper Powder roundup, described by Jack Flagg, was a reduced and dismal affair, with a mere four wagons in place of the twenty-seven which had assembled at the same spot four years earlier. However, the reduction must be attributed to the preceding two years' deflation, not to the winter just passed, since no one knew in advance of the roundup just how bad the losses were going to be. As it turned out, the grounds where 10,000 head of cattle had been gathered in 1883 now saw only as many hundred.

Wherever a creek bottom or a draw had offered a ghostly hope of shelter the dead cattle were piled in heaps, while the bark and small branches of willows and box elders were gnawed off as high as a starving animal could reach. "Teddy Blue" wrote of riding on the Maginnis roundup: "... we weren't getting a thing; we'd ride all morning and maybe only find a couple of weak-kneed, ganted steers.... The weather was hot, and the dead cattle stunk in the coulees ... pfew! I can smell them yet." The winter's tale was told in a piece of doggerel of unidentified origin and confused chronology, which yet gives some of the feeling of that terrible time:

> *I may not see a hundred*
> *Before I cross the Styx,*
> *But coal or ember, I'll remember*
> *Eighteen eighty-six.*
>
> *The stiff heaps in the coulee,*
> *The dead eyes in the camp,*
> *And the wind about, blowing fortunes out,*
> *As a woman blows out a lamp.*

"Dead eyes," indeed. It was said that for years to come the eyes of hard men who had been through that spring's roundup went bleak at the memory.

The loss estimates varied wildly; so for that matter did the losses, depending on local conditions and the class of cattle. Losses in the Big Horn Basin were tragically large, but one lucky owner who had moved his herd to a sheltered range in the foothills actually branded more calves next spring than usual. In hard-hit Montana a rancher on the Rosebud who was obviously kin to one of the Wise Virgins fed hay all winter and brought his herd through; but in northern Dakota equally wise ranchers who had planned to feed hay were defeated by the 'hoppers, who ate it up before they could cut it. The heaviest loss was suffered by the "through" herds from Texas which were dumped out in the fall without a chance to survive, and this is the grim story told by John Clay: "The Worsham folks never attempted to gather their remnant; ... out of [Major Smith's] 5,500 three-year-olds we got about a hundred head." Yet a brother of this same owner, who had brought his herd to a neighboring range a year earlier, lost only ten per cent.

A big outfit in Crook County, northeastern Wyoming, lost 11,090 cattle out of one herd of 12,000 and wrote off 22,000 head out of a total of 30,000. Skepticism was expressed over some of these hard-luck stories. Many managers of big companies, it was pointed out, had systematically overstated the size of their herds, at the same time understating the *normal* annual loss at the two per cent figure the rosy prospectuses had set forth, when everybody knew that ten per cent was more like it in an average year. Now the whole accumulation of lies was written off at once and blamed on the hard winter; which, said the cynics, saved many a reputation.[11]

But with all the discounts taken, murder it was. Next to the unacclimated cattle the worst loss was among she-stock; the cow with a calf in her belly or one at her heels, sucking what milk she had to give, was in no condition to stand this.

Horace Plunkett, for one, lost ten per cent of his steers and seventy-five per cent of his cows. With such a loss among the maternal stock the calf brand in Wyoming was variously reported down by fifty per cent; or seventy-five per cent; or four fifths as compared to the year before— and a calf tally is a count, not guesswork.

Experienced judges generally placed the over-all loss in Wyoming at around fifty per cent, Montana fifty to sixty, but no one really knew. It was generally felt that the growing class of homesteader-ranchmen who kept small herds and had a hayfield may have come through well enough to offset somewhat the spectacular losses among the big herds, but there were many mysteries. Why did such good ranchmen as Gregor Lang and his son Lincoln lose eighty per cent on the Little Missouri? Why did Stuart himself, after keeping cowboys at work all winter and generally doing everything humanly possible, lose two thirds of a wintered herd? His spirit never recovered.

Biggest mystery of all, however, was what became of the cattle. For the carcasses counted as they melted out from under the drifts, the carcasses which had rolled down with the spring floods, the lost cattle known or guessed at which had gone into air holes and been swept down under the ice—none of this came anywhere near approximating the total loss. Where had they gone? At first it was thought that they had drifted before the storms hundreds of miles, and that some would turn up on distant roundups. But they never did. Did their bones disintegrate among the grass stems so that riders combing the range could not find them? How? Anyway, they were not found. No one knew, or will ever know, the answer. Mother Earth, so-called, who had treated them so cruelly, had in some fashion taken back her own.

The roundups came and passed into mid-July, the reports were in, there was no concealing the facts now; and still the Cheyenne *Leader* kept as mum on the subject of losses as a Victorian mother on the subject of sex. On July 21 the *Weekly Leader* ran a story in bold headlines about a glittering gala at the Cheyenne Club, filled with socially prominent names. On another page was an inconspicuous item about Alec Swan being sued for three quarters of a million. But when September and the shipping season came, there was no concealing the truth even from the editorial self, as the black battering-ram headlines, on the front page now, hit home in blow after blow:

Sept. 22 THE CATTLE MARKET Receipts Show a Considerable Falling Off
Sept. 29 ON THE DOWN GRADE Range Stock Declines
Oct. 20 VERY DISCOURAGING The Cattle Market Still Tending Downward
Dec. 1 DOWN AGAIN Another Setback

Worse even than the headlines were the paragraphs underneath with their leaden monotonous insistence on a single theme: "...down... down.... Oversupply.... Very few buyers.... Heavy turn-off of the poorer grades.... Heavy receipts the cause of the decline.... No oversupply of choice beeves. [But who had any choice beeves?] Cattle from the ranges coming in at a rate of five to six thousand a day.... Prospects of more arrivals." And now the poorer grades were depressing the better ones; even "natives" were beginning to be dumped; the market was a shambles—all telling a story which he who ran could read. The bankrupt "barons" were scraping their ranges of everything left from the winter which could still stand on four legs and throwing it on the glutted market.

Wyoming, the "All's Well" state, was one of the heaviest shippers, and that too told its story.

The chapter was almost finished. One big cattle company after another closed out. Secretary Sturgis had resigned from the Wyoming Stock Growers' Association effective the spring of 1887. Back in his native New York, his charm and self-confidence unimpaired, he was financially and socially successful, a member of the Union League Club and a leader in many civic causes and good works. Among other things— a note in passing—he devoted himself to the American Society for the Prevention of Cruelty to Animals.[12]

And so goodbye to the Beef Bonanza. The lords had flown. But Wyoming went on.

2

A Maverick
Is a Motherless Calf
1884-1890

Many a cowman got his start with a long rope and a running iron.

—ARTICLE OF THE WESTERN CREDO

Three years ago a guileless tenderfoot came into Wyoming, leading a single Texas steer and carrying a branding iron; now he is the opulent possessor of six hundred head of fine cattle—the ostensible progeny of that one steer.

—BILL NYE in the Laramie Boomerang, 1883

Nowadays when they pray they consign the thief to a warmer place than southern Texas. It makes all the difference as to whose ox is gored.

—JOHN CLAY in My Life on the Range

SEVEN

Long Ropes
and Running Irons

ON THE open range, ownership of a calf was determined by the brand on the cow. But if the calf escaped the roundup and grew big enough to leave its mother without a brand, or if it was orphaned by causes natural or unnatural, there was no way of proving who owned it, and this simple natural fact led to more trouble and strife than any other one cause in the history of the West.[1]

The orphan was called a maverick. There are numerous legends as to the origin of the name, but all agree that it was derived from that of the well-known Texas family, and that somewhere, at some time, there was a man named Maverick who neglected to brand his increase. Hence a rider happening upon a slick-sided cow or bull would say "That's one of Maverick's," or simply "That's a Maverick." One version has it that this wily character deliberately refrained from branding and then said: "Anything without a brand is mine." The real story is told by J. Frank Dobie in *The Longhorns* and again by Robert H. Fletcher in *Free Grass to Fences*. A South Carolinian named Samuel A. Maverick had come to Texas and was practicing law in San Antonio some years before the Civil War. In 1845 he accepted 400 head of mixed cattle in lieu of cash on a note. Fletcher's account continues:

> The cattle were on long, narrow Matagorda Island four miles off the Texas coast. They were in charge of an irresponsible Negro family who seemingly came with the cattle as part of the deal.... The Negroes were not very conscientious herders and few calves were branded.
>
> During the Mexican war Maverick was up to his ears in business and political affairs. He paid slight attention to his island bovines and due to defections by restless members of the herd [who had waded ashore at low

tide] they still tallied four hundred after he had owned them for eight years.

In 1853 he had them moved from the island to the mainland where they mingled with the herds of full-time stockgrowers who kept their calves branded and who were forever on the lookout for slicks. When they found one it was a twenty-to-one shot that it was a Maverick critter, which didn't deter them from slapping their own iron on the beast. And so unbranded cattle became known as Mavericks.

In 1856 Sam Maverick sold his herd.... They were the only cattle he ever owned.[2]

Sam Maverick was a Yale graduate, and thus an eastern institution of learning became connected, albeit remotely, with one of the most controversial aspects of life in the Wild West.

Wyoming law defined mavericks as "all neat cattle, regardless of age, found running at large in this territory without a mother, and upon which there is no brand." Whose were they? Popular opinion had a ready answer: the unidentified animal belonged to the first man who dropped his loop on it. A "wide loop." A "long rope." The two terms meant the same thing. They meant trouble and loss for the owners of large herds.

Along with the long rope went the running iron. Respectable cow outfits imprinted their monogram on bovine hides with heavy stamp irons, but a slender rod with a curved tip would do just as well, in expert hands, to inscribe or burn over any brand. There were times and places where the mere carrying of a running iron on a man's saddle was considered prima facie evidence of guilt.

In most respects the honesty of the West was proverbial. Doors were never locked. Word-of-mouth agreements were accepted on transactions involving tens of thousands of dollars. But the West had an elastic conscience when it came to stock matters—it stretched like a piece of wet rawhide. Worse yet was the unsanctified sense of humor which made lawbreaking, which ought to have been a serious matter, a subject of infinite deadpan jesting on the part of everybody except the victim—unless the thief got caught, and then the joke was on him.

A whole family of yarns grew up around the assumption, which contained more truth than poetry, that no cow outfit on the roundup or on the trail ever willingly killed one of its own animals for meat. For instance there was the one about the Texas cowman who rode up to a neighbor's camp at dinner time, and was invited in with typical plains hospitality.

"Come in, come right into camp, John, and have some dinner," urged the host. "I'll give you something to eat you never ate before in your life."

"What's that?" the visitor asked, falling into the trap.

"A piece of your own beef."

The folklore rang countless changes on the theme, in vintage jests which grew warm with repetition. There was the one about the widow-woman who told her boys, when they brought in meat for the table, to be sure not to take an animal bearing their own brand, for she would as lief eat one of her little children as one of her own beeves. There were not-so-sly allusions to the cowman who was so extraordinarily honest, or extraordinarily tough, that he could eat a steak from one of his own animals without feeling queasy; conversely, there was the cowman who unknowingly ate a bait of his own beef and it made him deathly sick.

Another classic was the yarn about the dishonest foreman, which proceeded from the tongue-in-cheek assumption that the foreman of any large outfit was inevitably dishonest and stole from his employer, who had of course stolen in his turn from somebody else; hence arose this chestnut about the foreman whose employer's brand was a simple letter I. In time the foreman became ambitious and decided to start a herd for himself; he chose for his brand an IC.* As years went by he too became rich and respectable, and *his* foreman, becoming ambitious in turn, started a herd which he branded ICU. Finally, we come to the third foreman, following in the footsteps of the others, who branded ICU2. Pretty feeble, no doubt, but it remained good for a laugh after countless repetitions over coffee and beans in the cook tent.

It was a sagebrush axiom that all it took to start a cow outfit was a running iron and nerve enough to use it. To this day the barroom cynic in any cow-country town, always ready to enlighten the newcomer, is sure to offer half-seriously, half in jest: "Why, don't you know how old So-and-So got his start?"—naming the ancestor of the largest cattle owner in the area. "He got it with a long rope and a running iron." The remark has been made about every cattleman of any prominence from the Rio Grande to the Canadian line, and is so hoary with ancient usage that it is taken without offense. Since it is a well-known psychological principle that humor is generally a denial of some inner discomfort, the discerning will see in this enormous folklore of jests about stealing the symptoms of guilt.

There were rustlers and rustlers. Their methods varied and so did their community status. The distinctions among the various kinds of

* An easy way of stealing, before the era of tight brand-registration laws, was for a newcomer to move in on a range and start a brand which was like that of a wealthy neighbor except for the addition of a few lines. There are countless instances of brand conversion; a CY, for example, was readily changeable to an OX.

rustling were like the difference between professional prostitution and an occasional fling.

Branding a maverick, in the minds of the generality, was a crime without moral turpitude, if a crime at all—like violating the prohibition law or cheating on an expense account. No amount of legislation ever wholly changed this attitude, though a few jail sentences helped. Even under the law it was rated a misdemeanor, not a felony.

But it was one thing to slap your iron on a maverick when you happened on him in the course of a day's riding; this was a temptation few could resist, and men of the sternest antirustling persuasion have been heard to admit with the third highball: "Hell, I've done it myself." It was another thing to scour the country deep into another man's range looking for slicks on the pretext that you were merely out hunting strays, and to keep this up day after day. The more you made a business of mavericking the closer you came to the fine line that separated the mavericker from something worse. "'Mavericking,'" Frank Dobie has said, "graduated into a soft synonym for stealing."

When the natural supply of mavericks was not great enough to satisfy the ambitious mavericker, especially in view of the competition, the next step was to forestall nature by placing your brand on a big calf that was going to become a maverick in a few weeks. You took the chance that nobody would ride by and notice it in the meanwhile; indeed, you took a second chance, for the big calf, displaced by a younger sibling, would continue to hang around its mother for some time hoping to get another suck, and this was a dead giveaway. But what the hell. The country was big, riders were few, and if a stock detective hired by the Association did happen to come along, the likelihood was he would not know who owned your unregistered brand, called a maverick brand—and suppose he did; you could take care of yourself.

The third step was to make mavericks by separating calves from their mothers until they were weaned. Granville Stuart in *My Forty Years on the Frontier* mentions the case of the fortunate ranchman whose cows always gave birth to twins and triplets, while his neighbors' cows hung enviously around his corral lamenting their own childless state.[3] But as rustling went this was pretty crude stuff—settler stuff. Experts would pen the calves in some lonely corral in the foothills, then run the cows a long way off and hold them there until the calves were eating grass. This writer remarked to an old-timer that it must have taken a pretty good cowboy to run a cow off from her calf. "There were good cowboys," he said.

If the rustler stopped there he remained semirespectable, at least in his own estimation, and he might even have a certain Robin Hood dash. He was well above the line which divided the good bad man from the skunk. But others descended to such methods as slitting the calf's tongue so it couldn't suck, or killing the cow in order to make an orphan of the calf. During Johnson County's time of trouble, calves bearing a rustler's fresh brand were found still hanging about the dead body of the mother cow. Nothing dashing about that.

Finally the rustler might come to burning over other men's brands with a running iron, or "blotching" them so badly they could not be read. He was now a full-fledged thief. *Facilis descensus Averno.*

Between the practices described in the last two paragraphs and the milder forms of stealing the elastic conscience stiffened and became uneasy. A man who "made no bones" in later years about having branded any number of mavericks in his day would swear on a stack of Bibles that he had never altered a brand in his life. As for the other kinds of dirty business, we may quote the utterance of a likable reprobate who was well known in the Powder River country.

"I'm a thief and I've been a thief all my life," he declared with disarming frankness, "but there's one place I draw the line; I will not kill a cow to get the calf."

Butchering a steer on the range, burying the hide and taking the meat home to eat was a cheap form of stealing, fit only for thieving Indians and threadbare settlers. It was disapproved more on social than on moral grounds. Another two-bit operation was to separate a calf from the cow, take it home and let the women and children raise it by hand. This was called "finding a motherless calf."

There was considerable sympathy for the man so poor he had to steal in order to feed his family, even when that man happened to be an Indian. Charlie Russell painted a picture called "Caught in the Act," in which two bundled-up cowboys in the dead of winter have come upon a pair of Indians skinning a beef in the snow. One of the Indians points to his open mouth in the sign for hunger, and the uncertain attitude of the cowboys tells more plainly than words how they are torn between loyalty to their outfit and pity for the half-starved red men.

But the business of butchering beef on the range soon developed into a commercial enterprise, with the local meat market for an outlet. In western Nebraska in the eighties a member of a grand jury considering the case of a settler charged with killing a beef wanted to know whether he had killed it to eat or to sell!

To sum up the code, the man least condemned for rustling was the man who stole in order to build up a herd of his own and get a start, after which he would turn respectable. Most condemned was the thief so low he would cut the rope tying some settler's old bony milk cow to the tailgate of his wagon and steal the cow.

Finally, let us not overlook the curious double meaning which attached to the word rustler. A rustler was a thief. But he was also a man of energy, a hustler who rose early and rode far in order to get ahead in the world. A money-raising committee would be referred to as "the rustling committee." Newspapers called themselves *The Bonanza Rustler* or *The Big Horn County Rustler*. When a young boy won a prize for bringing in the largest number of subscribers to a local paper, the item was captioned A GOOD RUSTLER. An animal which sustained itself on the range under adverse conditions was "a good rustler" too, and a man arriving home late with a guest would ask his wife to "go rustle us up something to eat."

Moral confusion, or merely semantic?

But a horse thief was something else entirely. When you said horse thief you had better smile.

EIGHT

The Case of William Maverick

IT BECAME increasingly clear that the maverick question would have to be regulated, and so would the roundups. To responsible cowmen the chaos of each man for himself was intolerable. In Montana Granville Stuart protested what he called "the Texas system of everybody's placing his brand on every calf found unbranded on the range, without even trying to ascertain to whom the animal belonged.... From the first I took issue against this kind of business. It was only a step from 'mavericking' to branding any calf without a brand, and from that to changing brands. Cowboys permitted to brand promiscuously for a company soon found that they could as easily steal calves and brand for themselves." [1]

In an effort to bring about some order in the early eighties various rules of thumb were proposed, one being the so-called "law of accustomed range," which said that the maverick belonged to the man upon whose range it was found. Under this rule an honest cowman, if he came upon a maverick while riding in his neighbor's territory, would rope and brand it for his neighbor. This was called "courtesy of the range," and the idea was that the other man would reciprocate. However, the law of customary range was all too often neglected in favor of the law of the jungle. Before the maverick laws were passed, many of the big outfits were going at it with might and main; it was not uncommon for them to offer their cowboys five dollars a head for mavericks branded in the outfit's name, and this source of income helped many a laid-off buckaroo to get through the winter. Up to now it had been a case of tit for tat, one big company raiding another. It was a legal no-man's land, but when a cowboy started branding for himself he was called a thief.

Apart from the five-dollars-a-head consideration, zealous cowpunchers would sometimes brand for their employer just to show their efficiency, and many owners looked the other way while this was done.

But some did not. While Theodore Roosevelt was ranching in North Dakota in the early eighties, he was out riding one day with one of his men, a cowboy from Texas, when they came upon a "slick." The cowhand roped it.

"Hold on," said Roosevelt, "we're on the Langs' range. That calf belongs to them."

"Oh, I know my business," said the cowpoke, continuing his preparations to brand.

Once again Roosevelt snapped his order to desist, and followed it up by saying: "A man who will steal for me will steal from me. You're fired." [2]

The incident was related far up and down the Little Missouri. It may have opened a few eyes.

On February 5, 1884, the Laramie *Boomerang* rejoiced:

The stock business of the Laramie plains is so shaping itself of late ... that the ownership of herds is extending to a greater number of lesser ranchers, thus giving almost every ranchman a share in the profits of the lucrative business heretofore confined to a few wealthy owners.

But what pleased the *Boomerang* did not please the "few wealthy owners" at all. They were even less pleased when the same thing started happening in the vast reaches of northern Wyoming where, in the same year, spokesmen for the great 76 outfit were already scowling over the encroachment of a few small shoestring operators whose fifty or a hundred head were said to be exerting pressure on a range already overcrowded by the 76 and its neighbors' tens of thousands.

As settlers with a few cattle of their own began infiltrating on every range, the question "Whose maverick?" became increasingly moot. Soon the have-nots, the little fellows with fifty or a hundred or two hundred head, were proposing their own rule of thumb to the effect that any man who had cattle on the range was entitled to brand mavericks. That unbranded yearling whose sleek side gleamed so temptingly behind a clump of sagebrush might just as well be the offspring of one of his own fifty cows—so argued the settler—as of one of the neighboring "baron's" five thousand. Mathematically his claim was absurd, but it was useless to argue with him, and just as useless to argue with the "baron" that his exclusive so-called rights on the range, which had never existed, and with them his exclusive right to claim the mavericks, had gone to join the buffalo. Like it or not, they were now the people's mavericks.

There was chaos too on the roundups, as each owner gathered and branded at his own sweet will, and the cattle were so continuously "choused" that they could not gain weight. Agreements were made and resolutions passed, but every spring the roundup "sooners" were out notwithstanding, trying to get ahead of everybody else and take all the big unbranded calves.

Regulation was very much in order. In 1883, 1884, and 1885 Colorado, Wyoming, and Montana in that sequence passed laws to regulate roundups and provide an answer to the question *Who owns the maverick?* Colorado and Montana from the first placed control of their livestock affairs under a governmental commission which was supposed to administer them in the interests of all. The people seem to have been satisfied that this was the case, since the laws remained in effect with only minimal modifications until the turn of the century brought an end to the open-range system.

But in Wyoming the big stockmen won a Pyrrhic victory when they succeeded in passing, over heated public opposition, the maverick law of 1884. This vested control not in any public body but in the Wyoming Stock Growers' Association. One of the worst pieces of legislation ever inflicted on the West, it was hacked at and amended in every succeeding session of the legislature, going generally from bad to worse, until the first state legislature, meeting at the end of 1890, finally wiped the miserable thing off the books, leaving a void. But by that time it was too late. Bad trouble was ready to blow.

The maverick law of 1884 lit the powder train which led to the Johnson County explosion.

The eighth Legislative Assembly of Wyoming Territory convened in January 1884 on a note of soaring upbeat. To the "lords" of two continents who gathered in the icy, invigorating air, not a cloud was visible in the financial sky. Champagne and money bubbled at the Cheyenne Club, and to mention overstocking would have been equivalent to calling one's mother an evil name. The territorial capitol building had not yet started rising on the naked plain north of Main Street, so the legislature met in the ornate Commerce Block, and the first order of business was a bill with the twin objective of regulating the roundups and providing a solution to the maverick question.

The bill proposed to give the Wyoming Stock Growers' Association authority to organize all roundups in the territory. There were some loud objections on the part of diehards who resisted regulation on general principle, and out in the western wilds of the territory there was talk of hanging the roundup foreman if he ventured to appear, but on the whole criticism was directed less against rule by law than rule by the Association.

The second feature of the bill was to claim all mavericks on behalf of the Association, and this was what tipped the fat into the fire.

Whose mavericks were they? Nobody knew. The Association represented a majority of the cattle in the territory; it did not represent a majority of the owners. However, the bill provided that all unbranded cattle were to be taken up by the roundup foreman on behalf of the Association and branded with an M on the neck in token of same, and that they were to be sold at auction every ten days, the proceeds going into the treasury of the Association, "to be used in the payment of cattle inspectors and other like purposes." [3]

The "like purposes" were nowhere defined. Not a penny of the maverick money had to be accounted for. The three-dollar-a-day roundup foreman had to give a $3000 bond for the faithful discharge of his trust involving a few hundred dollars, whereas the officials of a private corporation who were responsible for the entire territorial maverick fund running into thousands were not asked for any surety, nor for so much as an annual report. None of this was lost on the opposition press: "... what 'other like purposes' may be are unknown to the world. This autocratic stock association is not required to report publicly any of its proceedings," sputtered the Laramie *Weekly Boomerang*.[4]

Nor was it lost on the cowboys, who were unlettered but not slow; and away out under the wintry skies, in untidy bunkhouses and bachelor cabins they spent hours around the stove discussing the maverick bill, came to the pungent conclusion that "other like purposes" included the upkeep of that rich man's club in Cheyenne.

Back in civilization, which for the most part meant Cheyenne and Laramie, public wrath exploded in the press. The bill was damned as unconstitutional, which it probably was, and as unenforceable, which it promptly turned out to be. "A leading lawyer of the territory," quoted in the Laramie *Daily Boomerang*, called it "one of the greatest outrages on human liberty ever attempted." Epithets such as "vicious" and "atrocious class legislation" flew through the air, while the *Boomerang* added its comment that the bill if passed "would work great injustice to the growers of little means and would place the business entirely in the hands of the few." Predictions were made on all sides that the monstrosity could not possibly pass.

While lawyers and editors had their say, the average citizen was bundling up to his nose to ride ten miles to his mailbox through the wintry weather, to pick up a skimpy folded newspaper and fume and swear over the goings-on in Cheyenne. A rancher at Elk Mountain on the Laramie plains gripped his pencil in hardened fingers and filled a column in the *Carbon County Journal* with his wrath. How dared the Association make rules for men who were not its own members? To read such a bill before an American legislative assembly in the year 1884, he concluded, was "enough to make a good American dog ashamed." [5]

A provision which particularly incensed the small owner was one to the effect that no cattle could be branded between February 15 and the start of the spring roundup, three months later.[6] The average owner of, say, a hundred head claimed that he knew every one of his few animals individually as well as he knew the members of his own family, and to the best of his ability he kept them ranging fairly close to his homestead. But suppose he had missed one on the roundup. If he branded it he would be charged as a thief. If he did not, it would be taken up at next spring's roundup and claimed by the Association.

The press fumed on about discriminatory legislation and confiscation without due process, and the *Boomerang* christened the unloved measure "William Maverick." The name stuck, then slid over by an associative process to include the little fellow who opposed its passage. Wrote the Buffalo correspondent of the *Boomerang* (whose column was of course captioned "Buffalo Chips") on February 19:

> By all means give our large stock interests all the protection consistent with their right of ownership ... but God save us from the law which will make the poor poorer and the rich richer. The universal sentiment of "William Maverick" and his kind here is, "Vote it down." We don't want class legislation.

As tempers rose higher some of the cattlemen stormed that nobody was opposed to the maverick bill except (the usual expression) "thieves and sympathizers with thieves." Yet the bill had its opponents even among the big ones, and the biggest was the glittering Alec Swan. He opposed the measure as unfair. He was on his way east when word of his scandalous deviation reached the ears of Secretary Sturgis. The latter wired a demand for an explanation. Swan wired back on March 2:

> I never agreed to support the maverick bill. Never read it until after leaving Cheyenne. Am ready to give full support to any measure which will give justice to cattle owners. Do not consider present bill just in its provisions and if passed will be unsatisfactory in results.[7]

It was one more instance to show that Swan, with all his financial trapeze work, had human sense.

Overconfident opponents predicted the demise of Bill Maverick up to the last, but on February 27 it slid through the Legislative Council, the upper house, with its worst features intact. On March 7, the day before adjournment, an amended bill was rushed through the assembly before its opponents could blink their eyes, by a vote of ten to two in the Council and twelve to six in the lower house. As one candid legislator remarked: "If we hadn't waited until the last day these sons of bitches of reporters would have got a whack at it, and it would have bounced." [8]

The public had read a naked and cynical declaration of intent in a clause of the maverick bill which provided that no man would be allowed to bid on mavericks without first making a bond of $3000 to the Association. This was grotesque. The animals, it was well understood, would not bring much if any over ten dollars a head, and as matters turned out they often brought less. Such was the uproar of protest over the bill that the bonding provision was dropped before passage, but the stock-men succeeded in restoring it four years later. [9]

To the cowboys far-flung in their great empty spaces, the new rules and their implications sank in slowly. Their bitter disappointment, when they learned the meaning of the new maverick law, was recorded by Jack Flagg:

"The cowboys thought that so long as the mavericks were to be sold to the highest bidder that they here had a chance to buy cattle, but they were sadly mistaken. A bunch of mavericks would be put up for sale, some boy who had a few dollars saved would make a bid on them. The baron who claimed the range, or his foreman who was acting for him, would then raise the bid, they would be run up so high the cowboy would have to quit. No matter how high the bid had been, the baron would be receipted for so many mavericks at $10 per head.

"It was impossible for an employee to buy a cow." [10]

The authors of the law had sought to legitimize the unusual step of turning over a territorial fund to a private association. They did so by providing, in Section 9, that membership in the Association should be open to "All persons who are directly interested in the business of cattle growing in this territory, and who have not been convicted of a felony or possessed of a reputation notoriously bad." The judgment of a man's reputation was left up to the executive committee of the Wyoming Stock Growers' Association.

More and more the small Wyoming rancher, who didn't have enough money or cattle to run his own roundup wagon, was forced into a shadowy no-man's land where he existed on sufferance of the neighboring big outfits. The small man with fifty or sixty or a hundred head— provided he was not on the blacklist or "possessed of a reputation notoriously bad"—was often permitted by the good-natured foreman of a big outfit to ride along with the wagon for a day or two and gather his cattle, even if he did not belong to the Association. But he had no real rights. He might be barred, for example, if he had "talked against us."

No one who studies the stock laws of Montana and Colorado can fail to see why these states had so much less trouble than Wyoming. Not only was authority over livestock matters vested in the government of the state or territory, instead of in a stock-growers' association, but the authority was decentralized and democratic. There was no fuss over maverick sales because they were left in local hands.[11]

"The usual Montana method of dealing with mavericks," according to Robert H. Fletcher, "was to sell them at roundup to the highest bidder, slap on his brand, tally them to him and turn them loose with his other cattle. The accumulated money went into the roundup fund that paid the horse wranglers and the reps who were sent to the other districts." A similarly simple system prevailed in Colorado. Anybody could understand this. The money was spent locally where everybody could see what became of it, and it benefited all alike.

No maverick fund was required because inspectors were paid by the state, and incidentally they inspected for all, not, as Wyoming's man in the sagebrush suspected, on a members-only basis.*

Many of the decisions which in Wyoming were made at the territorial capital and then imposed over 98,000 square miles were left in Montana to the saddle-hardened men of the roundup districts. In addition to handling maverick sales, they decided for themselves the time and method of working their own roundups, and they elected their own roundup captains, who ruled with a rod of iron and were respected by all. Montana's small owners could hold their own with the big ones, absentee or no, and they had no tolerance for rustling. The "soft synonym for stealing" got short shrift in Montana. So did big-owner arrogance.

* This statement refers to an old and troubled day long gone. For many years past, the Association has been rightfully proud of its skilled inspectors and its services to the cattle industry of the whole state in discovering strays at market points and sending the proceeds to the owner. In *Cow Country Cavalcade*, Maurice Frink wrote: "By legislative enactment the Association since 1931 has been recognized as a quasi-public organization vested with authority to represent the state of Wyoming outside the state in inspection of livestock to determine ownership, the Association books being audited annually by the state examiner.... This service, incidentally, is supplied to all stockmen in Wyoming regardless of membership in the Association." pp. 97, 99.

NINE

Who Is a Cattle Thief?

I

AFTER THE maverick law was passed, the excitement and name-calling which attended its passage died down and, so far as outward appearances went, the whole affair seemed forgotten. This was the spring of 1884; all Wyoming was riding the crest of prosperity; and everyone from the "lord" with his English thoroughbred and his English saddle down to the youngest horse wrangler on the roundup was too busy enjoying the thrill of the big herds and the big calf tallies and the high prices to leave any room for problems.

Only in nonpublic sources, mainly the correspondence and executive minutes of the Wyoming Stock Growers' Association, do we find any symptoms of trouble—a few differences with members over lenience toward brand-owning cowboys, and in the fall an unnoticed replevin suit was filed against two cowhands who were said to have appropriated some mavericks. Their names were Jack Cooper and Ed Lineberger.

Could anything be duller than a replevin suit? No criminal action was possible at this time because, inexplicably, the ardent proponents of Bill Maverick had neglected to provide him with any teeth in the shape of penalties. On second thought, the omission was not so strange to anyone who can read between the lines that the biennial sessions of territorial legislatures devoted as much attention to the cup that cheers as they did to legislating, with the result that some very careless legislation was passed.

Jack Cooper seems to have been a plausible scamp, if scamp he was, with a knack for winning friends and influencing the right people. He had formed advantageous partnerships with medium-sized stockmen, at least one of whom was a member of the Association. And when the case came up he and Lineberger somehow raised enough money to retain the leading lawyer of the territory. Clearly this Cooper was a hard man to keep down.

The pair had an associate named Tom Collins. He and Lineberger had been in trouble over branding mavericks as early as 1883, when they were both foremen of outfits on the Sweetwater, though there was then no maverick law for them to violate and the big companies were branding mavericks as fast as they could. But the Association took an unfavorable view of their activities.[1]

Between the fall of 1884, when the replevin suit was brought, and the spring of 1887, when Tom Collins was tried and acquitted on a charge of cattle stealing, the trio had dealt the Association a shellacking in court from which its Old Guard never recovered and never learned, and Cooper and Lineberger had come within an inch of upsetting the maverick law.

We hear of Jack Cooper directly for the first time in 1885, when in spite of the suit against him he shows up on the roundup as bold as brass, gathering his cattle and even buying mavericks, which was strictly *verboten*. The offense was reported to the executive committee, and the sequel was a stiff letter from Secretary Sturgis to James B. Jackson of Council Bluffs, Iowa.

July 18, 1885.... It is stated by a member of the executive committee and by other responsible parties that your foreman allowed Jack Cooper to accompany your outfit on the Bitter Creek roundup, that you carried his bedding, furnished him meals, and further that you allowed him to buy mavericks on your own range.

You are aware that the Association has regarded Cooper for the past year as a very dangerous man, and that the Association is now carrying on a suit with said Cooper for cattle which he stole in 1884.

Under the circumstances, to have one of our most prominent members in that section give him aid and comfort ... is a direct injury to the Association and offsets any effort we can make to protect your property and that of others from this class of men.

Mr. Jackson was reminded that he was responsible for the conduct of men in his employ, and was requested to discharge his foreman or see that the latter conformed to regulations in the future.

The secretary and the executive committee had a two-edged weapon for use in such a case. The employee charged with misconduct could be placed on the blacklist and thus deprived of a living without proof, accusation being sufficient.* At the other edge an owner who crossed

---

* In justice to the committee, appeals for reinstatement were readily heard and sometimes granted.

the secretary's will could be expelled from the Association. This was an extremely serious matter; since the victim would be barred thenceforth from taking part in the official roundups, it amounted to reading him out of the cattle business in Wyoming territory.

Armed with this double weapon, the secretary carried things with a high and heavy hand. On one occasion an order was printed and sent to all members advising them that they were required to furnish horses, wagons, and food, upon request, to inspectors in pursuit of criminals; penalty for noncompliance—as usual—expulsion. The undernote of grumbling over this sort of dictation was not confined to "thieves and sympathizers with thieves." [2]

The replevin suit dragged on for two years, and in the meanwhile Cooper and Lineberger were a hair shirt endured first by Mr. Sturgis and later by his successor as secretary of the Association, Mr. Thomas B. Adams. They were on and off the blacklist. They had enough influential connections to make them hard to handle, which is true of all crooks. But were these men crooks? Were they victims of persecution? Were they just enough brighter and more determined than the average cowpuncher or small ranchman to earn from Secretary Sturgis the adjective *dangerous?*

The names of Collins, Cooper, and Lineberger appear on the blacklist circular for September 2, 1885, the only surviving copy of that mysterious publication. All three made repeated appeals for reinstatement and Collins was restored to grace temporarily, but the other two were turned down. A subcommittee recommended clemency for Cooper, but the full executive committee, dominated by Sturgis, overruled the recommendation and voted to keep him in Coventry. Was this because of the aggravated nature of Cooper's offenses, or was it because this common cowhand had dared to fight the Association and attack the constitutionality of the maverick law? [3]

Merely turning down his appeal did not go far enough, however, for on November 30, 1885, a resolution was adopted by the committee which, reduced to plain English, meant that that body was determined to keep Cooper's name on the blacklist even if he should be cleared in court. Persecution begins to sound like the word for it.

Toward the end of October 1886 at Rawlins, Judge Samuel T. Corn of the third judicial district handed down his decision. By an act of judicial sleight-of-hand he managed to rule in favor of Cooper and Lineberger without passing on the constitutionality of the maverick law. But he denied the Association's suit to replevin the mavericks, and at the same time awarded the two men the sum of $1003.38 for an additional twenty-four head of cattle which they claimed had been seized by the Association. A compromise of $750 was agreed upon, plus removal of the names of Cooper and Lineberger from the blacklist—at last—and publication of a notice to that effect.[4] It was a ringing vindication of the two alleged cattle thieves.

Another point has been overlooked. Unrighteousness, strange as it may seem, was not the exclusive stigma of the mavericking class. The blacklist was in all probability illegal, and the Association's executive committee were so advised by their own attorneys. After the setback in the Cooper-Lineberger case the members had some sobering second thoughts as to whether they might be personally liable for damages incurred under too-free use of the blacklist, and they sought an opinion from their law firm on the question of conspiracy. The reply was that forbidding members to give employment did go too far toward a "combination," and the clause was accordingly stricken from the circular, but the members could still read between the lines, and knew what would happen to them if they hired a man on the list.

Judge Corn's decision was hailed with an outburst of rejoicing in the antistock press, which leaped to the conclusion that the maverick law had been ruled unconstitutional. "You Can't Take a Poor Man's Property Without Due Process of Law," exulted the Douglas *Advertiser*. But the rejoicing was premature.

Shortly after the decision was handed down Secretary Adams, accompanied by Hugo Donzelman as attorney for the defendants and territorial attorney general, called on the judge to ask him just what he had decided. The judge assured them that he had not passed on the question of constitutionality; he had merely ruled that a maverick was not a maverick for legal purposes until it had been taken up by the roundup foreman and branded with an M on the neck according to law; hence it did not until then become the property of the Association. Nobody seemed to know just what this meant, and both sides of the maverick controversy went on doing as they had before.

The names of Cooper and Lineberger had been removed from the blacklist as grudgingly as possible and only as part of the settlement in the case. It was not long, however, before the executive committee found an excuse to break its agreement and blacklist the pair once more. The excuse was furnished by the trial of Tom Collins on a cattle-theft charge the following spring.

Collins had been another hair shirt to the mighty. Like Cooper and Lineberger, he had influential friends. During his short period of restoration to grace he had written a letter to the secretary. Signed *Thomas*

H. Collins and penned in a firm, literate hand, it was so full of noble sentiments, high regard for the Association, and praise for its great work that this writer thought at first it must have come from some respectable rancher of the same name.

But no; it was from the scandalous Collins himself. The apple-polisher was desirous of having his brands recognized by the Association and entered in its brand book. Secretary Sturgis proved human enough to respond to flattery, and graciously granted the request. A year later Tom Collins was under indictment as a thief.

In what the antistock *Carbon County Journal* referred to disdainfully as "another of those farcical cattle cases," he was charged with running his own Staircase brand over a neighboring L 7 (L $_7$), a charge which if true was not farcical at all. Adopting a brand which was enough like that of a neighbor to make alteration easy was an old trick of the sleazy-morals crew. The evidence against Collins must have been fairly strong, because the jury were out five hours, but they returned a verdict of not guilty.[5]

As for Cooper and Lineberger, on May 26, 1887, we find all Association members notified that the pair are once again on the blacklist "in consequence of their behavior during and after the Collins trial."

What behavior? Did they exercise their constitutional right of testifying for the defendent? Talk against the Association? Shoot off their six-guns in the courtroom to celebrate the acquittal? We are not told.

But the fact stands that on such grounds as his "behavior," his "disposition," or his "record," a man could be deprived of his reputation and his living on the say-so of a little group of autocrats in the territorial capital.

The Jack Cooper story as we know it ends on the same note of vindictiveness and spite. In the fall of 1887 he appealed to the Association for recovery of the proceeds from two stray steers belonging to him which had been carried off during the roundup. This was a common occurrence, and it was the duty of the Association, under the responsibility delegated to it by territorial law, to identify all strays wherever possible and return the proceeds to any Wyoming citizen who happened to be their owner. However, Thomas B. Adams, who had succeeded Sturgis as secretary, quibbled over the proofs of ownership offered by Cooper. The latter called on J. R. Dixon, the prosecuting attorney for Carbon County, to ask his aid in pressing the claim, remarking rather pathetically: "I suppose they will want to beat me, owing to our former rackets."

Dixon examined the papers, satisfied himself that Cooper's claim was just, and forwarded it to the Association. When Adams still quibbled, Dixon sent back a sharp reply pointing out the unwisdom of requiring "extraordinary proofs" of Cooper. Under the prosecutor's pressure the secretary finally paid, "with considerable hesitation and reluctance," to quote his own words, the $74.90 which Cooper had coming to him.[6]

And that is the last we hear of Cooper, Collins, and Lineberger. Lives like theirs were writ on water. Their love and their hatred and their envy, their right and their wrong, the girls they made love to and the horses they rode, are now perished; and no man knows what they really were or what became of them. Except that Jack Cooper stopped a bullet on the Sweetwater in 1889.

TEN

Who Is a Cattle Thief?
II

REGARDLESS OF what the judge told the secretary and the attorney general, the sagebrush lawyers were convinced after the Cooper-Lineberger decision that the maverick law had been as good as thrown out of court, and they proceeded to act accordingly, as merry as mice when the cat is ailing. Being by no means unintelligent men, some of them had come to their own independent conclusion that the law was unconstitutional as early as the summer of 1886.[1] As to the spring of 1887, there must have been some cattle alive in that dismal season, for over in the vast wild reaches of the Big Horn Basin the long-rope artists were out early, and they were making a good haul. Frank Canton, the Association's star detective, was trying to police an area as big as a couple of small eastern states which was bisected by a range of mountains running down the middle. He wrote Secretary Adams on March 26: "... The lawless element up here have gotten the idea that they can brand mavericks with impunity and not be punished for it. I believe a great many of them are under the impression that the maverick law is unconstitutional, and think that by standing together they can beat any case of that kind. There is no doubt here that this combination have some good backing and could raise considerable money." [2]

From the time Cooper entered his defense in the maverick suit on constitutional grounds, Association insiders had been expressing private doubts as to whether their pet piece of legislation would hold, but they never voiced them publicly.[3] Never at any time then or thereafter could friends of the Association bring themselves to admit what is painfully clear on the record—that the maverick law of 1884 was at best a fatal mistake and at worst unconstitutional.

The acquittal of Tom Collins in the spring of 1887 was a second blow to the Association coming hard on the heels of the first. Secretary Adams was bitter. Already, on January 21, he had written: "It seems to be the popular thing at present to hamper the work of the Association in every direction.... After the expenditure of a great deal of money and our obtaining what we considered ample evidence to convict, the attorney for the defense, the judge on the bench and the jury, as well as the newspapers and the general public, seemed combined to place the Association in the light of criminals...."

The mutterings grew louder to the effect that the only cure for a cow thief was a noose at the end of a rope.

Assuming for the moment that Tom Collins was guilty, why was he freed? Was it because, as the stockmen always said, you couldn't get a jury to convict a cow thief no matter what the evidence? Their assertion, while partially true, has been overstressed, because outside of periods when feeling ran high there *were* convictions in cattle cases; while as for horse thieves, they were sent up time and again.

In the Tom Collins case, were there any special factors at work which would influence a jury to disregard evidence against him? The answer is yes. The average citizen of Carbon County was convinced that the Association operated on the principle of one rule for me and another rule for thee. The average citizen believed that stock-law violations were winked at when committed by a favored member, while the same "mistake" if made by an ordinary fellow would lead to his arrest.

The records of the executive committee for the years 1885, 1886, and 1887 unfortunately lend color to this belief. A deputation is appointed to see Mr. A. H. Swan and obtain payment for mavericks improperly branded and also balance due on those sold to Mr. Swan under average value. "Improperly branded" is sometimes called by a harsher name.

A communication from the Powder River Cattle Company (Frewen's 76 outfit) is discussed; it is in connection with gathering cattle before the general roundup. Such early gathering is forbidden under the roundup law, but who would suggest taking action against the mighty 76? Mr. A. B. Clark of Laramie County is charged with branding mavericks before the roundup. This is exactly the same offense of which Jack Cooper was accused, but Mr. Clark's "explanation" must have been satisfactory, since in his case we hear no more of the matter.[4] Mr. Clark is so hot on the subject of honesty on the range that in 1892 he takes part in an armed expedition against Johnson County to liquidate cattle thieves. A well-known member in the Sweetwater region is accused of appropriating and selling stray cattle and horses, but the charges are never investigated, and in the middle of the flurry the accused member is appointed bondsman for the roundup, a position of great trust.[5]

These cases were minor. Their effect sank in, but it was as nothing to the repercussions caused by the little matter of Heck Reel's cowboys and the matter of Mr. Corlett's "honest mistake."

Alexander H. Reel was not only one of the early birds in Wyoming, he also had extensive cattle-raising interests and was firmly entrenched as a power in the Wyoming Stock Growers' Association. Sometime in 1884 two or more of Heck Reel's cowboys in the Sweetwater area had —er—driven off a number of horses belonging to a neighboring ranchman without accounting to the owner of same.

Had Mr. Reel been an ordinary member of the Association, a short and ugly word would have sufficed. The employee of an ordinary member, as everybody knew, had to be considerably purer than Caesar's wife. He had to be so pure in fact that he might not even own a cow for fear he might be tempted to steal another one. An ordinary member might be summoned to the territorial capital from a far-distant point at great personal inconvenience to be reminded that he was responsible for the actions of his employees and to be called to account for their misdeeds.

But Mr. Reel was no ordinary member. He had served as treasurer of the Association since 1876, was to serve until 1889 and to remain a leading member of the inner circle up to and after the ill-starred invasion. One of the leading hard-liners, he was firmly convinced of the righteousness of the maverick law and contended that only "the rustlers" were advocating its repeal. The theft of horses by his cowboys kicked up such a scandal that the issue was raised openly at the following annual meeting of the Association, in the spring of 1885.[6] Mr. Reel huffed indignantly but still did nothing, either then or thereafter.

To say that the affair blew over would be a perilous understatement. Sagebrush memories were long. It too sank in. And then, in 1886 and 1887, there was the matter of Mr. Corlett's "honest mistake."

Arthur T. Corlett was a brother of the senior member of the Association's firm of legal advisers, Corlett, Lacey and Riner. At some time during the roundup of 1886 Mr. Corlett had evidently branded an animal under questionable circumstances—which were clear enough, however, to some of the local people to create a demand that he be prosecuted and to raise the question (since he was not prosecuted) why not?

By next spring the question was still hot and getting hotter. Mr. Dixon, the Carbon County attorney, was ready to go ahead, but the Association, speaking in the person of Secretary Adams, hedged with the excuse that there was insufficient evidence to justify the Association in going to the expense of a trial.

"The branding of which Corlett was accused was done in the presence of a dozen men and without the faintest show of deception on his part," wrote the perspiring secretary. "These cases of misbranding in the presence of witnesses occur on almost every roundup and are simply the result of honest mistakes. Such acts materially differ from the work which is going on all over the range about which there can be no doubt." [7]

"Differ how?" ran the murmur through the grass stems. For in that naked land where no man could keep a secret from his neighbor, every time a big owner branded in advance of the roundup and got away with it, every time one of the big ones was let off on a charge which would have been pressed against a little fellow, it became known all over the area and eventually all over the territory—known to every settler and cowboy; to every bartender and banker and businessman in town; known to every citizen who might ever be called to serve on a jury in a stock-stealing case.

There was at the time a rugged old-timer serving on the executive committee for Carbon County, Perry L. Smith. He had come in years earlier on a construction job for the Union Pacific, and like so many in his day had stayed to go into cattle-raising. In May 1887, at about the time of Tom Collins' acquittal, Smith called on Secretary Adams in Cheyenne to satisfy himself at first hand what was going to be done in regard to prosecution of the Corlett case. Upon finding that the answer was "Nothing," he slapped his resignation from the executive committee on the desk. It was accepted a few days later.[8]

The groundswell of discontent within the Association's own ranks was making itself felt on a wide front at this time; so much so that one may ask whether the sharp drop in Association membership during the bad years of 1887 and 1888 was all due to the hard times, or whether dissatisfaction among smaller members was not partially responsible for the dropouts. Some of the letter-writers heard from at this time were evidently unhappy over lack of protection and felt that they were paying for the support of a costly detective system which benefited only the large owner. There must have been a serious movement of rebellion on foot against the existing executive committee and officers, from President Joseph M. Carey and Secretary Sturgis on down, prior to the spring meeting of 1887, since Secretary Adams wrote a circular letter to the members urging them to remain loyal.[9]

However, the steamroller so familiar in political affairs was evidently in good running order since we hear no more of upsetting Judge Carey's regime. But later in the year a small member's wrath exploded in a letter to Secretary Adams, September 17, 1887:

> It seems to me that those who are the most wealthy have had all the protection, and the small fry the persecution.... Their mantle of wealth covers *mistakes*, which would be called *crimes* had they occurred in a poorer man's corral.... If this is the principal [*sic*] on which the association is to be continued, why us small fish had better keep our money for *self* protection, rather than pass it into the hands of monopolists to crush us with.[10]

The Heck Reel case, never forgotten, was now fresher than ever. Why had Reel's cowboys never been prosecuted, to say nothing of Arthur Corlett? Tom Collins had been acquitted, and more cattle-theft cases were coming up in an adjoining county. Safe in the seats of the mighty—the sacred precincts of the Cheyenne Club and the headquarters of the Wyoming Stock Growers' Association—Secretary Adams could not possibly comprehend what executive-committee member R. B. Connor suffered as he went about his business in a little town like Rawlins, running the gauntlet of the lank forms propping up the building fronts, stopping in at a bar; enduring the cool stares, the deadpan innuendos, the outright jeers. Why no prosecution?

The cattle-stealing cases were due to be tried in Lander, county seat of Fremont county, that summer. Connor continued to hammer at Adams about the Corlett case and "the case of Heck Reel's about the horses," which was, he noted in a letter, "another one that acts against us."

"The impression seems to be that the case against Corlett was dismissed simply because he was a brother of the attorney for the association," he wrote, "and that it was through the influence of the association that the case was dismissed ... it appears to me that if Corlett was innocent he would feel like demanding a trial instead of fighting it." Connor began to talk of resigning from the executive committee. "I have been laughed at more than once around here because I could not succeed in having an investigation of the Heck Reel affair." [11]

The secretary was in the middle, an uncomfortable spot. Still perspiring visibly, he pleaded first with Connor to be patient, and then with Reel to make some amends. Three years had elapsed since the horses had been stolen, and it was now too late to do anything about the matter except with the assistance of Mr. Reel himself. Would he not make some attempt to have his late or current employees, if they were still in his employ, settle for stolen property and thus remove a stain from the Association's record? "I understand," he wrote, "that this matter works against us in every case that we have in the courts west of here [Cheyenne]." [12] But Mr. Reel turned a deaf ear.

The cattle-theft cases were tried in Lander during the July term of court. The writer has been unable to learn anything of their merits or even their number; but their outcome was predictable, a string of acquittals. The matter became quite a *cause célèbre*, with the pro-stockmen press raising the usual hue and cry about the impossibility of securing a conviction no matter how strong the evidence, accompanied by the usual hysterical exaggerations, such implausible figures as "sixty cases" being freely bandied about. The Fremont county acquittals were even cited in extenuation of the hanging of a woman called "Cattle Kate," two years later. Yet the correspondence of the Wyoming Stock Growers' Association makes it crystal-clear that public outrage over the gross favoritism shown by that body to its prominent members was a contributing cause if not the sole cause of the jury's action.

Those damned rustler juries—you never could get them to convict a thief.

ELEVEN

"You Can't Get a Conviction"

EVERY HISTORY of the open-range period has dwelt on the unending drain and loss suffered by cattle owners through rustling. James Cox, in his *Historical and Biographical Record of the Cattle Industry of Texas*, speaks of "... one of the most extraordinary drawbacks any trade or interest ever encountered ... the systematic, continuous, day-in-and-day-out stealing of cattle." [1] Writer after writer has stressed the near-impossibility of getting convictions when the victim of theft was an unpopular cattle "baron," while the jury was made up of settlers most of whom were tarred with the same brush as the accused. The humor with which this unfunny matter was regarded by the incorrigible West has already been touched upon. One story tells of the trial of a settler in Colorado at which several witnesses testified that it was quite customary for calves to leave their mothers of their own accord and shut themselves up in a barn. The suspect was acquitted. Afterwards the sheriff asked loudly in a hotel lobby what else you could expect when a cow thief was tried by a cow-thief jury before a cow-thief judge. The judge heard about it and fined him $25 for contempt. [2]

On top of the frequently unfriendly attitude of juries, there was the difficulty of getting anyone to testify. Cowboys didn't tell. Whatever one of them might think privately of another's conduct, however honest he might be himself, he would not go to court as a witness against him. As one member wrote rather mournfully to the Association: "There is not a cowboy who will give another away on this range." [3]

But after making every allowance there remains another side to the question, at least in Wyoming, where the Association's purblind adherence to unwise and detested policies led directly to a disastrous series of acquittals in 1887, with more to come later. After the Fremont county acquittals in midsummer an even stronger demonstration that virtue was not necessarily on the side of the prosecution occurred at the end of the same year, in the shape of the notorious Horse Shoe cases.

But first, during the gloomy summer of 1887 with its financial failures and its mutterings of dissension a brief ray of good will lighted the gathering storm clouds over the affair of Jim Larson's cow.

"A couple of Larson boys who live out on the head of Separation creek [were] the owners of a milch cow. When the roundup was out in the neighborhood the cow was picked up and drove [*sic*] off with a bunch of cattle, although the foreman of the roundup was informed that the cow belonged to the Larsons, to which the foreman paid no attention but drove the cow over the Platte, where she was sold as a maverick. The owners being poor men cannot now recover their property. ... When such cases yearly occur, is it any wonder there is no conviction for stock stealing, when a powerful organization like the Wyoming Stock Association persists in stealing and appropriating the poor man's stock." Thus the *Carbon County Journal*, whose editor, J. P. Friend, was a notorious twister of the "corporate cormorants'" tails.[4]

As soon as the secretary heard about the onslaught he demanded to know why the owners of the cow had not complained to the Association instead of to a newspaper. Thus the Larson cow became for the moment a territorial issue. The carrying off of local owners' cattle by a big trail herd or roundup outfit moving through the country was a chronic complaint. Theoretically redress was provided under the maverick law, but practically the little owner with only a few coins in his jeans could not recover his animal. Mr. Adams, however, was determined to prove that the Association was in truth a friend to the small owner as well as to the big one, so he made heroic efforts to recover the cow and did recover her.

The whole affair ended in a burst of good feeling in the *Carbon County Journal* for November 20. Secretary Adams reported that "the notorious cow has been returned to Mr. James Larson, and the Association has in one instance at least kept its faith toward a 'poor cattleman.' This has been done at considerable expense and much trouble," and so forth.

The editor of the *Journal* fell all over himself to express appreciation:

We trust this honest and rightful act on the part of the Association will have the effect of bringing about a better feeling between the Association and the small stockgrowers of this county, and that the small growers will realize that the interests of the Association are their interests. Having interested ourselves in this case, we have become convinced that many of the complaints against the Association have no foundation in fact.

But the love feast was not to endure.

Horse Shoe was a tiny post office near Fort Fetterman which has long since disappeared from the map. Because it was also near the line of the Fremont, Elkhorn and Missouri Valley railroad it had received an early influx of settlers. In the latter months of 1887 a clutch of the yokels was arrested and haled into Cheyenne, to be greeted by the press, which soon changed its tune, as "alleged desperadoes" and "a gang of cattle thieves." One of them was more or less well known locally as a "good fellow" who had been arrested in a few minor saloon brawls; the rest were average settlers or cowboys.[5] All told twelve men were charged. All twelve were set free; and by the time the trials were finished three days before Christmas the public wrath had partially spent itself in the gales of laughter which swept the territory at the expense of the Association and its bungling detectives. Laughter is not to be underestimated; it is a brutal weapon.

The cases were tried in the first territorial district court in Cheyenne, Judge William L. Maginnis presiding, during the month of December 1887. The first was that of one Mark Ryan, who was charged with branding cattle not his own. It was testified that Ryan with detective Elam, the latter posing as a friendly neighbor, had captured three mavericks. The detective branded two to show how easy it was. Ryan hesitated when given leave to appropriate the third, but Elam urged him to go ahead, and the deed was done. The jury returned a verdict of not guilty.[6]

Such procedure on the part of an officer of the law in obtaining evidence is called entrapment, and is a recognized ground for acquittal under the common law. Moreover there was a reward of $250 payable out of county funds to an officer who obtained the arrest and conviction of a cattle, horse, or mule thief. To the judge it was apparent that the detectives had been motivated by a desire to collect the reward.

Judge Maginnis was a thirty-two-year-old Kentuckian who had only recently been appointed to a federal judgeship in the territory. In the words of the Laramie *Boomerang*, he "came here a tenderfoot, and being accustomed in the effete east to seeing the law executed by legally constituted agents of justice he was not prepared for the state of affairs he found existing in his new, wild and woolly jurisdiction." [7] His wrath descended and he ordered a grand jury investigation of the conduct of the detectives, A. H. Elam and J. W. Foster. In his charge to the grand jury on December 5 he condemned the action of "some stock inspectors, or stock detectives,"

[who] have been making it a business in this county to induce persons to

commit crime for the purpose of arresting them afterwards to obtain a reward. I regret very much to say it is doubtful whether such action on the part of detectives can be punished as criminal under the statutes of this territory, but such outrageous procedure by the officers of the law deserves the condemnation of the court and certainly of the grand jury. . . .[8]

Five days later the grand jury, well filled with cattlemen and their supporters, handed up its report, which consisted of a return slap at the judge. Far from condemning the detectives, it praised them for performance of their duty against "an organized band of rustlers," found that they had never induced any person or persons to commit crimes or misdemeanors, and added that they had "expected no reward only their monthly compensation from their employers," a curious statement in view of the testimony and the statutory fact, and one symptomatic of an increasingly ugly frame of mind.

On both sides tempers were rising throughout the Territory, while the current proceedings turned into such a carnival for enemies of the Association that a reporter was moved to comment: "It would sometimes be difficult for an observer to say who is on trial, the defendants or the detectives who have testified against them." Case after case collapsed amid whoops of derision.

On December 9 two more defendants, Joseph Huffman and William Lavelle, who had also been indicted for misbranding cattle, were acquitted on all counts by order from the bench. Next, on December 21, one J. S. "Doc" Howard was acquitted on the charge of killing a beef with the intention of appropriating same to his own use.

Howard did not deny butchering the animal. He stated that his supposed good neighbor, Detective Foster, had brought the beef to the ranch and induced him to kill it by assuring him that he, Foster, was the owner. It was after dark, so Howard was unable to read the brand. This might have been taken for a tall story had it not accorded with the already well-established facts regarding the operations of Foster and Elam, and some more witnesses testified to that effect.

A third Association detective, named August Pasche, though not directly involved in the cases, was raked over the coals by defense counsel because of some indiscreet opinions he had expressed in public the week before. His opinions are of interest because of an ugly and ominous note contained therein, a note which was being sounded often among the large stock-owning class as the bitterness of frustration and defeat—so well exemplified in the current trials—ate inward.

Defense counsel pursued the point as follows:

"I will ask you whether or not on an occasion last week in the saloon of West Moyer you said that the courts and juries ought to have been hung ten years ago?"

"I might have made such a remark as that."

"Didn't you say on the same occasion that the laws ought to be suspended and the Wyoming Stock Growers' Association could hang all those rustling — — —?"

"I didn't say that. I said it would come to that."

"That the Wyoming Stock Growers' Association would have to go and hang these people?"

"I said all honest people—"

"You are one of the honest people you refer to?"

Sullenly Pasche stuck to his guns. Under questioning he elaborated his remarks.

"Mr. Pasche, you said it was coming to the time when honest people would have to take the matter into their own hands and hang these fellows?"

"It seems to me so."

"Notwithstanding your explanation you did make the remark that the courts and juries ought to have been hung ten years ago?"

"I said simply if there had been a court and a jury hung ten years ago there would be some justice; I believe I have heard other people make the same remark." [9]

Two days before Christmas the Cheyenne *Leader* headlined yet another double acquittal. Two roving cowhands named Wilkes and Cavanaugh, well-known locally, had been apprehended in Utah on a charge of stealing a horse from a Laramie County citizen bearing the down-east name of Silas Doty. At first blush the evidence for the prosecution was conclusive. Ownership of the horse was established by Mr. Doty and others. The defendants were seen in possession of the horse and acted suspiciously. They might well have been convicted if the case against them had not rested upon the testimony of that comic-horse-opera gumshoe, Detective Elam.

Elam, like Foster, was ostensibly a good neighbor. He told of the stay of the pair at his ranch. They told of it too, but their version differed from his. Elam said the pair had expressed the ambition to become horse thieves, and he had attempted to dissuade them. They said they had bought Mr. Doty's horse from Elam right out of a stall in Elam's barn. The claim that an animal had been bought in good faith from a third party was all too familiar in horse-stealing cases. On the other hand, the average open-range character with a strong back and a weak head never learned to demand the bill of sale which was required by law. Who was telling the truth?

Elam described an exchange of gifts which was almost Oriental in its lavishness. One of the cowhands, he testified, had pleaded with him to provide him with a six-shooter from his armory; he, Elam, finally gave the fellow the weapon. In return the visitor presented him with a valuable saddle. Not to be outdone in generosity Elam presented his guest with another saddle. The two finally departed carrying a lunch they had requested Mrs. Elam to prepare.

According to the defendants the mutual admiration and exchange of gifts was a myth; the saddle trade had been a purely commercial transaction by which they obtained possession of Mr. Doty's horse, which Elam represented as his. After leaving Elam's they had worked for seventeen days for neighboring ranchmen, earning $34, which was applied in payment for this and other horses purchased from Elam.

After the acquittal the courtroom crowd adjourned to the bar of the Interocean Hotel across the street from the UP tracks, the shining double thread which linked a little episode called Cheyenne to East and West across the starlit plains. The rubies and emeralds of the railroad lights winked in the brilliant air. The bar was jammed with stock growers, businessmen, witnesses, jurors, reporters; everybody was there, including the attorneys for both sides and even a couple of traveling men fresh off the train, who had crossed the street from the depot and stomped the snow off their feet and were now getting an earful of life in the real West.

An argument developed between the prosecuting attorney, W. R. Stoll, and a ranchman who had been on the jury. Stoll observed in gentlemanly vein that he thought the sworn statements of a stock detective were as reliable as those of any other witness. The juror replied that he wouldn't vote to convict a dog on the testimony of those liars. The Association's chief of detectives took up the cudgels, several bystanders mixed in, and only the presence of a few cool heads prevented a free-for-all.[10]

Immediately after the trial of the two alleged horse thieves the prosecution entered a *nolle prosequi* in eight similar cases which hung on the testimony of the Association detectives.[11]

There is no indication that the guiding lights of the Association ever even entertained the notion that their conduct of the Horse Shoe cases might have been a mistake. Instead they appear to have withdrawn increasingly into the dangerous conviction that everybody was out of step but themselves—the press, the public, the juries, the judges—a state of mind which was to come to painful fruition in the years ahead.

From their point of view the timing of the Horse Shoe cases was particularly unfortunate. They were tried in December. The tenth Legislative Assembly of Wyoming Territory convened in January, and one of its first items of business was revision of the maverick law.

TWELVE

Bill Maverick Again

THE PUBLIC reaction to the Horse Shoe cases was so heated that even Association stalwarts became convinced of the wisdom of some pulling in of horns. During the summer Secretary Adams had exchanged correspondence with Secretary Russell B. Harrison of the Montana Stockgrowers Association, and had convinced himself that a territorial livestock commission similar to the one in Montana might "dissipate the prejudice now existing against the Association . . . a prejudice generally felt for the reason many suspect the large fund derived from the sale of mavericks is used for the protection of the few against the many." [1]

There was no doubt about it—the Association by this time was facing a thoroughly nasty press. Apart from the provincial weeklies, which always tended to favor the small stock grower and launched their feeble attacks in vain against the mighty entrenched in Cheyenne, there was the Laramie *Boomerang*, a powerful Democratic daily, now under an aggressive editorship. The *Boomerang* declared "The Tenth Legislative Assembly should afford relief, reduce the Wyoming Stock Growers' Association to a position comparable to that of an agricultural association, wipe out the detective system entirely and abolish the office of chief detective. . . . The Association is stronger in Wyoming than the press, the courts or even the legislature." It quoted "a prominent citizen" as declaring that "the custom of hanging a man who is suspected of stealing a $25 broncho and acquitting one who is known to have killed one or two men has ruled long enough, and it is time for justice to take off her tear-stained bandage and hang it up to dry." Even the stoutly Republican Cheyenne *Sun*, surprisingly, joined in the attacks, and agreed that the Association "was a nuisance which ought to be regulated if not entirely suppressed." [2]

When the tenth legislature convened in January 1888, it promptly developed into a tussle between the Association and Governor Thomas Moonlight. The press had discovered that in addition to collecting the juicy territorial maverick fund "to be used in the payment of inspectors and other like purposes," the Association was also enabled to draw on county taxes to pay stock detectives the enormous wage of $225 a month. (The average cowhand drew $40.) On top of this double revenue—with no accounting—the counties were being taxed under another old law which provided a reward of $250 for a sheriff or "other person" obtaining the conviction of a horse, cattle or mule thief. Hence, public opinion decided, the extraordinary activities of Foster, Elam, and company.[3]

When the assembly met the two old special-interest laws were promptly repealed,[4] but when the new territorial livestock commission was proposed it became evident at once that the Association did not intend to give up any of its real powers.

The talk had been of a democratic body with a member "from" each county; but the opposition speaker of the lower house found a sleeper in Section 2 of the bill, which defined the make-up of the commission. This was the innocent-seeming substitution of the preposition *for* for the preposition *from*, so that the section now read that instead of a member "from" each county there would be a member "for" each county. This meant that a complaisant governor—as soon as we can get rid of this fellow Moonlight—could pack the board with members of the Association's inner ring in Cheyenne.

"We note that the Stock Association is still up to its old tricks," grumbled the *Boomerang*.[5]

Discovery of this trick caused quite a little tempest and the prepositions were switched back again, but the bill passed both houses without any further change. It was vetoed by Governor Moonlight with a stinging message on January 21, 1888.

Moonlight, a bearded Kansan, had been appointed by President Cleveland. He was one of the farm-minded politicians of the type then riding high in Congress and government, who equated wheat-raising with virtue and stock-raising with sin. His regime did little to clear up the confused picture in Wyoming, but he was honest and well-meaning, and his veto of the new maverick bill scored several bull's-eyes.

He started off by discovering another sleeper in Section 3, which stated that members of the commission were to hold office "for the term of two years and until their successors shall be duly appointed and shall have qualified." To the governor's acute eye this meant "a direct challenge to the appointing power of the executive"; it meant—since the commission members had to be confirmed by the Legislative Council or upper house—that the Council, which was usually synonymous with the livestock interests, could keep men of its choice in office indefinitely by failure to confirm new appointees.

Moonlight was angry. "The commissioners are beyond the power of removal for none is provided; are absolutely free to do as they please. They draw no salary, give no bonds, acknowledge no responsibility and are subject to no authority. They may ride roughshod over the rights of others and there is no remedy save in the courts. They can appoint an unlimited number of subordinates and pay them out of the maverick fund." The sizzling executive called Section 20, creating the private army to which he particularly objected, "more dangerous to the lives and liberties of the citizens of Wyoming than all other sections combined." The unlimited number of stock inspectors and "assistants," appointable by the commission under the proposed law, would have had the power to summon a posse and make arrests in the same manner as sheriffs.

"These inspectors and assistants," the governor continued, "may summon their fellow citizens and drag them out of bed to assist in rounding up a maverick, and may arrest and imprison the citizens, but if in the discharge of the high and exalted duties of a sheriff they should accept of any bribe, they would be discharged and could be appointed again with a renewal of the powers and duties of a sheriff and stock inspector next morning." [6]

After all that, the bill failed of the necessary two-thirds majority to repass over the veto by only a single vote, though there were cries of trickery in the press.

In the end Moonlight was forced to accept Section 3 with its self-perpetuating feature for members of the livestock commission, but he did succeed in knocking out the two worst features of the bill. A denatured Section 20 now required stock inspectors, if exercising the power of sheriffs, to be deputized according to law; and Section 22 was toughened to ensure the discharge of any commission employee accepting a bribe and rule out his re-employment.

The governor signed the amended version, and a territorial livestock commission now replaced the Wyoming Stock Growers' Association as livestock authority in the territory.[7] But it was dominated by the same individuals and the same interests merely wearing different hats; a case of *plus ça change, plus c'est la même chose.*

January 1890 came, and with it the eleventh and last session of the Wyoming territorial legislature. The Wyoming Stock Growers' Association, with a heavy shrinkage in its membership base, had increasingly assumed the aspect of a rich men's club. At the spring meeting of 1885, Secretary Sturgis had proudly announced a membership of 400, representing two million cattle. By the end of 1888 the membership had dwindled to 183, and in 1890 the picture was so bad that no figure for membership was announced. According to a reliable source, it was down to sixty-eight. During this period there were from 3500 to 5000 cattle-owners paying taxes, but the handful of Association members owned eighty-five to ninety per cent of the cattle.

That was not all they controlled. During the 1890 legislative session, eight out of twelve members of the upper house were also members of the "declining" Association, as were all five members of the committee dealing with livestock.[8] The effect on legislation was predictable. The Association kept all it had gained in 1888, got back some of what it had lost, and added a new triumph.

Item: The democratic folderol about membership in the territorial livestock commission, one member "from" each county, was swept away. Although the number of counties had been increased from eight to eleven, the number of livestock commissioners was cut down to five, their qualification for membership merely being a resident of the Territory. This guaranteed that control of livestock matters would be kept in the hands of the clique in Cheyenne—under a more complaisant governor, who was not long in appearing.[9]

Item: Certain restrictions on maverick sales which would have the effect of shutting out the small bidder were retained.

Item: Since an arrangement for restricting would-be bidders had resulted in lowering of maverick prices and virtual disappearance of the maverick fund, an appropriation of $10,000 was obtained to provide for the expenses of the livestock commission. In a territory of vast expanse but only 60,000 population, ten thousand 1890 dollars was a sizable sum.[10]

It might be added that when the first state legislature convened at the end of the same year, the number of members on the state livestock commission was further reduced, from five to three. By this time the dwindling Association not only controlled the legislature, it had a friend in the governor's chair, friends on the bench, and a friend in the White House in Washington (President Benjamin Harrison) who were subservient to its wishes. It had, in short, or it was, a machine which ruled Wyoming.

Much has been written of the Association's decline in prestige, of its loss of members and money during the difficult years after 1887.

But if this be losing, who would not choose to lose?

A maverick is a motherless calf. A maverick is a motherless calf whose daddy has run off with another cow. A maverick is the rightful property of the man upon whose range it is found. A maverick is the property, rightful or not, of the first man who gets his rope on it. Since nobody knows whose property the maverick is, it may be declared the property of the commonwealth, to be auctioned off to the highest bidder, or the highest and best bidder, or the highest responsible bidder, or the highest responsible bidder whose personal qualifications are acceptable to the executive committee, without which acceptability he will find that his money is no good regardless of how responsible he is.

Once you have declared that the commonwealth owns the maverick you may not have solved much of anything after all, because someone is likely to ask who owns the commonwealth, and how it plans to conduct the sales and for whose benefit. To the big stockman the maverick is a symbol of property and the property is mine, not thine. To the little stockmen who came along later, the maverick is a symbol of his own rights on the public domain. The maverick is a source of hatred and strife. The maverick is a boil on the neck of the body politic. The maverick is a motherless calf.

The primary and ostensible purpose of the law dealing with maverick sales was to raise an inspection fund. But in addition to the declared purpose it had a second undeclared purpose which was just as visible between the lines as the devil's tail sticking out through the bottom of his trousers; the purpose of restricting the bidding to a few wealthy owners and shutting out the increasing number of new, small owners any one of whom might have had an animal get away unbranded, and would have liked a chance to bid it back or acquire a few bargain cattle.

Under cover of the excitement over the Horse Shoe cases, friends of the Wyoming Stock Growers' Association succeeded in slipping into the 1888 bill a provision which had failed of passage in 1884, that requiring a preposterous bond of the would-be bidder on mavericks. Originally $3000, it was now scaled down to $2000; but to the average cowboy or homesteader who wanted to bid on perhaps ten head of mavericks at the nominal prevailing rate of $10 a head, it was as prohibitive as a trip to the moon; which was the transparent intention.

Still in the grip of their extraordinary obsession with mavericks, the leading cattlemen and their friends in the legislature succeeded in establishing a new condition which did away with all bidding on mavericks on the range. Henceforth all the mavericks taken in each roundup district were to be bid on in advance, by lot, for the coming season, at a sale to be held on the steps of the capitol building each spring before the roundup, at a date which was timed to coincide with the annual meeting of the Wyoming Stock Growers' Association. The total number of mavericks which might be taken in each entire roundup district were to be bid on at this sale at so much a head, the purchaser not knowing of course just what number he was contracting for.[11] To a rich man a few head one way or the other made no difference; to a penny-scraping homesteader they did; even if he had the money to bid on fifty head or more; even if he had been able to raise the $2000 bond; even if he had managed to make the trip to the capital from his log-cabin homestead, which of course he could not do. The maverick obsession on the part of the then-leading cattlemen of Wyoming amounted to a collective neurosis; especially in view of the fact that losses from mavericking were a drop in the bucket compared to winter losses. Yet in all the records, little concern is expressed over winter losses, in comparison with the overriding fixation against letting any outsider gain possession of a maverick, even though he was willing to pay good money for it.

When legal restrictions on maverick sales failed to go far enough to keep out the small buyer, restrictions were imposed by on-the-spot fiat without benefit of law. In Johnson County, according to an early informant, "a certain cowboy working for an outfit by custom was not supposed of course to own any cattle. He told me he had about $1000 saved up, would like to invest in mavericks that were offered for sale and so informed his employer. The latter agreed that he would be glad to have him do it, but nevertheless, if he did, he would be told to cut out his string of horses and leave the outfit and be listed among those blackballed from now on."

In 1884 a roundup foreman on Cheyenne River, east of Powder River, sold a few mavericks to a pair of partners for better than $15 a head. He had supposed that what he did was legal under the "highest and best bidder" clause. But after making his report to Secretary Sturgis he received a stiff reply stating that "it was not the intention of the law to sell those yearlings to little thieves like M. and W."

And during the strike disturbance in the summer of 1886 an executive committee member recommended a man for the blacklist, not so much because he had taken part in the strike, which he had, as because he had bought mavericks on the same roundup.[12] When a man found out that if he purchased mavericks with his honest dollars he would be rated a criminal almost as if he had gone out and branded them on the range, what would you expect him to do then?

That was just what some of them did.

THIRTEEN

Exit Bill Maverick

SUDDENLY, AT the beginning of 1891, there was no more maverick law—none at all. In the most inexplicable gesture of seven years of wrangling over the maverick question the first state legislature, meeting at the end of December 1890, had reversed all previous policy *in toto*, erasing the word *maverick* from the books, leaving a void. The Cheyenne *Leader's* comment is hardly adequate to explain such a drastic change of front, but whatever the reasons they are lost.

"The usual tinkering with the stock laws," the *Leader* sneered on December 23. "It seems rather remarkable that with all the experience that has been had in the stock business, that legislation to protect it should invariably prove both expensive and inadequate. Neither the large nor the small owners have received adequate protection."

But those who supposed that in view of repeal just anybody would now be free to brand mavericks soon learned their mistake. "It is understood," the *Leader* continued, "that [the mavericks] will be claimed by the men who own [*sic*] the range on which they are found." Nobody except the United States government "owned" the ranges, but the big stockmen were constantly forgetting this, and their "understanding" left the small stockmen out in the cold as usual.

Early in May the Northern Wyoming Protective Association, Johnson County branch of the WSGA, effected a permanent organization and elected Fred G. S. Hesse president. An agreement was reached whereby, in the absence of a maverick law, the mavericks were to be divided up daily by the roundup foreman in the ratio of the number of calves branded by each outfit. This arrangement of course excluded the small owners, many of whom were barred from the roundups anyway. As for the part of the year outside of the roundup season, it was held that the maverick was the property of the fellow who caught him, just the same as in the good old days, with the understood proviso that the maverick be caught by an insider, not an outsider—a settler or black-balled man. The latter soon found that the law had not been repealed for *their* benefit, and if they branded mavericks they would be in just as much hot water as ever.

An air of jollity prevailed at the Johnson County stockmen's meeting, according to the *Bulletin;* and no wonder. The demise of Bill Maverick, who had caused even these allies to fall out over many a year, was occasion enough for a few extra drinks.*

* Buffalo *Bulletin,* May 14, 1891.

3

No Promised Land
1875-1890

The search for the mysterious treasure of the West
had been going on for full four hundred years and indeed much longer. What mattered the aim of the
quest; whether it was the golden apples of the Hes-
perides, or a short cut to the riches of Ind, or the
Fountain of Youth, or the Seven Cities of Cibola, or
a fast fortune in the cattle business? Or an unknown
dream burning in the fires of the sunset, a dream too
potent to be extinguished by realities of blood and
privation and sudden death, which captured the souls
of adventurers like Captain Stewart; of priests like
Father de Smet, whose declared aim was to save the
souls of the heathen—but any good priest knew it
was not necessary to cross half the world to find souls
to save, when there were sinners enough at home; or
the lure of the Sisdakee, where there were dusky
women and danger, but there were women and danger
in other places; or the beckoning finger of "opportunity" but "opportunity" was often a mirage; or the
urge to escape from the stale complexities of ordinary
life into something else—but to what, what, what?

The lure of the West—what was it?—a question
never answered, nor ever likely to be.

—ANONYMOUS

The Cattlemen Come—
and So Do the Settlers

POWDER RIVER was famous for its quicksands. They would bog a saddle blanket, the cowboys said, and for miles and miles the only place you could get a horse or a roundup wagon or a bull team or a stagecoach across was a spot where a streak of hard limestone underlay the river bed. This became the Powder River crossing of the Bozeman road, or just Powder River Crossing. The cluster of log shacks at the crossing housed saloons, stables, road ranch accommodations such as they were, a store, a blacksmith shop, and a post office. At this crossroads of the West, Lords and Honorables rubbed elbows with the most villainous types. Newcomers investing in the cattle business, visitors from the eastern seaboard or the British Isles and their ladies, caught up in the excitement of this great New World adventure, had but one way to get to the Powder River country and that was by stage northward from the Platte, over the old Bozeman cutoff route to the gold fields of western Montana, the old Indian-fighting road called after John M. Bozeman who pioneered it in 1864 across some of the wickedest Indian country in the world—and lost his own scalp on it a year or so later.

The stagecoach—safe enough now for what that was worth—jolted along at a snail's pace over the dusty, sagebrush-freckled miles from Fort Fetterman. The passengers cramped hip to hip and thigh to thigh in the narrow seat were so hot they couldn't even perspire. The midday sun beat the dreary landscape into flatness. The gravelly hills with their everlasting pimples of sagebrush had about as much beauty in them as a slag heap. Why couldn't the Creator have thought of some other form of vegetation when he made the West? What's wonderful about the West? Why didn't I stay home?

But it's not far to the crossing now. The shadows are beginning to creep out of their hiding place and some magic is touching the slag-heap hills with wonders of color and contour. The laboring faithful horses strain up the last rise before the drop down onto Powder River, and now at the top, with a gasp and a gulp, the traveler inhales his first view of the Big Horns.

There they are, a frieze of dreaming blue and silver hanging in the western sky, so far away, like a vision of the promised land. Which will never be fulfilled. The driver, who of course, is something of a showman, pauses at the top to let them take it all in while he points out Black Tooth and Cloud's Peak with the streaks of snow on their sides. Then the stage rattles on down the slope toward the cluster of log buildings at the bottom, and soon the horses, freed of their sweaty collars and traces, are having a good roll in the dirt, and the passengers are stretching their legs at the bar.

The first herd Frewen turned loose on Powder River in 1879, believing he and his friends had twenty years in which to expand and prosper, was the start of a rush which soon swept him and all the boom-time hopefuls off their feet. How fast the others came! By 1881 the country was filling up with cattle; nearly 80,000 east of the Big Horns, and more coming in on the western slope. In 1884, which was the second peak roundup year, an estimated 181,000 cattle were gathered east of the Big Horns in Johnson County, of which 123,000 were British-owned.[1]

For nine years two social systems as far apart as the poles co-existed with almost no contact of persons apart from the cowboy whom the growing colony of Britons hired and fired, and none of understanding. When contact did come it came in the unpleasant shape of quarrels over land matters. On one hand there were the manners and customs of the old world transplanted to the new, with luxurious hunting trips, gay house-parties, and titled guests. On the other there was this preposterous breed of peasants who came to the front door if the ranch house had one, and who expected to be invited to sit down at the table with the family.* Although clearly akin to that slightly subhuman species the nineteenth-century Englishman categorized as "the poor," they seemed not to know that they were "the poor." This was confusing; it was irritating; and in the end it spelled total defeat.

Early in 1881 Horace Plunkett, on a trip to Fort McKinney, stopped

* The degree of flexibility in the face of novel circumstances varied greatly with the individual Englishman. Folk memory in Johnson County still cherishes a tradition of parties at the Bar C at which titled ladies danced with spruced-up cowboys, greatly to the gratification of the local folk, since your independent western American was just as susceptible to the charms of a title as anyone else.

overnight with "a small haygrower" (homesteader) and noted with a flicker of surprise that the man would not accept pay for his hospitality. Was this a first flash of recognition that the social customs of a free frontier were not those of an old feudal country? If so it died out; for he soon determined that what he called the "open house system" or "free board system" must go from the ranges governed by himself and his friends.

The cattlemen came at the peak of a wet cycle which dated at least as far back as the middle seventies and lasted longer than the period covered by this book, except for the gunpowder-dry summer of 1886. Bluestem was everywhere, growing so tall and thick in lowlying meadows that pioneer homesteaders could cut wild hay even in valleys which bore such inauspicious names as Dry Fork and Salt Creek. Small watercourses long since bone-dry ran water; tiny lakes, with reeds at the edge and the curlews crying over them, shone sapphire on the distant prairie and rippled under a vagrant breeze; even the old buffalo wallows could still be seen.

"When you were working on the roundup the river would be 'swimming' for six weeks at a time. There were lakes where you don't see any today. Even the sagebrush grew taller—tall enough in lots of places to hide a man. It was a country worth fighting for then." Thus an old Johnson County resident whose father fought for it, on the side of the invaders.

And no wonder, for it rained—how it rained!—making fords impassable, washing out bridges, keeping a whole roundup camped in idleness for a week or longer by the side of a raging torrent while a hundred cowboys passed the time in horse racing and playing cards, waiting for the river to go down so the wagons could cross. It snowed too; and the snows which lay deep on the mountains and filled the gulches level-full and blew into great drifts and were scoured by the wind off the ridges were not an unmixed curse, for while they killed cattle they also built moisture for next spring's grass.

Horace Plunkett's diary tells the story. May: "Rain, rain . . . never saw so much rain in three days." June: "Roundup camped on an unfordable river. . . . Mountains have been so covered with snow that game is scarce and scattered. . . . A deluge washed away our garden. . . . Intended to cross mountains but a heavy rainstorm made it almost impossible. . . . Lots of snow still accumulated at 8000 feet." July: "Rained cats and dogs—again." August: "Rained torrents."

The bounties of nature which caused the land to be overrun with rich men's cattle brought other men as well, and by now homesteads were appearing by the sides of streams. The large owners had at first neglected to make entries, but by 1884 they were being forced to make them to protect their holdings and improvements, which included irrigation ditches; and a new, questioning, exasperated note creeps into the letters and diaries as they discover that the law is on the side of the interlopers and there is nothing they can do in the long run. They fought against the inevitable, however. In September of that year Plunkett was noting: "The lands we can irrigate [on the North Fork] are extensive. The whole question for us now is will the desert entries, made as we have to make them through third parties, be held good." In December he fumed: "Our home ranch has been jumped. Buffalo and its gang are the curse of the country."

Faced by unrealistic land laws which were framed to suit humid-area farmers and then modified, late and reluctantly, by unrealistic compromises, the cattle-grower almost universally engaged in shenanigans of some sort in order to gain control of the land he needed in order to operate. It was going on all over the West: dummy entries, jumped claims, contested filings, sound and fury in Washington. The foreigners were no worse than anybody else. But when the cattle-owner, whether foreign or American, used force or threats to drive bona-fide settlers off the land, then popular feeling swung against him.

Moreton Frewen was writing to Fred Hesse in April 1884 about "doing all we can to take up the water on North Fork.... I know a firm of land sharks in Colorado who seem to have undue influence with the land department and through them for a consideration I hope to do it; only keep this dark." So far it was standard procedure, but Frewen was arrogant. A month later he was writing furiously to Plunkett: "We have got to face this invasion of fresh Texans boldly and at once. I am going to 'war.'" Who were the "fresh Texans"—who could they have been but former cowboys of his own and his neighbors, who had decided to settle?

Shortly before he himself was ousted from the Wyoming management of the Powder River Cattle Company, Frewen was writing Fred Hesse what to do about the interlopers on his range. "As to this hound Tisdell, split him like a rail ... pull his fence all over the place and have the wire cut in short lengths. He is the kind of man to make an example of." And later: "Do not fail to bounce that fence of David's. : ... I have no patience with these bullheaded fellows who are coming in, in spite of all remonstrance." One of the fellows proved less bullheaded than discreet. His story, first told in the Cheyenne *Leader* in March 1885, was of starting to set up housekeeping at a location only some thirty miles from Frewen's home ranch. He was descended upon at once by a party of imported cowboys from Britain whose speech he could hardly understand. He got the main idea however, when he stated that he planned to settle. "You cahn't do that, you know, this is the Frewen brothers' cattle range," he was told. He moved on.

For a man who not only had no legal title to the land he occupied but was not even a citizen of the country in which it lay, Moreton Frewen was certainly asserting himself.[2]

Buffalo was growing. It was romping on its bawdy and unsanitary way, which did not amuse Britishers like Plunkett and Frewen. They had been reared on the topside of a centuries-old caste system, and they detested Buffalo and never visited it except when forced by matters of business necessity. It took a robust American sense of humor—like that of Theodore Roosevelt, who found Medora, North Dakota amusing, and Buffalo was no worse—to appreciate items like this concerning the funeral of one Whiskey Bill, which was sent by the Buffalo correspondent of the Laramie *Boomerang* early in 1884. It gave the text of a notice posted on the door of the Occidental Hotel, reading:

The friends of the late Whisky Bill are respectfully invited to attend his funeral—he having gone up the flume on Friday—which will take place from Sam Tompkins' saloon on Sunday. The best ecclesiastical talent has been engaged, and the services will be of a varied & interesting character.

COMMITTEE

The town had its periodic morality waves, typical of frontier communities where preachers as well as morality were scarce. Couples who had been living together in open and unwedded bliss were haled before the court and told to get married, or else. In one such action the judge stated that one or two or even a greater number of occasional offenses were not sufficient to justify a verdict of guilty; it must be *habitual* cohabitation; an important distinction, since it exempted one of the town's major industries from danger of prosecution. The outcome ranged from "Case dismissed" to a fine of $25 apiece. The latter was exceptionally severe, since the double standard of morality then prevailing in the East was reversed in the chivalrous West, the "lady" generally drawing a "case dismissed" out of hand, while the offending male might be bound over to the next session of court.

In 1889 a couple was hauled before the court on complaint of both fornication and adultery, she being single, he married. The conclusion as recorded in the Criminal Appearance Docket of Johnson County reads as follows: "Parties marry in opin [*sic*] court and case dismissed."

Evidently bigamy was rated a matter of no consequence in the good old frontier days.

From 1882 to 1886 Johnson County had a famous and efficient sheriff whose name was not Frank M. Canton though he was so known then and for the rest of his life. He had spent his early years in Texas under his real name, Joe Horner, which he changed when he left Texas after a shooting scrape or two, with the heel flies after him—to borrow two expressions which were in frequent use at the time. He bossed a trail herd of twenty-five hundred head to Ogallala, Nebraska, in 1878 when he was twenty-nine years old, and from then on Frank Canton enters the story. He went farther north, and is listed as serving from 1878 to 1892 as a range detective for the Wyoming Stock Growers' Association.

He was energetic, liked, and feared. He put several stage robbers out of business and after a considerable display of courage arrested the notorious outlaw, Teton Jackson, who later dug his way out of the jail in Boise, Idaho. A scribe in Buffalo—one of those fluent young men who invariably turned up in the remotest frontier spots—eulogized in the Laramie *Boomerang:* "Sheriff Canton and his men never seem to sleep. There have been no escapes from our apology for a jail this winter." [3]

It was proof of his popularity that he served as sheriff for two consecutive terms, until in 1886 he chose to devote himself solely to the work of the Wyoming Stock Growers' Association. But those were the happy far-off times when, apart from the normal personal frictions, hardly anybody in Buffalo was fighting with anybody—yet.

FIFTEEN

Never the Twain Shall Meet

"THE MAJOR adjustment any upper class Englishman in the West had to make was to accept absolutely social equality." Thus Robert G. Athearn in *Westward the Briton*. Among the majority who never learned to make it was one of the ablest and finest men ever lured to the West by the hopes of a quick fortune in the cattle business—the Irishman, Horace Plunkett.

The Colorado University professor has stated the case with brutal directness. It was conform or get out. In the end they got out. There were brilliant exceptions, and quiet exceptions too, but the majority of the English, the wealthy and conspicuous among them, that is, had come for the novelty and the money. When the money vanished and the novelty wore off, they departed. While they remained they made some appalling mistakes.

By far the most prominent of the Anglo-Scottish-Irish colony on Powder River, excepting only the meteoric Moreton Frewen, was Horace Curzon Plunkett, who was no meteor. His energy and ability would have made him conspicuous anywhere, and he went on to ever-increasing prominence throughout his long life. The mistakes he made in the West were those of his class, his nation, and his age. They would not have been mistakes in India where the sahib ruled supreme, but they were disastrous in Wyoming, which was not a healthy habitat for sahibs. It is not surprising that snobs like Frewen and a whole host of lesser snobs could not adapt themselves to the equalitarian West; the surprising thing is that a man as enlightened and high-minded as Horace Plunkett could not do it either. For years he was chiefly remembered at the forks of Powder River for his part in three violently unpopular moves which helped bring on the deluge five years after his departure, One was the partially abortive wage cut; another the abolition of the old rule of hospitality on the range—"the free board system at ranch houses," as Plunkett called it disapprovingly; and the third was the roundup boycott which he was said to have been instrumental in introducing. For a foreigner to come and occupy American soil and then proceed to throw these monkey wrenches into its social system was, when you stop to think of it, a not unnatural irritant, even in the hospitable and easygoing West.

In 1903, fifteen years after he last saw Powder River, Horace Plunkett was knighted by King Edward VII for his distinguished services to Irish agriculture. In 1881 he had begun keeping a diary, which he continued until his death in 1932. The Wyoming portion is a remarkable self-portrait of a man of energy, zeal, and honor. It also presents an almost perfect case history showing why British cattle companies had trouble and made trouble in Wyoming.[1]

By October 1879, just before his twenty-fifth birthday, Plunkett was established on a ranch on the North Fork of Powder River, in partnership with Alexis and Edmond Roche, brothers of Lord Fermoy. Thereafter for nine years he returned every year, no longer a stranger but never at home.

"He was never sure whether he liked the country or not," his biographer wrote. "He was intermittently appreciative of the landscape but it remained strange and unfriendly to him." In this he differed from two famous Americans each of whom liked, the one Wyoming, the other the Dakota badlands very much indeed. He saw the West with the bleak eye of the black-and-white camera which recorded the flat landscape, muddy, rutted streets, and mean buildings of the cowtowns but missed all the magic of color and light, to say nothing of the human spectrum. Of that uproarious inhibition-smasher, Ogalalla, he wrote: "A poor place, just country accommodations.... Bad water and poor food... treeless and barren.... I suppose nowhere is such business done in such a miserable place." Cheyenne was "a bleak and dusty spot but with a champagne mountain air which relieved the sense of desolation."

Owen Wister raved—there is no other word—about "the particular moment of sunset when the light that never was on land or sea, except in Wyoming, turns not only mountain and plain but dry ditches of mud and ash heaps into objects of enchanted splendor." Plunkett never saw it. The hot gold and blue of the Wyoming summer; the brilliancy of spring, when the snow still lay dazzling on the mountains and the fresh little white faces of baby calves were showing up everywhere; the distances that stretched the soul into infinity—all this said nothing to an inward eye which remained constantly turned toward the green fields of Ireland.

Yet April of every year found him on board ship, westward bound from Queenstown. In October or November he made the return voyage. He spent the five or six winter months at home in the great Tudor pile of Dunsany castle, with trips to Dublin and to London; hunting, looking after family affairs, and devoting himself to his father. The old lord loved this faithful younger son, whose venture in far Wyoming always seemed strange and terrible to him, and from 1881 onward kept begging him to give it up.

Your English import in the West was one up on the average American tenderfoot; he was an expert horseman to start with. Horace Plunkett very soon ceased to be a tenderfoot, and by 1884 he was a cowman. We find him tallying horses, classing cattle, driving the remuda over the mountains on the way back to the home ranch after the roundup was over. A do-it-yourself man, he mastered surveyors' techniques and laid out his irrigation ditches himself. When his cattle were shipped in the fall he rode the cattle train to market like any cowhand, got off at the stops and walked along the cars with a prod pole to prod up the unfortunate animals which had gotten down. Then, since there was no uniformed conductor to shout "All abo-oard" when the engineer jerked the train into motion without warning, the aristocrat from overseas grabbed the nearest handhold and scrambled up the monkey ladder to the top, to walk back along the catwalk over the swaying, rattling cars to the rear of the train, where he climbed down into the caboose.

But while he learned the techniques of the cattle game fast enough, he never understood its spirit. On the whole he disliked cowboys and the feeling was regrettably mutual. He was frequently vexed by "insubordination," which rarely troubles a good schoolmaster or a good leader. "A crowd of cowboys who had been lying around the ranch waiting for the roundup moved out which was a great relief," he wrote on May 31, 1886. A little later the same year, which was the year of the wage cut and strike, occurs this dismal entry—written when he rode to the roundup: "They were not cordial at all. They have been talking about shooting me all winter because I have been made the scapegoat of the attempt to reduce wages. I expect I shall live through it, but it is unpleasant being scowled at and talked at by the blackguards."

Cowboys were drunken and profane—except on the job, when they were merely profane; but worse than that, ten centuries of feudal overlordship had not conditioned Plunkett to understand a kind of man who would flounder through snowdrifts at forty below and stay with the herd in a stampede, but who would not "serve."

Yet understanding them was vital to the success of a cow outfit. The good will of neighbors too—especially small neighbors—was a must for any ranching enterprise; the wreckage of such good will through the folly of the big outfits was what brought Johnson County to flaming disaster. Yet Plunkett seemed to have no awareness of neighbors other than his fellow Britons. Again in contrast to Roosevelt, who took such huge delight in the human spectrum along the Little Missouri, Plunkett's Wyoming scene was an irritating, almost faceless blur of drunken or "insubordinate" cowhands and hostile settlers who jumped his claims. Yet an occasional lightning flash of awareness showed him the same personalities in a truer light. A kind and compassionate man himself, he was quick to recognize these qualities in others. During the summer of 1884, a wayfarer riding through the country shot himself accidentally in the stomach and was brought at daybreak to the Peters and Alston ranch, where he lingered for ten days and then died.

"The cowboys were kindness itself to the patient," he wrote, with a hint of surprise in the brief entry; as though a man who had kept his eyes shut suddenly opened them and saw something which had been there all the time. Plunkett hated suffering; the diary notes with an almost audible sigh of relief that the unfortunate fellow "died without pain."

On another occasion in 1886 a glimpse of the human virtues in his rough surroundings flashed like a comet across his mental photographic plate. In September he had set out to join the beef roundup. "Overtook a cowboy and a miner en route from Sundance to Washakie. . . . We heard the roundup was on West Bridger Creek. . . . Night overtook us while searching for the roundup, and supperless and bedless we had to camp out and wait through the long night for the guidance of the sun." The night was chilly. "In the division of saddle blankets the cowboy and miner insisted on my having a third share, as I had only one and they had two each and overcoats." A new world, well named. A new world.

After a sleepless night they found the roundup—of course—only three quarters of a mile away.

He had not intended to let his own cowboys know about his mishap, but he might have known he couldn't fool them. Gravely they asked whether the hotel where he had spent the night last night was run on the European or the American plan.

In the summer of 1884 the firm of Plunkett and Roche was expanded and reorganized into the Frontier Land and Cattle Company. But a single ranching enterprise could not begin to satisfy Plunkett's restless spirit, and he was soon involved in a network of companies, partnerships, affiliates, directorates, and salaried supervisory posts of bewildering complexity. But the biggest mistake he ever made was consenting to take over the management of Frewen's calamitous Powder River Company. This embroiled him in a bitter and long-drawn-out quarrel with both Frewen brothers, on top of a thankless grind of travel back and forth, back and forth from Alberta—where the 76 herds had been moved after all—to Sherman Hill on the Union Pacific, where Moreton had dreamed up a packing plant without ice; to the feeding sheds on Lake Superior which were connected with another abortive scheme for shipping live cattle by boat. Needless to say his own ranches suffered accordingly.

Worst of all was his inability to hold an outfit together. To use an Americanism, he couldn't get along with the help. "The foreman makes or loses money in this country," he had written, with his curious kind of double vision which enabled him to see mistakes even while he was making them. Yet he was never able to find and keep a good foreman.

The ramrod, as he was sometimes called, was a peculiar breed. He drew three times as much pay as the ordinary hand; he thought well of himself, and on the whole with reason. Wyoming had foremen who could have bossed a herd from Red River to the North Pole and brought it through without loss, but since most of them had been limited to a fifth-grade education in Texas, bookkeeping was not their strong point. Plunkett required bookkeeping. He also disapproved of "intractability." In nine years in Wyoming, except for the few early, happy years in which he was pleased with Jack Donahue, he never found a satisfactory man to run the EK herds, and the break with Donahue was the saddest case of all. The big, tough Texan had worked faithfully for him for four years, but in 1884, when the original outfit was expanded and rechristened the Frontier Cattle Company, Plunkett decided that Donahue was not up to the new, enlarged responsibilities. He hesitated, finagled, finally decided to let him go, and ended by replacing him with an inferior man. The tough cowboy was hurt and showed it, and Plunkett penned a sad little eulogy on the departed, uncertainty breathing in every line.

"With the wagon no man in the country can outwork him and he is honest as far as I know too. But about the ranch he was intolerable being careless of property and negligent of all work except cowpunching pure and simple. He was a strange character—a desperado by nature and by education. But he had his good points too. He had no respect for anyone and was very intractable. So on the whole it is best to replace him. His strange western humor—terribly profane and blasphemous at times—was generally amazing. He thoroughly understood the expressiveness of the western language and some of his sayings will long be remembered by Plunkett, Roche and Co.!"

"He had no respect for anyone." To the son of a noble house, this was a new and unsettling phenomenon. Yet how many leaders in the West, from Sir William Drummond Stewart of the fur-trading caravans to Charles Goodnight of Texas to Granville Stuart of Montana to Theodore Roosevelt, could have told a different story of these frontier "desperados" and their alleged want to respect. They could have told that respect was freely given to those who earned it; it was not built in as part of an imported social system. The imported system was fatally self-defeating from the moment it crossed the Mississippi. Those who looked for respect on the basis of rank, wealth, or position simply never got it at all. . . . Never the twain shall meet.

Except when they do. Among the many men who came from magnificent feudal backgrounds to the West there were many exceptions, and the exceptions managed to shed the system with its habits of a lifetime as easily and gracefully as they would shed a cloak, without sacrificing an iota of themselves.

But Horace Plunkett brought the system with him to Wyoming, where it enveloped him like an invisible cocoon. At home or in the West, he was involved with the same little closed circuit of friends and neighbors whose families had dined, hunted, and danced together; frolicked through the London season, attended coronations in their ermine-lined robes, intermarried, and sometimes quarreled, for generations. His cattle enterprise staggered under a plethora of partners, shareholders, office holders, who were all old Eton chums, County Meath neighbors, and the like, and who had to be kept busy somehow because they were all eager to play at being cowboys until they got tired of it or until it interfered with their normal pursuits. The idea prevailed that any scion of the gentry was qualified to operate a cattle "ranche," and it was long before Plunkett was disabused of it. At one point two of the partners, left in charge while he was away, fouled up the books just as badly as an ignorant foreman might have done, but after all, one can scarcely discharge an old friend who wears the same school tie.

A vice-president "imagines that he can run the business up here [the EK] from Cheyenne." Later, when the same vice-president was wheeling and dealing around Omaha in connection with some of the company's business interests, Plunkett remarked rather leadenly: "He is much better at this sort of work than range work."

That was it. They were all better at wheeling and dealing than at range work. It was a case of too many chiefs and not enough Indians.

Every spring it was the same story. Plunkett returned from Ireland to be greeted by a state of affairs ranging from a major mess to the verge of disaster. In May 1883: "House left in a filthy condition by the cowboys. Spent the whole day doing housemaid's work." Then: "We have installed Yup Mi, a celestial, as cook. Hope the cowboys won't shoot him."

A year later, after arrival at the ranch: "Found everything that hadn't been stolen in a state of filth. One Jennings and his wife are in possession. She is a dull apparently sulky woman who does not seem to be one for doing any work. There is however next to nothing to eat. Possibly when we feed her she will work."

In 1885, in Cheyenne: "May 10. Gilchrist [vice-president] came in from Powder River and reported terrible anarchy during the winter in the EK outfit. Business badly conducted and much money lost." In August the same year: "Drove to EK ranch. Never saw the range so terribly eaten off. Yet the cattle look well. Found old Pete cooking for a crowd of passers-by. Everything filthy. Have to go out to a tent to sleep." 1886 was the year of another foreman fiasco, the quarrel with Frewen, the wage cut, and the year Plunkett was glared at on the roundup. In the cattle business troubles never came singly.

The partner who appears to have been at Plunkett's ranches most regularly and done the most damage was a large investor and charter member of the firm, Alexis Roche. Alexis was arrogant, spoiled, and incapable of conducting himself decently toward anyone under him. Plunkett knew all this—but Alexis was an old family friend! Two of his brothers were also partners or investors in the concern. The family were in somewhat straitened circumstances. To discharge Alexis was unthinkable. So he clung to this misfit until the very last gasp.

The gasp occurred in the spring of 1887. The annual bad news from Powder River reached him in Cheyenne, but this time it was so much worse as to be a catastrophe. Alexis had managed to make the outfit so hated throughout the countryside, besides alienating its own men, that—Plunkett wrote—"we shall have to do all our work ourselves." At long last he reached the painful decision to fire Alexis. However the latter, although the principal architect of the wreck, had not achieved it alone. Another partner had wintered at the ranch with him. He had obviously been no better.

If the EK picture was at all typical, it is apparent that many of the well-heeled British cattle companies were not run as a business but merely as a form of extended nepotism. If half the hangers-on they retained drew pay commensurate with their uselessness, it is no wonder that the companies went broke.

The summer of 1887 was a sad time. Plunkett spent melancholy days at the ranch burning papers and packing up, and he gave away all his cowboy clothes except one suit, as he did not expect to need them again, but in the summer of 1888 Horace did, after all, pay one more brief visit to straighten out the affairs of the EK. It was the last time he ever saw the Powder River country. Early in 1889 his father died and Horace, though a younger son, came into a large fortune which enabled him to ride out financial storms in which many others were going under. His next older brother, "Johnny," became the seventeenth Baron Dunsany, and his son, Horace's nephew, was the Lord Dunsany who won worldwide renown as a poet and playwright.

Back home for good in his beloved Ireland, the restless and somewhat unadjusted young man of Wyoming days very soon found his destiny. He threw himself heart and soul into the cause of improving the Irish farmer's lot, preaching rural cooperatives with the zeal of an evangelist. His success in this led to his knighthood.

He paid one last visit to Wyoming in 1889, but it took him only as far as Cheyenne—"dull and doleful—surely the glory has departed." And on this visit he found a colleague who had fallen, alas, into a pit more universal than regional.

In Omaha "I unearthed E, in a saloon where he had been living the life of a low-down 'sport'—whiskey, gambling, women etc. I tackled him about the debts he had left in Wyoming greatly to the discredit of the English contingent and shamed him into making an assignment of all he professed to have in England or Ireland for the creditors."

And so Britannia retreated from the West in some disorder, though not entirely. For to this day, from Montana to Texas, you will meet older men with good, hard outdoor faces and the bowed legs of a cowboy, who are ranching, buying and selling cattle, cowpunching, just like their neighbors. The accent they brought with them has almost disappeared; they never mention their family connections, nor the check which some of them still receive once a month from an English bank; it is only when you visit them in their homes and see the crested silver tea service on the sideboard, or the picture of the Tudor manor house where they were born, that you really come to know these quiet ones who are at home under two flags.

Horace Plunkett had a strain of pessimism and self-doubt in his nature which led him to look back dubiously on his Wyoming venture.

"I don't think the ten years in the west were wholly wasted," he wrote many years later, "but certainly they might have been better spent."

In perspective they appear anything but wasted. His Wyoming experience with its lessons, some of them painful, was like an inoculation with the American spirit. It was uncomfortable in its earlier stages and rather slow to "take," but "take" it did. In an introduction to Miss Digby's biography, a colleague who had served under him in the Department of Agriculture and Technical Instruction in Ireland, which Sir Horace founded, wrote: "His ten years of ranching laid the foundation of his deep understanding of the United States. . . . The ten years in the west . . . vitally affected the whole thought and course of his life." Among other things it led to his work for Anglo-American understanding and to intimate friendships with such leading American statesmen as Theodore Roosevelt, Gifford Pinchot, Colonel House, Walter Hines Page.

"East is east and west is west, and never the twain shall meet," Kipling wrote. "But there is neither east nor west, border nor breed nor birth"—given certain conditions. Horace Plunkett ended by fulfilling them. To his biographer he was "an Anglo-American Irishman."

SIXTEEN

If You Call a Man a Thief

*The line between stealing and honorable warfare is
very indistinct in the war between the cattlemen and
the homesteader.*
—EVERETT DICK *in The Sod House Frontier*

THE VACUUM left by the withering away of the old big outfits was soon
filled not by cattle, which never overran the Powder River country in
such numbers again, but by men—and conflict. New men, new issues—
you didn't hear so much about land contests and claim jumping now,
but you heard a lot about "blackballed men" who were not allowed to
take part in the roundups or get a job. You heard about settlers and
rustlers, and sometimes the terms seemed almost interchangeable, except
that which one was used depended on the party doing the talking.

By 1889 the Powder River contingent of "lords" were all gone:
Plunkett, Winn, Windsor, Peters, Alston, and the entire clutch of Plunkett
partners and protégés. All the outfits were in receivership and closing out
with the exception of Plunkett's EK, which had been cushioned against
the jolts of adversity by its owner's fortunate inheritance; the EK alone
still had a wagon on the roundup in 1892 as a reminder of happier days.

But while the English money was gone (and so was most of the
eastern money), there was still plenty of Omaha and Chicago money
invested in northern Wyoming. Henry Blair, banker of Chicago, still
had his Hoe outfit below the forks of Powder River, and William Pax-
ton of Omaha still had the Ogalalla Cattle Company in the field with
William C. Irvine as manager. Two Tisdale brothers, J. N. and Robert—
the former the "Tisdell" Frewen had ordered "split like a rail"—were
firmly established on the South Fork despite the Englishman's neighborly
intentions. They were Canadians with good financial backing; * they
too had a big outfit as size was counted in these latter days, and none of

---

* No relation to John A. Tisdale who was murdered in 1891.

this group were any more hospitable toward settlers and blackballed cowboys than their English predecessors.

Also in 1889 the last of the great 76 herds, now down to some 10,000 head, were sold to Pierre Wibaux of Montana for $18.50 around. This astute Frenchman had begun winter-feeding his cattle when Plunkett and others were still only talking about it, had weathered the storms of 1887, gone back to France and raised more money, and was now buying when everyone else was selling. By the early 1900s he was one of the biggest cowmen Montana had ever seen, although the books all tell you that the range-cattle business was finished by that time, but his is another story, with a happier ending. The Powder River Company was long since in bankruptcy and the firm of Windsor and Kemp of London and Omaha had been appointed receivers. The few 76 cattle left on the range after the sale to Wibaux were put in the charge of Fred G. S. Hesse, who had been foreman for the Frewens ever since they brought in their first herd in 1879. He had before this taken over the remnants of the Bar C, WP, and other English-owned outfits, and he now fell heir to the Frewens' range and buildings on Crazy Woman, made over to him in payment of a large debt which the company owed him for services and supplies. For the next three years, until he was taken prisoner with the invaders, he was the most influential man on Powder River.

A product of the sturdy mercantile middle class, well educated, he had come to America in 1875 at the age of twenty-one, intending to go on around the world to visit a brother in Australia, but he got no farther than San Antonio, Texas. Working his way north by the usual trail-herd route, he had eventually reached Cheyenne, where he met Moreton Frewen and was hired. He was a man of great ability and great rigidity, and the Johnson County war was to a considerable extent his personal war.[1]

The end of the depressed roundup season of 1885 saw the heaviest winter layoff of cowboys yet known. The following fall there was a still further reduction in the working force, and the spring roundup of 1887 brought disaster in more ways than one. Only four wagons instead of the twenty-seven four years earlier; the figure told its own story. It meant, on Upper Powder alone, some three hundred fewer cowboys employed on the range, and this reduction was not seasonal, it was for keeps. The 76 alone had turned off seventy-five men.

Winter unemployment, now merging into permanent unemployment, had always been a problem in the northern cow country. Now the companies in their wisdom decided to put a stop to the practice called "riding the grubline." In the fall of 1886, with more men out of work than ever before, the "free board system" condemned by Horace Plunkett was abolished, and signs reading "Road Ranch: Meals 50 Cents" were posted at ranch houses. To an out-of-work cowboy the price was prohibitive, as it was meant to be. It was also three times as much as the owners charged each other; since the prevailing rate for a "rep" looking out for his outfit's strays on another roundup was not fifty cents a meal, but fifty cents a day.

Up to now the laid-off hand had had three ways of getting through the winter. He could hole up in an abandoned line camp with others who were waiting it out for spring and the start of the roundups, running a trapline or—since this was slim pickings—shooting a beef on the range from time to time and selling the meat at local markets under the transparent pretense that it was elk meat—"slow elk," the wits called it. The latter was shady and risky. If he still felt a prejudice in favor of honesty he settled for the three to five dollars a head which was the going rate for mavericks branded in the name of his summertime employer.

The more ambitious cowboy would file on a homestead and put in his winter months improving it, but those who took this course soon found that they got the cold shoulder when they applied for a job next spring; the big outfits did not welcome such small-fry competition on the range and justified themselves by taking it for granted that the ex-cowboy was a thief.

The third way of getting through the winter was to "ride the grubline." Mounted on his best horse and packing his bed and his "forty years' gatherings" on another, he would visit from ranch to ranch, living by the old law of hospitality in the West. There were a few chronic "saddle bums" and there were worse, but the average grubline rider was a decent sort who avoided staying too long in one place, carried wood and water for the cook, and was always welcomed by the bored and isolated men on the premises because he was a new face and he brought the news of the range. So he got through the jobless months somehow until the uncertain sun of April shone again and it was time to rehire the crew, bring in the horses and break the broncs, replace broken corral poles, clean irrigation ditches, mend gear; and generally get everything in readiness for the late May morning when the driver-cook would crack his whip in the air, the mules would strain at their collars, the squadron of rude cavalry would start moving in the half-light, and the wagon would pull out on one more roundup.

The invitation to " 'light and eat" had softened many an economic hardship. But the foreign aristocrats and the smart eastern businessmen found it a nuisance, especially now when the shoe was pinching the financial foot. So they decided to put a stop to it. This penny-wise smartness saved them a few dollars, cost them untold thousands in ill-will.

The order did more than outrage the jobless man who didn't have fifty cents to spend; it outraged the foremen and cooks who were forced to carry it out, and set up a groundswell of rebellion among permanent employees. Fifty cents a meal! "Them's the orders," mumbled the cook, who might have ridden the grubline himself in a less fortunate winter, hating himself, hating the unaccustomed sensation of not wanting to look a fellow in the face as he took the coins; or worse, watched the fellow ride away. *Hungry!*

Once again the Montana stockmen started to make the same mistake as their Wyoming neighbors and once again they thought better of it. At the semiannual meeting of the Montana Stockgrowers Association at Helena in August 1886, the members voted to charge road-ranch prices for visitors as Wyoming was doing. They had a legitimate cause for concern, since a number of bad characters were at large in the country, riding horses of doubtful ownership; the cattlemen understandably did not want their ranches turned into way stations for thieves. Hence a resolution was passed to the effect that all visitors should pay for meals. But again the Montanans quickly reconsidered. For at the next meeting, in April 1887, Theodore Roosevelt moved to rescind that resolution and substitute one requiring merely that foremen keep a record of all suspicious persons visiting their ranches and of the brands on their horses. His motion was adopted; in Montana and North Dakota the "road ranch" idea was consigned to oblivion and the old friendly custom of the grubline held sway once more.[2]

By 1887 many of the old-time cowboys who had been in northern Wyoming for as long as five and six years were giving up and going away; others were filing on government land and fencing hay meadows and starting to run a few head of cattle, moves not welcomed by the successors of the old big outfits.

Settlers from outside were trickling in, and they were no more welcomed than the "fresh Texans" had been by Moreton Frewen a few years earlier. Among the so-called Nebraska farmers who started coming into Johnson County at this time were a young fellow called "Ranger" Jones and his brother Johnny, both cowpunchers and both shortly to be accused of rustling. Ranger, who was a daredevil bronc-buster, came in 1887, rode for the EK in 1888, later took up a homestead on the Red Fork, still later was shot in the back while driving homeward from Buffalo with a wagonload of floorboards for his new house.

In the fall of 1886, at about the time he made his land entry on the Red Fork, Jack Flagg had bought the Hat brand from a man named W. E. Hathaway at Powder River Crossing, at the same time buying a dozen head of "emigrant cattle"—cheap, worn-out work stock sold by freighters and movers. It was always suspected that such little bunches were acquired "to draw to"—to give their owner an excuse to brand mavericks. Frank Canton was watching, and was exchanging comments with Secretary Adams in Cheyenne.

"I know Jack Flagg very well. I am confident that the gentleman is crooked. . . . I think there is two others who intend to go into this business with him. Jack Flagg is an old-timer here and is a hard man; he is cunning and it will take some good work to send him over the road."

And from Adams: ". . . the mavericking is being done rather openly." Openly—openly—how often that word occurred.

Of 1887 Flagg wrote: "That spring I was blackballed and not allowed to work for any of the outfits because I had bought cattle and taken up government land.[3] [As] I could not work for any outfit on Powder River; and as I had a string of horses of my own, and as what few cattle I owned were ranging in the Cheyenne River and Antelope country, I decided to go to that roundup." After a few days the foreman, J. B. Moore, offered him a job. Later Flagg asked if he could buy mavericks. 'Much to my surprise he told me he would sell them to any man who had the money to pay for them." Flagg thereupon bought seven heifers for ten dollars a head and brought them home with him when the roundup was over.

He seems to have been unaware that the 1866 legislature, in an unprecedented move, had liberalized the maverick law. For the moment they were available to the highest bidder with no strings attached, and they could be bought in any number desired, down to one head. This lasted only until the next legislature met. There was grumbling in Cheyenne about some of the mavericks having "fallen into dishonest hands"—doubtless a reference to Flagg himself—and at the next legislative session the maverick sales were more tightly restricted than ever.

The war on the Wyoming range was a variant of the long, hard-fought war between the cattleman and the homesteader which took place all over the new lands of the West. Late in 1891, when the murder of two Johnson County settlers was attracting nationwide attention, the Omaha *Bee* observed that "the shooting in Johnson County last week was the outcome of the bitter conflict which has raged incessantly between large and small owners as classes for six years." Before the passage of the 1884 maverick law, the paper went on, "the little fellows had been allowed to work on the roundup with the large outfits," but that afterwards, "by a new arrangement, they were compelled to collect their cattle as they could." The "new arrangement" to which the *Bee* referred was the increasing application of a roundup boycott.[4]

It was easy for the owners to justify this measure by calling every man on their list a rustler, but was he? Maurice Frink says in *Cow Country Cavalcade*, an authorized history of the Wyoming Stock Growers' Association: "The big ranchers blacklisted *those who thus came into competition with them;* that is, they barred the upstarts from Association roundups. The men thus ostracized then got together with their sympathizers and other small operators and rounded up what they called their own cattle" *—unlawfully, of course. They had no other way.

In 1887, according to Flagg, "the barons all signed a paper, taken around by Horace Plunkett, agreeing to boycott all boys who had gone to ranching." [5] Plunkett himself makes no mention of any such incident, but certain it is that the tension between large and small operators was rising steadily and so was the number of blackballed men. Often the roundup was spitefully scattered when the big outfits were through. In the unlikely event that the independent meekly waited to "gather his cattle as he could," he would find precious few of them after the roundup had passed.

In a letter to Elmer Brock some years ago, a ninety-year-old former resident of Johnson County wrote: "Most of the regular cowpunchers were friendly with neighbors. There was one Foster working for the EK outfit. He was repping. He was cutting out EK stuff, he saw a Hat cow and calf. He cut them out with his stuff. Someone went and told the roundup foreman. He sent for Foster and said to him, cut out your string of saddle horses, go back to your outfit. You can't work on this roundup any more."

The vicious circle went round and round. First men were shut out of work for wages, either because the work no longer existed or because they were accused of some real or suspected offense. Next these men took up homesteads and started raising cattle on their own in order to live. Thirdly, they were barred from the roundups. Of course they were "compelled to collect their cattle as they could," unless they proposed to starve. Conceivably some of them by this time were no longer particular whether the cattle were theirs or not. It was a system guaranteed to make outlaws even out of angels, and there were very few angels on Powder River.

If you call a man a thief, treat him like a thief, and deprive him of all chance to earn a living honestly, the chances are he will oblige you by becoming a thief.

* P. 135.

The Hat Outfit

THE HAT brand bought by Jack Flagg soon became a storm center in Johnson County. In 1888 Flagg took four partners, selling each of them a one-fifth interest in the outfit. They were all good cowmen and good fighting men; they were all blackballed and sworn enemies of the big outfits, and they proceeded to give the latter all the trouble in their power. Some of them came from decent backgrounds in Texas, substantial in a modest way, with enough money behind them to invest in a few cattle apiece. Their reputations varied locally from good to bad.

Al Allison, whose real name was Martin Allison Tisdale, was the black-sheep son of a respectable family who had avoided education and other restraints and had left Texas under a change of name for the usual reason. The other partners were Billy Hill, L. A. Webb, and Thomas Gardner. Hill eventually moved to Canada, with a faint unpleasant odor of a liking for bad company clinging to him; but Tom Gardner and Lou Webb settled down into becoming prosperous ranchers and pillars of the community, respected even by their former enemies, in Johnson County's peaceful aftermath.

Such was the Hat outfit, most celebrated or most notorious of all of Johnson County's rustlers, not even excepting Nate Champion, who was aligned with them. They were the rustler elite. Theirs was no fly-by-night "maverick" brand but one duly registered with the county, and their advertisement—showing the likeness of an enormous cowboy hat etched across the ribs of a woodcut steer—was flaunted insolently week after week in the columns of the Buffalo *Bulletin* alongside those of respectable outfits. To explain the paradox of such a group J. Elmer Brock, who made a lifetime hobby of research into Johnson County lore, wrote: "Men ordinarily honest stole cattle from the big outfits and did not consider it dishonest but an act justifiable in a war of classes." [1] They used the weapons available, the rope and the running iron. But one member of the partnership, Jack Flagg, had a weapon more sophisticated and dangerous than all the ropes and irons in the world. He could express himself.

Jack Flagg was a tall, fine-looking man with a hearty laugh, addicted to black hats. He had taught school from time to time and was "of good address," his enemies admitted; overaddicted to drinking and gambling, his friends admitted. By nature he was contentious, quarreling even with neighbors; by instinct he was a politician and a rabblerouser. Immediately after the invasion he bought a newspaper, the Buffalo *Echo,* the previous editor of which, a stockman sympathizer, had fled to a friendlier clime. Flagg remained an editor for several years, drifted around, and eventually returned to ranching in another part of the state. The stockmen gave him credit for being the brains of the "outlaws." He and Fred Hesse were enemies to the knife.

Flagg put on paper the thoughts which hundreds of men did not know how to express. He was speaking for many besides himself when he penned this bitter accusation in the *Bulletin* of June 9, 1892:

I had cattle on the range that I had as clear a title to as a person could possibly have; yet I was not allowed to buy a maverick that was put up and sold ostensibly to the highest bidder, nor was I allowed to claim and brand any for myself, even though they should be ranging within a stone's throw of my fence.

These dictatorial autocrats, some of them not owning a foot of land, could say: "We have defined our boundary lines, every maverick within those lines is ours, if you have cattle keep them in your private field, the public domain is ours; if your animal gets out of your field unbranded, we will neither allow you to take it, nor will we allow you to buy it when, according to our law, it is put up for sale."

The cattle barons of Wyoming were unable to enforce a monopoly on the free public domain, though for eight years, beginning with the first maverick law in 1884, they did their level best. Their industrial counterparts in the East were oily and rich. They built monopolies and engaged in labor-busting, and the packinghouse combine and the railroad combine put the squeeze on their country cousins, the western meat shippers, in a most unfeeling way. But unlike immigrant labor in the East, the homesteader was a free man and could not be busted. This resulted in a case of maddening frustration on the part of the cattle barons clustering around Cheyenne, so that they arrived at a state of emotionalism bordering on hysteria, in which hardly one of them could tell a fact from a hole in his head. Therefore they ended by believing their own propaganda, which is always fatal.

Cattle-stealing flourished in Johnson County during the era of bad feeling which came in after 1887, and for several years convictions were impossible to obtain, but the facts have been obscured and the cattlemen's case damaged by a farrago of nonsense compounded of gullibility and lies. Statements regarding the number of acquittals in cattle-stealing cases were put out by the cattlemen's propaganda machine, in the effort to justify the invasion, with the most reckless defiance of truth.

"Of two hundred cases brought for stealing cattle and horses [in Johnson County] only five convictions were secured." . . . "About three hundred indictments recorded against cattle thieves [in Johnson County]. . . . Several hundred indictments have been found against [cattle thieves in Johnson County] during the past few years, but juries have promptly acquitted them." . . . "The Johnson County attorney nolle prossed seventy-five cattle-theft cases at one time, alleging the county's lack of ability to stand the expense." . . . "In Johnson County alone, out of 180 indictments in four years, only one conviction had been secured." Another statement. pushed the number of indictments up to 435, with, of course, no convictions.[2] Such statements have been repeated over and over again by writers of pseudo-history down to the present without any attempt at verification, although the facts were easily available in the court records of Johnson County. The fact is that during the whole ten years from the time the court of the Second Judicial District held its first session in Buffalo in 1882 until the year of the invasion the total number of criminal cases in every category including cattle-stealing, horse-stealing, assault, illegal cohabitation, fornication, murder, and ordinary burglary had barely passed the two hundred mark. So much for the tall tales.

During the early years of the court the livestock cases were more or less evenly divided between horse theft and cattle theft, possibly a few more of the former, with frequent convictions and sentences to the penitentiary at Joliet, Illinois, Wyoming then having no penitentiary of its own. Eighteen eighty-five serves well enough as a typical year, with four horse or mule cases, five cattle cases; two acquittals, two cases dismissed, and five convictions. Two presumably unsavory characters (since use of an alias may be considered presumptive evidence of bad intentions) drew stiff sentences of six and five and a half years at Joliet for horse-stealing. A man got two and a half years for stealing a cow from the livery-stable man. The only case involving theft from a large company was that of two luckless Indians who butchered a beef belonging to Horace Plunkett's Frontier outfit, presumably to eat, and got one year apiece.

In 1886 there were no cattle cases, five horse-theft cases; three convictions, one case with outcome not stated, and the fifth dismissed. Since the party whose case was dismissed was already doing six years in the pen the righteous had little cause for complaint. It is clear that up to now the large cattle-owners of Johnson County had nothing to cry in their beer about.

Eighteen eighty-seven saw the first maverick case in Johnson County.* A cowboy branded a maverick unlawfully, not for himself but for a company, presumably his employers. Case dismissed.

The next year was when things began to look rough for the cattlemen, as the blacklist and the boycott inflamed public sentiment against them. In 1888 there were five cattle indictments, four dismissed or not found, and only one conviction, for petty larceny. But the last carried a hundred-dollar fine—three times the value of the animal.

Eighteen eighty-nine was the first of four black years for Wyoming. It was so bad that the five file boxes of incoming correspondence for the Wyoming Stock Growers' Association have been stripped virtually empty for reasons best known to those who did the stripping, and from that time onward the carefully kept records of the Association for all practical purposes cease to exist. It was the year a talkative road-ranch keeper and a prostitute were hanged on the Sweetwater by five prominent and wealthy ranchmen, four of whom had originated in the civilized East. In Johnson County it was the year the rustlers swept the boards.

At the first term of court seven individuals were tried on six charges of stock-stealing and every one was acquitted. That was when the presiding justice, Judge Micah C. Saufley, made his oft-quoted remark on the courthouse steps to the effect that the four men (no indication which four) were as guilty as any men he had ever tried, and he did not know how the stock interests were to protect themselves. At the second term of court, after the roundup, insult was added to injury by the dismissal of the Hat maverick cases.

That impudent crew, the Hat oufit, who infuriated their opponents by acting in open disregard of roundup regulations and behaving at all times as though they had a perfect right, decided to answer the boycott against them by putting their own wagon on the roundup. They could

* In a letter of January 25, 1893, Fred G. S. Hesse stated that during 1883 a man named Eb Stewart with other men "did a very extensive business" of branding mavericks in the Powder River and Antelope countries; also stole a considerable number of cattle and sold them near the South Dakota line; that they were brought back for trial but failed of conviction. Mr. Hesse was mistaken on two counts. The name of Eb Stewart, a notorious character, appears nowhere in the court records of Johnson County. As for branding mavericks he could have branded all he pleased in 1883, since there was as yet no maverick law on the books to violate.

not eat at the larger outfits' wagons, nor could they get any help in gathering their cattle, so they brought their own.

"We each of us owned a string of horses," Flagg wrote, "and we had a team and wagon and so, as we only had to hire a cook, we concluded that the cheapest way would be to put a wagon on the roundup." [3]

It was a cool move. There was no way to keep the upstarts out except by shooting; and the owner class were to demonstrate in the next three years that they were not partial to shooting unless numbers were on their side or a man could be shot in the back. The roundup worked south up the South Fork until it reached the Carey range and met the Platte roundup, when a fist fight took place between Flagg and Mike Shonsey, then foreman for the CY, over Flagg's charge that Shonsey was "blotching" his calves—burning over the Hat brand and rebranding the animal for his own employer. No damage resulted except a bloody nose and a pair of torn pants, but Flagg of course being a writer had the last word, and he claimed the moral victory.[4] Shonsey was an Irishman from Ohio who hated the Texas contingent and was one of the few men working on the range who sided with the big owners. When he moved to Johnson County a year or two later a festering grudge moved with him.

After the roundup was over the five Hat partners and a cowboy who had already been charged in a cattle case were indicted in eight cases. One was for stealing "one head of neat cattle," but the rest were for branding mavericks. All six of the defendants were charged for each of the eight animals alleged to have been misbranded or stolen. Branding a maverick was never a felony (a penitentiary offense) under Wyoming law, but a misdemeanor carrying a hundred-dollar fine and six months in the county jail. The wrathful prosecution generally treated it as a felony just the same. Bail was set at $1800 for each defendant, a sum totaling in excess of $10,000. They raised it, however, and regained their liberty. In the fall the cases were dismissed on motion of the prosecuting attorney.

The repercussions were enormous. Coming on top of the acquittals in the spring, it led to wild charges about the breakdown of law in Johnson County. There had been a breakdown in the courts for the past two years; that was plain, but silly statements and crazy exaggerations did the cattlemen's cause no good in the long run. One such statement was the one to the effect that the county attorney had nolle prossed seventy-five cases at one stroke, an obvious reference to the Hat maverick charges. By an arithmetical *tour de force* it would be possible to multiply the six defendants by the eight animals they were severally accused of branding and arrive at a grand total of forty-eight cases. But that is not the way it appears in Criminal Appearance Docket No. 1,

District Court, Johnson County, Wyoming, where the Hat cases are listed as Numbers 168 and 172 through 178, inclusive. Not seventy-five cases; not forty-eight cases; not three hundred cases. Just eight.

This is as good a time as any to wind up the history of the most famous—and, curiously enough, semirespectable—rustler outfit in the history of the northern range. There was some falling out among the partners, and in 1890 the Hat partnership was dissolved, dividing something under five hundred head of cattle.[5] The brand was retained by Lou Webb and Billy Hill and continued to carry the flag for defiance and insubordination in common with other leading spirits among the rustlers, until peace was declared after the invasion, when the Hat wagon went peaceably to the roundup in company with the wagons of surviving big outfits.

If incendiary Jack Flagg and the rope-wielding Hat crew and Nate Champion were the focus of trouble on the rustler side, the focus on the other side was Fred Hesse and Frank Canton, who worked together. Canton had long since established himself on a ranch in a lovely well-watered spot south of Buffalo, snuggled in against the Big Horns, but when his second term as sheriff ran out in 1886 he was not interested in running again. He had received an offer from the Wyoming Stock Growers' Association to serve as its chief detective in northern Wyoming, with several assistants and what was then a very fancy salary—$2500 a year. He accepted. But by the time the disastrous autumn of 1887 arrived, when the grim tally of the hard winter was in, he was asked to take a salary cut, and in the spring of 1888 the Association regretfully let him go, still owing him money.

He now very much wanted his old job as sheriff back, but times had changed. The fearless, popular, and efficient sheriff of the early eighties (handsome too, as a famous photograph reveals) was now known as a tool of the unloved Association. Of course his appointment as top Association detective for the northern half of the Territory was supposed to be a secret, but there were few secrets in that naked land. As a Texan under any name, Canton was naturally a Democrat, but the rustler element in the county, who were Democrats too, had in 1888 found a candidate much more to their liking in the person of sandy-mustachioed bartender W. G. "Red" Angus—"a man who has lived in a saloon and house of prostitution all his life and his associates are thieves and cutthroats of the worst type," Canton fumed in a letter to Secretary Adams of the Wyoming Stock Growers' Association. Fuming did no good. With the backing of Jack Flagg, Angus was nominated and elected. Canton nursed his wrath.[6]

Next year a new ingredient was added in all innocence to the stew of trouble now simmering in Johnson County. A settler named John A. Tisdale took up a homestead at the head of the Red Fork, above Jack Flagg's. Tisdale was a Texan. He had bossed three herds up the trail and for a few years had been established in North Dakota where he worked for a while for Theodore Roosevelt (who presented a high chair when his first son, Martin A. Tisdale, was born), had served later in charge of the Northern Pacific stockyards at Mandan. When he moved to Wyoming in 1889 he was a solid family man forty years old, with a wife and two little children and a very fair supply of this world's goods as they were counted in a poor frontier community—two fine big work mares and a few cattle and a saddle horse and $1200. He was well educated, too, the product of a small Texas college. He does not sound like a rustler, but that is what he was called, especially after he was dead.

But he was the older brother of the dark-gray sheep Al Allison, and he is said to have advanced some money for Allison's entry into the Hat partnership. He could have had no idea what he was getting into when he moved onto Powder River, but he and the Hat boys and Nate Champion had all come from the same county and had known each other since boyhood, and with Texas clannishness they stuck together. Tisdale had known somebody else in Texas—Joe Horner, latterly known as Frank Canton. The rest is a tale repeated by the fireside through many an evening over many years and passed on by local note-takers; not history but a sidelight on history, worth repeating on its own account; the tale being that two persons whose demise was attributed to the then Horner were friends of John Tisdale's. The tale continues that when Tisdale and Canton first met on the street in Buffalo there was a flare-up and Canton saved his life by ducking into a store. Tisdale calmed down afterwards. Regardless of details, the truth seems to be that bad blood existed between the two men for some reason; and it remained, like an explosive mixture sitting on the back of the stove.[7]

EIGHTEEN

The Crime
on the Sweetwater

THIS IS a tale of the bad old days in the West, when wrong went unrighted and crime went unpunished and the good guy did not win, but went down in sickening defeat. As for the good girl, there is none. It is the story of the hanging of Ella Watson and James Averell on the Sweetwater in 1889.[1]

The hanging was probably the most revolting crime in the entire annals of the West. There is plenty of competition for the title, but the Sweetwater affair had every element of infamy, with nothing left out. To begin with there is something peculiarly offensive to a normal mind in the spectacle of a lynch mob of men strangling a woman, regardless of what she has done. And the question of this woman's guilt is clouded. Ella was a prostitute who accepted recompense for her favors in the form of stolen yearlings and may have gotten in deeper. That is the accusation against her.

Allegations connecting Averell, her one-time paramour with whom she was no longer living, with cattle-stealing are based on the flimsiest sort of hearsay. There is substantial testimony, however, to the effect that he had made himself a good deal of a nuisance to local big stockmen by stirring up trouble for them in land matters, so they determined to get rid of him.

And finally there is the matter of the missing witnesses. Three persons witnessed the abduction of the doomed pair from their ranches, and a fourth followed the men and witnessed the actual hanging. Yet by the time the grand jury met three months later the four witnesses had all disappeared—one dead under circumstances never explained, one fled from the territory, and the other two vanished from the known earth.

One streak of honor shines through the sickening affair, the courage of the cowboy Frank Buchanan, the brave fool who tried in vain to stop six murderers single-handed, who tried again in vain to bring them to justice, and who paid for his rashness probably with his life.

Out in the sagebrush near the Sweetwater River Ella kept what the West prettily called a hog ranch. That is, she catered to her customers in their own wild and woolly surroundings instead of amid the lights of town. Twenty-eight years old at the time of her death, she was a farmer's daughter from Lebanon, Kansas, who had gone west and gone wrong as many another young woman had done without getting hung for it. There exists a picture of her, a full-bosomed wench astride a horse with her full calico skirts flowing over the saddle and a sunbonnet on her head. Not bad-looking in a common way, and bright too, according to one who had made her acquaintance, she looked plenty good to woman-starved cowboys who would cover many a mile over dry sagebrush for such an inducement. She died at the end of a rope on July 20, 1889.[2]

Dead with her, hanging from the same limb, was Jim Averell, storekeeper, saloonkeeper, postmaster, and justice of the peace. Averell ran a road ranch on the Sweetwater at the point where the Rawlins–Lander stage line crossed the old Oregon trail. It was three miles east of Independence Rock, the storied landmark, the "register of the desert" which figured in hundreds of emigrant diaries, the great gray hump of stone which lay like a sleeping elephant beside the trail. It was a good location for business and Averell prospered. Neighbors said that he owned no cattle at the time of his death.

He had served a ten-year hitch as a private in the Army, part of it with the 9th Infantry at Fort McKinney; he was discharged in 1881.

In civilian life, according to Flagg, he became a surveyor. He turned up on the Sweetwater a few years after his Army discharge and filed on a homestead February 24, 1886. Shortly afterward he picked Ella Watson up out of a bawdyhouse in Rawlins and brought her out to the Sweetwater to boost business for his road ranch and brighten his personal life besides. The moral tone of the place was not very high, but neither was the moral tone of the West at the time.

Ella took up a homestead a mile or so west of Averell's on March 24, 1888, on a trickle of water called Horse Creek, and improved it, they say, very creditably.[3]

Both the Watson and Averell entries were in the middle of the huge tract of land claimed by Albert J. Bothwell, largest and most arrogant of the local big stockmen, as his range. The intrusive road-ranch keeper had a gift of gab and was a natural agitator, and his good education, wherever obtained, sharpened the edge of his tongue. He called Bothwell and the rest of them tyrants and usurpers and land sharks and other names, and opposed their grasp on the Sweetwater valley. Ella too was an open and noisy enemy of the big stockmen. She was also a strumpet with a vocabulary to match. According to one of her associates Bothwell came to see her a number of times and tried to buy her out. She told him he could keep his money.[4]

There is something shivery about the casual behavior of people who don't know they are going to die in a few hours. About two o'clock on the hot, sunny afternoon of July 20, a Saturday, Ella and John De Corey, a cowboy in her employ, drove down to the river to buy some moccasins and beadwork from a party of Indians camped there. The six men passed them, some in a buggy and some on horseback, probably checking their movements, then turned back, and when Ella and the cowboy returned to her homestead the men were there ahead of them.

"I was at Ella's trying to catch a pony when the men rode up," said fourteen-year-old Gene Crowder. "John Durbin took down the wire fence and drove the cattle out, while McLain and Conners kept Ella from going to the house. After a while they told her to get into the wagon and she asked them where they were going. They told her to Rawlins. She wanted to go to the house and change her clothes but they would not let her and made her get into the wagon. Bothwell told her he would rope her and drag her if she did not get in.

"She got in then and we all started toward Jim's. I tried to ride around the cattle and get ahead, but Bothwell took hold of my pony's bridle and made me stay with them." The party went on and found Jim Averell, who was starting for Casper with a team and wagon, at his second gate. They made him throw up his hands and told him they had a warrant for his arrest. When he asked where the warrant was Durbin and Bothwell drew their guns on him and told him that was warrant enough." Then he too was forced to get into the buckboard and they set off toward Independence Rock.

To the Crowder boy's account, John De Corey added: "I started to follow them, but Bothwell pointed his gun at me and called me a bad name and told me to go in the house and not show up that day." [5]

He and the boy spurred on to Averell's, and in the darkly odorous interior of the store and bar, cool after the July heat, they found several idlers to whom they imparted the news that Bothwell and Durbin and the other four men had taken Jim and Ella and were driving around the Rock with them. Their hearers were too terrified to make a move, all except the cowboy Frank Buchanan, who jumped on his horse, armed only with a six-shooter, and took the trail alone after a lynch mob of six men carrying Winchesters.

He cut around the west end of Independence Rock, keeping the party in sight as they went toward the river; saw them drive into the ford and follow up the bed of the stream for about two miles. Once they stopped a long time in the water and argued loudly, but he could not hear what they said.

Afterwards one of the accused lynchers talked. He told people that when they started out to get the pair they intended only to scare them; that they took them first to the river and told them they would be drowned if they did not promise to leave the country; that the man and the woman only laughed and replied with oaths and insults that there was not enough water in the river to give a dirty land-hog a decent bath; that they were then taken up Spring Creek canyon to a point about five miles above Averell's ranch, and there with nooses around their necks were given one more chance to leave the country before being swung out to their death.[6] But this alleged last-minute offer of mercy does not agree with the eye-and-ear witness of Frank Buchanan.

At deadliest risk to his life, Buchanan followed the six armed and ugly men as they pulled up the gulch of rocks and sagebrush and scrub timber, rode around to the south, keeping out of sight; then dismounted and tied his horse and crawled under cover of rocks and brush until he was so close he could hear what they were saying. They were disputing and shouting.

"Bothwell had the rope around Jim's neck," Buchanan said later, "and had it tied to a limb. He told him to be game and jump off. McLain was trying to put the rope around Ella's neck, but she was dodging her head so that he did not succeed at that time.

"I opened fire on them but do not know whether I hit anyone or not. They turned and began shooting at me. I unloaded my revolver twice but had to run as they were shooting at me with Winchesters. I ran to my horse and rode to the ranch and told them Jim and Ella were hung."

The sagebrush telegraph had carried the news of the kidnaping, and as the afternoon wore on men rode up to Averell's and tied their horses to the hitching rack and gathered inside to cut the dust out of their throats and wonder and wait. The sage was throwing its purple shadows, a sunset was building, and the Ferris mountains looked like the ramparts of heaven, which they were not, when Buchanan returned. Bothwell had ordered De Corey and the Crowder boy to get into the house and stay there; there was no need to repeat the warning to this ashy-faced crowd; they were all scared spitless. Nobody offered to ride into Casper with Buchanan to get the sheriff. So it was Buchanan again, alone again, who set out on his grim Paul Revere's ride to carry word of the hanging.

He rode through Bothwell's big pasture, and cowboy though he was, got lost in the dark, stumbled around for hours before finding the trail, and finally reined in his exhausted horse at Tex Healy's homestead shack at three in the morning.

Healy's place was a twenty-five-mile ride east of Averell's if you didn't get lost, and an equal distance west of the log-shack village of Casper, on the North Platte. Buchanan got Healy out of bed and told his tale of horror while the pale, clean summer dawn lightened the prairie. Then he returned to the Sweetwater while Healy pounded into Casper with the news.

Healy arrived at eleven o'clock Sunday morning, the twenty-first, but not until Monday did the posse get under way. Warrants had to be sworn out and deputies sworn in; a fitting amount of whiskey had to be consumed; since the principals were dead there was no reason to hurry, and the West never hurried in any event.

Fifty miles is a long day's ride, so it was after dark on the evening of Monday, the twenty-second, when the posse reached Averell's ranch. Frank Buchanan guided them five miles farther to Spring Creek gulch. There in the darkness of early Tuesday morning their lanterns found the dangling bodies which had been there in the July heat for two and a half days.

"Hanging from the limb of a stunted pine growing on the summit of a cliff fronting the Sweetwater River, were the bodies of James Averell and Ella Watson. Side by side they swung, their arms touching each other, their tongues protruding and their faces swollen and discolored almost beyond recognition. Common cowboy lariats had been used, and both had died by strangulation, neither having fallen over two feet. Judging from signs too plain to be mistaken a desperate struggle had taken place on the cliff, and both man and woman had fought for their lives until the last," wrote the first reporter to talk to members of the posse.[7]

The bodies were cut down and carried to the Averell ranch. On the morning of the twenty-third, an inquest was held by an impromptu seven-man coroner's jury, impaneled by an acting coroner who was normally a justice of the peace in Casper.[*] The jury took the testimony

---

[*] While it is not revelant to the guilt of the accused, it is relevant to the issues of these troubled times that two members of the coroner's jury belonged to a notorious interstate horsethief gang which operated out of Casper into Montana and was broken

of Gene Crowder, John De Corey, Frank Buchanan, and Ralph Cole, returned a verdict that "the deceased came to their deaths by hanging" by six individuals who were named, with the addition of an alleged "unknown man," who has remained a shadowy figure. The six men were later arrested and admitted to bail in Rawlins on July 25. They were Albert J. Bothwell, R. B. Connor, John Durbin, R. M. Galbraith, Ernest McLain, and Tom Sun.[8]

The remains of Jim Averell and Ella Watson were given a hasty burial in one box. Water seeped into the shallow grave. All signs of it soon disappeared and the coyotes scattered the bones. Casper was not to acquire a church until a year later, and there were no good people in the town who cared enough to go out to the dismal spot, to set up a marker and say a prayer, but curiosity-seekers took photographs of the tree at the edge of the gulch. The moccasins Ella was wearing—the moccasins she had bought from the Indians that carefree sunny day down on the river—fell from her feet during her death struggles. They lay on the ground for a few days, and were then picked up by the wife of a nearby ranchman, who took them home for a souvenir.

In the meantime George B. Henderson had turned up in Cheyenne. Henderson was manager of John Clay's 71 Quarter Circle ranch which had its headquarters on the Sweetwater near the historic Three Crossings. He was a Pennsylvanian, a former Pinkerton man, and a former member of Pennsylvania's coal and iron police. Although the story of the "unknown man" at the hanging was as full of holes as a fishnet it refused to die, and the finger of suspicion pointed insistently at Henderson. That he was mixed up in the lynching somehow is true, Clay having stated—with unusual candor even for thirty years later—that Henderson "was not a party directly to this business but he was indirectly connected with it" (p. 272).

On Monday, July 22, Henderson "happened to be in the capital," in the words of a *Leader* reporter, where eager interviewers were told that news of the double hanging had been telegraphed to him from Rawlins. It is likely that Henderson, abetted by news toadies, played an important role in laying down the swift and effective smoke screen from Cheyenne which blotted out the real issue in the murders so completely that only a few students of history have raised it from that day to this. By the time the bodies were found and cut down in the dark early-morning hours of the twenty-third the wires out of Cheyenne were

---

up by the good work of law officers only two months later. The two men were E. J. Healy and Jess Lockwood. There is nothing on the record to show that the stockmen who eliminated a drab and a storekeeper did much to get rid of this gang. Reported by Mokler, p. 310.

sizzling with sensation and dripping with gore, and before the leisurely posse jogging on its way up the Sweetwater had had time to make any arrests, good people in all parts of the nation were shuddering with delicious horror over their coffee cups while they read about the crimes of the deceased.

The man and woman had imposed a reign of terror on the Sweetwater valley for years, and especially on its "honest, law-abiding people," the Cheyenne *Sun* singling out Messrs. Bothwell, Durbin and Sun for special mention in that category. "Honest men" went in constant fear of their lives. "Averill [(*sic*) was] a murderous coward [who] constantly threatened death to those who interfered with him." He had "killed his man"; "two men"; "several men, one of whom he shot in the back. [No names mentioned.] The woman was as desperate as the man, a daredevil in the saddle, handy with a six-shooter and an adept with the lariat and branding iron . . . a holy terror [who] rode straddle, always had a vicious broncho for a mount and seemed never tired of dashing across the range"; though in another version she was "slouchy and filthy in appearance . . . an arrant coward . . . could not ride horseback." . . . "A neighbor" had seen "Mrs. Averill" round up two of his steers on the range and deliberately shoot both of them. . . . "Desperadoes!" howled Cheyenne. "A case of life and death between honest men and cutthroat thieves!"

And all this blossomed in the press, not only of Cheyenne and Laramie but of New York, Chicago, Omaha, Denver, and a great many other places—three papers in Denver alone gobbling up this filth—on the twenty-third when the bodies were scarcely buried, the inquest had only just been held and, let us repeat, there had not yet been any arrests. It was fast work. Too fast to have merely happened.

In fact, so swiftly was the propaganda barrage laid down, within hours after Henderson reached Cheyenne, that the marks of advance planning are unmistakable, and in more ways than one. It is hardly likely that Henderson did the whole thing alone. His role was probably to supply local color and circumstantial detail, but distribution would have been handled better by an office in the capital, and it is not hard to guess which office. Everything in the stories, aside from their Cheyenne origin, stamps them as coming from a common source (a handout prepared by a party or parties who were interested in stifling any questions concerning the Sweetwater murders): the similarity of tone, which was one of ranting diatribe, the repetition of details and even of identical phrases which were used over and over, and the misspelling of the name "Averill," a dead giveaway. All of this hints strongly of premeditation, involving how many individuals no one now can say. It demolishes the convenient theory that a group of righteously outraged cattlemen, who had intended only to frighten the pair with threats, had somehow allowed the business to get out of hand and had hanged them by mistake, so to speak.

While the outlines of the "reign of terror" yarn were uniformly the same, this imposed no check on the reportorial fancy, and the palm for offensive fiction writing goes to Ed Towse of the Cheyenne *Leader*, later of the Cheyenne *Sun*, who was to cut an ignominious figure in the invasion three years later.

"Word was passed along the river," he wrote, "and early in the night from ten to twenty men, made desperate by steady loss, gathered at a designated rendezvous and galloped to the Averill ranch. They approached the place cautiously, for Averill had murdered two men and would not hesitate to shoot, while the woman was always full of fight.

"Within the little habitation sat the thieving pair before a rude fireplace. The room was clouded with cigarette smoke. A whiskey bottle with two glasses was on the deal table, and firearms were scattered around to be within easy reach"—et cetera. A little of Ed Towse goes a long way, and that is enough except to add that "Averill . . . showed himself a cur. He begged and whined and protested innocence, even saying that the woman did all the stealing. The female was made of sterner stuff. She exhausted a blasphemous vocabulary upon the visitors, who essayed to stop the vile flow by gagging her but found the task too great. When preparations for the short trip to the scaffold were made she called for her own horse and vaulted from its back to the ground." *

But while in the *Leader* and elsewhere she "died with curses on her foul lips," in the Chicago *Interocean* and the Omaha *Bee* she remembered her mother and asked that her ill-gotten gains be used to found a home for wayward girls. In New York the *Police Gazette* put in its two cents' worth with BLASPHEMING BORDER BEAUTY BARBAROUSLY BOOSTED BRANCHWARD. Death itself offered no surcease for the poor wretch as the "very best people" held a witches' sabbath over her remains and the press tore her to pieces in such an orgy of indecency and fakery as can seldom have been equaled even in the nineteenth century.

By the second day of the orgy plain Ella Watson with her sunbonnet and calico had been metamorphosed into "Cattle Kate Maxwell," a

---

* Towse's authorship of this work is established by the *Carbon County Journal*, which sneered on August 10: "Ed Towse's fame as a dime novel writer has crossed the Atlantic. We find nearly half a column of his Sweetwater romance published in the *Dublin Times* of July 24." The story was doubtless cabled to Dublin as a particularly juicy example of life in the wild, wild U.S.A., a subject popular with Europeans.

former Chicago dance-hall queen who wore silks and diamonds, rode like a demon, imported race horses to the prairie, shot a drunken Mexican dead for insulting her, and so on and on unto columns of trash. It started harmlessly as a case of mistaken identity when a reporter in Douglas picked up a local rumor and named Ella Watson, the prostitute involved with Averell, as being identical with "the person who recently figured in the dispatches as 'Cattle Kate,' who held up a faro dealer at Bessemer and robbed him of his bank roll." This hint was enough, and a new yarn gushed out from Cheyenne in time for the papers on the twenty-fourth. Ed Towse is suspected, but there is no proof. "Kate" had poisoned her husband, shot a colored boy who made off with her diamonds, winged a retainer who presumed to call her "Katie"; she had stolen more cattle than any one man in the West; and—an ingenious touch of plausibility—had staged a big spree at her ranch on the proceeds of the Bessemer holdup! The purpose of this dreary twaddle was obvious. It was to distract attention from the only question that mattered—whether the woman who was hung had ever done anything to justify hanging, and whether the six men arrested were guilty of murder. It worked. Clearly this blaspheming, gun-toting jezebel had gotten just what she deserved. What nice people could think otherwise? [9]

The Laramie *Boomerang*, always cynical about the Cheyenne ring and all its works and ways, yawned mightily over the Cattle Kate yarn. "Farewell, Cattle Queen Kate!" it perorated at the close of some editorial remarks, "Thou didst never exist, but vale anyway."

After the burial of Jim Averell and Ella Watson and the meeting of the coroner's jury on the twenty-third, the posse pushed on westward up the Sweetwater. Frank Buchanan was a member of it. Buchanan, the brave fool, the faithful fool, slogging along in the lead, still simple enough to hope for justice and rash enough to stick his neck out trying to get it. The posse passed the deep cleft in the rocks called Devil's Gate and turned into Tom Sun's ranch beside the sliding river.

Sun was an old-timer, the only real frontiersman in the crew. He coolly accepted arrest, admitted his part in the hanging, and named the others. The posse went on to Bothwell's. The latter informed members of the posse that they would "go over the range" the same way if they did not get out of the country, and on being told that he was under arrest he advised them to take a good look at every tree they passed on their way back to Casper, as they would be likely to find six or eight more rustlers hanging by the neck.[10]

Warrants were served on Albert J. Bothwell, Tom Sun, Ernest McLean, Robert B. Connor, Robert M. Galbraith, and John Durbin, and they were taken to Rawlins for arraignment. Described as "a farce" in the provincial press, the hearing was held not in court but in a hotel room. Although first-degree murder under the law was an unbailable offense, the six accused stockmen were admitted to bail in the trifling sum of $5000 each. They were even permitted to sign one another's bonds. There was a flurry of indignation in the press over the irregularity of the proceedings, and some wishful predictions made of a new arraignment to be held "soon," but nothing came of it.[11]

Legality became suddenly important, however, in the matter of the impromptu coroner's jury which had named six prominent citizens as hangmen; after a clamor in Cheyenne a second inquest was held under the regular coroner; no witnesses were called, and a verdict was returned that James Averell and Ella Watson had met their deaths at the hands of parties unknown. "This," exulted the Cheyenne *Weekly Sun*, on August 1, "is more like it!"

As the carnival of ghouls subsided, a note of sanity and puzzlement crept into the territorial press outside Cheyenne. Even the Denver papers had some sobering second thoughts. What, after all, had the man and woman done to deserve hanging? Were they really thieves?

"The woman was never accused of using a rope and branding iron by anyone near her." "Her reputation has not been that of a cattle rustler but of a common prostitute." Mused the *Carbon County Journal* on August 3: "It is reported that [Averell] lived with this woman Watson at one time and was not married to her, but if this is sufficient cause for mob law what a glorious field Wyoming presents for hanging parties."

And on July 30, the Laramie *Boomerang*: "If disputes over land matters had anything to do with their taking off . . . then the *Casper Mail* is justified in referring to the strangling of the couple as 'cold-blooded murder.'"

The newspaper stories planted by Cheyenne to whitewash the hanging were made up of epithets and abuse. They have been the sole basis of accusations against the deceased man and woman for seventy-five years. And the newspaper allegations are all hot air with no specific charges, with one exception. "A cowboy" who had paid a stealthy visit to "their place" reported that "their corral held no less than fifty head of freshly branded steers, mostly yearlings"; or forty head, or forty-seven head "which had been taken in the thieving rampages by these freebooters of the range"; or a hundred head or twenty-five; in the "Averill and Maxwell herds"; or "in the Cattle Kate pasture where her brand could be put upon them." *

---

* According to a recent investigator, Professor T. A. Larson of the University of Wyoming, Ella Watson never had a brand recorded with the Carbon County

But the Cheyenne *Tribune* went further and stated that the cause of the raid was the determination of stockmen to take back forty head of mavericks which "the woman" had gathered and held in her pasture, the mavericks having been purchased at a regular sale of the territorial livestock commission by John Durbin, who repossessed them—an allegation which stands out with a sharp little click of plausibility. For there were cattle in Ella's pasture that day, John Durbin did drive them out—and they may well have had no business being there. But while this bit of evidence—at least it sounds like evidence—implicates Ella, it does not implicate Averell.

The case against Averell as the dangerous night-riding leader of a gang of rustlers is based on nothing but the imaginings of pulp fiction. No alleged fact was ever offered to support the charge. At this point a psychological footnote is in order. Averell was much too gabby to be the mastermind of a gang of crooks. As every reader of Wild-West fiction knows, the bad man is a cur, but he keeps his mouth shut. Averell was an agitator, and he talked constantly. The two types seldom inhabit the same skin.

According to Cheyenne, "When the roundup reached Averill's ranch Averill refused to allow cowboys to inspect his pasture, threatening to kill anyone who tried to enter. The roundup was forced to leave his pasture uninspected"—a statement so idiotic as to write itself off in the mind of anyone familiar with roundup procedures. In the *Leader's* version it had been "rumored" lately that "the woman and Averill were engaged in a regular roundup of mavericks and would gather several hundred for shipment this fall"—irrelevant bosh. What had they actually done before they were hung? The absence of any direct criminal charge against Averell is a conspicuous feature of the case.

If there is virtually no evidence to show that Averell was a thief, there is a formidable body of testimony to show that he quarreled with the biggest stockmen in the Sweetwater valley, those accused in his lynching. Jack Flagg, who was well acquainted on the Sweetwater, wrote three years later: "The reason for murdering him was the direct result of trouble he had with Bothwell over some fine meadow land that Bothwell was holding illegally. Averell, a surveyor, had detected the fraud and had contested Bothwell's right to the land and the contest had been decided in his favor only a short while before he was hung."

According to Frank Buchanan, as quoted in that interview in the

---

brand committee, though she applied. Averell applied five years running, 1885 through 1889, and was turned down each time by the committee. The question is *Why?* Averell's supporters stated that he owned no cattle except a milk cow or two at the time of his death.

Casper *Mail* in which he talked too much for his own good: "Averell had contested the land Conners [*sic*] was trying to hold. He had made Durbin some trouble on a final proof and kept Bothwell from fencing the whole Sweetwater valley."

Some admissions by supporters of the hangmen helped confirm the case against them: that their real motive was not so much suppression of stealing, as they contended, but the determination to get rid of interlopers on the range. Charles A. Guernsey wrote in *Wyoming Cowboy Days,* "Bill Averill and Cattle Kate [*sic*] were lynched for being too free with a lariat and branding iron and occupying land claimed either rightfully or wrongfully by more powerful interests." [12] Guernsey was an important stockman and a longtime member of the Cheyenne Club and the Wyoming Stock Growers' Association, and he approved the lynching.

The editor of the Casper *Weekly Mail* wrote: "James Averell was not a cattle thief, and if this business is sifted to the bottom it will be found that his death was caused because he opposed the gobbling up of the public domain by individuals or corporations. ... He held that a bona fide settler had a right to enter an enclosure fraudulently held or covered up by a large land owner. He favored the settling up of the rich valley of the Sweetwater with small ranches and the making of homes for hundreds of families, instead of having it owned or controlled by one or two. Averell stealing cattle—all bush and buncombe. The writer was personally acquainted with him and knew that he expected serious trouble over land affairs in the valley." [13]

There is also the letter Averell wrote to the Casper *Mail* which appeared on April 7, a little over three months before his death. It was a well-written letter; too well-written. In it he talked of "land-grabbers, who are only camped here as speculators under the desert land act. They are opposed to anything that would settle and improve the country or make it anything but a cow pasture for eastern speculators. ... Is it not enough to excite one's prejudice to see the Sweetwater River owned, or claimed, for a distance of seventy-five miles from its mouth, by three or four men?"

The heavy hand of money and power crushed the law and crushed investigation. It also crushed the witnesses, in the most brutal and shocking aspect of the whole affair.

The local small fry, ignorant and leaderless, made a pathetic attempt at prosecuting the case. A fund was raised by subscription. Ella Watson's father, poor man, came from his farm in Kansas, determined to stay until after the trial which never took place. A brother of Jim Averell's who lived in Tacoma, Washington, appeared on the scene to pursue investigations, and it was announced that he had obtained five witnesses. He did not have them long.

The disappearance of Frank Buchanan was first reported, prematurely it turned out, on July 27; but as late as September 13 he turned up, working quietly as a mule-puncher in the employ of the Niobrara Transportation Company. That was the last ever seen of him.

The grand jury met in Rawlins on October 14, and the state asked for the indictment of Albert J. Bothwell, R. B. Connor, John Durbin, R. M. Galbraith, Ernest McLain, and Tom Sun on a charge of murder. The accused were represented by the firm of Corlett, Lacey and Riner, for many years the leading attorneys for the Wyoming Stock Growers' Association. But by that time the witnesses had all disappeared, so the six men went free.

Frank Buchanan, forfeiting a $500 bond for his appearance, had vanished from the known earth. In the complacent words of the proper Dr. Penrose of Philadelphia, an intimate of the leading stockmen, "he had to be put out of the way that he might not testify." [14] Ralph Cole, one of the three who had seen the couple forced into the buggy, had also disappeared. John De Corey had been in Steamboat Springs, Colorado, on August 30, but no one knows what became of him after that. The boy Gene Crowder, later described as "a sickly boy" or "an invalid," though there had been nothing noticeably sickly about his actions on the day of the hanging, was dead. According to Mokler he died of "Bright's disease"; according to Mercer "he was taken in charge by the cattlemen. He lingered some weeks and died—rumor strongly insisting, at the hands of his protectors by the administration of a slow poison." As for Ralph Cole, Mokler says that when he left Averell's ranch after the hanging he was followed by George Henderson. "Cole reached a surveyor's camp late at night and remained until morning. The next day, while trying to make his way to a station on the Union Pacific railroad, he was overtaken by Henderson, who shot him and the body of the victim was burned to ashes. Whether or not this is true can not be verified, but the fact remained that Cole has not been seen since, although every effort was made by friends to find him." [15]

No attempt was ever made to investigate these three disappearances or the boy's death, nor were any questions ever asked of the men most likely to be involved. Upheld by most of the money and all of the influence in the Territory and openly applauded for what they had done, they were completely immune to consequences and their arrogance knew no bounds. They were even rewarded. Bothwell and Tom Sun had been named to the executive committee of the Wyoming Stock Growers' Association in the spring of 1889; Sun served until 1910 and

Bothwell until 1902. John Durbin was appointed to the committee the following spring. Murder in all its forms, whether by hanging, dry-gulching, or massive armed assault, was the method of range control favored by the most powerful livestock interests and "very best people" of Wyoming.

Owen Wister, not yet a famous author but just another proper young Philadelphian enjoying his summers in Wyoming, wrote in his diary for October 12, 1889: "Sat yesterday in smoking car with one of the gentlemen indicted [sic] for lynching the man and the woman. He seemed a good solid citizen, and I hope he'll get off. Sheriff Donell said, 'All the good folks say it was a good job; it's only the wayward classes that complain.'" Young Mr. Wister did not comment on the little matter of the vanished witnesses.

After the pair were dead Bothwell got what he wanted, possession of their land. He did this by the time-honored method of having their land entries contested by a third party, one Henry H. Wilson, who then made entry himself and after proving up, allegedly "sold" both tracts to Bothwell. So the latter was once again lord of the Sweetwater valley.

After gaining possession of the property he moved Ella's little shack from its original location to the bank of a small creek near his ranch buildings, where he could see it from the house. He used it as an ice-house; a delicate touch which was not lost on the bystanders.

In 1915 he retired to Los Angeles, where he spent his declining years in a state of prosperity. He died in Santa Barbara in 1928, in bed.

Like the ballad of Frankie and Johnny, this story has no moral. This story has no end.

4

1891: The Story of a Year

NINETEEN

"Caught on the Market"

In the fall of 1891 the state livestock commission thought of a new move in the war against rustlers. The powers of the commission were by now fully concentrated in the hands of the ruling clique in Cheyenne. Membership was reduced to three, and democratic claptrap about the desirability of any representation for the state outside the capital on this powerful body had been silenced.[1]

When the fall shipping season came on, the commission issued an order to inspectors at market points to seize all cattle shipped by certain men "known to be rustlers" and hold up the proceeds of sale. This was not a question of estrays; the cattle were clearly branded and their owners known. In cases where an innocent second party had bought cattle in good faith from one whom the livestock commission regarded as a rustler, the bill of sale was disregarded and the proceeds were held up anyway. Any shipper of seized cattle was privileged to come to Cheyenne and submit proofs of ownership (i.e. of innocence), to an *ex parte* board which had already decided against him.

"Such an action by the board," in the words of one historian, "so at variance with the fundamental principle of Anglo-Saxon justice, could not fail to inflame public sentiment and bring the honest ranchman and granger into line with the cattle rustlers."[2]

During the shipping season that fall about five carloads of cattle were seized from owners alleged to be rustlers and the proceeds, amounting to $4239.79, impounded. Although the charges of rustling covered parts of six counties, it was noticeable that only Johnson County residents' cattle were seized. The question was on what basis. According to information furnished by the commission itself later, the tip supplied on rustling activities came from a "northern protective association" which

137

could have been none other than the Northern Wyoming Protective Association, which was equivalent to Fred Hesse. It was a perfect triple play—Hesse to the commission to the market, and the rustler was out.[3]

On October 28 the Cheyenne *Leader* ran a story headlined CAUGHT ON THE MARKET, in which it waxed enthusiastic over what it called the new method of circumventing the rustler. "The outcome," the *Leader* concluded brightly, "will be watched with a good deal of interest."

The outcome was not slow to appear. In December a visitor from Johnson County reported more rustling done in one week since the seizure plan was put into effect than in any six months in years. The stolen cattle were being driven out to Idaho, Utah, and Montana. It was said that one herd of two hundred fifty head and another of three hundred had been rounded up and driven openly across half of Wyoming without even the bother of hanging the brands; an exploit worthy of Robin Hood and his men. Like Robin Hood, these outlaws had popular support.[4]

The repercussions continued after the first of the year. In February a group of Johnson County citizens, including men who had never before aligned themselves with the rustler faction, sent the livestock board a petition requesting that body in no very humble terms to return the impounded money withheld from "good and reputable citizens and taxpayers of said county" in connection with the seizure. Johnson County was closing ranks.[5]

And in Cheyenne the *Leader,* which had up to now been a vociferous supporter of the stockmen, did the kind of about-face which was not unknown in the frontier press; it came out on March 22 with a stentorian editorial headlined TIME TO CALL A HALT in which it denounced the policy and called on the commission to return the impounded funds. Never tolerant of opposition, the strongmen of the Wyoming Stock Growers' Association were furious, and Secretary Ijams was heard to declare publicly that "the only thing left for us now is to knock out that damned outfit." An advertising boycott of the *Leader* was declared.

Nothing could have played better into the hands of editor John Carroll, who retaliated by flaunting a patchwork of blank spaces on his pages to show where advertising had been withdrawn. Up to then the public had been displaying its customary indifference to the plight of Anglo-Saxon justice, but opinion now began to sizzle, and letters were received reading: "I believe in free speech. Double my space." The advertising boycott was abandoned, and the commission even weakened to the point of summoning the editors so it could explain its action. But it never relinquished its grip on the seized funds until the owners sued to recover.[6]

Joe DeBarthe's Buffalo

FOR THE little northern metropolis of Buffalo, 1891 opened on a high note of rejoicing and hope. It ended in terror and tragedy.

At the end of 1890 Buffalo was a coming town of a thousand people despite its distance from the railroad. It had two weekly newspapers, two banks, a sawmill, a flouring mill; and the saplings in front of the courthouse were beginning to look like trees now, they had reached the second story. At the center of town Clear Creek rippled and purled under the Main Street bridge beside the Occidental Hotel. Up hill to the south, just past the scarlet iniquities of Laurel Avenue, a modest little Episcopal church lifted its cross to the sky.

In the fall of 1890 the Buffalo *Bulletin* was taken over by a roving frontier editor, Joe DeBarthe, who bought an interest and became its editor. Born in Connecticut in 1854, DeBarthe had worked on the Springfield (Mass.) *Republican* before moving west. He had a little capital and bought a printing press; the names of two of the Wyoming papers with which he was connected between 1888 and his move to Buffalo reflect some of the jauntiness of that youthful era: *Wind River Mountaineer* and *Bonanza Rustler*. In Buffalo he was editor of the *Bulletin* for not much over a year and a half; but that year and a half was the longest in Wyoming's history.

The tragedy of the invasion was DeBarthe's personal tragedy. Ill, he left the *Bulletin* afterward. There were stories of his losing weight, of heavy drinking. But before long he pulled himself together and fulfilled an old ambition; he wrote the life and adventures of Frank Grouard, the famous scout who was then stationed at Fort McKinney. The book became a classic of the West and is now in print in a new edition.[1]

In his short period as editor in Buffalo, Joe DeBarthe left a living portrait of a frontier town.

The first number of the *Bulletin* under his editorship appeared on October 9, 1890, and plunged into big news soon after; the Ghost Dance excitement among the Sioux and Cheyennes, then the bloody affair at Wounded Knee, and finally the death of Sitting Bull at the Standing Rock agency on December 15. Joe DeBarthe was one of those who believed that the only good Indian was a dead one, and with all his might he beat the tom-toms about the continuing redskin menace, partly out of sincere conviction but also to convince the authorities that northern Wyoming still urgently needed the protection of Fort McKinney against the whipped and demoralized Sioux.

For a scare worse than Indians had now arisen. News coming out of Washington said that Buffalo was threatened with loss of its Army post, its economic lifeblood and reason for being during the whole twelve years since the town was founded. The three companies at McKinney had already been reduced to two, and somewhere upstairs in the War Department the order deactivating the post had been issued and only awaited a second order carrying it out.

But at the last gasp, heroic efforts by Wyoming's two senators in Washington succeeded in having the order reversed. VICTORY AT LAST, the *Bulletin*'s headlines exulted on January 22. The post was to be not merely retained but enlarged! Three companies of the 6th Cavalry and two of the 8th Infantry were coming to take over, including the latter's headquarters' company and its famous band.

The arrival of the 6th Cavalry on one of the first days of February inspired a piece of emotional reporting which almost brings tears to the eyes of a sentimental reader and evokes a scene straight out of Currier & Ives. Main Street was draped with flags; the Protection Hose Company had decorated its cart; the Hook and Ladder boys had done the same. At 11:30 A.M. bugle calls from both ends of town gave the signal that the three troops of the 6th had been sighted in the Red Hills east of Buffalo. Soon the merchants, the officials, the preachers, the saloon men, the housewives, the children, and the girls from Laurel Avenue with their silks and velvets and nodding plumes, well bundled up against the cold—every soul in town except bedridden invalids, if there were any—were filling the board sidewalks or driving out in buggies to meet the oncoming heroes. Kids and cowboys galloped around on their ponies. The sun sparkled on the snowcovered Big Horns. At last they trotted into view, sunburned and frostbitten after a hard trip, their weather-stained blues contrasting with the natty new uniforms of the militia escort. Cheer after cheer rent the air, and "the sun smiled down on the happiest thousand people in the state of Wyoming as, amid the lively strains of the Buffalo band, the gallant 6th Cavalry was escorted through the most progressive little city in the west."

After a soul-filling reception in front of the courthouse the troopers, "two miles from the loveliest spot for a garrison in the country, struck out at a sharp gallop for Fort McKinney." Six days later the whole performance was repeated in honor of the 8th Infantry. The *Bulletin* was ecstatic over the business prospects all this entailed for the city. Just think—five companies of soldiers with their $25.75 every two months, clear, plus the civilians who would add up to a total of five or six hundred persons at the post! But Joe DeBarthe made it clear that his enthusiasm rose above such crass considerations even while he entertained them.

"All are gentlemen," he exclaimed, "men of high attainments, enlisted as well as officers. We will make due allowance for a reasonable amount of hilarity, gaiety and funny business, but if not carried to an extreme you will find that an enlisted private is treated as well as we would use the secretary of war."

The troops were surprised and moved by the warmth of their reception. They were accustomed to being fleeced, tolerated, taken for granted, and Tommy Atkined generally, but Buffalo's wholehearted greeting was something new in their experience. It set the tone for an *entente cordiale* between post and town and led to their emphatic if unofficial sympathy with Johnson County, from the commanding officer on down, when the invasion took place fourteen months later.

It wasn't only the troops who liked Buffalo. In midsummer even the Cheyenne *Leader* went out of its way to pay Buffalo a compliment. In mid-August, the *Leader* ran an editorial praising Buffalo as a model place of residence because of its peaceful character, no one being allowed to carry firearms within the city limits. "The result of two years of the law has been to make Buffalo as peaceful as a New England village and absolutely safe. . . . No cowboy starts for Buffalo without leaving his revolver at home." The Bulletin replied with a modest disclaimer as to *nobody* carrying firearms, but admitted that anyway we're a pretty peaceable place.

You can read the old files of the *Bulletin*—still published in Buffalo, which will be brought out of the safe upon special request by editor Frank Hicks; you can read those precious old files and lose yourself in the day-to-day existence of a world of yesterday.

The weather makes news. Powder River is very high, and there is no crossing between Buffalo and Douglas except by cable ferry. A number of passengers were almost drowned when the ferryman lost his grip on the rope and the ferry was swept downstream, but luckily a number of mounted soldiers, who were escorting the McKinney paymaster back to the railroad, were close at hand and they rode into the river, saving all before the rapids were reached.

The camp at Bald Mountain, where a minor gold rush has been in progress, is snowed in, with snow as high as the eaves of the houses. Only five people remain in town. The *Bulletin's* correspondent at Fort McKinney complains about slow mail service at the post and is reminded that mud and snow are hub-deep between here and the railroad and the horses can barely flounder through. Our Ono correspondent reports that spring is springing, only to follow up a week later with the sad word that the report had been premature; the ground is now covered with five inches of "the beautiful," and it's still snowing.

Transportation makes news. A new stage line is going in between the Belle Fourche and Buffalo; it will make the 120 miles in twenty hours. The stage between Buffalo and Douglas, with good roads and careful drivers, "rolls in on time with almost as much ease and order as a limited." The Burlington railroad is being graded from Gillette to Powder River. The grading is a great boom for this part of Wyoming, since it opens a market for the farmers of Johnson, Sheridan, and Crook counties. It also opens a market for rustled beef, but we don't mention that.

Horses make news. A carousing cowboy bucks his steed down the length of Main Street and into Bob Foote's store; two troopers are fined for riding too fast through the streets; and the never-ending recurrence of horse accidents should disabuse the modern reader of any notion that the horse was a safe and sane mode of transportation. We read of two runaways in one week in March. Later a terrible spill is reported from Fort McKinney, when a soldier trying to overtake a team of runaway mules on horseback got tangled up with the vehicle and came down to disaster. Still later a private of the 8th falls from his wagon under the horses' hoofs, and is seriously hurt just a few days before his discharge; and the week after that another Army teamster is thrown out and badly hurt. Those horse-and-buggy days were certainly slow.

Churches and society and business and oddments make news. There are balls and parties at the post for the townspeople, with dancing to the music of the distinguished 8th Infantry band, under the skilled leadership of Professor Carlsen. The officers and their ladies drop in during the early part of the evening and then withdraw, but the ball continues "until the purple streaks of the rosy dawn were visible in the eastern horizon."

The prohibition argument is raging, and a Methodist divine in Laramie is quoted as saying that he has seen more drunken women in Wyoming than men. A sensitive saloonkeeper—proving that such a being can exist—denies that he is a fiend in human form whose only motive is to corrupt the public morals. Some cowboys in nearby Sheridan, after indulging in "that which is not prohibited," are arrested and locked up in the cooler together with several "commoners [*sic*]." The summary court at the post is busy with soldiers who have been visiting Buffalo and taking on too much O B Joyful.

Two wolves have been killed north of town. The McKinney ball club is starting spring practice, and the Buffalo club is advised that it had better look sharp, or it will be in the soup again as it was last season. There has been a verdict of not guilty in the Few Tails murder case. (Who is Few Tails?)

Jokes and tall stories brighten the columns. Drunk attempting to smite rattlesnake falls flat. Snake bites drunk. Drunk recovers; snake dies. Winter rolls around again and the street below the board sidewalk is a sea of mud and slush. Passerby sees a hat floating on the ocean of muck below the hitching rail and stoops over to retrieve same. A muffled voice says: "Never mind the hat. Get me and my horse out."

Lest anyone forget that this is still the rowdy West, an attack by the Nez Percés on a stagecoach is described. It is not clear whether the story is contemporary or picked up from some old exchange, but never mind. The cavalry riding to the rescue were mistaken for more Indians by the male passengers, who cut the traces, mounted the coach horses and fled, leaving a woman passenger behind. She took to the brush, discarding her clothing as she went; when found she had nothing on but her shoes. It turned out that she was a widely known character called Yellowstone Fan; her peculiar actions were accounted for by the fact that in view of her profession she probably just took her clothes off on general principles anyway.

But the biggest, most glowing, omnipresent news is the rosiness of the present and the even rosier future. Buffalo, the reader is told on April 2, is destined to rival Colorado Springs as a health resort; and on May 21: "We are in the center of a large and rich farming country, thickly settled." We are planting wheat, corn, potatoes, beans, buckwheat, sorghum, rhubarb, and fruit trees. "Wyoming's vast resources"—of which, needless to say, Johnson County has a lion's share—include coal, iron, oil, copper, silver, gold, asbestos, and many other minerals; also an abundance of fine farming land with a never-failing supply of water for irrigation. "Hustling grangers" are planting potatoes. Somebody is going to set out a $3000 orchard. John R. Smith of Crazy Woman expects to start plowing on his ranch Monday; he will put in a hundred acres to grain, eighty of which will be oats.

Yes, but (the reader asks in growing bewilderment) what about cattle? Although cattle-raising was by far and away Johnson County's leading industry, almost—in real terms—its only industry, although it added up to fourteen times the value of all the farm products in the county put together, it is mentioned in Joe DeBarthe's columns virtually not at all. Is it prospering or not? What is the condition of the range? Are the cattle fat or poor? What kind of prices are they bringing at the big eastern markets? We are not told. To judge from the *Bulletin's* persistent avoidance of the subject, its blind spot of a magnitude which could blot out fourteen-fifteenths of the local economic picture, one would judge that grazing was not a synonym for wealth but a species of dirty word.[2]

In addition to a portrait of a western town, Joe DeBarthe painted a portrait of a fallacy and a state of mind.

Both were so current among the frontier boosters of the period as to be well-nigh universal. The fallacy was that by dint of legislative fiat and loud talking you could make it rain, and could cause springs to spring out of the ground on every hundred and sixty acres ("Farm Homes for Poor Men") of tinder-dry sagebrush. Anybody who denied this was a tool of the corporate cormorants and the cattle barons, and a traitor to our fair state—or county or region—besides. There were places—though this was not true of Wyoming—where even the word *irrigation* was taboo; do you dare insinuate, sir, that our supply of natural rainfall is any less than that bestowed on the Garden of Eden?

The state of mind was that the cowman was a symptom of backwardness along with the Indian. He was a stumblingblock in the way of population and progress, and like the Indian he had to go.

If there was no other way to get rid of him you could pretend he wasn't there. Is there an extra-heavy fall of snow on the mountains? The reader is reminded that it spells "plenty of irrigation medicine" for the farmers, but nothing is said about grass medicine for the cattle. Does a stockman over Lander way arrive in Casper with a squadron of cowboys and a trainload of cattle to ship out? The scribe from the Casper *Derrick*, as like Joe DeBarthe as one pea in a pod is like another, is deaf and blind to the bawling of the cattle and the chuffing of the engine and the figures in the cowman's little book, which indicate that his shipment may bring, say, a good $16,000 at current prices—very roughly estimated—in Omaha; instead the reporter asks about the crops the farmers are harvesting on Wind River and the two new flouring mills in Lander, all this picked up in the *Bulletin's* exchanges.

In the meanwhile Johnson County's real industry, its livestock industry, was ill of a terrible malady which would soon erupt into murder and civil war beneath the people's feet.

The year dozed on into summer. In the *Bulletin's* pages Buffalo appeared one of those happy countries which have no history except for the timeless rhythms of birth and death. Joe DeBarthe went prospecting for gold in the Big Horns. There were picnics up the canyons in the lovely weather. There were sorrows too, as a young wife died of a hemorrhage while on a picnic in Tongue River canyon. Tuberculosis? The white killer was raging in those days even in this salubrious climate, but its name is not mentioned.

The stars that fell on Alabama conferred no greater blessing than the moisture which fell on Wyoming in that lush, lovely summer, but it had its drawbacks. One day in July Frank Canton and a pair of colleagues started over the mountains with a wagon and team for a visit to Lander. Finding that recent rains had made the road up Crazy Woman canyon impassable, they tried the ascent next day by way of the sawmill road, "which at best," observed Ye Ed, "is like crossing Niagara Falls with a locomotive on a slack wire." There had been a waterspout, there were washouts and finally a chasm. Three days running they set out from Buffalo; three evenings running they returned, "weary, worn and wet; moist, muddy and mad."

The mountains dreamed on the hot blue haze. The bars were cool, with a reek of beer. But under its somnolent exterior Buffalo was racked by feuds; Frank Canton against John A. Tisdale; Fred Hesse against Jack Flagg; Canton against Flagg; Canton against Sheriff Red Angus, who had beaten him to the office he wanted; Mike Shonsey against Flagg, against Champion; Champion and Flagg defying the big outfits, and the big outfits by now with plans getting set to get them. Enemies met and exchanged curt nods, their boot heels clumping on the board sidewalks; or they leaned elbow to elbow over the long mahogany at Zindel's, the handsomest bar in town, watching each other through slitted eyes; biding their time.

In midsummer, when Joe DeBarthe was still lost in his visions of prize rutabagas and the railroad coming, there was a rift in the outward calm. On July 25 the Cheyenne *Leader* suddenly and violently denounced "the audacious organized system of cattle stealing now not merely prevalent but rampant on nearly every cattle range in Wyoming.... Men who before this year have borne and deserved good characters are now openly engaged in preying upon the public ranges.... All their neighbors and acquaintances are perfectly aware of the fact and the practice is oftentimes not merely winked at, but applauded.... There are only two horns to the dilemma, either the thieves or the cattlemen must go." [3]

The *Bulletin's* reply two weeks later showed some cognizance of the situation but denied that "we" were any worse than our neighbors. At about the same time an item from Trabing landed like a petard on the *Bulletin*'s own doorstep. "A party of blackballed cowboys held up a portion of the roundup a few days ago and took out and branded thirty of the finest calves in the herd. Say, fellow citizens," drawled the Trabing scribe, "who are the people?" [4]

The whole county knew that the leader of "the party of blackballed cowboys" was Nate Champion. It knew that the man whose herd was held up was Bob Tisdale, of the big stock-owning Tisdales, and that he and Champion had had a quarrel. The county knew a number of things which were not yet appearing in the *Bulletin*. That paper was kept busy denying unfavorable stories: "The reported stealing of cattle right and left is a mistake. We do not know what excuse can be given for starting such reports." More to the point, as of mid-October, Johnson county had an agricultural fair, with first prize going to a Mr. Sonnerberger who had raised a record crop of grain two miles south of Buffalo.

On the first of November Nate Champion and another man were attacked in their beds at dawn by a party of armed men with intent to kill, but this symptomatic incident was barely mentioned in the *Bulletin*. The townspeople had better things to think about than a ruckus involving a pair of blackballed cowboys up at the head of the Middle Fork, and some of them even asked Joe DeBarthe what he was trying to do, make a hero out of Nate Champion? But the homesteaders scattered miles apart away up there in the red-wall country started locking their doors at night, a thing never before heard of.

Before these things happened Frank Canton's wife and her two little girls had narrowly escaped death in a runaway.

The Canton ranch was a dozen miles south of town, close in against the first low range of the mountains called the Horn, which made a battlement extending for many miles west of the valley. On this day Mrs. Canton had driven into town on some errands. She was driving a buggy with a team of gentle horses, as the West reckoned gentle horses, and the little girls, three and five, were beside her on the seat. On the way home, in the lane leading to the ranch, she got out to open a gate. [5]

Everyone who knows the West is familiar with the gates which present an obstacle course on all ranch roads. You get out or dismount, as the case may be; struggle with an obstinate contraption of poles and wires or let down some bars, lead your horse through or your team through, or, if you are in a car, get in and drive through. Then you go back and close the gate, to leave one open being an unspeakable crime, since livestock would escape. In the old days when you were driving a team and wagon this left you in an unfavorable position if anything should happen, because you were in the rear.

Having led her team through, Mrs. Canton went back to replace the bars. While she was lifting them into place the three-year-old clucked to the horses, and they started out at a walk. The mother spoke to them and they quickened to a trot. She ran and tried to get in, but they became frightened and were soon going at a gallop. With one foot on the step, the frantic woman clung to the buggy for half a mile, until finally her skirts became entangled in the wheel and she was dragged until the skirt tore off and she was left lying unconscious in the road.

The crazed horses galloped on. One child was bounced out, but with the miraculous resilience of children landed almost unharmed; the other one clung to the seat of the careening buggy and was still clinging to it when the team was finally stopped.

At a ranch house a mile away a children's party was in progress, and over the flat intervening meadow the runaway was seen. Neighbors Charles Basch and George Washbaugh jumped on their horses and tore across the field to the rescue, got mired, had to pull down part of a barbed-wire fence to make a gap, finally got through and brought the runaway team to a halt three quarters of a mile beyond the Canton house. Others in the meantime had run to the scene, found Mrs. Canton lying in the road, and carried her indoors. In the middle of the excitement Frank Canton arrived home. George Washbaugh had already left for town to call a doctor, but Canton told Charlie Basch to take Old Fred and go.

The horse called Fred—*old* being merely a term of endearment—was a leggy sorrel with a blazed face and two white stockings, and was the fastest thing on four legs in that part of the country. Basch and the flying Fred overtook George Washbaugh and made the twelve miles into town in thirty-five minutes, as he later had occasion to remember well. The doctor was found; Mrs. Canton recovered; Frank Canton was profuse in his thanks to all concerned, especially to Charlie Basch. He said he never would forget what Basch had done. In a curious fashion he kept his word.

Five months later Frank Canton, Charlie Basch, and the horse Fred were involved in a grimmer triangle of life and death.

The Weather Breeder

*We don't know why it is but for years there has been
a prejudice against the cattle growers that has done
as much to encourage the rustler as the booty he secured. Another remarkable feature is the unfriendly
disposition of the cowboys toward the cattle owners.*
—CHEYENNE *Daily Sun,* DECEMBER 4, 1891

ON THE RANGE the hot cloudless summer of 1891 was like a pot getting
ready to boil over.

It began with the Waggoner hanging. Thomas Waggoner was a settler
living near Newcastle, in the northeast corner of the state. On June 4 he
was taken from his home by three men in the presence of his wife and
children. Fifteen days later his body was found hanging to a tree only two
miles from his house, Mrs. Waggoner having evidently neglected to
pursue any inquiries when he did not return. Upwards of a thousand
horses were found in his pasture—a very considerable number of horses,
worth considerable money.

There are three theories to account for his taking off. The first is that
he was an innocent settler hanged by wicked cattlemen. This theory is
favored by those writers to whom all settlers are innocent and all
cattlemen wicked. The second and silliest theory is that he was an innocent settler slain by wicked rustlers because he knew too much. The third,
and the only one supported by most surviving evidence, is that he was a
receiver of stolen horses.

When the coroner and party arrived from Newcastle to investigate the
death they found a scene worthy of *Tobacco Road.* The two-room log
house contained not a chair nor a bed; only bunks, a bench, and boxes to
sit on. "Everything indicated that not a dollar had been spent that could
possibly be avoided," wrote the Newcastle *Journal.* "The dinner was so
rocky that none of the visitors could eat. Everything was squalor and
misery and filth. Mrs. Waggoner and the brother John spent most of the
time weeping and wailing. There were two children, one a bright boy of
three or four years old, the other a baby.

"During the last term of the district court an indictment was found against Waggoner for living with this woman without being married to her. She had been living with him four or five years and had one child by him. Tom rushed out there with Justice Shively and the marriage ceremony was performed. Since that time another child was born to them."

This squalid wretch with his obviously mentally defective wife left an estate estimated by rumor as anywhere from $17,000 to $70,000 in a bank in Newcastle. (These sums grow rapidly with repetition.) That he did leave an estate, however, is a fact, since an administrator was appointed by the court. According to a few local contemporary reports—the only ones worth any credence—Waggoner's ranch was a headquarters or relay station for a band of horse thieves operating out of Montana and Nebraska. It was further stated a few days after the discovery of the body that several stockmen had looked through his horse herd and identified their horses.[1]

Two of the men named by rumor in connection with the hanging of Waggoner—trigger men, professional gun-toters, one of them a stock detective employed by the Wyoming Stock Growers' Association—were indicted some months later in connection with the dawn attack on Nate Champion. Interestingly enough, one of these men, Fred Coates, was named as administrator of Waggoner's estate—which suggests some very murky local possibilities. The Waggoner affair was too far from Johnson County to awaken any repercussions there at the time, but it struck the keynote for a bad summer.

On Powder River the state of guerrilla war was intensifying and both sides were fighting fire with fire. "A new blackball list had been made out by the Northern Wyoming Protective Association that spring," Flagg wrote, "and it included nearly every man in the country who owned a hoof of stock, and the foremen had had strict orders not to allow any of them to eat a meal at their wagons, or to turn any one of their cattle, or to allow a man in their employ to assist them in any way in handling their stock."

The boycott was clearly illegal. Roundups were a state function conducted under an agency of the state government—the Livestock Commission—which was liberally financed by the taxpayers' money. For a group of private citizens by force and personal fiat to keep other citizens out of the roundups in the absence of any proof of wrongdoing or formal charges was without justification. But it was not until a year later, after the invasion had torn the state in two, that the ostracized small owners acquired enough sophistication to challenge the roundup procedure in court.[2] In the meanwhile they came to the roundups anyway—with guns.

That was not the only reaction. The latter half of 1891 saw more stealing on the range than ever before, and a worse form of stealing. Burned-over brands were appearing everywhere now, as were dead cows, whereas the milder mavericking had been the only kind of theft complained of through 1887. There were men who did a brisk business of killing other men's beeves and selling the meat to the Burlington grading crews; a good deal of "slow elk" was sold to the fort, and there was at least one well-known saloon man in Buffalo who was said to be grubstaking ex-cowboys to engage in this kind of enterprise, on the usual fifty-fifty basis.

The regular rustlers, as their supporters called them, still confined themselves to what a newspaper termed "the more humane and gentlemanly methods of rustling," boasting in after years that they had never blotched a brand, or killed a cow to wean the calf. "Unfortunately," Elmer Brock pointed out, "associated with these men were a number of common thieves. They thrived here where they could work behind a screen of respectability and honest people." Matters had reached a point where a measure of acceptance was accorded to any enemy of the big stockmen, however low his character might be.

Below the "regular rustlers" those on the scene could discern two other classes in the rustling hierarchy. The second class were common thieves in the range-country sense because they descended to the lower forms of stealing but they were not otherwise criminals, since cattle were the only form of property they bothered. Unlike the first group, neither during the rustling era nor at any future time did they rise above the level of wage-earning cowhand. "Some of them would drop their maverick brand on a big calf with no particular idea of what they were going to do with it," an old Johnson County resident said, "but just because it was the smart thing to do. Everybody else was doing the same."

Overlapping the second class and the genuine criminal class was the scum which always boils to the surface where trouble brews. These were the hoodlums who shot livestock on the range for spite; who despoiled the houses of fugitive cattlemen after the invasion; who made threats against friends of the invaders and half intended to carry them out, and in one case—the George Wellman killing—did so. They were drifters, and they ranged from worthless to villainous. They shaded into the third class, whose hangers-on they became, the bank robbers and train robbers of the Hole in the Wall gang. The latter did not rise to prominence until the late nineties, but some of its lesser members were around to make trouble in 1891 and 1892.

The rustlers worked in twos and threes, carrying their beds and grub, skillet and coffeepot on pack horses. They worked ahead of the roundup, throwing bunches of cattle over ridges and up little pockets in the hills where the drive on its prearranged course would pass them by, going back later to brand the big calves and separate the smaller ones from their mothers until they were weaned. Although the foremen had orders not to feed them at the wagons they often turned up at dinner time just the same, taking for granted the customary hospitality of the range with the suave insolence possible only to a cowboy carrying a fast gun on his hip. They were fed.

It is told of Al Allison that one day he rode up to the wagon of a roundup on the Antelope range and addressed the owner. "Mr. K, you've got some of our cattle in that roundup and I'd like to go in and cut them out." He was observing the outward form of range etiquette, he was asking permission, and besides he was armed and no one cared to stop him. He thereupon rode into the herd and cut out a sizable number of big unbranded calves, remarking with a final flourish of impudence: "We had a big loss last winter and all our old cattle died, but we've sure got a lot of good young ones." Even from the standpoint of some of the rustlers, Al Allison was too much. His own relatives held no particular brief for him.

"These men worked together with sufficient force, armed with Winchesters and revolvers," Fred Hesse wrote, "so as to intimidate the owners and even the foremen [*sic!*] of the outfits. They did their work openly—going so far as to wait until the roundup was made and then tying down and branding anything they chose." The cowboys were thoroughly disaffected by this time, even in sympathy with the rustlers, and they had no intention of interfering. As another of the invader captains described it: "The men working for the cattle outfits seemed to have an understanding among themselves that they were being paid so much a month for working, not fighting, and it was up to the owner or manager to do his own fighting." [3]

The owners offered no resistance whatever, the Al Allison incident being typical. In the whole record of preinvasion troubles there is not a single instance of an owner standing up to a rustler in defense of his property and having it out man-to-man; not an instance in which he did what, from his own point of view, he would have been amply justified in doing: took armed men and went after his cattle and recovered them at gunpoint, if necessary. On the other hand there are at least two reported instances in which a cattle-owner, coming upon a thief red-handed in the midst of his work or a party coming upon a group of thieves, simply turned tail and rode away.

One brave man did go after stolen cattle and bring them back but this is no part of the invasion story, as it happened five years later. The man was Bob Divine, foreman of the Carey outfit, who rode into the Hole in the Wall, which had become a bandit-rustler stronghold by that time, on the trail of some CY cattle which had been stolen. The incident occasioned the famous Hole in the Wall fight, and a rustler was killed. It is interesting though unprofitable to speculate on how the course of events might have changed if one of the Johnson County cattlemen or his foreman had shown the courage of a Bob Divine and had it out with the rustlers on the spot, instead of coming with an army at his back to terrorize a whole community. The writer surmises that in such a case public opinion, however violently against the cattlemen, would have turned around and approved his course, and if a few rustlers had happened to get killed in a fair fight no one would have cared very much except the relatives and friends of the deceased. Such a show of force might have discouraged rustling.

Western opinion was a peculiar thing. It kept hands off what it considered private differences to a point which was downright anti-social. It cared next to nothing about the law as such, and as for that hifalutin affair known as "a matter of principle," the West had never heard of it. But it cared everything for the Code which decreed that a man should act like a man. Fighting for your rights as a man should was acceptable under the Code even when they were not your rights. Vigilante action was approved when it was felt that the ends of justice had been achieved. But shooting men in the back was unfavorably regarded, and so was wholesale assassination planned in secret.

There were open quarrels on the range that summer as well as seething undercover hatreds; there were showdowns in the fall, and Nate Champion was mixed up in most of them. Looking back, it seems almost to have been Nate Champion's year. It was also his last.

By 1891 the outfits with wagons on the Upper Powder roundup were down to two, the 76, of which Johnny Pierce was foreman, and the EK, with Mike Shonsey (sometimes spelled Shaunsey) in charge. The EK and NH had always been one outfit under Plunkett's Frontier Cattle Company, but now what was left of the Bar C had been added to the fold, and Shonsey was looking after all three.

"Two or three wrangles came up during this roundup over the unfair treatment of the blackballed boys by Pierce and Shaunsey," Flagg wrote. "On one occasion Nate Champion had four or five head of cattle in

Shaunsey's herd that had gotten in accidentally. He went to Shaunsey and told him they were in there and he would like to get them out, as he supposed that he [Shaunsey] did not want them in his herd.

"Shaunsey told him that it did not make any difference, that he could leave them in and he would hold them for him, that he would work the bunch in a day or so and then he would get them out. As soon as Nate was gone he had the bunch rounded up and cut Nate's cattle out and ran them off.

"That, of course, vexed Nate and he had some words with Shaunsey over the matter. Shaunsey never forgave him, though apparently afterwards he was very friendly."

The two-faced behavior of Shonsey puzzled the blackballed men for many a year. Enmity would break out of him one moment, followed by gestures of seeming friendliness. He even made one to Flagg, who was surprised to find his name suddenly taken off the blacklist that spring, while Shonsey invited him to go on the roundup and gather his cattle. Not in Jack Flagg's time, nor for years after, did the reason for the Irishman's mysterious behavior come to light, and then it was in an interview with a Wyoming historian in his old age. In addition to his regular work he was drawing pay from the cattlemen to report on the movements of the rustlers. Shonsey was a spy.[4]

There was a second feud that summer between Nate Champion and Robert Tisdale, one of the brothers who had established themselves on the South Fork and were now sitting high in the seats of the mighty. Their first clash occurred over range rights in the red-walled valley of Buffalo Creek, which was later to become famous as the Hole in the Wall, but at this time was still prosaically known as the Bar C pasture. The celebrated valley ran thirty miles north and south, bounded on the west by the Big Horn mountains and on the east by a red-rock wall which for its entire length had only four narrow openings through which cattle or a man on horseback could pass. It was a valley designed by nature for purple-hued fiction or an outlaw's retreat, but at this time it was just some hundred thousand acres of good range which had been left vacant since the Bar C folded in 1889. Robert Tisdale turned 2000 head of cattle into the red-walled valley, and shortly afterward Champion turned his little herd of two hundred head into the same great pasture.

"Just as soon as Tisdale knew of Champion having put his cattle in," Flagg wrote, "he began to raise the devil and said that he did not see what right Champion had to put his cattle in where he had his. He blustered around awhile and finally rounded his cattle up and drove them out, taking a good many of Champion's with him."

It may be that this encounter provoked the "say, fellow citizens" affair in which Champion swooped down on Bob Tisdale's roundup on the South Fork, seized the big calves, and scattered the rest of the herd. The incident is described by Robert B. David in *Malcolm Campbell, Sheriff*, and is here partly paraphrased and partly quoted. Robert Tisdale was rounding up on his range, when he found himself camped across a creek from an independent roundup being conducted by Nate Champion and his friends. Next day, after Tisdale and his men had gathered fifteen hundred head of wild range cattle, "Champion and his men rode out leisurely on fresh mounts, armed to the teeth, and ignoring Tisdale's cowboys completely, they proceeded to rope, throw and tie all the calves, after which they scattered the remainder of the herd.

"Tisdale was quite powerless in the face of desperate odds, and when on the following morning the rustlers branded the calves and departed, he was obliged to submit and accept the incident philosophically." [5] Tisdale, it is obvious, had no support from his cowboys.

Who was Nathan D. Champion?

He was born near Round Rock, Williamson County, Texas, cradle of cowboys, September 29, 1857, and the assumption is that he came north with a trail herd. Since he was killed by the cattlemen in circumstances which made him a hero to a large element of the population, efforts have been made to establish him as a bad man, a man with a criminal record who, as the saying went, "needed killing." For this reason it is worth while tracing his moral pedigree.

An oft-repeated story has it that he was an old hand at cattle-stealing who had worked for a cattleman near Brush, Colorado, and been chased out of the state for rustling. The source of this tale is a now forgotten Chicago newspaper, the *Saturday Blade*, where on March 12, 1892, there appeared a concoction captioned "Four Bad Men," evidently based on an interview with a Wyoming cattleman passing through Chicago and so wonderfully garbled it appears to have been written by a reporter who lost his notes and then wrote his story while drunk. Among the "bad men" mentioned was one Lee West, who never existed and was apparently an amalgamation of Lee Moore and Lou Webb. But the main point is that "Nat Champion" (*sic*) was described as an "unhung scoundrel" who had worked for a cattleman near Brush, Colorado, under the name of Charlie Taylor and was fired for rustling.

Since there was a real Charlie Taylor who infested Wyoming in her time of trouble, since he had indeed departed in haste from Colorado circa 1891 for killing a man, the foregoing can be dismissed as a case of mistaken identity. [6]

In the interview the writer had with James C. Shaw many years ago the question of Nate Champion came up and Mr. Shaw, who came from Williamson County too and had known Champion all his life, said "he was never run out of anywhere."

The bad man story is bunk.

The facts of Champion's career are now well established. He had been in Wyoming ten years when he was killed. In June 1882 he was working for the EK and was mentioned in Horace Plunkett's diary, and since no trail herd could have reached Wyoming so early in the season he must have arrived the year before. In 1884 he was a wagon boss for the Bar C—as attested both by Jack Flagg and by the caption of a photo in the Wyoming archives—and in 1886 he was again a wagon boss for the EK. At the end of that roundup Horace Plunkett let him go with regret, remarking: "He is a good man."

In 1888 he was back with the EK again, but toward the end of that season there was a flareup of some sort and the foreman Curt Spaugh was fired, together with three cowboys of whom Nate Champion was probably one.[7] That is the last we hear of him until 1891, when he was blackballed and running cattle on the range.

There is a Brock story about him. At one point while the settler Albert Brock, in his steady growth as a man of affairs, was away on a trip, he hired Champion to look after the house while the family were gone, the deal being that Champion was to board himself. Brock arrived home, joined his caretaker for a meal, and the latter apologized for the lack of potatoes, stating that he had been unable to get to town.

Brock said: "There's a ton of them in the cellar. Why didn't you help yourself?" Champion replied: "Yes. I know, but they weren't mine."

Nate Champion is described as stockily built, with steely blue-gray eyes; a quiet sort, people said; laconic, soft-spoken. He was also a lion of a man who feared nothing and would stand up to anybody, and he was lightning with a gun. The cattlemen hated him very greatly. Four of them couldn't kill him even in his bed. It took fifty men to do the job.

The summer of 1891—its cloudless days and silvered nights—was what old-time people called a weather breeder. It was too perfect. Work on the roundups was hot under the blazing sun, but sweat evaporated in the dry air and men's faces shone like oiled wood. The mountains lifted their great blue heads above the dusty scene. Moisture had blessed the land. The alfalfa fields, more of them every year now, were patches of emerald on the golden earth, burnt gold everywhere with the color of sunburnt grass, except for the azure cloud shadows lying on distant uplands that looked like the pastures of heaven. The grass was rich and the cattle were fat. Despite all the to-do about rustling, one large owner on Piney Creek, near Buffalo, had bought six thousand head of cattle and was turning them out on a range no longer overstocked.

On the Fourth of July John Clay, who had been elected president of the Wyoming Stock Growers' Association at the spring meeting, was visiting Major Frank Wolcott at the VR ranch on a tributary of the North Platte. The VR was owned by the Tolland Cattle Company, another overseas concern, and the doughty major was its resident manager.

"Major Wolcott and I were walking across a beautiful alfalfa meadow on Deer Creek a short distance from his house," Clay wrote, and described the scene as work went on despite the holiday, the hay fell in windrows, the rakes gathered it and the lifters elevated it into great, sweet-smelling stacks. As they strolled along the edge of the meadow with the purple blooms as yet uncut brushing their knees, the major divulged information of such a startling nature that Mr. Clay departed for Europe very soon after. Major Wolcott had told him of the plan to take a large body of armed men and march through northern Wyoming, exterminating all who were thought to be rustlers.[8]

Clay enjoyed his European holiday, and would have us believe that the matter concerning which Major Wolcott had spoken to him completely left his mind. It was not until his ship reached Queenstown, Ireland, on his return voyage in early April, he tells us, and the mails came aboard, that he received his first intimation of a fight between cowboys and cattle-owners in Wyoming.

TWENTY-TWO

Blood on a Tarpaulin

NATE CHAMPION had never filed on a homestead, but he had his brand on about two hundred head of cattle, as attested after his death. The end of October 1891 found him and a fellow named Ross Gilbertson, a rather blurred, rather unsavory figure in the record, holed up together in a two-by-twice one-room cabin way up on the headwaters of the Middle Fork, a mile or less from the old Bar C headquarters. The rented cabin, known as the Hall cabin, was in an oval pocket of a valley, one of those perfect places of concealment which a few years later was to make the Hole in the Wall famous as an outlaw's retreat. It was not over half a mile long, cut off on the north side by the heavy growth of trees and brush along the Middle Fork, on the south side and the west end by the sheer red sandstone walls which run every which-way at that point. The only way into it—unless you and your horse were to fall over the cliff—was by a hidden trail down a narrow draw.

Nate Champion was not hiding from anybody—he was not the type; he had picked out a cozy spot for the winter, and the outlines of his cabin can be paced off by the foundation stones still half-buried in the earth.[1] It was unbelievably small; barely room for a built-in bunk and a stove, and so low a medium-sized man had to stoop to get through the door. I once asked a man who had lived there a long time why the wretched dimensions of those cabins. Was it shiftlessness? He answered: "No. If you had to lift those logs into place by yourself you'd stop as soon as you could."

Nate Champion and Ross Gilbertson were attacked in their bunk bed at dawn November 1, 1891, by four armed men. Four (some people thought six); their object at any rate was clear—to kill Nate Champion.

The preceding afternoon, October 31, a man named Nick Ray was riding up Beaver Creek on his way to the Riverside post office when he saw two men camped in a bend of the creek. Their horses were grazing nearby, and he recognized one as belonging to Joe Elliott, the Association stock detective.[2] The same day Mike Shonsey had ridden up to Champion's cabin on some pretext of a parley about a horse trade. It was a curious gesture in view of their recent quarrel, and Champion received him coolly, concluded later that the purpose of the visit was to spy out whether Champion was at home.

Next morning Champion woke at daybreak and petted the cat, then went back to sleep, winter being the time for sleeping. The next time he woke was when the door was burst open and three men sprang into the room, one of them saying: "Give up—we've got you this time."

"What's the matter, boys?" he replied coolly, affecting a yawn. As he stretched, his left hand found his six-shooter hanging from the bedpost —"they forgot I was a left-handed man." He and one attacker fired within a split second of each other. The shot just missed Champion, though the pistol was so close that his face was powder-burned. A second shot buried itself in the blankets between the two occupants of the bed. With a second shot from Champion the men turned and ran, and as they piled out the door he fired another shot at about the right height to hit the last one in the middle, looked out the window and saw "a short dark fellow" running into the brush, holding his stomach. At no time did Gilbertson appear much interested in fighting, but Nate ordered him to get his six-gun and watch the window while Champion looked out the door. The first thing he saw was a Winchester leaning against the cabin and another one beside the woodpile a few feet away. They needed the guns as they had only six-shooters; Champion took a chance and stepped out to get them when a fourth man, whom he identified later as Joe Elliott, sprang around the corner of the house with pistol aimed. Champion jumped back inside and fired a shot through the chinking of the cabin, looked out again and saw the man disappearing into the brush.

He and the unenthusiastic Gilbertson, who was not on hand to be a witness when Joe Elliott was charged with assault a few months later, followed the assailants and about seventy-five yards from the cabin found four overcoats and other personal belongings. It was still early morning when Tommy Carr,[3] then a ranch hand at what was left of the Bar C and who lived to be an old man with a long memory, was in the barn milking a cow. He felt someone looking at him, turned to face Nate Champion, who had entered noiselessly, Winchester in hand, to see if anyone was hiding in the barn. Carr was the first man to hear about the attack.

The timing after seventy-odd years is a little confused, but no matter. At some point Nate Champion and friends pursued the trail of the assailants and found a hastily abandoned camp on Beaver Creek within three quarters of a mile of the NH headquarters, where Mike Shonsey now lived as foreman for the combined remnants of the three old British outfits. This proximity was sufficient evidence to any western mind that Mike Shonsey had been privy to the attack; which he almost certainly was, being a paid informer for the cattlemen. At the abandoned campsite they found numerous articles scattered about which gave evidence of hasty departure, and a tarpaulin heavily bloodstained. One of Champion's shots had found its mark.

That same day he loped across country to the home of his friend John A. Tisdale, found him at home with his wife, who was carrying a child, and told of the attack. His words were remembered by Mrs. Tisdale, who repeated them many times to the son born after his father's death. "There's going to be trouble," Champion had said. "If it comes to fighting I can fight, but I can't lead a fight." Brave as he was, he was aware of his own deficiencies in education, and turned to the friend, who had what he lacked.

Not long after Champion's prediction of more trouble he and Tisdale were riding together when they met Mike Shonsey. Champion whipped out his gun and demanded to know the names of his attackers. "I know who they were but I want to hear you say it. Don't lie to me or I'll kill you." Shonsey told.

The story was repeated in several versions, but the above is the one Johnny Tisdale heard over and over from his mother in later years. It is probably correct. This version continues, with a little less certainty, that Frank Canton was named by Shonsey, at gunpoint, as one of the attackers; and local tradition insists that one of the rifles left by the cabin was Canton's.[4]

Nor was that the end of the Champion–Shonsey feud. According to another local memory or winter's tale or what you will, not long after Champion, Shonsey, and Tisdale had words, Mike Shonsey and his men had gathered some cattle and were working them on a flat meadow near the present site of Kaycee. In any such gather, cattle of various owners are likely to be mixed in. Champion rode up and, without a word of by-your-leave started cutting out certain animals.

According to range etiquette this was a deliberate insult which could have had only one purpose; to provoke Shonsey to go for his gun. But no man cared to tangle with Nate Champion in a gun encounter, and Shonsey swallowed the affront.[5]

As for Shonsey and Tisdale, the sagebrush telegraph carried the news of some sort of confrontation; carried it far and wide if somewhat confusedly, so that a garbled version of it even turned up in the Cheyenne *Sun*. Moreover, it was said that Tisdale expressed openly, freely, contemptuously his opinion of cowards who went around trying to kill people in their beds.[6] The old hatred between him and Frank Canton flared up again.

Two nights before the attempt to kill Nate Champion a meeting was held in Buffalo. It was a totally unprecedented sort of meeting for this unsophisticated little western community, since its purpose was to organize the settlers and small stockmen of Johnson County, none of whom were of a type who had ever previously lent themselves to organization. It was a very large meeting, attended by virtually every citizen east of the Big Horns with the exception of Champion and Ross Gilbertson, who had not made the fifty-mile trip to town. The object was to deal with common community problems, one of which was the recent stock-seizure move. Another object was consideration of ways and means to deal with a much older grievance, that of big outfits moving through the countryside with their large herds, carelessly knocking down settlers' fences and trampling their garden plots. The big herd also had a way of collecting the cattle of small owners as it went.

The meeting was both large and enthusiastic. The name chosen was the Northern Wyoming Farmers' and Stock Growers' Association. A declaration of purposes was adopted which for lofty sentiments and high-flown phraseology, for endorsement of virtue and abhorrence of sin, for dedication to patriotism, home, and mother could not have been bettered by a church convention, and some of the worst scamps in northern Wyoming voted *Aye*.[7]

During the next few months of rising tensions throughout the state, the new organization held open meetings and advertised a reward of $500 for the apprehension of anyone found shooting livestock on the range—an answer to recent charges. But toward the end of March it flung down the gauntlet in a gesture of defiance which caused the greatest excitement in Cheyenne; it announced that the Northern Wyoming Farmers' and Stockmens' Association would hold an independent roundup this spring, with Nate Champion as captain. And the date set was a month ahead of the authorized roundup!

Recriminations broke out anew against the damnable rustlers. It was true that the move was in open violation of state law. It was scarcely the furtive behavior of ordinary thieves.

TWENTY-THREE

The Reader Is the Jury

I

EARLY IN December Buffalo was rocked by two murders. It was as though a land mine, buried in the roots of the social and economic system since the early eighties and giving ample warning of its presence, had finally blown up, leaving the people torn and bleeding.[1]

The end of November and the beginning of December were always a great time in town. Court was in session and the ranchers came from far and near to transact business, see friends, and lay in the winter's supplies. Among those who came was the young settler, cowboy, and bronc-buster called Ranger Jones—Orley E. Jones—twenty-three years old. Afterwards he was called a rustler, but who knows? The charges were windy and vague. Anyway, he had filed on a homestead on the Red Fork a few miles below Jack Flagg's and next above one filed on by his brother Johnny.

According to one scrap of local tradition Jones had had some sort of a feud with Fred Hesse. Like many of the local folk he resented what he considered the arrogant ways of the Englishman, and the story is that he threatened him. Ranger was something of a blusterer, and the story continues that on this occasion he collected a gang of cronies outside a saloon and told them he was going to go in and pick a quarrel with Hesse, who was inside. "I'll tell him what a son of a bitch he is until he pulls his gun, and then I'll shoot him." It sounded like a typical drunken brag, but Ranger Jones never took a drink.

He did go in and offer some taunts to Hesse, who simply ignored him and walked away.

About November 20 he left the Red Fork, telling his brother he would be back in four or five days. But he had a good time and stayed longer than he intended, going to a dance at Piney, north of Buffalo, on Thanksgiving night. He finally set out for home on the afternoon of the twenty-eighth. He was going to be married and he had bought flooring for his house, and the bundle of boards stuck far out at the back of his two-horse buckboard, swaying and dipping as the conveyance jolted over the road.[2] The road he followed veered south and west, hugging the low first ridge of the mountains called the Horn until it turned west near the southern end and threaded a low pass to the now-obliterated settlements of Barnum and Riverside. Then he planned to turn up the Red Fork and start to lay that flooring in readiness for his bride. He never arrived.

By the time his frozen body was discovered five days later, Johnson County had a second murder on its hands.

John A. Tisdale had come to town the same week, and it took no great hindsight to see that during his stay he was acting unlike himself. Normally a sober man, he was drinking heavily.

"It was the first time the people of this city had ever seen him in his cups," said the *Bulletin* later. He talked freely, telling several people that he was afraid an attempt would be made on his life on his way home. Although he had a six-shooter, he went in and bought a shotgun from George Munkres the hardware dealer, to whom he again expressed fears. This strange choice of confidant in itself showed that Tisdale must have been drunk, since he would have known that Munkres was a great friend of Frank Canton's, and an inside member of the clique from whom—if Tisdale had to fear anything—he had most to fear. A story went the rounds later that he had overheard a remark made by Frank Canton to Fred Hesse that Canton would "tend to him" (Tisdale), but this was never confirmed. The hardware dealer presented Tisdale with a pair of dogs, a bitch and a pup.

Tommy Carr, who had had enough of working for Shonsey and had quit his job at the Bar C, was in town buying horses. Carr was a friend of Tisdale's, and Tisdale told him too of his dread and asked him to wait until Tisdale was ready to leave so they could go together. Carr did wait for him several days, but since Tisdale was still drinking and delaying on the morning of November 30, he left without him.[3]

Whatever John Tisdale had heard to reduce a brave man to such an agony of fear, there was nothing unreasonable about the fear itself. For his sixty-mile road home, the same one Ranger Jones had taken, wound among hills and gulches which offered countless places of concealment for an assassin. The surest aim, the fastest draw, cannot stop a shot in the back.

Tisdale finally started out of Buffalo the afternoon of Monday the thirtieth, his wagon loaded with a winter's supplies, with sacks of flour and sugar and beans and sides of bacon; there were Christmas toys for his children and presents for his wife, there were the two dogs and a little red sled was on top of the load. He was driving a team of a gray horse and a brown. About sundown he made an unexpected move which threw some plans momentarily out of gear; he decided to stop for the night at the Cross H ranch, four to six miles south of town—estimates as to the exact distance vary; and all unknowingly, by so doing, he gained another fifteen hours of life. He did more; he forced his murderer to do the deed in broad daylight.

Elmer Freeman, the cowboy in charge at the Cross H was one more witness to Tisdale's premonitions. He said he "expected to have some trouble before he got home"; again expressed fear for his life and shut the window curtains. He "didn't lie quiet in his sleep." Next morning before leaving he made another reference to coming trouble, but this time it was merely the remark that he supposed he'd get stuck on the road with his heavily loaded wagon. There were slightly conflicting statements between Freeman and another overnight visitor at the ranch as to what time Tisdale left, whether it was eight or eight-thirty or nine; but subsequent testimony made it clear that he had left after eight.

His strange behavior had made such an impression on Freeman that Freeman himself was nervous and upset when he left some two hours later to ride to Buffalo—as he himself testified: "I was excited." This in itself was unusual, since cowboys did not become "excited" easily. They were distinctly not the worrying kind. After leaving the ranch he overtook Charlie Basch, riding in at a slower gait, and what he heard from the older man did nothing at all to allay his "excitement."

Meanwhile John Tisdale had creaked and crawled along in his heavy wagon, making not more than two or three miles an hour. Three miles or so south of the Cross H and eight miles south of Buffalo the road dipped into one of the countless waterworn draws which seamed the prairie, this one called Haywood's Gulch. Shortly before reaching it Tisdale was overtaken by Sam Stringer, the mailman, driving a span of mules hitched to a light buckboard. Stringer had the mail route to the settlements at the head of Powder River; he stopped and made arrangements with Tisdale about carrying some express up there from Buffalo, then he drove on. Like all country mail carriers he operated on schedule and was positive to a dot as to time and distance. He testified that he overtook Tisdale about nine o'clock two miles on the north or Buffalo side of the gulch. It was therefore approximately ten o'clock when John Tisdale reached the gulch and met his death.

The assassin was waiting a few yards from the spot where the road, running north and south, dipped into and crossed the gulch, which ran east and west. He had tied his horse about a hundred yards off the road and out of sight. The place he had picked to do the shooting was down in the gulch at a point where a clay abutment about six feet high offered concealment close to the road. Some seventy-five yards from this point was higher ground, from which he could see the road and watch for Tisdale's approach; footprints in the snow showed that he had walked back and forth several times from the gulch to the brow of the hill while waiting, and the snow was trampled behind the clay abutment as though he had waited there some time.

Finally Tisdale reached his rendezvous, braked his wagon down into the bottom of the gulch, and started the pull up the other side. The murderer waited until the horses began to climb the hill and then, John Tisdale's back presenting a perfect target, he stepped out from his hiding place and fired from a distance of twenty feet.

The first shot struck the handle of the six-shooter which Tisdale was wearing in a shoulder sling under his coat and glanced off, hitting one of the horses in the jugular; the animal bled heavily but did not fall. The second shot found its mark and John Tisdale fell back dead on his load of Christmas toys.

The killer took his time. First he walked up to the brow of the hill, the southern lip of the gulch, apparently to look around and see if anyone was coming. It so happened that someone was, but he ignored this. Then he returned to the gulch, mounted his horse and led the team and wagon, with the wounded horse and dead driver, a few hundred yards eastward down the gulch to a point out of sight of the road, where he shot both horses. Later on when the sheriffs got there, John Tisdale's new shotgun was found where it had fallen between the wagon tracks, with both barrels full of mud and one indented cartridge showing that after the first shot missed he was trying to cock and fire the gun when the fatal shot struck him.

With his work finished the killer took off for Buffalo on a course which led diagonally straight across country to the town. The bitch tried to follow him and he shot her dead.

By eleven o'clock he was back in Buffalo, cool as an icicle, mingling with the pre-Christmas crowd.

Charlie Basch—Charles Franklin Basch, forty-one—finished his chores that morning at nine-fifteen and left his ranch, sixteen miles south of Buffalo, to ride to town. It was a lovely sunny winter's day; a melting day, and Charlie Basch didn't have a thing on his mind beyond a matter of business about some cattle which he intended to transact with a ranch-man on Rock Creek, a few miles north of Buffalo. As he approached Haywood's Gulch he met Sam Stringer and passed the time of day with him. The two men agreed as to the hour; it was about ten o'clock or a little after. Some twenty minutes after meeting Stringer, Basch reached the gulch.

The saddle-horse trail he was following left the wagon road at that point and cut straight across. As Basch approached the cutoff he saw a man leading a horse on the brow of the hill above the gulch. Basch recognized the horse as he had good reason to, since he had ridden him; it was Frank Canton's famous sorrel, Old Fred. He recognized the man too. It was Frank Canton.

Basch said many years after that his first thought was to ride up to Canton and ride into town with him. The two men were neighbors; they had been friendly for years, especially so since Basch's part in stopping the Canton runaway. But the man drew out his gun. Then he put it away again. Basch quickly decided to keep on going.

That wasn't all Basch saw and heard up there on the saddle trail. All told he saw the man he later identified as Frank Canton over a total of five minutes, saw him four times as he appeared and disappeared in the hollows. He saw the team standing in the road—then he saw the man, on horseback now, lead the team off the road and out of sight. Basch testified that he saw no one on the wagon, which was not surprising since the driver was on his back, dead. Some minutes later, while Basch tended strictly to his business and kept moving, he heard two shots. They were the shots which killed the horses. Shortly afterward he had his last sight of the man, riding at top speed toward Buffalo.

It was a few minutes before eleven when Elmer Freeman left the Cross H to come to Buffalo, and a half-mile or so away from his ranch he overtook Charlie Basch. Freeman was still "excited" over what he had seen of John Tisdale's behavior. The younger man, it would seem, was the first to blurt out his fears, and then Charlie Basch told. With a shudder of common consent the two men avoided turning back to see whatever Thing was lying in the gulch, but pushed on into Buffalo, carefully not hurrying—"we rode at the usual gait." It was twenty-five minutes to twelve when they reached Buffalo and put their horses in the livery barn—Basch looked at his watch.

Basch left it to Freeman to alert the authorities. He remained in town long enough for dinner and for the drink or two which he may have needed, saying nothing to anyone. Then he got on to attend to his business on Rock Creek. Charlie Basch had some thinking to do. It is unhealthy to come upon a murderer in the midst of his work.

Freeman hurried to Sheriff Angus, who was in court, and reported "that I thought something had happened." By twelve o'clock Freeman and the two undersheriffs, Howard Roles and Jack Donahue, with Tom Gardner were on their way back to Haywood's Gulch. They found the great pool of blood in the road where the horse had been hit; four hundred yards to the east they found the wagon with the dead man's body lying on it and the two dead horses, the gray with his back downhill and the brown with his head lying on the gray.

The sheriffs studied the tracks; found that the horse led by the dismounted killer was "barefoot"—unshod. They found the tracks of a man, made by a Number 8 boot or shoe; a rubber shoe but not, they thought, an overshoe. The measurements were never checked with footgear worn by the suspect, just as other clues were neglected in some police work as slovenly and incompetent as was ever seen in any part of the country, East or West.

Freeman didn't spend much time looking around, just a few minutes. They sent him flying back to Buffalo to fetch the coroner, and he made the sixteen-mile round trip, counting time out at the gulch, in little more than an hour. He left Buffalo again in a buggy with the coroner at one-thirty or two. Not until the coroner reached the scene did the strangest find of that grim day come to light; a very small, very grateful puppy, wrapped up in an overcoat on the wagon seat. That the puppy was not noticed sooner, with all the stir around the wagon, reveals an astounding piece of dog behavior, for a pup left alone for several hours would normally have crawled out of the overcoat and welcomed the first human beings to appear with tail-waggings and joyful cries. All the lie-down-and-obey know-how bred into the working dogs of country people could hardly account for this. The little thing must have sensed, with inherited wisdom far beyond his weeks of life, that things were very, very wrong. So he cowered and kept quiet.

Tom Gardner pushed on up the road to carry the word to the foothill settlements and above all to break the hard news to the wife of John Tisdale. He arrived at Jack Flagg's at midnight, rested a few minutes, and then went on to the Tisdale ranch, which was at the very head of the Red Fork, up under the divide, to get Mrs. Tisdale out of bed in the small hours of the morning and inform her as best he knew how that she was a widow. By sunrise the people were beginning to collect at Flagg's place as the word was sped by courier from one ranch to another, and in the afternoon they started for town in a body, a somber but orderly crowd, the widow among them.

On the same day, December 2, the coroner's inquest had been held, a slipshod affair which developed nothing of interest beyond some transparent red-herring attempts on the part of friends of Canton to make it appear that the death of Tisdale had been the result of a quarrel among "the rustlers," stories which were promptly refuted. Also at the inquest Charlie Basch, on the stand, floundered painfully, denying that he had recognized either Frank Canton or the horse Fred, while admitting, oddly enough, that on the way into town he had told Freeman he had recognized both of them. He was to change his witness on both points of recognition within the next two weeks

Upon learning of the murder of Tisdale, Johnny Jones became alarmed for Ranger and came into Buffalo to start a search for his overdue brother. By early morning of December third a party of a dozen armed men were out on the road to the south, combing the draws and gulches all along the route by which Ranger had started for home. In the evening one of their number rode into Buffalo at a mad gallop and reported breathlessly to the sheriff that fourteen miles south of town he had followed the track of a wagon leading off the main road; at a distance of about three hundred yards from the highway, concealed from it by a divide, he had come in sight of a wagon with the body of a man lying across the seat. No, he had not investigated. He started out with the sheriffs, leading them to the spot; and by midnight they were back in Buffalo confirming the public's belief that a second victim had been assassinated.[4]

Buffalo was a small, poor country town, and one murder at a time was more than it could handle. Nothing was ever done about solving the killing of Ranger Jones; not a suspect was ever arrested or named publicly, though there were plenty of people who were willing enough to offer their private opinion; not a witness was ever called so far as we know, and if an inquest was held—as it must have been—both the Buffalo *Bulletin* and the Cheyenne press were too busy to mention it. Buffalo was completely absorbed in the Tisdale case, which would have come down in history as beclouded as the Jones affair if it hadn't been for Charlie Basch's ride into town that morning.

Jack Flagg, who was a good reporter whatever else some people called him, has left us every fact that survives on the murder of Ranger Jones, and all subsequent accounts have been drawn from his. About sundown on November twenty-eighth a well-known sheepman, D. A. Kingsbury, had met Jones just north of the crossing of Muddy Creek, fifteen miles south of Buffalo. A minute earlier Kingsbury, heading for town, had crossed the bridge over the creek and had seen a man with a rifle in his hands, whom he had taken for a freighter looking for his work animals. At this point we stumble across one of those little fragments of reminiscence: a housewife from south of Buffalo was driving toward town with her little boy on the seat and in her purse a very large sum of money as money went in those days; she had two hundred dollars with her, because like everybody else she was going in to get supplies for all winter. She too met Ranger Jones; and she too saw the man, or a man. He had a handkerchief tied over his face, which frightened her. She dropped her purse and kicked it under the loose hay which covered the bottom of the wagon to help keep feet warm. But the man wasn't interested in purses. He rode in front of her team a short distance and then turned out to let them pass. As he rode ahead she was sure she recognized that ramrod back, so different from the casual slouch of the westerner. You can't call this kind of thing evidence. Just another winter's tale, but it has been told for seventy years.

The man—the same man—anyway, the man Kingsbury had seen near the bridge—concealed himself under it and waited for Ranger Jones to drive across. Then he shot him in the back, the standard practice. Jones was shot three times.

"The murderer was not more than six feet away when he fired," Flagg continues. "The first shot struck a large cartridge belt worn by Ranger and did no harm. The other two shots were both mortal; one in the side and the other in the chest.

"There must have been two men present when the shooting was done. The road, twenty feet after leaving the bridge, goes through a short cut between two banks, and in there a man must have stood to stop the team, for one of the horses was a wild one and would have run when the shot was fired, and the man under the bridge could not have caught them. They had been stopped at once, for there were no marks of the buggy or team outside of the road before entering the cut. After the team was stopped it was then driven out of the road and there stopped under a bank, and out of sight of the road." The horses were then turned loose in a nearby pasture, where they were found.[5]

So the killing of Ranger Jones was a two man job. If Jones, why not Tisdale? A question never asked in court. The case against Frank Canton never came to court. Affronted by gossip that his horse Fred had been seen near the murder site, he demanded a hearing in order to clear himself. The horse, he said, was kept in a locked stable at all times and he alone had the key. Therefore it could not have been his horse. A hearing or arraignment of Frank Canton, which was not a trial, was held before a justice of the peace in Buffalo on December 8, 1891.

TWENTY-FOUR

The Reader Is the Jury
II

THERE IS an idea haunting the conscience of all civilized peoples that an unsolved murder is an unlaid ghost.

The hearing on the charge against Frank Canton began the morning of December the eighth before a hushed, orderly crowd. Elmer Freeman described Tisdale's nervousness the night before his death. The sheriffs told of finding the body. A Mrs. Oliver Condert or Olive S. Conrad told of driving into Buffalo that morning and seeing a man on horseback riding very hard from the south, too far away to describe; she had noticed him because he was riding so fast, had thought it must be someone going for a doctor.

Sam Stringer the mailman told of overtaking John Tisdale two miles this side of the gulch and of meeting Charlie Basch on the other side. After passing Tisdale he saw a man on a black horse, off to the left, riding slowly along in the direction the victim had taken. The man was some distance away and he did not recognize him. Basch saw the man too, but that came out later.

Basch, on the stand, was still showing signs of a mental struggle. Just as at the inquest his testimony differed from what he had told Elmer Freeman on the way into town, so at the hearing he changed his testimony from what he gave at the inquest. While again stating that he was unable to recognize the man he saw at the gulch, he now swore that he had recognized the horse. After all, a horse with those markings—the blazed face, the white stockings on the hind feet—would be hard *not* to recognize, even for a person who had not spent his whole life with horses.

"It was to the best of my knowledge and belief Mr. Canton's horse Fred." Yes, he was positive about the horse. Yes, he had been a witness at

169

the coroner's inquest; yes, he had said then he wouldn't swear positively about the horse, "am willing to so swear now."

The man was wearing a drab-colored overcoat and a black hat creased down the middle; he had a scarf around his neck, wore it wrapped around the lower part of his face. He did not know who the man was or what he was doing with the team. Yes, he knew that the defendant had worn an overcoat such as he described and a hat similar to the one he described, a black hat doubled down on top. He was fifty or sixty yards from the man. Why didn't he go closer? "Because I never ride up on a man with a gun in his hand. The man had a gun in his hand. I thought it was none of my business."

He had a conversation with the defendant on Wednesday (the day after the killing) "after my return from Rock Creek. It occurred in Mr. Round's [livery] stable. We were alone; he asked me what was this he heard about his horse; I told him I had said it was his horse. He said his horse was under lock and key and he could prove it; he said it was a very serious matter to get out on a person."

Later, a good long time later, Basch modified this story and enlarged it, because the passage of forty-four years will do things to any man's memory, or because he had felt it healthier not to tell too much at the time, or because of a combination of both. He and Canton were not exactly alone since one of the undersheriffs, Howard Roles, was lingering at the door of the barn, which put a crimp in the conversation, but some of it went like this.

" 'Did you hear about Tisdale being killed?' I said: 'Yes.' He said: 'They laid it onto me.' I said: 'I saw you out there all right.' " That was all at that time, but the day before, according to Basch's later account, the day of the killing, he had had a meeting with Canton in Buffalo and the following conversation took place.

" 'Did you see me out at the gulch?' I said: 'Yes.' 'Well,' he said, 'that wasn't me you saw at the gulch.' I said: 'It wasn't?' He said: 'No.' "

Basch went on out to Rock Creek doing, as we have already suggested, some deep thinking. He had obviously not finished his thinking when the hearing was held on December 8. He went on thinking for another four or five days after that, and the upshot of his thought will appear in due course.

He had cut a rather sorry figure on the stand, and when Frank Canton followed him to testify in his own defense Basch looked even worse. To his wavering semi-identification Canton opposed an almost bulletproof alibi; just almost. With witnesses supporting him at each step he described his every movement on the day in question, a normal day of a prominent citizen leading the leisurely life of the old West.

"On the first day of December I was not out of the city of Buffalo, nor was my horse Fred." Thus Frank Canton on the stand.

He had been up at six at the home of his father-in-law, W. E. Wilkerson, where he and his family were staying that winter. The home was on the west side of Main Street, uphill from the church. Behind the house there was an alley running parallel with Main Street, and the horse was kept in a stable in the alley. The stable was locked at all times.

He went downtown to the post office; it was not as late as seven o'clock and the post office was not open; went on up the street to Dr. Lott's office but the doctor did not come in, though he waited half an hour; then back to Wilkerson's where he had a cup of coffee and some breakfast about seven-thirty. He then took the horse out to water him and cleaned the stable. The horse was out only twice that day, the second time being when he took him to be shod in the early afternoon.

"The boys" had been interested in that trip to the blacksmith's because the killer had ridden a barefooted horse, and a few days earlier several of them had had a conference with Canton in the back of Conrad's store, among those present being Jack Flagg, Lou Webb, Tom Gardner, a couple of highly respected middle-of-the-roaders, and a Canton ally, but the conference of course got nowhere one way or the other. Canton's morning went on; he went back to the post office and got his mail and then dropped into Eggleston's drugstore to read it; went to Conrad's and ordered some hay, meanwhile greeting friends on the street who inquired about his health, as he had recently had a bout with rheumatism and had just returned from Dakota Hot Springs.

He greeted his friend George W. Munkres in front of the latter's hardware store about nine o'clock; returned to Eggleston's and spent a pleasant half-hour chatting with friends, the timing in here a bit vague; went to the clubrooms and read the papers—the businessmen and cattlemen around Buffalo having their own junior version of the Cheyenne club. He went up the street again and met esteemed early settler and former roundup foreman Hank Devoe, who asked after his rheumatism and invited him to take a drink; saw Rob Tisdale, walked up to the courthouse with him and sat down and chatted a while with the sheriff. According to Canton it was "then after ten o'clock"—quite an understatement, since Devoe fixed the time of his meeting with Canton as "before dinner," as late as eleven o'clock.

A court of posterity sitting seventy years after the event has certain advantages over a real court, but more disadvantages. It has the advantage of hindsight, but it cannot call witnesses, and much if not most of the evidence has been lost. It cannot investigate; it can only speculate. What would a smart cross-examiner have made of the soft spot in Canton's alibi? Indeed, closely examined, it was full of soft spots.

Most of the ten major defense witnesses were respectable business and professional men of Buffalo who were identified with the cattlemen's party through sympathies if nothing closer; some doubtless were, and others were not, privy to all that was going on.

The druggist Eggleston swore to seeing Canton first that morning in his store about eight-thirty; saw him again in his store in the neighborhood of nine, when a pleasant little gathering of friends took place. It is a fact long known to jurisprudence that persons not knowing they are going to be called as witnesses in a murder case are uncertain as to their observations of time. A Dr. Holland testified to meeting Canton in the drugstore at about nine. James T. Craig, well known as a businessman-cattleman, swore that he had met Canton in Eggleston's drugstore "between nine and ten." I. N. Pearson, the steward of the club, testified to seeing Canton in the clubrooms "between nine and nine-thirty," and Robert Dunn, not otherwise identified, swore to meeting him in another drugstore "between nine and ten A.M."

Subsequently both Hank Devoe and Dr. Lott testified to seeing Canton at eleven. Between this hour and the vague preliminary testimony as to "between nine and ten," only one witness swore positively to seeing him near ten, the hour the murder was committed. That was the hardware dealer, whose credibility would have been open to attack on grounds of his extremely close identification with the cattlemen's faction.

The hypothetical cross-examiner would have had a few more' questions. When you say "between nine and ten," which do you mean, nearer nine or nearer ten? When you say "between nine and nine-thirty," do you mean 9:01 or 9:29? It could make a lot of difference. It could make just this much difference: a man owning a fast horse could have slipped away from the social scene on Main Street, ridden out of an alley and made the eight miles to the gulch in half an hour or less, to be there in plenty of time to await the coming of Tisdale, plodding toward his rendezvous with death at 10 A.M.

One more question from the cross-examiner, this one addressed to Canton. You say you reached the post office before it opened. You have lived in Buffalo eleven years; don't you know what time the post office opens? Then you went to Dr. Lott's offce, and arrived there half an hour or more ahead of the doctor. Why were you up so early? Were you perhaps a little nervous that morning? Were you awaiting a message, brought by a messenger from the vicinity of the Cross H ranch, to let you know that a victim marked for your bullet had started on his fateful way, and it was time for you to get on your horse and go?

The prejudiced conduct of the Canton hearing by Justice of the Peace Carroll H. Parmelee aroused repercussions even in Cheyenne. Parmelee, an influential local lawyer, was a creature of the cattlemen and an aide-de-camp to Acting Governor Amos W. Barber, who was also a creature of the cattlemen. The prosecution pleaded for continuance a second day, in order to give it time to produce rebuttal witnesses—the last thing the powers wanted to see produced. The presiding justice allowed the hearing to run on until ten in the evening and then adjourned it, leaving a host of unanswered questions. Next morning at nine he announced his decision, and Frank Canton walked out a free man.

Next to the prejudice on the bench the worst feature of the case was the laxity of the sheriffs, Angus and his deputies together. Both sides in the bitter and bloostained controversy were furious over the negligence of Angus in the matter of Frank Canton's horse.

The sheriff was in court all morning. Why didn't he demand at once to inspect Frank Canton's horse Fred? That was what everyone wanted to know, including the Buffalo *Echo,* which was on the side of the cattlemen and was sticking up for Canton's innocence. What was the matter with Angus? Was he cowardly or merely stupid? If he had acted at once, the condition of the horse—whether cool and rested or showing signs of a recent hard ride—would have settled the question of Frank Canton's innocence or guilt once and for all.

But Angus stalled and did nothing, and when Canton took the horse out to be shod several hours later the signs, if there had been any signs, had evaporated forever.

The deputies were if possible even worse. When undersheriffs Howard Roles and Jack Donahue were dispatched by Angus to the murder scene —Donahue was the picturesque villain who had both fascinated and appalled Horace Plunkett—they found the body, studied the ground for tracks, took note of footprints and measured distance. Among other things they found the clear tracks of the killer's barefooted horse where they left his gruesome handiwork and took off in a north by westerly direction toward Buffalo, straight across country. Until the curious converged in hordes there was little likelihood of their being obliterated by other tracks. The conditions were perfect; the soft ground, a mixture of mud and melting snow, held every imprint as though carved in marble.

The sheriffs never followed the tracks.

The distance to town was about eight miles, certainly not more than seven on the short cut followed by the assassin. Donahue testified at the hearing that on the *following day*—not the first—he had followed the tracks of the barefooted horse with his wide-spaced hoofprints of a dead gallop "probably two miles." Two miles only! And even at that he was lying to cover himself, for it was not until *six days after the murder* that the body of the dog shot by the murderer was discovered on the killer's trail, *not over half a mile* from the spot where the dead man had been found with his wagon and team!

The reader may wish to go back to his television set. For in real life three noble western sheriffs, types who have figured as heroes of many a screen epic, proved too lazy and worthless to follow a killer's fresh tracks in the snow.

And now for the questions which never were asked except by thwarted citizens hungering for justice; which never were answered except by that pale, pale shadow of a court, public opinion. It took two men to kill Ranger Jones. How many did it take to kill John Tisdale? Two men? More than two? Was there a general plot?

A general plot? Hindsight lends insight. During those late November days, when court was in session and the town was teeming with visitors, the townspeople noticed an odd circumstance, thought nothing of it at the time, connected it up later, and thought hard. They noticed the frequency with which members of the cattlemen's club would come downstairs from the clubrooms above a store and cross the street to the livery stable on the corner by the creek. Later they recollected that this was while Jones and Tisdale were in town. Were the agile club members, so busy watching the stable, checking on the teams of first Jones and later Tisdale, to spot the departure time of these marked men from the town? [1]

That wasn't all; there was Hank Devoe's odd encounter on the night of November 30, when the reluctant Tisdale with his premonition of fate had finally left, only to make that unexpected stop at the Cross H ranch. That evening Devoe, heading north into Buffalo, met a rider with a handkerchief over his face heading south at considerable speed. This was the sort of thing you don't think too much about at the time—the fellow might have just been trying to keep the cold air out of his lungs—but later when a body is found in a gulch you think plenty. On December 13 the Cheyenne *Sun* reported that Frank Canton was known to have taken a long hard ride on the evening of the thirtieth.

After the hearing the state of affairs in Johnson County began inciting some lifted eyebrows even in Cheyenne. The *Leader* wrote on December 24: "There are four men suspected to have been concerned (to the extent of instigation if no further) in the recent assassinations."

The plot theory again.

It was the morning of December 9 when Justice Parmelee made his ruling and Frank Canton left the courtroom free. Within a few days afterward something new and startling had entered the case, its nature not divulged at the time. The friends of the dead man were busy, and at some time between the sixteenth and the nineteenth a new warrant for Frank Canton's arrest was issued by a different justice of the peace in Buffalo, a man named Reimann.

On the seventeenth, Frank Canton and Fred Hesse fled Buffalo in hot haste, not to return until they came with the invading army. There are three different versions of this hegira. The first, told by Fred Hesse himself and by numerous friends and admirers of both men, was that on their 110-mile ride to the railroad at Gillette they were chased by seven rustlers determined to kill them; that only the superior speed and bottom of their horses saved their lives; besides which they outwitted their pursuers by taking a cutoff route. They were accompanied by a brother-in-law of Fred Hesse who went with them to take the horses back. The seven rustlers were never named.

Frank Canton, turning up in Cheyenne as cool as ever the day before Christmas, told a different story. He and Fred Hesse had been in no hurry when they left Buffalo; no hurry at all. They had left town on horseback at ten o'clock on the morning of the seventeenth, after spending a leisurely couple of hours bidding goodbye to friends. They had followed the main stage road, meeting teams and men on horseback but encountering no interference.[2] Certain emphases in Canton's story sounded almost like an answer to something. He had been on his way east to join his wife, who was visiting relatives in Illinois. When the train reached Crawford, Nebraska, he learned that Al Allison, John Tisdale's brother, had obtained another warrant. He had then abandoned his trip, returning to Denver and later to Cheyenne. It is worth noting that he did not return to Buffalo. He who had been so eager to face his accusers the first time that he demanded his own arrest was by no means so eager to be arrested now.

The *Bulletin* had a third version of the flight. Those alleged seven rustlers who had chased Fred Hesse but for some unaccountable reason had not chased Frank Canton were not rustlers. According to the *Bulletin* the pursuers of the departing citizens were Deputy Sheriff Howard Roles and Special Deputy John Round the livery-stable man and a posse, who were trying to serve that second warrant.[*]

Canton resumed his trip to Illinois. In March the county attorney

---

[*] *Bulletin* February 4, 1892. The statement that Canton, at least, was fleeing Buffalo to escape arrest is unexpectedly confirmed by Charles H. Burritt, cattlemen's attorney, who wrote in a letter of May 14, 1892, that he had assisted in Canton's *escape* from the town—not in his leisurely departure. The reason for the precipitate departure of Fred Hesse has never been cleared up.

wrote the acting governor, Amos W. Barber, pointing out that a new information had been filed against Canton based on new sworn statements, and requesting that the governor issue a requisition to obtain his return from Illinois. To one one's surprise the request was denied.[3]

But on the first of April Canton appeared in Cheyenne, and on the third he appeared before Judge John W. Blake of the Second Judicial District in his chambers in nearby Laramie, the Second District including Johnson County, where he was charged with first-degree murder and admitted to $30,000 bail. The story was that some new evidence had turned up.[4]

New evidence, rather! Thirty thousand dollars worth!

What was the nature of the new evidence against Canton? It was simply that Charlie Basch had decided to talk.

On May 11, 1935, forty-three and a half years after the murder of Tisdale took place, Charlie Basch, then eighty-five, gave an interview to the indefatigable local historian J. Elmer Brock. The interview was stenographically transcribed and was put away, put very thoroughly away. Elmer Brock died a few years later. Since it was his commendable wish and the wish of his family not to hurt any innocent people, the interview, along with other Brock papers dealing with those troubled days was filed away in the Wyoming archives at the state university in a container marked *Not To Be Opened Until 1973*.

The trouble with this sort of precaution is that it is generally useless. A secret which is known to a number of people is no secret at all; before the interview was so solemnly locked up in the archives a copy or two or three had leaked out; the writer has a photographic duplicate in her possession.

What Basch stated in the interview was that when he rode up over the brow of the hill above the gulch he was not any fifty or sixty yards from the man he saw there. "I wasn't a hundred feet from him." The horse—could he read the brand on the horse? "Yes, I could see the 111 just as plain, and I knowed the horse well for I had rode him."

Why had the sudden unlooked-for intruder not been shot then and there? "When I came up on the hill he drew out his gun that way, and put it back and went right on up the hill. He never said anything."

"It was a wonder he didn't shoot you."

"It was."

"Hadn't you always been real good friends?"

"Yes. One time the team ran away with his wife and I saved her. He said that he never would forget me. So I guess that is the reason he didn't."

"That is the only reason you didn't get killed that day?"

"I imagine it was. We had been great friends always before this."

One can picture defense counsel having a great time with this story. An old man's recollection, taken down forty-four years after the event! An old man's memory, always subject to error; an old man who in the intervening lifetime had been flattered, coaxed, worked on, urged to tell his story over and over again, with the pressure always on him to tell what the local rustler faction wanted to hear and remember what they wanted him to remember. An old man who had made demonstrable mistakes as checked against his testimony at the time. He had said that the suspect he identified had worn a red-and-gray scarf over the lower part of his face; forty-four years later he said it was a handkerchief. He confused the identity of the prosecuting attorney.

But the old man's memory does not have to stand alone. For on December 12, 1891, Sheriff Red Angus had arrived in Cheyenne in charge of a couple of prisoners on the way to the pen, and he was interviewed by the Cheyenne *Sun*, the interview appearing next day, the thirteenth. The interview naturally bore down hard on the Tisdale murder and the case against Frank Canton. What evidence was there? That was when Angus let something slip, and it seems clear that it was a slip, since the warrant was not yet out.

"Basch, who almost witnessed the murder of Tisdale, was within less than a hundred feet of the killer after the shooting," said Angus.

Not fifty or sixty yards but less than a hundred feet, established publicly eleven days after the murder. At that distance even a modern nearsighted bookworm can identify anybody, especially a man he has known for nine years; and the men who rode the range every day were not nearsighted; they had almost telescopic vision. This one little line in a long-forgotten newspaper story is what clinches the case.

Months later, in the spring of 1892, after the invasion excitement was beginning to subside slightly, but while the invaders including Frank Canton were still in jail, an indictment against Frank Canton for murder in the first degree in the Tisdale case was found, Case Number 210 in the Criminal Appearance Docket of the District Court, Johnson County, State of Wyoming. A motion for change of venue was entered on October 4, and the motion was granted November 1, change being to Uinta County in the remotest southwest corner of the state. Letters to the court clerk in the county seat of Uinta County obtained no response and the writer was never able to learn the exact date and nature of the disposition of the case. It seems clear, however, that it was dismissed.

It would have been worth any amount of money to a large number of influential people in Wyoming to see that the Frank Canton murder case, especially with its implications of other men involved, never came to trial, and it never did.

There was a reign of terror in Johnson County, but it was not the same as the one so graphically pictured by the Cheyenne propaganda machine. The country people who lived in the foothills and up at the head of the forks of Powder River went about literally in fear for their lives, not knowing who would be next but convinced in their own minds, every mother's son of them, that they had not seen the end to this business. They were afraid to travel on the roads because the roads dipped into gulches, but instead followed the tops of the divides where they could see before and behind them. They loaded themselves with everything they possessed that could shoot, powerless though weapons had been to save either Jones or Tisdale.

The Cheyenne propaganda machine had a name for this state of affairs. It was "murderous rustlers going armed to the teeth."

Roundup scene. The riders in the foreground are getting ready to cut out cattle from the main herd.

Moreton Frewen.

The Cheyenne Club.

Main Street, Buffalo, Wyoming, about 1884. New courthouse appears in background.

Ella Watson, the woman remembered as "Cattle Kate," who was hanged by cattlemen in 1889.

Frank Canton with his favorite horse.

The only known photo of Nate Champion in existence, at the right. At the left, his twin brother Dudley Champion, who was shot dead by Mike Shonsey, one of the invaders, after the prisoners were released. Al Allison, brother of John A. Tisdale, is in the middle.

Gulch where John A. Tisdale was murdered on December 1, 1891.

"THE INVADERS"
JOHNSON COUNTY CATTLE WAR TAKEN AT F♭. D.A. RUSSELL
(FRANCIS E. WARREN) MAY 4ᵗʰ 1892

No 1 TOM SMITH
2 A.B. CLARKE
3 JN. LESLIE
4 FR. WHITCOMB
5 D. BROOKS
6 W.B. WALLACE
7 CHAS FORD

No 8 C.R. POWERS
9 A.D. ADAMSON
10 C.A. CAMPBELL
11 FRANK LABERTEAUX
12 PHIL DUFRAN
13 FRANK WOLCOTT
14 W.E. GUTHRIE

No 15 W.C. IRVINE
16 BOB TISDALE
17 JOE ELLIOTT
18 JOHN TISDALE
19 SCOTT DAVIS
20 FRED DE BILLIER
21 BEN MORRISON

No 22 W.J.C. KANE
23 L.H. PARKER
24 TESCHMACHER
25 B.C. SCHULZE
26 W.H. TABOR
27 J.A. GARRETT
28 W.A. WILSON

No 29 J. HARLI
30 M.A. MC NA
31 MIKE S
32 DICK AL
33 FRED HES
34 FRANK CA
35 WM LITT

ABOVE. A. S. Mercer after he shaved off the famous beard which had distinguished him most of his life. The transformation occurred at about the time he wrote the "Banditti."

NE 16 JEFF WYATT
27 BOB BARLING
38 B. SUTHERLAND
39 BUCK GARRETT
40 G.R. TUCKER
41 J.M. BENFORD
42 WILL ARMSTRONG

Some of the invaders at Fort Russell after they were taken prisoner.

The KC ranch barn soon after Champion's death.

The TA ranch house as the cattlemen left it after their rescue by federal troops.

TWENTY-FIVE

Banquo's Ghost
and Other Omens

In 1890 two fast operators bearing the alliterative names of William Kingen and Kinch McKinney were making a good thing out of interstate cattle-stealing between Nebraska and Wyoming at the head of a dozen-member gang. At the end of the same year they had the book thrown at them in the first district court in Cheyenne (where the Horse Shoe cases had been laughed out of court just three years before), drawing stiff sentences of eight years apiece. These convictions ought to have encouraged the cattlemen and eased the tightening tensions, but nothing of the sort happened, for the tensions were now concentrated in Wyoming north of the Platte and east of a line running roughly down the center of the state.

All through the fall of 1891 the hue and cry over stealing on the range increased. The Cheyenne *Leader* lamented the loss to the state of "several important herds," which had been driven out by rustler depredations or were about to be driven out, to Montana or Nebraska, "where safety is assured." The worst "infected area," as the cattlemen called it, was defined as the counties of Johnson, Converse, and Natrona.[1] All three counties were marked by very bad relations between their leading stockmen and the rest of the population.

Yet Oelrichs, South Dakota, a short distance across the Wyoming line, exulted at the end of November 1891 that "the cattle stealing business in this part of the state has practically come to a close," with three local ranchmen sentenced to prison and more convictions expected. About a week later a dispatch from Deadwood reported "two noted cattle and horse thieves" shot by cowboys with the comment "This makes four thieves shot within seventy-five miles of here lately." Evidently South

Dakota stockowners were not afraid to pull a gun in defense of their rights and had cowpunchers who would back them up. As far away as Texas it was noted that by the early nineties "juries and judges are getting so incredulous that the boys have been having considerable trouble to explain their mistakes, and the consequence is that many of them have been sent east [the state penitentiary in east Texas] to work under the supervision of the state." [2]

One of the most vocal sufferers was John Durbin of Natrona County, who said he was being forced to close out a three-quarter-million-dollar business and move to Montana because of the depredations on his herds; the annual loss to the state—so the press lamented—would be $3,000 in taxes plus the local business done by the firm. This was a symptom of direst import for the state and its economy, and the editorial writers tore their hair. [3] Mr. Durbin of course had been one of the stockmen prominently identified with the hanging of the Watson woman and James Averell only two years before, and he said he was being stolen blind. Oddly enough the editorial writers never noticed the connection.

After the December murders of Tisdale and Jones the tensions increased a thousandfold. A spate of articles began reaching the press of the nation, denouncing what was referred to as the "reign of terror" in Johnson County. This newspaper reign of terror had nothing to do with the terror of people whose neighbors had been shot in the back and who feared that the same thing might happen to them. No overt acts—as distinct from the case of two very dead men—had been performed. But since public opinion held the stockmen responsible for the double dry-gulching, it was obvious that some sort of a propaganda backfire was necessary in order to divert attention from the crimes already committed and to soften the public's mind in preparation for coming events. The publicity machine which had laid down such a swift and effective smoke screen over the hanging of Ella Watson and Jim Averell now sprang back into action with the time-honored diversionary technique of denouncing your opponent for the same crimes you have committed or are planning to commit yourself—"those Jews attacked me." A rash of releases, under the usual Cheyenne dateline, appeared in the eastern press.

"The rustlers have begun the naming of cowmen who are to be put to death," cried the Washington *Star* early in January 1892, a date when the cowmen's own plans for wholesale liquidation were well advanced. The Chicago *Herald* chilled the blood of its readers by telling of "the most outrageous assaults on honest employees that refused affiliation with [the rustlers] and who in many cases were shot down in cold blood for remaining faithful to their trust."

Yes, but who? When? Where? No names are mentioned, but for years after the invasion its apologists kept reiterating the same childishly transparent charges. Dr. Charles Bingham Penrose of Philadelphia, writing his reminiscences, spoke of rustlers who "killed men who interfered with them," who drove out by threats and sometimes by assassination the inspectors and agents of the cattlemen." W. E. Guthrie, who took part in the invasion, repeated the same woolly allegations; by the winter of 1891–1892, he said, "several" innocent men "had already been assassinated." [4]

But does anyone suppose that if a cattleman or "faithful" employee had thus been assassinated, the cattlemen's press would have overlooked it? In fact, not a scrap of evidence exists to show that a single cattleman, or "inspector" or "agent" of the cattlemen had so much as a hair of his head harmed by "rustlers" prior to the invasion.[*]

In the summer of 1891 George Henderson, manager of John Clay's Seventy-One Quarter Circle ranch on the Sweetwater, already mentioned in connection with the Averell–Watson hanging, was shot and killed, and in his book *My Life on the Range,* Clay states that he was killed by "a rustler." This is a flat falsehood. Henderson was killed by John Tregoning, alias Smith, a disgruntled ex-employee he had fired for unsatisfactory work, in a quarrel over severance pay. Clay could scarcely have been the victim of an honest mistake, since the facts of the Henderson killing were thoroughly aired at Tregoning's trial, in sworn testimony which was reported to the tune of column after column in the Cheyenne press. Tregoning was convicted of second-degree murder and received a life sentence.[5]

The newly formed Northern Wyoming Farmers' and Stockgrowers' Association had attracted little attention at first, but after the December murders it became a leading target of propaganda attacks. It had been active—expanding its program, holding meetings which were announced in the press in advance, and to which the public, including the ladies of the community, were invited. Now there was a furor about the supposed sinister motives of this "secret" organization. On or about December 11 a story emanating from Cheyenne proclaimed that after one of the "secret" meetings "it was declared on the streets that H. B. Ijams, W. C. Irvine, Fred Hesse, Frank Wolcott and three or four others who had resisted the rustlers should be killed." It was a textbook case of paranoid projection, since nobody was planning assassination but the parties named.[6] It was Banquo's ghost all over again; the greenish transparent specter at the

---

[*] A gentleman who served for many years as secretary of the Wyoming Stock Growers' Association told the writer that no inspector or detective employed by them had ever suffered bodily harm in line of duty.

feast, filling the seat at the head of the board, wearing the gruesome aspect of John A. Tisdale, fallen back dead on his load of Christmas toys, or of Ranger Jones with the grimace of death on his face, his blood-matted hair frozen to the buggy seat.

By the beginning of the year the "reign of terror" in Johnson County was horrifying good citizens in all parts of the United States, and the coming "campaign of extermination" was being all but openly talked of. An article in the Billings *Gazette* on March 10 forecast the invasion, now less than a month away, with the words: "The opening of spring may be more red than green for the horse thieves and cattle thieves of Wyoming."

All this aroused Joe DeBarthe to a peak of editorial eloquence and fury. On April 7, the following editorial with its overtones of *Macbeth* appeared in the *Bulletin.*

Certain paid lickspittles who claim to represent all the virtue and honesty in Johnson County have been writing lies to the outside world about the thieves in this locality. No man who has not sanctioned murder has escaped the calumnies of these vipers. They have even written notes of warning to each other, taken them down to Cheyenne and cried: "See what I received through the mails." . . .

The reign of terror they yell about raged in their own breasts. The only thing they had to fear were the ghosts of the men who had been murdered. And this fear grew to such proportions that they saw daggers in the eyes of every man who was not numbered in their coterie, and they have left the country.

Two days after the editorial appeared Nate Champion and Nick Ray were surrounded and met their death.

5

"An Insurrection
in Wyoming"
1892

An insurrection exists in Johnson County, in the state of Wyoming, in the immediate vicinity of Fort McKinney, against the government of said state.... I apply to you on behalf of the state of Wyoming to direct the United States troops at Fort McKinney to assist in suppressing the insurrection.

—TELEGRAM FROM AMOS W. BARBER, ACTING GOVERNOR OF WYOMING, TO PRESIDENT BENJAMIN HARRISON, APRIL 12, 1892

A WHO'S WHO
OF THE INVASION

All those listed below, except where otherwise indicated, surrendered to federal troops at the TA ranch and were later transferred to the state penitentiary at Laramie, pending trial on first degree murder charges.

I. THE CATTLEMEN

ADAMSON, A. D.   Manager of the Ferguson Land and Cattle Company in southern Wyoming.

ALLEN, RICHARD M.   Assistant manager of the Standard Cattle Company, range in southern Wyoming; address Cheyenne.

CAMPBELL, C. A.   Converse County rancher (central Wyoming); had financial interests and was an intimate of John Clay. Canadian-born. Residence Cheyenne.

CLARKE, ARTHUR B.   Rancher in Laramie County, southern Wyoming. Address not given but probably Cheyenne.

CLARKE, W. J.   Water Commissioner for Johnson County. A newspaper comment at the time the invaders were put under arrest stated that "he had no enemies in Johnson County, no wrongs to right and no old scores to settle." He had been a roundup foreman in 1885. Probably drawn in through his membership on the executive committee.

DAVIS, H. W.   Known inevitably as "Hard Winter." Owner of a ranch at the mouth of Salt Creek on Powder River. "Hard Winter" deserted the invaders at Tisdales' when the decision to surround the KC and kill Champion was taken.

DE BILLIER, FREDERIC O.   Partner of Hubert E. Teschemacher, in their Duck Bar ranch on the Platte, in southeast central Wyoming. He was

185

a New Yorker and a Harvard man. Residence Cheyenne.

FORD, CHARLES   Foreman or resident manager of Dr. Harris' TA ranch about twenty miles south of Buffalo.

GUTHRIE, W. E.   Prominent ranchman, member of the legislature, partner in the Guthrie and Oskamp Cattle Company with a range on LaBonte Creek in Converse County, east central Wyoming. A longtime employer of Mike Shonsey, who had recently taken other employment.

HESSE, FRED G. S.   Manager of the 76 remnant and owner of the 28 ranch, both on Crazy Woman Creek, near Buffalo.

IRVINE, WILLIAM C.   Organizer and manager of the Converse Cattle Company and the Ogalalla Land and Cattle Company, both very large concerns; a director of corporations, including the Cheyenne and Northern Railroad, which later became the Chicago, Burlington and Quincy; member of the state Livestock Commission at the time of the invasion. His ranching interests were east of Powder River, in the Antelope Creek and Cheyenne River country.

A Pennsylvanian, he branded a keystone in honor of his native state.

LABERTEAUX, F. H.   Foreman and resident manager of Chicagoan Henry Blair's Hoe ranch on lower Powder River.

PARKER, LAFAYETTE H.   Manager of the Murphy Cattle Company on Piney Creek, north of Buffalo.

POWERS, A. R.   Manager and partner, Powers-Wilder Cattle Company, range on Crazy Woman Creek and Powder River. No further information, except that the company was an old one going back at least to 1884. Since he rode on the roundup as his own foreman, the outfit must have been relatively small.

SUTHERLAND, S. Brother-in-law of Fred Hesse. Like Phil DuFran he joined the invaders when they reached the TA, was taken prisoner with the rest, and released because there were no charges against either.

TESCHEMACHER, HUBERT E. Partner with Frederic O. de Billier in the half-million-dollar ranching enterprise at Bridger's Ferry on the North Platte; one of the most influential men in Wyoming from his arrival in 1879 until his departure after the invasion. He served the longest term on record as member of the executive committee of the Wyoming Stock Growers' Association, 1883–1892.

The son of a California Argonaut of Swiss descent, he was a Harvard graduate; wealthy and widely traveled. After leaving Wyoming following the invasion he gave the Somerset Club of Boston as his permanent address.

TISDALE, D. R. Known as Bob or Rob, brother of John N. Tisdale. Ranch on Willow Creek, a branch of the South Fork.

TISDALE, JOHN N. A state senator in the first state legislative assembly, 1890–1891, was criticized subsequently for holding onto his seat after selling out his Powder River holdings to his brother and moving to Salt Lake City. He returned to Wyoming to take part in the invasion.

WALLACE, W. B. A young Englishman then ranching or visiting in Colorado, who met Van Tassel when the latter was buying horses for the invasion near Longmont. Little else is known about him.

WHITCOMB, ELIAS W. The oldest of the invaders, known as "Pappy." He was also the only genuine pioneer among them, having come west in 1857. He worked for many years for the famous freighting firm of Russell, Majors and Waddell. He lived in Cheyenne and his range was on Hat Creek.

WOLCOTT, MAJOR FRANK   Manager of the VR ranch owned by the Tolland Company, Scottish, on a tributary of the North Platte in Converse County. A Kentuckian who had served on the Union side in the Civil War, and an old-time territorial official.

II. DETECTIVES AND OTHER EMPLOYEES

CANTON, FRANK M.   Residence Buffalo.

DAVIS, SCOTT   Nicknamed "Quick Shot." Formerly a captain of the shotgun messengers guarding gold shipments on the Cheyenne–Deadwood stage line, he served as detective-inspector for the Wyoming Stock Growers' Association 1890–1895, and was latterly known as W. C. Irvine's bodyguard.

DUFRAN, PHIL   An Association detective operating in Johnson County. He was taken prisoner with the rest, but as there were no charges against him he was released.

Previously served as foreman for Horace Plunkett and as roundup foreman; still earlier he had been mixed up in the settler-cattleman troubles in Nebraska, on the cattlemen's side.

ELLIOTT, JOE   Association detective and stock inspector serving northeastern Wyoming, around Newcastle and Gillette.

His name was mentioned in connection with the Waggoner hanging, and at the time of the invasion he was out on bail for the assault on Nate Champion.

MORRISON, B. M. (BEN)   Longtime Association detective.

SHONSEY (OR SHAUNSEY), MIKE Of Canadian-Irish extraction, he came to Wyoming from Ohio. He worked for several outfits as foreman over a period of years.

TABOR, W. H. Stock detective.

III. THE MERCENARIES

The following were recruited in Texas, in the vicinity of Paris, Lamar County:

ARMSTRONG, WILLIAM
BARLINGS, J.
BENFORD (or BEUFORD), J. M.
BROOKS, D. Also known as the Texas Kid, the youthful sharpshooter who was accorded the honor of killing Nick Ray.
DUDLEY, JIM, alias GUS GREEN. Died of wounds at Fort McKinney.
GARRETT, BUCK
GARRETT, J. A.
HAMILTON, ALEX
JOHNSON, J. C.
LITTLE, WILLIAM
LOWTHER, ALEX. Died of wounds at Fort McKinney.
MCNALLEY, H. C.
MARTIN, BOB (? PENROSE?)
MYNETT, J. D.
PICKARD (or RICKARD), K.
SCHULTZE, B.
SMITH, TOM. Leader and recruiter of Texans.
TUCKER, D. S.
TUCKER, GEORGE R.
WILLEY, B.
WILSON, W. A.

DUNNING, GEORGE. Recruited in Idaho.

IV. THE CIVILIANS

Three teamsters: William Collum, George Helm, and Charles Austin. Not present during the killing of Champion and Ray; not implicated and not taken prisoner.

Two newspaper correspondents: Sam T. Clover of the Chicago *Herald* and Ed Towse of the Cheyenne *Sun*.

One surgeon: Dr. Charles Bingham Penrose of Philadelphia.

TWENTY-SIX

The Willful Men

WYOMING IN 1892 was no longer a frontier, except for a few picturesque embellishments and some habits of mind. It was a state—modern, laced with railroads and telegraph lines. In Wyoming the decade from 1885 to 1895 was part of the same decade everywhere else. The glorious equality of man and man under western skies was not exactly a myth, but it was circumscribed by the same harsh realities which prevailed in the country as a whole.

In the industrial East it was a decade of ferocious class hatreds and savage industrial strife. It was the decade of the Haymarket riot and the Pullman strike and the two Homestead strikes. It was a decade when the ten- or twelve-hour day and the six- or seven-day week prevailed in many industries, and public opinion, in the press and in the drawing room, condemned the "conspiracy of labor."

Such was the national background of the Johnson County war.

During 1891 "an expedition of some kind" was decided upon. The words are those of W. C. Irvine, who with Major Frank Wolcott was one of its most active leaders. The excuse later offered, that its purpose was to forestall the illegal "rustlers' roundup" by serving warrants on the rustlers, was an afterthought which does not accord with the timing nor with any other known facts. For on July 4, when Major Wolcott told John Clay of the projected march into northern Wyoming, the "rustlers' roundup" had not only not been thought of but the very organization which was to plan it, the Northern Wyoming Farmers' and Stockgrowers' Association, was not yet born.

The planning was done by what opposition newspapers called "the

Cheyenne ring"—the little group of wealthy insiders who dominated the
Wyoming Stock Growers' Association, the cattle business, and, for the
most part, the politics and government of the state. The ringleaders without exception belonged to the little coterie of early comers who had been
running the affairs of Wyoming since the dawn of the beef bonanza in
1879, and before. "Lords" could come and go—even Tom Sturgis came
and went—but this little handful of early birds, the Old Guard of Wyoming politics, had fairly well kept the reins of power in their hands during
the whole period, and even the failure of the invasion only momentarily
loosened their grip. The incredible project of marching an army through a
peaceful countryside to shoot, hang, and burn was planned and financed
by this group. Of those who took personal part at least eight had been in
Wyoming since 1879 or earlier, while nine served on the executive committee of the Wyoming Stock Growers' Association either during, before,
or immediately after the invasion.[1]

It is not necessary to resort to avowed enemies of the cattlemen to
hear evidence as to the nature and purposes of their project or find out
who was involved, since the appalling facts stand starkly revealed in their
own words and those of their friends. With rare exceptions we have used
only such evidence as is furnished by themselves. An important source is
Dr. Charles Bingham Penrose, wellborn Philadelphian and a close friend
of Governor Barber, who started out with the "expedition" in the capacity
of surgeon but fled before the shooting started. Some twenty years later
he wrote his own version of the affair with the assistance of long, detailed
letters from W. C. Irvine.[2] Another source is John Clay, Jr., who was not
personally present on the invasion but who knew all about it, including its
cost in one hundred thousand 1892 dollars before it was finished, and who
pulled remarkably few punches in discussing it.

A third authority speaking from the invader side is Robert B. David,
whose book entitled *Malcolm Campbell, Sheriff*, published in 1932, is the
second full-scale history of the Johnson County affair, coming out thirty-
eight years after Mercer's *Banditti*, but from the opposite point of view,
the cattlemen's. Mr. David is the son of Edward David, manager for
Senator Carey in 1892, who played an important role in the invasion
preparations, and he obtained information from the only two members of
the cattlemen's party who were surviving when he wrote, Mike Shonsey
and W. E. Guthrie. It would seem that what he says about the invasion
planning may be taken as authentic.

In January R. S. Van Tassel of Cheyenne, one of the inner ring of
sooners who had long ruled the affairs of the Association, was sent to
Colorado to buy horses for the expeditionary force, a move made to
bypass the questions which would certainly be asked if any Wyoming

ranch owners started working their horses so early in the year. Tom Smith, a stock detective, was sent to his native Texas to recruit gunfighters. In Paris, Lamar County, he had no trouble picking up twenty-two fast guns who were told that they were to serve warrants on a gang of dangerous outlaws. There never were any warrants, but the Texans found that out later. The pay was $5 a day with expenses, plus a $50 bonus for each man killed, and they accepted readily.

The transaction violated Section 1, Article XIX, of the infant state's constitution, which read:

No armed police force, or detective agency, or armed body of men, shall ever be brought into this state for the suppression of domestic violence, except upon the application of the legislature, or of the executive when the legislature cannot be convened.

Strangely enough, in a part of the country nurtured on violence and only just awakening to law, this particular violation shocked public opinion as mere killing had never done. It was even remarked that Hubert E. Teschemacher of the invaders' party, who had sat in the state constitutional convention, ought to have known what was in the constitution, since he helped write it.

The garrulous H. B. Ijams, successor to Thomas B. Adams as secretary of the Wyoming Stock Growers' Association, went on a recruiting mission of his own to Idaho, but after a good deal of talking around he obtained only one volunteer, a tough young man named George Dunning. He might better have stayed at home. George Dunning, who had had skirmishes with big stockmen in his own Owyhee County, accepted the offer with the privately avowed purpose of warning the rustlers if possible, and of dealing the stockmen invaders all the grief he could. He succeeded notably well.

Otherwise no detail was overlooked. Arrangements were made with railroad officials to move a special train carrying fifty armed men and a heavy load of munitions from Cheyenne to Casper, whence the party would set out to liquidate all the rustlers in northern Wyoming along with their local supporters. There was no pretense as to the purpose of the train. One official of a minor connecting line threw up his hands. "Gentlemen, gentlemen," he exclaimed, "this railroad will have nothing to do with an expedition of this kind, nor will I, and my advice to you gentlemen is to drop it." He was Horace G. Burt, later president of the Union Pacific for seven years.

His intransigence made the cattlemen very angry. They had no trouble perfecting their arrangements with other rail executives, however, including those then in charge of the UP.[3]

Another step taken in advance was to tie up the state militia so as to prevent local authorities from calling it to their aid against the invaders. Wyoming law provided that in case of civil disturbance a call for the national guard might be issued by county sheriffs and other local officials if the legislature or the governor did not act. But on March 23, 1892, Adjutant General Frank Stitzer of the Wyoming National Guard issued General Order No. 4 to Colonel DeForest Richards, commanding the First Regiment of Infantry, to instruct his company commanders that "they shall obey only such orders to assemble their commands as shall be received from these headquarters, to assist the civil authorities in the preservation or enforcement of the laws of the state of Wyoming." The adjutant general was of course under direct orders from the then chief executive, Acting Governor Amos W. Barber.° Seventeen days later, when Sheriff Angus of Johnson County tried to call out the local militia company to halt the invaders, he was stopped by this order as intended.⁴

That planning of such a scope could only have taken place on a very high level is obvious on its face; that many if not most of the leading men of the state were mixed up in it was charged at the time. The charges were denied with passion, almost with panic during the summer of 1892, which was an election year, but evidence coming to light since has confirmed most of them. John Clay named Ijams (secretary of the Wyoming Stock Growers' Association), former territorial governor George W. Baxter, and of course Wolcott as among the leading planners. He added: "They were backed by every large cattleman in the state and behind them they had the moral influence of the two senators, Warren and Carey."

Dr. Penrose wrote twenty years later: "Governor Barber knew all about the expedition and he advised me to go on it." . . . "Willis Van-Devanter, who had been Chief Justice of the Supreme Court of Wyoming 1889–90, and was appointed by Taft Associate Justice of the Supreme Court of the United States in 1910, knew all about it. . . . I had at least one interview with Barber and VanDevanter before going on the expedition, and we talked the matter over and either Barber or VanDevanter (I think the latter) gave me a telegraphic code by which to communicate with them if I found it advisable to do so on the trip. This code I tore up and threw into the Platte River on my way to Douglas."⁵

The invaders planned to kill a considerable number of men in northern Wyoming, but there are differing versions as to how many. W. C. Irvine wrote Dr. Penrose: "We had the record of every man we intended

---

° Barber, a physician and a Pennsylvanian, as secretary of state, succeeded under the law to the governorship when his predecessor, Francis E. Warren, became one of the first United States senators from Wyoming in 1890.

to kill or drive from the country. We have never tried to deny that, and I for one have never had the slightest regret, or made the slightest apology for my part in it." Penrose placed the number of intended victims at nineteen. George Dunning placed it at thirty in Johnson County, with additional victims to be finished off by small squads of regulators on visits to other counties. A widely accepted story tells of a death list of seventy, including the sheriff and deputies and all three county commissioners. This was a piece of strategy as old as Rome; get rid of the leaders and the populace will give up. According to a letter from Buffalo which was written in the midst of the excitement, the list, found in Frank Canton's suitcase, also contained the names of townspeople, including merchant Robert Foote and editor Joe DeBarthe.[6]

The most explicit account of the plans in all their spine-chilling cold-bloodness appears in David's history of the invasion:

> The records of the suspects were considered carefully by all the cattlemen at the meeting, lest innocent men be included in the number of the doomed.... Every man was weighed, and when the list was finally completed of men of whom there was no doubt of guilt the number stood at an even seventy.
>
> It was then decided that these must be exterminated, either by shooting or hanging, and that the best manner of reaching these seventy men was by undertaking a quick invasion, conducted with all secrecy up through the Powder River country to Johnson County first, where the sheriff, W. G. Angus, would be eliminated together with the three county commissioners, so that a proper set of officials could be put in their places.
>
> Then the invaders planned to swing south and east, down through Converse County then west through Natrona, ridding the country of those on the list as they proceeded.[7]

The intention of the planners was to march to Buffalo, seize the courthouse and the arms of the militia stored there, and then proceed with their gruesome work. Massive reinforcements had been promised from sympathizers in and around Buffalo to help them take the town, but they never showed, and when the invaders fell into serious trouble their frantic calls for help went unheeded. There is a story in Struthers Burt's *Powder River* about a local cowman, not named, who had not wanted to offend his friends in Cheyenne by refusing the wagons and men they had asked for. But when the time came an extraordinary thing happened; a crew of experienced cowhands mislaid every one of their horses on the vast starlit plains one night, even to the wrangling horse, and the outfit was plumb afoot until the invasion was over.[8]

The final step in the preparations was cutting the telegraph line so that Johnson County would be cut off from the outside world while the work of assassination was being carried out. Senator Carey's manager Ed David was put in charge of the line cutting. The method was to cut the wire between two poles, hitch one end to a saddle horn and drag it two or three miles into the hills. David had been counted on to go along on the expedition, but when the time came he backed out, pleading his wife and children as an excuse, to the disappointment and wrath of the invaders. They would have liked Senator Carey's man to lend prestige to the party. But suspicion lingered that while the canny Senator was willing to help his friends up to a point, he did not want to go so far as to risk his political future; hence was quite willing to heed the tearful pleas of Mrs. David and tell her husband to stay home.

Never at any time did the willful men entertain the thought that their scheme might fail. Soaked in their own wishful thinking, they had convinced themselves that no "honest men" opposed their cause unless through intimidation by the rustlers. "The sympathies of nine-tenths of the people of Wyoming are with the cattle growers," boasted one of the ringleaders in Denver on April 12 when, unknown to him, his party was already in desperate straits. The day before Ijams had boasted that "the rustlers cannot muster as many men by far as our party will have in the field very soon." Just where this expected army of reinforcements was to come from is not clear, but there were rumors of pressure being applied in Washington to have a large number of deputy U.S. marshals ordered into the fray.[9]

The leaders anticipated no opposition. Their only fear was that the rustlers would fly to the mountains, and that some marked for "severe treatment," as it was politely put, might escape.

TWENTY-SEVEN

The Secret Special

THE FAMOUS train, the "secret," "mysterious" invasion special, got away from Cheyenne in the late afternoon of Tuesday, April 5, 1892, amid a flurry of rumor and speculation. While the leaders congratulated themselves that their preparations had gone unobserved, the train's departure was undoubtedly one of the worst-kept secrets in the history of the West.

Early Tuesday afternoon the regular train had come in from Denver carrying a special Pullman car with all the blinds down. Inside were the twenty-two Texas gunfighters and Major Frank Wolcott, who had gone to Denver to fetch them and was to be the commander in the field. If the stockmen had wanted to attract the attention of every yardman and station loafer in Denver and Cheyenne, that car with the blinds down was the way to do it; and in fact news of its departure reached Cheyenne by wire about as soon as the train itself. One bystander was so persistent in his questioning that he wormed out of the stationmaster something approaching the truth. He tried to send a telegram of warning to Angus, but the wires were cut by that time. He then wrote a letter, which did not reach Angus until Friday.

After the annual stock meeting adjourned, the members of the expedition sauntered down by twos and threes to the railroad yard, where the special train was by now made up and waiting. The horses were loaded in three stock cars, three brand-new Studebaker wagons were attached to a flatcar, the baggage was stowed in a fifth car, and the Pullman carrying the passengers made a train of six cars in all. "About five-thirty we pulled out," Dr. Penrose wrote twenty years later, "none but the initiated knowing that such an expedition had left Cheyenne." For days the bustle of preparation had been going on in the yards, with branding of horses, stowing of gear and loading of wagons, while uptown the gun store favored with the patronage of the Stock Association members had been doing a land-office business. It is hard to see how any full-grown citizen could have failed to note that something unusual was up, but the doctor's remark was typical of the self-deception which enfolded the venture from the first.

Fifty-two men were on the train. Nineteen were cattlemen, including the owners or managers of six large outfits in Johnson County; five were stock detectives, Frank Canton among them; and twenty-two were hired gun-fighters, all from Texas with the exception of George Dunning of Idaho. There were also six noncombatants on board—Dr. Penrose, three teamsters and, believe it or not, two newspaper correspondents, one of them being Sam T. Clover of the Chicago *Herald*. Acting on the tip received in Chicago, Clover had turned up in Cheyenne armed with a letter of introduction from Henry A. Blair, the Chicago tycoon who owned the Hoe ranch on Powder River, and whose manager was a member of the expedition. Although suspected at first of being a spy, Sam was glib enough to parlay himself without much trouble into an invitation to join the party, by using the time-honored newsman's pitch: "I will see that your side of the story reaches the public." He was a bit put out at first to find that another newspaperman had been included, the second correspondent being Ed Towse of "Cattle Kate" fame, now city editor of the Cheyenne *Sun*. But Sam need not have worried over the loss of his precious exclusive, for poor Ed Towse didn't last long.[1]

The train was to go as far as Casper, a hundred and fifty miles northwest of Cheyenne, then the party would proceed overland on horseback. As it jolted on its sleepless way that night dissension broke out. Major Wolcott was at work stowing gear in the baggage car when Frank Canton came in and the peppery major ordered him out. Whatever one may think of Frank Canton, he was not a man to be ordered around. Wolcott had been chosen as commander of the expedition for no visible reason except his military title and experience thirty years earlier and perhaps for the violence of his opinions. He was temperamentally unfit to lead men, and his stubbornness and bad judgment on two separate occasions doomed the expedition to failure, "for which," wrote an onlooker grimly, "they should now thank their God." It would have failed anyway, although it was armed, as David wrote, with "enough ammunition to kill all the people in the state of Wyoming."

The train arrived at the outskirts of Casper in the dark of four A.M. on April sixth. The horses were led off; each man picked his own and galloped away, except for the few who stayed behind to get the wagons off and loaded.

Around nine o'clock, while breakfast was being eaten out of sight of the town behind some hills north of the Platte, a number of saddled horses which had been loosely picketed to sagebrush broke loose and stampeded. It was several hours before they were rounded up and recovered, and well past noon before the column was on its way. Penrose's horse, he said, was among those not recovered and thereafter he rode in the wagon. By this time both he and Irvine were developing an acute dislike of Clover, whom the doctor described as "a fresh young man with a disposition to take other people's things ... he took my bridle—an unusually fine one—and never returned it." [2]

The going was awful. The wagons bogged; the horses slipped and fell repeatedly in the greasy gumbo and whitened with lather under their collars. One of the wagons broke through a bridge. In the afternoon two innocent bystanders put in their appearance. One was Bert Lambert, a line rider from a CY camp who was on his way into Casper when he was seized, placed in front of the party with a Texan on each side of him, and told not to look back on pain of instant death. At about the same time Oscar Lehman, a sheepherder, was picked up and placed in the rear. Both were freed after about three hours when each was warned to stay out of Casper until the following day, go to camp, and keep his mouth shut. Both obeyed with mad eagerness; and both headed for the camp of Oscar Lehman, where the latter had left his bride of a few months, neither knowing that the other had been made prisoner.

Lehman set out at a gallop, spurred on by fear because he had seen the other horseman heading toward his camp and feared for his wife's safety. Lambert, hearing hoofbeats behind him, thought the party had changed their minds and were sending a man to kill him. The breakneck run for camp ended in recognition and the hysterical laughter of relief. This was on the sixth.

The column plopped on its sinister way. A German sheepherder named Koch sighted it in the distance and was so scared that he left his herd of sheep and ran all the way to Casper. Two young boys had a shivery experience. Riding along in the dusk they saw on a nearby ridge, silhouetted against the afterglow, an army riding—horsemen, wagons. "The boys didn't know what this was," wrote Struthers Burt in *Powder River*, "but it looked bad to them. They waited, breathless, hidden, fortunately, by willows. Two days later they heard about the invaders." [3]

Between the bad going and cumbersome equipment—every comfort needed for men fresh from the armchairs of the Cheyenne club—the column was not making very good time. "They had tents, camp stools and mess wagons and were taking it awfully easy," one of the captives reported. That was the last word. Then for five days the sagebrush waste swallowed them up.

A cyclone of rumors swept the state. Casper, Douglas, Newcastle, and Gillette were spouting wild stories which reached the Denver, Omaha, and Chicago papers before they reached Cheyenne; only Buffalo with its cut telegraph line was silent. Casper had seen the three four-horse teams drive through the outskirts of town on the sixth and had taken them for a surveying party, but on Friday, the eighth, it wired the Chicago *Herald:* "The cattle army that left here a few days ago is one of the heaviest armed expeditions that ever passed into the Big Horn country. They have a small cannon with them and have announced their intention of carrying a war of extermination against the men they term rustlers who, however, claim to be peaceful ranchmen."

Everybody was buzzing by this time about the special train and the now-not-so-mysterious army. A cowpuncher with a good imagination saw a man hanging from an oil derrick between Casper and Tisdales' ranch. The telegraph line was still down. On Sunday the tenth rumors began flying about a big battle on Powder River. The report came from a line repairer on top of a pole who tapped out a message about a fight, but the line worked so badly that the operator in Cheyenne could make out nothing except the words "killed," "burned," and the name Flagg. Cheyenne was going slowly mad.

On the eleventh, Monday, Champion and Ray were two days dead, the cattlemen were surrounded and in mortal danger but no one knew it. Ed David, Senator Carey's manager, had received orders to cut the telegraph line and keep it cut, and he did; at the same time someone in Johnson County had discovered that two sides could play the game of wire-cutting as well as one, with a length of wire fastened to the saddle horn and dragged far out into the illimitable sage. No sooner did the line go up in one place than it went down somewhere else. In Denver ex-governor George W. Baxter and other cattlemen were still talking about what they were going to do to the rustlers. Out in the sagebrush-covered hinterland people were seeing things. Gillette talked with a stagecoach driver who had positively passed two wagonloads of dead and wounded being taken to Fort McKinney; Casper heard that twenty-eight men had been killed on one side and eighteen on the other; Gillette heard that Nate Champion and fifty men were surrounded at the TA ranch by a hundred men under Fred Hesse!

The telegraph line was working long enough—this is still the eleventh—for acting mayor Hogerson of Buffalo to get a wire through to acting governor Barber asking for troops, but since Barber didn't know yet whether his own side was winning or losing, he dragged his feet. Besides, the regular mayor, a stockmen's supporter, had fled and Mr. Hogerson, a member of the board of county commissioners, was definitely under suspicion and perhaps marked for death. By the time the governor got around to telegraphing a friend in Buffalo requesting information, the line was down again.

Also on the eleventh, Sheriff Red Angus in Buffalo got a wire out to his opposite number in Douglas, informing that official that a fight had taken place and requesting him to station guards at the Platte River bridge to arrest suspicious persons. Two terrified and bedraggled fugitives turned up in Douglas, riding fine horses, badly jaded, and stating that they had come from the scene of a battle; they were telling the truth, but naturally no one believed them. Kid Donnelly, who ran the road ranch at Powder River Crossing, reached Antelope Springs, thirty miles north of Douglas on the main traveled road to the north, with word that Nate Champion and Nick Ray had been killed; this too was true, but in all the uproar who knew what the truth was? On Tuesday, the twelfth, the Cheyenne *Sun,* sticking up to the last for the cattlemen, made disdainful reference to "stories of the silliest character" which were being circulated. One was that seventy-five *rustlers* had the *cattlemen* surrounded and that a terrible battle would soon be fought. Fancy such an absurdity!

Then the floodwaters broke. CAUGHT IN A TRAP, the *Leader* headlined on April 13. "The Invading Stockmen Regularly Besieged in a Ranch House in Johnson County." Next day followed the one word, SURRENDER.

What had happened? [4]

TWENTY-EIGHT

The Death of Nate Champion

THE INVASION army plodded along on the sixth of April toward its first destination, an overnight rest halt at the Tisdale ranch sixty-five miles north of Casper. They camped that night and had supper late. The road was still clogged with gumbo and on the second day, the seventh, it began to snow. After a noon halt still only thirty miles out of Casper, the main body left the floundering wagons and pushed on through the snow-storm to Tisdales', arriving exhausted long after dark, minus the commander of the expedition, Major Wolcott, who had gotten lost in the storm and had to sleep in a haystack. The men were told that they could rest all next day while waiting for the wagons to come up; the stockmen retired to the main house, the Texans to the bunkhouse.

It had been a mean trip in more ways than one. The quarrel which broke out on the train between Major Wolcott and Frank Canton had intensified. Tom Smith sided with Canton, and the Texans he had re-cruited followed Smith. On the morning of the second day Wolcott, in a huff, went through the motions of resigning his command, but this was a meaningless gesture.

The wagons did not reach Tisdales' until five o'clock on the afternoon of the eighth. They now had two passengers, Dr. Penrose and poor Ed Towse, who was suffering dreadfully from piles and could no longer sit on a horse.[1]

At about the time the wagons got there Mike Shonsey arrived, bringing news. He reported, according to Irvine, that fourteen or fifteen rustlers were at the KC ranch—where Nate Champion had moved his winter quarters after the attempt on his life at the Hall cabin—and Shonsey urged an immediate attack.[2] This piece of intelligence led to a

201

fresh outburst of quarreling in the party. Irvine and Wolcott were for marching at once to the KC and finishing off the rustlers they could catch then and there. Canton and Fred Hesse and the rest of the Johnson County men wanted to stick to the original plan and get on to their main objective, Buffalo. Most of the leaders were drinking heavily in the crowded, smoky room, and one at least was in an ugly mood. The Texans were becoming restless and several demanded to see the warrants they had been told they were to serve. Of course there were no warrants. A vote was taken, and the die was cast in favor of turning aside to the KC. This diversion, made at the insistence of Wolcott and Irvine, promised a day's delay and, almost inevitably, a warning to the people of Buffalo—which was just what happened.[3]

Mike Shonsey and three of the Texans were sent ahead to scout out the KC ranch * and make sure that the intended victims were still there. By midnight the main body were on the march.

Some consternation in the party followed the decision to proceed at once to the KC, as the prospect of cold-blooded slaughter, not just sometime but tomorrow morning, struck like a dash of cold reality in the face. Dr. Penrose wrote that when the army left at midnight, he was directed to stay with Ed Towse—by now completely *hors de combat*—and follow with the wagons in the morning. But when morning came he lingered on at Tisdales', and with him remained one of the cattlemen, "Hard Winter" Davis, who pleaded as an excuse that his horse was "played out" and could not go on. They were simply too frightened to move. During the day and evening of Saturday the ninth, various neighboring ranchmen turned up at Tisdales' all terrified and angry, and all armed, as the news of the killing and burning spread like a prairie fire. Some had seen the smoke as the cabin burned. Next morning, the tenth, Dr. Penrose fled with his companion, Davis, and they headed for the latter's ranch.[4]

From there the doctor continued south alone, hoping to reach Cheyenne. Posing as a Dr. Green from Fort McKinney and traveling in a buckboard, on Thursday the fourteenth he crossed the Platte River bridge at Fort Fetterman, throwing into the river as he crossed everything that might compromise or identify him, including the special telegraphic code given him by Governor Barber. In spite of these precautions he was recognized and arrested in Douglas, where a local reporter described him as "all broken up" over his arrest and incarceration. Still shaken and panicky, he told interviewers that he proposed to make a clean breast of

* The KC—one of Moreton Frewen's innumerable brands—was originally a Frewen line camp. Later it was homesteaded by a onetime wagon boss of Horace Plunkett's, Johnny Nolan.

the matter, testify fully, and throw himself on the mercy of the court. Later when a lawyer reached him he backed down and denied it. Attempts to hold him as a material witness failed, as a U.S. Marshal from Cheyenne got him out of durance on a writ of habeas corpus and restored him to his friends.⁵ Dr. Penrose devoted much time and effort in later years to justifying the events which had so horrified him at first blush. So ends an ignominious story.

Sam Clover described the miseries of that night ride to the KC "in the teeth of one of the worst gales of snow and wind that ever swept over the country. For six hours horses and men breasted the fearful storm, scarcely a word being exchanged during the entire journey.... The frozen snow beat with savage violence against the exposed faces of the men, blinding their eyes so that it was impossible to see a foot beyond their horses' heads, while beards and mustaches quickly became solid masses of snow and ice. Chilled to the marrow and stiff in every joint, the determined men yet pushed ahead and at daybreak * were within four miles of the ranch containing the thieves." Clover was so stiff he had to be lifted from his horse.

The distance from Tisdales' to the KC was fourteen or fifteen miles. The army stopped in a deep gulch four miles from their destination, where they built sagebrush fires and thawed out while waiting for the return of the scouts. Shonsey and the others came back in an hour or so to report all quiet at the cabin; in the words of George Dunning, "they said the parties were not expecting anything, and that they were playing the fiddle and having a good time generally." ⁶

After an hour or so of rest and restoring circulation, the order was given to march, and before daybreak the party had dismounted again on the river bluff half a mile south of the still-sleeping KC. When light came they looked over the bluff on a scene of countless repetitions all over the West: a cutbank stream with cottonwoods and box elders and willows marking its course, in summer the only green in sight, on a morning like this black against the snow; in the foreground was a little huddle of log buildings. Major Wolcott took charge of the deployment of forces and placed his men so as to surround the house; they were concealed in the stable, along the loop of the Middle Fork, and in the brush of a draw which came down to the river. Meanwhile the discovery of a freighter's wagon and a buckboard standing near the house threatened to disarrange the plan of attack; it was clear that the two rustlers were entertaining company, and the invaders, who thought of themselves as executioners,

* "Daybreak" is wrong. It was still some hours before daybreak when they stopped in the gulch.

were determined to kill no man they regarded as innocent. There was nothing to do but wait and see.

Whatever had happened to Mike Shonsey's original fourteen rustlers, by this time the "parties" at the KC were down to four, only two of whom were wanted—Nate Champion and Nick Ray. The other two were the innocent bystanders, Ben Jones and Bill Walker, who had chanced to stop at the KC ranch for the night. Always referred to as "the trappers," in fact they were both out-of-work roundup hands who were trapping in order to get through the winter, Bill Walker a cowhand, Jones a chuckwagon cook.

But the occupants of the house were enjoying a long winter's sleep, and for nearly two hours the besiegers lay prone with Winchesters ready, watching the cabin for signs of life; the products of eastern culture side by side with the Texas sharpshooters, sharing one aim: "the plan being," in Clover's words, "to shoot them [the rustlers] down as soon as they stepped outdoors.

"Presently an old man appeared, evidently one of the visitors who, tin bucket in hand, sauntered down to the river to get water for breakfast. He was permitted to pass the stable unmolested, but the moment he was out of sight of the house two Winchesters were pointed at him and he was ordered to make no outcry, but to keep on toward the river. Luckily for himself the old man soon satisfied the questioners that he was innocent, and he also told them that the men they were after were still in bed but that his partner, another freighter [*sic*], was already up." [7]

The "old man" was Ben Jones. After another wait of perhaps half an hour Bill Walker, his younger partner, appeared, and after he passed the stable he too was taken prisoner. Then Nick Ray came out of the house, gazing around him suspiciously. He was shot by the Texas Kid, who fired on Wolcott's order after Ray had gone ten or a dozen steps from the door. Then half a dozen Winchesters cracked simultaneously and he staggered and fell. With great effort he started crawling on hands and knees toward the house; as he reached it another shot took him in the back, and with a groan he fell forward on the doorstep. Nate Champion, who had been appearing in the door at intervals to fire at the stable, opened the door again and dragged the wounded man inside.

For an hour or two the besiegers kept pouring lead into the open windows of the house; finally, having decided that they were only wasting ammunition, they withdrew to their camp for consultation. Sam Clover meanwhile was right in the forefront; he had taken his place in one of the forward positions without asking permission from Major Wolcott, reasoning that the latter might refuse, and according to Irvine, who was bitterly hostile to the newsman, he borrowed a gun from one of the invaders and banged away with the best of them. The captive Bill Walker led all the invaders' horses down to the river to water—horses are neutral—as Walker figured that Nate Champion would recognize him and not shoot. All this while Champion was writing in a pocket notebook the record of a brave man's last hours:

Me and Nick was getting breakfast when the attack took place. Two men was with us—Bill Jones and another man. The old man went after water and did not come back. His friend went to see what was the matter and he did not come back. Nick started out and I told him to look out, that I thought there was someone at the stable would not let them come back.

Nick is shot but not dead yet. He is awful sick. I must go and wait on him.

It is now about two hours since the first shot. Nick is still alive.

They are still shooting and are all around the house. Boys, there is bullets coming in like hail.

Them fellows is in such shape I can't get at them. They are shooting from the stable and river and back of the house.

Nick is dead. He died about 9 o'clock. I see a smoke down at the stable. I think they have fired it. I don't think they intend to let me get away this time.

Meanwhile, the leaders of the war party had decided that the only practicable way to dislodge Champion was set fire to the house, so they sent some men to George Baxter's Western Union Beef Company ranch a few miles away for a load of hay. The men came back two hours later to report that no hay was to be had, and another council of war was held. Champion was still writing:

It is now about noon. There is someone at the stable yet. They are throwing a rope at the door and dragging it back. I guess it is to draw me out. I wish that duck would go further so I can get a shot at him.

Boys, I don't know what they have done with them two fellows that stayed here last night.

Boys, I feel pretty lonesome just now. I wish there was someone here with me so we could watch all sides at once. They may fool around until I get a good shot before they leave.

The leaders, still undecided, resting and some of them snoozing, had called in their pickets who were watching the road above and below the house. Apparently no clear-cut orders had been issued about stopping chance visitors, but there were still men behind the stable and around the house to guard against Champion's escape. It was now about half past two in the afternoon.

A few hours earlier Jack Flagg had left his Red Fork ranch eighteen miles west of the KC, on his way to the Democratic state convention at Douglas to which he was a delegate. Accompanying him was his seventeen-year-old stepson, Alonzo Taylor, driving a team of horses hitched to the running gears of a wagon on which were Flagg's suitcase and a rifle with three bullets in it. He had no inkling of trouble as he rode along, black hat settled over his brows, with slack reins and a busy mind, while the quick-footed sorrel stepped along over the frozen ruts at the effortless, mile-eating cow-horse gait. Because of the lull there was no sound of firing to warn him as he came abreast of the KC; the team and wagon were fifty yards ahead of him by this time. Then suddenly all hell broke loose, and as usual there is no agreement as to just what happened except that Flagg was not recognized at first.

According to one version Flagg took the armed men lounging about for friendly cowboys and when one of them called "Halt" cried: "Don't shoot me, boys—I'm all right," taking it for a joke. All at once there was a yell of "Jack Flagg! Jack Flagg!" and Charlie Ford, foreman of the TA, fired a Winchester at him and missed. The boy had already whipped up his team and sped on to the bridge. Under a hail of bullets Flagg, in his own words, "threw myself on the side of my horse and made a run for it," caught up with the wagon, seized his rifle, and stood off seven pursuing horsemen while the boy cut one of the team loose and mounted. Then he and the lad made their miraculous escape.[8]

Nate Champion was still writing in his notebook:

It is about 3 o'clock now. There was a man in a buckboard and one on horseback just passed. They fired on them as they went by. I don't know if they killed them or not. I seen lots of men come out on horses on the other side of the river and take after them.

I shot at a man in the stable just now. Don't know if I got him or not. I must go look out again. It don't look as if there is much show of my getting away. I see twelve or fifteen men. One looks like [name scratched out]. I don't know whether it is or not. I hope they did not catch them fellows that run over the bridge toward Smith's.

The invaders were chagrined and infuriated by Jack Flagg's escape, knowing that he would spread the alarm through the countryside. They did not know that the warning was already out, since a neighboring rancher named Terence Smith had heard the firing that morning and, looking down from the high ground north of the river, had seen enough to send him on a Paul Revere's ride for help. Once again the invaders were faced with a decision—whether to get on at once to their main objective, Buffalo, before the whole country could be aroused. Once again an argument broke out in the party; and once again it was the obstinacy of Major Wolcott, who insisted: "No, we will do one thing at a time, we will finish this fellow first," which prevailed and doomed the expedition to failure.[9]

The wagon left behind by Jack Flagg in his flight was now put to use to seal Champion's doom. The invaders chopped up some pitch-pine posts which were around the hay corral and what little old hay could be scraped up was added, until the load was piled high enough to protect the men who were to push the wagon against the house on the river side. Six men volunteered to back it against one of the windows, and while this was going on a hail of bullets was poured in at the windows to keep Champion from firing back at the attacking party. Once the combustible load was lodged against the house the attackers sprinted back to cover, while the wind from the river drove the flames through the open window.

Champion had kept on writing:

They are shooting at the house now. If I had a pair of glasses I believe I would know some of those men. They are coming back. I've got to look out.
Well, they have just got through shelling the house again like hail. I heard them splitting wood. I guess they are going to fire the house tonight. I think I will make a break when night comes, if alive.
Shooting again. I think they will fire the house this time.
It's not night yet. The house is all fired. Goodbye boys, if I never see you again.

Nathan D. Champion

The rest of the story is Clover's:

The roof of the house was the first to catch on fire, spreading rapidly downward until the north wall was a sheet of flames. Volumes of smoke poured in at the open window from the burning wagon, and in a short time through the plastered cracks of the log house puffs of smoke worked outward. Still the doomed man remained doggedly concealed, refusing to reward them by his appearance. The cordon of sharpshooters stood ready to fire upon him the instant he started to run. Fiercer and hotter grew the flames, leaping with mad impetuosity from room to room until every part of the house was ablaze and only the dugout at the west end remained intact.

"Reckon the cuss has shot himself," remarked one of the waiting marksmen. "No fellow could stay in that hole a minute and be alive."

These words were barely spoken when there was a shout, "There he goes," and a man clad in stocking feet, bearing a Winchester in his hands and a revolver in his belt, emerged from a volume of black smoke that issued from the rear door of the house and started off across the open space surrounding the cabin, into a ravine fifty yards south of the house, but the poor devil jumped square into the arms of two of the best shots in the outfit, who stood with levelled Winchesters around the bend waiting for his appearance. Champion saw them too late, for he over shot his mark just as a bullet struck his rifle arm, causing the gun to fall from his nerveless grasp. Before he could draw his revolver a second shot struck him in the breast, and a third and fourth found their way to his heart.

Nate Champion, the king of cattle thieves, and the bravest man in Johnson County, was dead. Prone upon his back, with his teeth clinched and a look of mingled defiance and determination on his face to the last, the intrepid rustler met his fate without a groan and paid the penalty of his crimes with his life. A card bearing the significant legion [sic] "Cattle thieves, beware," was pinned to his blood-soaked vest, and there in the dawn [sic] with his red sash tied around him and his half-closed eyes raised toward the blue sky, this brave but misguided man was left to lie by the band of regulators, who——

The finish of Sam Clover's purple paragraph has already been quoted in the introduction.

The Chicago reporter did not choose to tell the whole story. It was Clover himself who wrote the sign and buttoned it on the dead man's vest.[10] One of the gang took his six-shooter and belt—the six-shooter turning up later in the desk of a stock-association official in Cheyenne. Pawing over the warm and reeking corpse, the invaders found Champion's bloodstained notebook. It was taken from his body by Frank Canton in the presence of Irvine and several others, who read it and then, within less than two hours, Major Wolcott presented it to Clover. It was published in full in the Chicago *Herald* of April 16, along with the rest of the reporter's tale. Clover wrote in his fictionized autobiography that after copying the diary in a sort of shorthand he tore it up and threw the fragments into the sagebrush on his way into Buffalo, fearing to be found with the blood-soaked memento on his person. That version sounds plausible enough, but the truth of the matter appears to be what he wrote five weeks later to his patron, Henry A. Blair of Chicago, thanking the latter "for the return of Champion's diary pages," and adding: "I shall keep them as long as I live." Whether he did or not, there is no record of the diary's ever being seen again.[11]

By the time it was all over the three wagons had come up and (in Clover's words) "a hearty supper was eaten" half a mile from the burning cabin where Nick Ray's body was being incinerated. A good appetite was enjoyed by all. But while the majority wanted a hot meal and were determined to have it, it led to another wrangle between Irvine, Wolcott, and company on one side and Canton and Hesse on the other, the latter warning that success now depended on pushing with all speed for Buffalo before Jack Flagg could get there and arouse the town. But the Cheyenne Club contingent loved their creature comforts and were still quite unable to entertain the idea of failure. So the stop was made, which lost another hour.

The wagons were ordered to follow as fast as possible and head for Fort McKinney, where a rendezvous was to take place. In the evening the ponderous, slow-moving expedition once more got on its way.

TWENTY-NINE

A Surprise
for the Regulators

THE PARTY rode on until they reached a friendly ranch, George Baxter's Western Union Beef Company headquarters on the North Fork, six or seven miles from the KC. Here they changed horses, stopping just long enough to make the change, then resumed their sinister march—arrogant, mulish, confident in their overwhelming strength, and with no sense of urgency. The dark countryside around them was wide awake and furious, but ranches were few and far between, and they met no one and heard nothing except once, as will be described.

In the meanwhile Jack Flagg, whom we last saw spurring up the road under a hail of bullets, had raced for Trabing, fifteen miles out of Buffalo. Arriving at John R. Smith's ranch at nine o'clock at night, he and the boy found the storekeeper Robert Foote and two other men from Buffalo, who with Smith and Flagg had been headed for the state Democratic convention at Douglas, where they were to be delegates from Johnson County. Needless to say they never got there. As soon as Flagg had dropped his bombshell on the unsuspecting group, he and the boy Alonzo started back with three others to the assistance of the men they thought were still besieged at Nolan's. They had gone less than half the distance —it was over thirty miles—when at the Carr ranch they found twelve more armed men, who had heard the news from Terence Smith as he rode pell-mell for Buffalo.

It was now midnight. "Just as we rode up to Carr's ranch," Flagg's story continues, "someone exclaimed: 'There they are on the flat, a hundred strong.'" In the eerie light of a setting moon; in the terror which by now gripped the country, it is no wonder if the invaders looked a hundred strong; no wonder if the sight struck fear into the hearts of fifteen men on a naked flat.

Just before Flagg's arrival at Carr's, he reported, "the twelve men there had started to go to the KC and had seen the murderers coming and were preparing to ambush them, when one of the boys let his gun go off and the murderers swung off to the left and went through Carr's field. We laid at the ranch till daylight and then followed them up, passing them at the TA ranch and going on to Buffalo." [1]

Miles and hours after leaving the Baxter ranch, as Will Irvine told the story twenty years later, the avenging cattlemen approached the Carr ranch, which was seventeen miles from the KC.

"Somewhere along the road," he wrote, "I do not know where it was, as it was night, Jack Tisdale and Will Guthrie, who were our outriders, came galloping back to us saying there was a body of men ahead. There was much excitement among our men at once. Wolcott and myself got down afoot and walked ahead, he having a pair of field glasses, and after going a considerable distance and listening intently we had about decided that the boy had run into a bunch of range horses, when a gun was discharged ahead, which gave Sheriff Angus [sic] and his party away, and clearly indicated there was more or less excitement in both parties."

That accidental shot might have warned the cattlemen of what was in store for them, but they were like the royal house of Bourbon, they never learned anything. Instead Major Wolcott huffed mightily over the disgraceful state of discipline in his forces. "When we got back to the bunch," Irvine continued, "we found our men in such a state that Wolcott at once assumed command. . . . He rode out in front of us and gave us a good blowing up, saying, I can take ten good men and whip the whole damned bunch of you, and then lined us up and proceeded to drill us by moonlight." [2] This disciplinary move by Wolcott, which Irvine evidently approved, made one more delay.

The party detoured to the left, cut fences on the Carr ranch, and again struck the main traveled road to Buffalo. At 2 A.M. they reached Fred Hesse's 28 ranch twenty-two miles south of Buffalo, where a halt was made for coffee and a two-hour rest, the mercenaries sleeping in the barn loft. By four they were again on the road. They had reached the TA ranch fourteen miles from Buffalo, of which one of their party, Charlie Ford, was foreman, when they paused again, this time because Ford wanted to see his wife, according to Clover. While there one of the Texans suffered an accident which cost him his life.

He was Jim Dudley, a big man of 225 pounds; an excellent rifleman but one who because of his weight, which was too much for the average horse, should have been disqualified for such an expedition as this. When the change of horses was made at Baxter's that night, Dudley had trouble finding one to suit him. After Shonsey had tried him with five different horses the major became impatient at the delay and gave the order to march. Fearing the ill-dispositioned mount he wound up with, the big Texan elected to keep the horse he had ridden all the way from Tisdales', and the result was that when the party reached the TA the animal had given out and he was virtually afoot. Here he tried to get another horse. According to Irvine, "Charlie Ford loaned him an old gentle gray horse that had never been known to buck." But when Dudley mounted the animal promptly bucked, or bolted; his Winchester left its sheath and when the butt struck the ground it was discharged, the bullet striking poor Dudley in the knee.

The wounded man was eventually started for the Fort McKinney hospital in a spring wagon of Ford's, with two TA cowboys in charge. But when they reached Buffalo the town was already aroused, and the excited crowd refused to let him go on, suspecting that he was a spy. Not until the coroner, Dr. Watkins, had examined his wound was he finally allowed to proceed. Arrived at Fort McKinney, there was some official demur about admitting him to the hospital, but since he was obviously so ill that turning him away would be murder, Colonel Van Horn gave the order to admit him. Gangrene soon set in. In his delirium he babbled about the wife he had left behind in Texas, whom he would never see again. He died in a day or two, a pathetic sacrifice to a lost and worthless cause.[3]

The expeditionary forces were proceeding slowly on the road to Buffalo while expecting Ford and Dudley to rejoin them, when they were met by a messenger on a lathered horse who told them that Buffalo was in an uproar and urged them frantically to keep out of there at all costs. They thereupon determined to fall back on the TA.

Versions of what the messenger said and why the decision to retreat was taken vary according to who is telling the story. According to Irvine, who identified the messenger as a well-known Johnson County cattleman, James Craig: "He told us the people did not understand our intentions, that many were arrayed against us who honestly thought we were trying to run the honest settler out of the country, people who were honest good citizens and a class of people we did not want to injure; and that we could not possibly have a fight in Buffalo without killing and injuring many that had not harmed us or our property." [4] Thus related, the decision to turn back to the TA was purest philanthropy. It was otherwise according to Sam Clover, who reported that the messenger yelled:

"Turn back! Turn back! Everybody in town is aroused ... the rustlers are massing from every direction.... Get to cover if you value your lives." Another dispute broke out among the leaders, with Canton, Hesse, and the Texan Tom Smith insisting that they go ahead and fight, but again the Cheyenne Club contingent headed by Wolcott and Irvine overruled the bolder counsel and the party turned around and took refuge at the TA. The messenger in the meanwhile had been sent back to Buffalo under urgent entreaties to get ammunition and food supplies out to them, but he was unsuccessful and according to one report he was jailed. That afternoon Phil DuFran, stock detective and onetime roundup foreman, got out of Buffalo with Sutherland, Fred Hesse's brother-in-law, and joined the hapless crew, warning them to get ready to fight two hundred fifty men.[5]

Smart Sam Clover was too fast to get caught in this trap. Always a fool for luck, he had learned from the messenger that one of the officers at Fort McKinney was none other than his old friend Captain (now Major) Fechet, with whom he had campaigned at Fort Yates. Trusting to this information he now determined to ride on into Buffalo and take his chances with the rustlers, telling the leaders of the expedition that he must get on in and file his story, a move Irvine resentfully described as "desertion." With Clover went Richard M. Allen, assistant manager of the Standard Cattle Company of Cheyenne. To his friends he explained that he had payments coming due on some cattle which he simply had to meet, but to Clover on the ride into town he cursed his folly for ever getting mixed up in this miserable affair. Once in Buffalo the poor fellow did not last long. Giving his name as Carpenter, he left his horse at a livery stable and made a beeline for the Burlington stage, which was on the point of departure. But the brand on his horse was recognized or his actions were suspicious or both; John R. Smith was the man who spotted him, and he was snatched from the coach and thrown into jail.[*]

Sam Clover meanwhile was fast-talking himself off a very hot seat by maintaining that he was merely an innocent Chicagoan on his way to visit his friend the major at the Fort, having met "Carpenter" purely by accident on the way. The major was sent for while Sam did some sweating in the sheriff's office, and when the big handsome officer entered he was a welcome sight. He was also quick to grasp the real state of affairs.

"Well, I'm glad to see you," boomed the major, rising to the occasion. "I was beginning to think the regulators had got you too. Tell Sheriff Angus I'll vouch for him," he added heartily to the no-longer-suspicious undersheriff.

And with that, safe under the wing of the military, Clover rode off to

---

[*] He was not taken from the coach by "seventy-five armed rustlers," as the oft-repeated version has it, but by the city marshal. *Leader*, April 24.

the fort to luxuriate in hot baths and clean sheets while the wretched invaders prepared to stand siege for their lives.[6]

To a people with nerves rubbed raw by the December first murders and the four months of tension which followed, the news brought by Terence Smith on the evening of Saturday the ninth was enough to throw Buffalo into turmoil. The KC ranch was surrounded! The people were now convinced that the cattlemen intended to drive them from their homes, seize their small herds, and repossess their homesteads by fire and sword. Sheriff Angus lost no time in calling upon Captain Menardi of Company C, Wyoming National Guard, which was stationed in Buffalo, to supply men and arms. But assistance was refused, thanks to the secret order which had been issued from the state capital in anticipation of just such a request. At eleven o'clock Sunday morning Angus and a posse of half a dozen men set out for Nolan's ranch, sixty miles away, to verify the report. They reached the smoldering ruins of the KC ranch at dusk, stayed just long enough to identify the bullet-pierced body of Nate Champion in a draw some distance from the house and the charred remains of Nick Ray in the ruins, then started back to Buffalo. They got in at 1 A.M. Monday, a sensational ride of 120 miles in fourteen hours.[*]

Meanwhile on Sunday Jack Flagg had ridden into town at the head of the party from Carr's ranch, passing the invaders who were already holed up at the TA and missing Angus and the posse en route. Flagg had scarcely finished telling an excited crowd of his escape under a hail of bullets when a cowboy on a foam-covered horse rode frantically up Main Street with the news that the Nolan ranch was fired and he thought both occupants were dead.

Buffalo went wild. The streets were filling with armed men from the nearer ranches, while riders were sent to distant parts of the county for help to repel the murderers. In town the leading merchant, a venerable Scotsman named Robert Foote, "mounted his celebrated black horse, and with his long white beard flying to the breeze, dashed up and down the streets calling the citizens to arms," with appeals to patriotism, honor, and "your common manhood," "to protect all that you hold dear against this approaching foe." Thus the scene was described by A. S. Mercer in *The Banditti of the Plains.* According to less flowery press reports the old man dashed up and down roaring: "Come out, you so-and-sos, and take sides." In the cattlemen's books he was rated as a rustler and a receiver of stolen beef and was almost certainly on the famous death list. To the people at large, who felt that their homes and lives were threat-

---

[*] It is only forty-six miles by the modern road from Buffalo to the village of Kaycee which sprang up on the site of the old KC ranch, but the old-time road was less direct.

ened, he was a patriot and a hero. He threw open his store to all Johnson County defenders, offering guns, ammunition, blankets, slickers, warm clothing, flour, bacon, and general food supplies to all who were going to the siege of the TA; "Come in and help yourself" was the order of the day. Churches and schoolhouses were opened as headquarters for incoming recruits, while the good women of the town rallied to cook and bake for the home forces, with the sure and ancient knowledge of women that in any crisis the first need of men is to be fed.

Rumors of forces coming down from the north to relieve the cattlemen added to the turmoil. They never materialized, but in the first hours of excitement nobody knew what was going to happen. Jack Flagg obtained reinforcements in Buffalo Sunday evening and started back to the TA with forty-nine men, arriving at midnight. They posted pickets and waited for daylight. Red Angus, getting in from his fourteen-hour ride in the small hours Monday, presumably needed a few hours sleep, but before daylight he too was back at the TA with forty more men, to take up positions in the fold of the hills looking down on the ranch house. All night long as armed men kept coming into town, party after party of them moved out on the southward road, to wage war on the killer "whitecaps." [7]

The whitecaps! All at once the name was on every tongue. From nowhere it appeared in the very first dispatches. Whitecaps—a term of contempt, of hatred—but whence had it come and why? At the time it would seem that nobody knew or bothered to ask. Not until a few years ago did the writer learn from a very old resident of Buffalo that the reference was to the hooded and sheeted murderers of the Ku Klux Klan.

When a chilly morning dawned on Monday, April 11, the men in the TA ranch house looked out and saw little ragged outposts stationed here and there on the high ground across Crazy Woman creek. By this time perhaps they numbered a hundred and fifty, but they increased hourly. The whitecaps opened hostilities with a defiant rifle shot. The last act of the war had begun.

The "rustlers and citizens," as they were now being called, established their headquarters at the Covington ranch, a mile and a half or so on the Buffalo side of the TA. It was a hot, crowded, cozy place, with steaming men inside and steaming horses outside; lots of good hot coffee and a plentiful supply of good things to eat, sped out by the loyal women and girls of Buffalo to their defenders. Promptly elected as commander in the field was Arapahoe Brown, so called as a result of an early squaw alliance, and in many ways a strange choice. Rising unexpectedly from the ranks to the post of command, he was a huge, unwashed, bearded man, definitely not of Buffalo's better element, though he was manager of the flouring mill. An unsavory aura clung about Rap Brown, composed of various disappearances and unmarked graves in the vicinity of his homestead; it was said that one whole family had disappeared. He was one of those strange characters who come to the fore in a time of crisis and are not heard of again, or not favorably. But in the words of a reluctant tribute paid him by Major Wolcott at the time, he turned out to be "a great general."

If Rap Brown was the field commander for the rustlers, the much-respected Elias U. Snider—rancher, businessman, and pioneer—was chief of staff. From the first he was on hand at the Covington ranch to help organize the siege. Sheriff Angus could be termed the commander in chief, but he spent much of his time in Buffalo to organize and direct the recruits.

All that day and the next they kept flocking into town, an unshaven, tatterdemalion army on wiry horses, wearing six-shooters and carrying rifles. As new reinforcements from distant points kept coming, they were formed into bands of twenty and escorted out to the Covington ranch by deputy sheriffs. The local forces were all out there by that time, even young boys and old men manning outposts and carrying rifles. A young Methodist preacher named Marvin A. Rader was in sympathy with the people of Johnson County, and he rode in from Big Horn to help inspire and organize them to resist attack; he was thereupon called a rustler and denounced in sensational terms by the Cheyenne group and their subservient press.

The businessmen of Buffalo were for the most part on the side of the cattlemen, though they remained prudently silent in public; but the homesteaders and farmers and small ranchers of northern Wyoming rose in a tidal wave to crush the invader. Out of this sparsely populated region of rugged mountains and empty expanses of sagebrush some three hundred men had gathered to surround the TA ranch, and by the time of the surrender Wednesday morning their number was closer to four hundred. Even after that they kept coming for another twenty-four hours, as word of the termination of hostilities did not at once reach the outlying districts; and after that still more armed ranchers kept coming from all directions, the fear now being that through influence the prisoners would be turned loose.[8]

Yet the highest contemporary estimate of known rustlers in Johnson County, and a remarkably consistent one on the whole, placed their number at not above thirty. Such an uprising could hardly be written off as a mere affair of rustlers, thieves, and outlaws who had set out to ruin honest men.

The invaders were dumfounded. They had never looked for anything like this. They seem to have supposed that a private army could march through the countryside at will, burning and shooting, without arousing opposition. More than once they confessed that no thought of failure had entered their minds. But Major Wolcott, undeterred by experience, continued to blow as hard as ever from in prison, announcing that the only mistake made by the regulators was not coming in sufficient force. He said they would be back later with plenty of men and would get all these people yet.

At nine o'clock in the morning of Monday, the first day of the siege, the pickets posted at the Covington ranch sighted the three wagons of the invaders on the brow of a hill a mile or two away. They were promptly captured; when unloaded were found to contain several thousand rounds of ammunition, two cases of dynamite, fuses, and handcuffs, besides Frank Canton's suitcase which was said afterwards to have contained the death list. The word that poison was also found spread through the countryside and heightened the prevailing excitement; the whitecaps, it was said, had been planning to poison all the wells and thus kill off as much of the population as they were unable to mow down with dynamite and rifle fire. Actually the poison, found in Dr. Penrose's surgical kit—which had been lent him by the acting governor, Dr. Barber— was bichloride of mercury intended for use as an antiseptic in dressing wounds, but this explanation, offered by the doctor many years later, was not publicized at the time and would not have been believed if it had been.

The three teamsters, Charles Austin, William Collum, and George Helm, offered no resistance and suffered no harm. It is highly unlikely that they were surprised by their capture since they had already been stopped and questioned by Sheriff Angus when he and his posse were on their way to the KC. They had been instructed to tell anyone who asked that they were with a surveying party bound for the gold camp at Bald Mountain, but by the time Angus stopped them that little fiction was a trifle out of date, and these men were no fools; they knew it. With the marvelous equanimity of their kind they jolted on over the road, each man serene in the company of his four good horses, talking to them, cajoling them, reminding them once in a while with a gentle flick of the whip to pull harder over a rough spot; proceeding philosophically toward the fate that awaited them at the end of the line and knowing full well— being no fools—that it was not going to be a very hard one. And it wasn't.

Shorty, Bill, and Tex—if they were typical of the cook-teamster species—were graying and slightly paunchy and had punched cows in their time. They were also endowed with a bulletproof philosophy and the pungent wit of the western—shall we say, peasant? (We'd better not.) Speaking of the sudden defection of H. W. (Hard Winter) Davis just before the party marched to the KC, one of them observed that Hard Winter was took sick with the gunarrhea. The trio was conveyed to Buffalo where they bellied up to the bar and consumed more drinks, it is safe to say, than they ever paid for, while they told all, not once but over and over again. Buffalo held no grudge against the teamsters. Perhaps, like the agile Sam Clover, they didn't know what kind of a show they were getting into. The hell they didn't, when everybody else knew including half Cheyenne; and Buffalo knew they knew.

But Buffalo was a very human place. There was hardly a man in the town who could cast a stone without hitting himself. The teamsters were freely forgiven for what they had not done and the town took them to its heart and vice versa. When the captive cattlemen were removed to Cheyenne all three refused an offer to go back to their former employment, though it was accompanied by a proffered bonus of a hundred dollars; stating that they preferred the society in Buffalo to that of their late companions.[9]

A *Leader* reporter identified only as "E. T. P." had been sent out earlier in the year to tour the state and describe its glorious resources and glowing future. But he fell ill, and was still convalescing when he heard that "a band of supposed Pinkertons" had left Cheyenne for the north. He hurried to Buffalo. At a late hour on Monday he caught a ride with a wagonload of slickers and other paraphernalia bound for rustler headquarters, through a nasty storm of rain, sleet, and snow; spent the rest of the night in the jam-packed, stuffy little ranch house, talking with the leaders, listening to the crack of rifle fire and watching the flashes of the guns from the hills and gulches surrounding the TA.

By this time the situation was deadlocked and everyone knew it. The raiders had been lucky in the place of refuge fate provided them, for the TA was a good, solid ranch house; all through the first night they had worked like mad at strengthening their position, and when the siege began at dawn on Monday they were ready. The house was built of heavy squared logs ten by twelve inches. West of it a hundred yards was a log stable and a corral; west of that a short distance was a high knoll commanding a sweep of six hundred yards in every direction; an ideal place for a fort. An icehouse north of the main house was another good place to fortify; and ready at hand—another piece of luck—they found a supply of heavy lumber which had recently been brought from Buffalo.

A "fort" was built on top of the knoll, where deep trenches enclosed a space twelve or fourteen feet square, and all surrounded by a wall of heavy timbers, with firing portholes. At the house doors and windows had been logged up to a man's height and portholed, with only enough space left above these barricades to admit light. Around the house triangular redoubts were constructed in the same way as the fort, with trenches and palisades. The icehouse was reinforced like the house with heavy beams and loopholes; and all of these emplacements were manned by men armed with the finest of repeating rifles. The place when finished was practically impregnable to rifle fire. Whatever his failings as a leader, Major Wolcott was impressive as an engineer.[10]

All Monday night the besiegers were busy digging rifle pits and by Tuesday morning they had approached considerably nearer the house. But it was becoming plain that only a cannon could dislodge the defenders, and there was none except at the fort. Merchant Robert Foote, representing the citizen rustlers, went out to the post to call on Colonel Van Horn and ask for the loan of a cannon, even offering $500 for it. He was courteously refused.

Ammunition and supplies in the beleaguered garrison were fairly low, but the besiegers had no sure knowledge of this. Hence there was no answer in sight except ingenuity. Fortunately for the rustlers, they had plenty of that.

Tuesday, the twelfth, dawned under a lowering sky. It was going to be a long, long day.

THIRTY

"I Will Surrender to You—"

THE COURSE of hostilities at the TA was indissolubly bound with the ups and downs—and we use the words literally—of the comic-opera telegraph line which linked Fort McKinney with Douglas by way of Buffalo. It is comic only in retrospect. At the time it had little humor for those whose lives were at stake.

Maintained precariously by the Wyoming Inland Telegraph Company across mile after mile of empty sagebrush, the line had always been subject to hard luck. The year before the invasion the Buffalo *Bulletin*'s McKinney correspondent had whiled away a dull Sunday afternoon in the absence of news at the post by relating the troubles of the much-abused line. It was frequently struck by lightning, and when a soaking rain softened the ground where the poles stood the wind blew them down. Cowboys and hunters amused themselves by taking shots at the blue-green glass insulators. Emigrant parties chopped down the poles for firewood, and an indignant public denounced the company for bad service. But all of this was as nothing to what the line suffered after the invaders started their northward march.

To begin with, it was very thoroughly cut at the behest of Wolcott, Irvine and Co. on the fifth and sixth of April, to prevent the marked men of Buffalo from learning of their coming extinction. E. T. David and others were instructed to go on cutting the wire and keep it cut until further orders, and this was one more in the list of blunders which have led some commentators to refer to the Johnson County invasion as a gruesome farce. For their instructions were very thoroughly carried out, and though repairmen labored over the line all week, it remained dead through Sunday the tenth.* By this time the invaders were in very hot water and could have used the line to summon help for themselves, a contingency they had not looked for.[1]

On Monday the eleventh, when they were surrounded, a correspondent in Buffalo who could only have been Clover reported to Chicago: "The telegraph people have just got a wire through but it is liable to go down again any time." It did, promptly. The same day a man trying to repair it was shot at. It was apparent that other parties were now having a go at wire-cutting for their own purposes. During the short time the line was working on Monday, word reached Cheyenne for the first time directly from Buffalo. It was a telegram to Governor Barber from Acting Mayor Charles J. Hogerson, stating that an armed force had invaded the county, and requesting that the militia be called out for the protection of the citizens. Barber remained calm.

For Hogerson was known as a "rustler"; and his name, together with that of the other two members of the board of county commissioners, was thought to be on the list of those marked for extermination—of which the governor may or may not have had a copy. Cheyenne, personified by Barber who alone could act, was in a fog; a fog compounded of scanty information, disbelief of what it did hear, and an overweening confidence that nothing could possibly have gone wrong for its friends the regulators—who were now facing extinction themselves.

Upon receiving Hogerson's message Barber stalled. He wired Captain C. H. Parmelee of Company C of the National Guard in Buffalo asking for particulars. Then, possibly feeling that as governor he ought to make some sort of gesture for appearance's sake, he telegraphed National Guard officers some rather ambiguous orders to have their commands ready to move; in the next breath virtually nullified these orders by recommending "extreme caution" in making any move. Governor Barber was plainly determined to avoid interfering with his friends' program of liquidation, which was still assumed to be proceeding according to plan. Then the line went down again.[2]

As Tuesday dawned Rap Brown and E. U. Snider, at rustler headquarters, were putting their wits to work. They had learned by now that the enemy could not be dislodged by rifle fire, and they had no cannon. But they did have the wagons captured from the invaders, and these they put to use, being too busy no doubt to notice that history was repeating itself, for wasn't it Jack Flagg's abandoned wagon which these same now-surrounded men had used to burn Nate Champion out to his death?

Lashing the running gears of two wagons together they proceeded to

---

* This was the day a repairman tried to send a message from the top of a pole, but the suspense in Cheyenne was heightened when only three words got through.

build what was variously termed a movable fort or breastworks, an "Ark of Safety," or a "Go-Devil." The idea was to push this contraption close enough to the TA fortifications so that dynamite bombs could be hurled into the fort. The dynamite had been captured along with the wagons.

The "Ark of Safety" was built up of two thicknesses of eight-inch logs fastened together by wire and mounted on the wagon gears to a height of six feet. Baled hay made the wings. This awkward contrivance could be moved by five men with difficulty; by fifteen men easily. It would protect forty men. During the day it was inched over the bumpy ground toward the "fort" or redoubt which protected the west side of the ranch house. Also during the day Angus, fearing a breakthrough attempt, ordered sharpshooters to pick off as many of their horses as could be seen in the corral near the barn. At least five were hit and they went down, kicking. In the wars of the West, whichever side won, the horses always lost. The riflemen on the hills overlooking the ranch had gotten the range, and the openings above the barricaded windows were by now so perforated that they looked like a pepper box, and bullets had been coming through the cracks between the logs. There were any number of hairbreadth escapes and near-misses, yet when the fighting was finished, with the exception of Will Irvine, who was creased in the foot and hobbled for a few days, not a single one of the leaders and instigators of the expedition suffered so much as a scratch. Ironically, it was the Texas mercenaries who paid. A second unfortunate named Alex Lowther was crawling on hands and knees with a cocked six-shooter strapped around his waist when the gun went off, hitting him in the groin. He died at the post hospital a couple of days later.

While Governor Barber dawdled in Cheyenne—"a weak-kneed ass, inept and overly smart," snapped Clover in retrospect; while telegraph repairmen galloped up and down the line between Buffalo and Powder River crossing, stringing wire which went down again behind them as soon as they had passed, the men dug in behind their homemade fortifications were growing hourly more desperate. They still had a hundred rounds of ammunition apiece, which would not last long in heavy fighting, and a cellar full of potatoes to eat. But they knew that their situation was hopeless. They were bitter at the failure of the reinforcements they had expected to spring to their aid around Buffalo, but their local allies had evidently felt more enthusiasm for hanging rustlers than they did now for rescuing invaders. At least one direct appeal for local help went out from the TA, since Irvine relates that "a messenger" was sent to one John Winterling of the Big Red Ranch, Sheridan County, who had been very keen on promoting the invasion back in the fall and had promised to be on hand at the proper time. He was now urged to come at once with all possible manpower. The messenger reached him and succeeded in getting back to the TA, but nothing more was heard from Mr. Winterling.

A desperate mass sortie was talked about by the besieged men. Irvine wrote: "The second night [Monday] Wolcott, who had a foolish idea the rustlers would not fight, wanted to take twenty men on foot and make a night attack on about three hundred. This I opposed. He became very angry and called me a damned mutineer." It was a typical piece of Wolcott strategy, dictated by temper rather than judgment. The next night Wolcott again proposed a break. The time was set for 2 A.M., and again the plan was to include only the twenty or so of "the Wyoming boys," the idea being apparently to leave the Texans to their fate.*

But before the hour arrived the moon came out and shone so brightly on the snow that the attempt was canceled, as it would clearly have been suicide. It would have been in any case. Still suffering from cocksureness, the invaders had no idea of how fully they were surrounded.

The cattlemen's friends in Buffalo, aware of their plight, were doubtless doing whatever they could to bring help, yet their role remains a mystery. Tuesday afternoon several of them called on Colonel Van Horn and implored that officer for troops to disperse the rustlers and bring the cattlemen to the post. He replied that he could do nothing without orders.

But why, during the hours on Monday when the telegraph was working, had they not sent a wire to Governor Barber informing him of the true state of affairs? Were they too frightened? Then why did they not speed a courier to Gillette, where a telegram could be sent with safety? Why for that matter was he not dispatched on Sunday as soon as the invaders had retreated to the TA and their danger was plain to all?

They may have sent a courier on Monday, but that is speculation. According to one report a messenger did get out from the desperate men bottled up inside the TA. He must have slipped through the rustler lines in the dark and stormy early hours of Monday morning, when the lines were still forming and were thinly manned. He had a hundred-mile ride ahead of him to the telegraph at Gillette. It was undoubtedly this message which finally reached the indecisive Barber and jolted him into action.

We do not know what time on Tuesday the word finally penetrated to Governor Barber's sanctum but all at once he was moving heaven

---

* Several observers reported that the expedition leaders were cold in the extreme to their Texas hirelings. They seem to have regarded them as social inferiors and when all were in prison together treated them with disdain. This curious behavior on the part of one group of men toward another, when all were in the same boat, was only one of many oddities which marked the great antirustler crusade. A modern mind would interpret it as a projection of guilt feelings.

and earth to get the troops at Fort McKinney sent to the rescue of the cattlemen. At some time during the day he dispatched his famous telegram to President Benjamin Harrison:

An insurrection exists in Johnson County in the state of Wyoming, in the immediate vicinity of Fort McKinney, against the government of said state. The legislature is not in session and cannot be convened in time to afford any relief whatever or to take any action thereon. Open hostilities exist and large bodies of armed men are engaged in battle. A company of state militia is located at the city of Buffalo near the scene of said action, but its continued presence in that city is absolutely required for the purpose of protecting life and property therein. The scene of action is 125 miles from the nearest railroad point from which other portions of the state militia could be sent. No relief can be afforded by state militia and the civil authorities are wholly unable to afford any relief whatever. United States troops are located at Fort McKinney, which is thirteen miles from the scene of action, which is known as the TA ranch. I apply to you on behalf of the state of Wyoming to direct the United States troops at Fort McKinney to assist in suppressing this insurrection. Lives of a large number of persons are in imminent danger.

Amos W. Barber, Acting Governor.

In this remarkable message the question of just who was in insurrection was not clarified.

As hours passed with no reply from the President the Governor, becoming increasingly frantic, sent telegram after telegram to Brigadier General John B. Brooke, commanding the Department of the Platte at Omaha, to Colonel Van Horn at Fort McKinney, to Captain Parmelee and even to Mayor Hogerson of Buffalo, apprising them that he had asked the President for troops and urging the military leaders to hold themselves in readiness.

Late in the evening he finally reached Wyoming senators Carey and Warren in Washington. The senators hastened to call on Acting Secretary of War Grant, and the party repaired to the White House where they got the President out of bed (Carey and Harrison had been old Senate friends). In a matter of minutes orders were on the way, and from that time forward all the heavy artillery of influence from Cheyenne to Washington and back again was brought to bear to rescue the cattlemen from the consequences of their act, whether physical or legal.

At 11:05 P.M., at last, the President wired Governor Barber:

I have, in compliance with your call for aid of the United States forces to protect the state of Wyoming against domestic violence, ordered the secretary of war to concentrate a sufficient force at the scene of the disturbance and to co-operate with your authorities.

The rest was like the ending of a B-grade western motion picture, except for a few cynical overtones. At 11:37 P.M., thirty-two minutes after the President's telegram was sent, General Brooke wired the governor confirming receipt of the presidential order and adding that the commanding officer at Fort McKinney had been directed "to prevent violence and preserve peace." According to Washington sources his instructions were to co-operate with Governor Barber "in suppressing the rustler disorder"—no word being mentioned of disorder on the part of anyone else. Colonel Van Horn unwittingly injected a sour note in his telegram of acknowledgement with the comment: ENTIRE COUNTRY IS AROUSED BY THE KILLINGS AT THE KC RANCH AND SOME OF THE BEST CITIZENS ARE IN THE POSSE.

The telegraph wire had been restored just in time. The colonel received his orders at 12:05 A.M. Two hours later Troops H, C, and D of the 6th Cavalry under Major Fechet, with Colonel Van Horn in command, clanked and jingled out of Fort McKinney in the freezing night in a thoroughly disgusted frame of mind, because they had just come in that evening from chasing a band of marauding Crows back to the reservation and did not relish being ordered out again at two in the morning. Also they were heartily on the side of Johnson County and would rather have left the whitecaps to their fate.

Inside the TA ranch that Wednesday morning, April thirteenth, there was gloom. The distant figures which showed up once in a while on the skyline and then ducked down again were not going to go away. The clumsy "Ark of Safety" had been manned and was moving, and those inside the ranch house could watch it as it lurched over the uneven ground, coming gradually closer to the log-and-earthworks "fort." It had been moved about a hundred yards when the soldiers came in sight. There was agreement on both sides that this was the day of showdown, but the showdown could only come out one way. The men in the TA were talking again about a rush for freedom—a rush which would have ended in death for most of them.—But hark! A bugle call. It is the troops.

Colonel Van Horn's command arrived at the scene of the fighting at 6:45 A.M. and halted behind a hill 800 yards from the ranch. The besiegers had become aware of their approach and redoubled their fire on the buildings, but after the halt, the Colonel requested Sheriff Angus to order a cease fire, and the order was promptly obeyed. At a conference between Colonel Van Horn on one side, and Angus and Arapahoe Brown on the other, the latter stated that they had no objection to seeing their foe surrender to the military, provided only they received assurance that the stockmen would be turned over to the civil authorities in the near future for trial. Satisfied by the Colonel that this would be the case—and unaware that, through no fault of Colonel Van Horn's, there was a joker in it—they raised no more questions and the truce proceeded.

A bugle blew. The guidon bearers were called to the front, and drawn up in line between them were five men; Colonel Van Horn, Major Fechet, Captain Parmelee as aide-de-camp and representative of the governor, Sheriff Angus and—the fifth man?—none other than Sam T. Clover. The line seven abreast swept down the hill to the first of the rifle pits followed by the column of troops. Someone was waving a white handkerchief.

"Presently a head appeared above the breastworks, followed by a hand that fanned the air with a soiled rag, and almost at the same instant a white emblem fluttered far down the slope at the house. In a few minutes Colonel Van Horn and his staff ranged alongside the rampart, inside of which were gathered a dozen of the most grimy yet most determined looking specimens of humanity ever seen." So Clover wrote. "All cast at Sheriff Angus looks of malevolent hatred." At almost the same moment Major Wolcott came out of the house and advanced briskly toward the troops, his short legs moving in soldierly rhythm. Colonel Van Horn explained that his orders were to quell disturbance and to prevent loss of life and destruction of property. Would the major's party surrender quietly?

"I will surrender to you," returned the doughty major, "but to that man [indicating Sheriff Angus] never. I know him well. Rather than give up to him we will all die right here."

Completion of the formalities took about two hours. The official count of men and arms taken at the surrender, as reported by Colonel Van Horn, was forty-five men including one wounded; forty-six horses, forty-five rifles, fifty revolvers, and five thousand rounds of ammunition. While the arms were being turned over a party of about two hundred horsemen collected to watch the proceedings, coming as close as the cordon of troops would permit, but without offering to make any disturbance. At a quarter to nine the march to the post was begun, with the prisoners closely guarded by troops before, behind, and on either side of them. Again the besieging party gathered to watch, this time from the hillside near the road, but according to the Colonel "without any attempt at disturbing or molesting the movement. In fact," his report continues, "their conduct insofar as relates to their intercourse with the troops was extremely moderate and creditable to themselves." [3]

In a letter to the governor Captain Parmelee reported that small bodies of armed men had followed the party to the fort, and taunts, jeers, and yells of hostility were heard. The main body, however, disbanded at Angus' order, and the most prevalent manifestation observed was one of intense curiosity coupled with a kind of satisfaction. The troops, who had been briefed to expect trouble, were pleasantly disappointed.

Two men were left behind in the empty and bullet-pierced stronghold. One was the Texan Alex Lowther, badly wounded the day before. He was soon removed to the post in an ambulance. The other was George Dunning, known as "Idaho," who had been recruited in his native state by Colonel H. B. Ijams. This strange, relentless young man had known exactly what he wanted when he signed up with the invaders, and now was his chance. He hid out in the hay in the barn loft until everybody had gone; then he walked to Buffalo. There are stories that he was considerably roughed up when he got to Buffalo, but he persisted in his purpose, which was to give himself up to Sheriff Angus and then tell all he knew about the invasion; perhaps somewhat more than he knew. He was soon safely locked up in Angus' custody. Dunning spent the summer guarded and in hiding, writing on that document curiously entitled "The Confession of George Dunning." *

* See A. S. Mercer's *The Banditti of the Plains.*

How Buffalo
Lost the Railroad

A WAR has been defined as a difference of opinion among groups of people which cannot be settled except by shooting. According to this definition the fracas in Johnson County, however limited in scope, qualifies as a war.

For the owners were convinced that theirs was a crusade of honest men against thieves and that all their deeds were cloaked with righteousness. The local inhabitants, looking at what had happened—two men shot in the back, two more men riddled with bullets and their cabin burned—came to the conclusion that the purpose of the expedition was to burn their homes, seize their livestock, and kill anybody who resisted. Three days after the surrender a committee of Johnson County citizens headed by the acting mayor, Charles J. Hogerson, protested to President Benjamin Harrison:

We do solemnly affirm that, contrary to all law of God and man, an armed body of capitalists with hired war men, have entered our country with the open and avowed intention of taking possession of and controlling the same in their own interests; that we believe their aim was to terrorize and depopulate the country to their own aggrandizement, to murder and kill any and all persons resisting them, regardless of reputation or calling; that they have been detected in the act of commitment of such murder and killing; that they have resisted arrest by the civil authorities and have defied all law....[1]

"To murder and kill regardless of reputation or calling"—Mr. Hogerson himself was a businessman and a solid citizen, head of the board of county commissioners, owner of the leading blacksmith shop in town, and no rustler. But he was a friend of Angus', and his case hovers on the always fine razor edge which divides a political difference of opinion from crime. His message concluded with an appeal for justice and a reaffirmation of loyalty to the President of the United States.

In Cheyenne the prisoners' friends huffed that the undeniably respectable names among the petitioners, of whom there were quite a few, were there because the signers had been intimidated and coerced, along with those "honest farmers" who had unexpectedly sided with the rustlers. If half the threats and intimidation charged by Cheyenne had been real, the invaders would have been welcomed as an army of deliverance instead of being met with a mass uprising of wrath.

Outside observers, from Colonel Van Horn on down, remarked on the degree of forbearance shown by the community in spite of the popular excitement. The *Leader*'s special correspondent, "E. T. P.," arriving in Buffalo on the first evening of the TA siege, was agreeably surprised to find that the town was quiet. "I went where I pleased unarmed. Others did the same and I noticed at least one woman on the street alone."

But Governor Barber was working to get the prisoners out of the toils of civil justice, and he fed the flames of propaganda by expressing repeated fears for their safety. At the same time the *Herald* was pumping artificial respiration into the mob-violence theme with hysterical frenzy. "RUSTLERS WANT BLOOD," hissed the *Herald* on the sixteenth. "*May* Murder Captured Cattlemen. A Thousand Armed Men Waiting for an Opportunity to Shoot the Prisoners Down." The "thousand armed men" were more than double the number reported on hand at the height of the TA hostilities. "MAY LYNCH CATTLEMEN," (April 17). "EAGER FOR VENGEANCE. Rustlers Bound to Shed Blood. Armed Stock Thieves and Their Friends Wrought up to a Pitch of Excitement Where They *May* Attack the Soldiers to Secure the Captive Cattlemen" (April 19; italics supplied). Other linguistic devices were the familiar "It is feared" ... "It is apprehended that" ... "It is freely predicted here that Angus and his supporters will never permit the captive cattlemen to leave that country alive"—and, of course, "rumored" and "expected"; "Six Companies Escorting the Captive Cattlemen to Fort McKinney [*sic*] Followed by Hundreds of Desperadoes Who Are Expected to Make an Attack."

Day after day this sort of thing was served up to the public without a single overt action to justify it. It was ugly; it was typical of the times. And it worked. The little citizens of a big remote county had no comeback. And the most grievous consequence to them was the loss of the long-awaited railroad.

The Burlington and Missouri, which was building northwesterly through Wyoming, decided to bypass Buffalo in view of the numerous offenses charged against that community. First, two of its citizens had been shot in the back while going about their business by parties not altogether unknown; later the community had compounded its felonies by resisting an armed attack. This would never do, and the B. & M. backers, who were financially not unrelated to the backers of the big Wyoming cattle companies, refused to endanger their goods and passengers in transit through a hotbed of cutthroats, desperados, and outlaws. So the railroad went to Sheridan instead. And that hurt.

The surrender of the invaders and cessation of hostilities brought no peace to the town on Clear Creek, as crisis followed crisis in the next few days, yet without any disorder. The first crisis was the funeral of Nate Champion and Nick Ray. The day before the surrender a coroner's jury headed by Dr. John C. Watkins had set out to review the remains of the two men, still lying in the desolation of burning and bloodshed at the gutted KC ranch, and bring them back to Buffalo. But the strain was too much for the frail, fifty-year-old physician who had come from New England some years before.

"My dear brother was not very well and was much excited over all this," Miss Mary S. Watkins wrote. "He went in discharge of his duty to hold an inquest upon the bodies of the murdered men, but died of apoplexy before he reached them." Taken ill on the way, he died at that already-famous way station where everything happened, Carr's ranch. The bodies of all three men were brought back into Buffalo.[2]

On the fourteenth the remains of Nate Champion and Nick Ray were placed on public exhibition. The charred and roasted trunk of Ray, with head and limbs gone, the bullet-pierced body of Champion caused intense feeling. The next day services for Dr. Watkins were held in the morning; those for the KC victims at two in the afternoon, in a vacant store building on Main Street. The room was so jammed with women, most of them in tears, that only a few men could get in to hear the young Methodist preacher, Marvin Rader, counsel the people to abide within the law and hear him repeat the Biblical text: " 'Vengeance is mine,' saith the Lord, 'I will repay.' " The procession then moved up Main Street to the cemetery, followed by carriages, wagons, men on foot; mounted men, women, and boys, to a total of perhaps five hundred persons.

Strangely enough it was Clover who commented—somewhere under the RUSTLERS WANT BLOOD headline: "There are no dangerous indications. The community has shown itself to be remarkable for its patience and order."

In the meanwhile Dick Allen, who had left his friends and been snatched from the stage as he was trying to get out of Buffalo, was still languishing in the county jail. Governor Barber, to whom virtually full power over the military had been delegated by the powers in Washington, requested that they take custody of Allen, and ordered the sheriff to turn his lone prisoner forthwith over to Fort McKinney. Colonel Van Horn, who was taking no chances, inquired of Angus whether he thought one troop of cavalry would be sufficient for the protection of the prisoner during the transfer, or whether he should send three troops.

The sheriff replied: "If you send cavalry the chances are there might be trouble. But if you want your man, send one soldier."

The colonel took the sheriff's advice. An open wagon manned by a sergeant and a private drove up before the courthouse. Two hundred armed men lined the sidewalk and pressed close to stare, but when Angus came out they fell back, leaving a lane open to the door. The three men went inside and let Allen out of his cell, a receipt was signed for him, and they started to leave the building. Allen was frightened when he saw the crowd and tried to turn back into the jail, but the soldiers, by now thoroughly confident, hustled him across the sidewalk and into the wagon. A voice said: "Oh, you murderer." Another voice said: "You keep quiet." The first speaker was identified as a brother of the murdered Nate Champion; the second as Deputy Sheriff Howard Roles. And that was all.[3]

Such was mob violence, Johnson County style.

Yet the county, like other communities, had its dregs of crime and disorder. They had always been there; transient stage-robbers and horse thieves; outlaws of the Teton Jackson stripe, and the tattered fringe of the rustler element who appropriated other men's cattle mainly out of a liking for trouble. They were visible in Johnson County at the time of the invasion; bullies and scum. Some demanded the death of all the invaders. A clerk in a drygoods store was beaten over the head with a pistol "for what you said last winter." The leading druggist, known to be friendly to the cattlemen, was threatened in an ugly manner; the father-in-law of one of the invading force, marching in the funeral procession for Nate Champion and Nick Ray, was hit in the face with the butt of a quirt, although he was in the act of paying tribute to one of the invasion victims.

This contemptible crew, not numerous enough to constitute a threat to the captured cattlemen, was composed of bona-fide bad men. They were two-bit bad men to be sure; a far cry from the two-gun elite of western heroics, if such ever existed. But they were bad enough to engage in looting and disorder in the weeks after the invasion, which the Johnson County authorities to their everlasting shame failed to control; bad enough to commit a particularly vicious and senseless murder less than a month after the events described in this chapter.

There were stories within the story. One of them was that of the *Herald* correspondent himself.

A few years ago the writer proposed a magazine-length article on the Johnson County invasion to a very distinguished editor. Since a "gimmick"—something different by way of an approach—seemed to be in order, the suggestion was made that the article be built around Sam Clover as a key figure. The editor turned it down. "Frankly, I think Clover was a detestable character," he said. The article duly appeared, but minus the *Herald's* star reporter.

Detestable he may have been, but he *was;* he can no more be overlooked in telling the Johnson County story than you can overlook a cinder in your eye. He was an early-blooming product of the yellow press, which was shortly to burst into full flower in Chicago and New York, and he had all the vices and virtues of his kind; he was unscrupulous and a liar—and he got the story. On the morning the cattlemen surrendered at the TA ranch the *Leader* correspondent, who had been up half the night filing his first day's dispatch, overslept, had trouble getting hold of a horse, arrived late at the scene of the siege, and missed the surrender. Clover would have stolen a horse. That about sums him up.

Clover's byline never appeared in his own paper, though toward the end he himself was mentioned once or twice as a newsworthy item in his own right—which doesn't often happen to a reporter. With anonymous correspondents filing dispatches to the *Herald* from here, there, and everywhere in Wyoming how can we follow Clover's movements or identify his stories? The answer lies in the piecing together of clues. Clover himself referred to his rescue by Major Fechet in the paper, and described it in his thinly disguised autobiography *On Special Assignment.* And since the brash young man from Chicago was not easily overlooked he came in for considerable mention by other correspondents.

From the time he left the invaders to their fate at the TA ranch and took his chances on getting away with it in Buffalo until he got safely out of range a week later—in a word, for as long as he sojourned in the vicinity of the rustler capital—Clover was careful not to reveal by so much as a line that he knew more than was healthy for him about the KC killings.

For almost a week, still posing as a wandering correspondent who had innocently come to see Wyoming, he busied himself with sending items of the kind that anybody could pick up during the excitement in Buffalo. At the same time he stuck closely to the protection of his friend Major Fechet. Having all the facilities of the post at his command he was able to employ its civilian scouts as couriers. Then on Saturday, April 16, the *Herald* appeared with one of the great eyewitness reports of the century, Clover's account of the double killing and burning at the KC. The story was datelined Buffalo, April 15, but the dateline was a fake. Would anyone take Clover for that kind of a fool?

Not only had the dispatch not been sent from Buffalo, but Clover had not risked his freedom by sending it from anywhere inside Wyoming. It was telegraphed on the fifteenth from Edgemont, South Dakota, about three times as far as Gillette, and the presumption is that a Fort McKinney scout was again pressed into service as courier. Ask us not how, but the *Leader* somehow obtained the facts, and a few days later it reprinted the great Clover special, with his name and the Edgemont dateline, thus giving the whole thing away.

And now consider the delicacy of the timing. The news of Clover's KC revelation, appearing in Chicago on the sixteenth, could not even under the best of conditions—that is, with the telegraph working—be expected to reach Buffalo in less than twenty-four hours, and anyway Clover was snugly ensconced at the post. Early next day, the seventeenth, before indignant citizens had time to start demanding his scalp, he was shaking the dust—or rather the mud—of northern Wyoming off his feet forever, in the company of Major Fechet and the three troops of cavalry, on his way to the outside world, the railroad, and escape. The captured cattlemen were being returned to the tender care of Governor Barber, and Clover was going back to the Loop.

But he wasn't there yet, nor was that the end of his cynical saga. However, at this point a sort of obituary is in order. For gall, guts, and reporting know-how—and for scurrility, bias, and shameless distortion —the *Herald* correspondent rates a special two-headed medal of his own.

THIRTY-TWO

And Marched Them Down Again

The King of France
He had ten thousand men.
He marched them up a hill one day
And marched them down again.

—NURSERY RHYME

ON EASTER SUNDAY morning, April 17, Major Fechet's command left Fort McKinney with the prisoners, bound for Douglas and ultimately Cheyenne. The order of march was the same as before. The captives were flanked by half a troop of cavalry on either side, with a second troop in the lead and the third troop bringing up the rear. The military, who behaved in an exemplary manner throughout, were equally determined to prevent a rush on the prisoners by local bullies, or any attempt at escape, and a Hotchkiss gun carried in the lead of the column underscored the point.* Between the front and rear guards there plodded and ploughed through the mud ten four-horse teams including an ambulance, which was soon filled with the frostbitten, alkalied, and half-snow-blind casualties of the fearful march.

The cavalcade squelched out of the post at 10:30 A.M. in a cold downpour of rain which did not deter a large crowd of spectators from Buffalo from gathering to see the last of their enemies. Inside the post women and children and remaining soldiers, slickered against the rain, also gathered to stare. On the outside the onlookers pressed close to the marchers; too close to suit Major Fechet.

"Get back!" he shouted. "All you boys; you ladies and gentlemen in carriages too, everybody move back!" All but a few tried to obey but they moved too slowly, and Captain Stanton of C Troop ordered his troopers to slam their horses broadside on into the crowd to clear it. A squadron of "the boys" dashed up to the prisoners with a flourish of bravado, yelling threats.

"Cut them away!" the major shouted again, and Angus and his depu-

* "General Brooke has instructed Colonel Van Horn that there is no intention of making the situation worse by enabling the cattlemen to slip away. They will surely be brought to trial." Chicago *Herald*, April 17.

234

ties galloped in and cut them back the way cattle or horses are cut out of a herd.[1]

Taking the old Bozeman road of bloody Indian memories, the column plodded on its way toward its first night's halt at the crossing of Crazy Woman, twenty miles to the south and east. This was the one-time site of Gus Trabing's freight stop and road ranch, where Moreton Frewen came into the picture—how many eons before? Not fourteen years. In the raging currents of the West, where one West vanished almost before it had arrived and was swept out by a new torrent, fourteen years equaled fourteen decades anywhere else. Between the dashing adventurer with his Cambridge accent and the dreary party of cattlemen being herded back to Cheyenne, a continent had changed. They had failed to recognize it.

From the time Major Fechet's command left Fort McKinney, for almost five days it was swallowed up in silence. The telegraph line was cut to pieces again.

After being restored just long enough near midnight on the twelfth to let orders get through to Colonel Van Horn to take charge at the TA, it was down again, up again, down again for the next three days, until it looked in places as though pieced together with bits of baling wire. Then on Saturday the sixteenth, a party of unidentified horsemen rode out to the line and pulled down poles and cut wires over so much of its length between Buffalo and Douglas that it was almost a week before a message could get through.

The motive for the new outbreak of wire-cutting was not clear. One explanation was that the hoodlum element had destroyed the line from spite because the cattlemen had escaped their clutches; another was that the "rustlers" had done it to keep their "movements" from becoming known, but since the rustlers never made any movements at all that seems hardly likely.

A third theory was generated in the heavy air of mystery which now enveloped Cheyenne. Dapper Governor Barber looked bland above his mustache and didn't know a thing about the whereabouts of prisoners or troops, or even whether they had left McKinney. Neither did General Brooke in Omaha. It was all very strange, since two companies of the 17th Infantry from friendly Fort Russell had already been ordered to Douglas to receive the prisoners. Hence the third speculation was that Cheyenne, professing fear of popular excitement and a rustler attack, had possibly gone back to cutting wires on its own account. Whatever the reason, the command was five days out of communication on the terrible march, the worst in the combined memory of four seasoned West Pointers.[2]

From the time the troopers and prisoners left McKinney Sunday morning in a freezing rain which soon turned to sleet and then into a blizzard, the weather, which had been bad enough all month, outdid itself in a performance of sheer hell. On the second day there was more snow, third day more rain and snow, on the fourth day, Wednesday, there was rain, hail, sleet, and snow. It was not very cold, but the wind-driven sleet cut through Army overcoats and stung faces like needles. The prisoners of course had no overcoats, but wore a motley of ragged trousers, gunny sacks, slickers, and Army blankets draped around their shoulders. The suffering of the Texans was especially severe, for they were used to a warm climate and had come dressed for April—but not April in Wyoming. The party struggled through snowdrifts up to their stirrups in some places and in others squelched through fetlock-deep mud; splashed across roaring, bank-full streams. At the night camps the supply wagons were slow in arriving, and after they did the howling wind drove the snow under and into the tents, making sleep all but impossible. The alkali water had, in the words of a victim, "a chain lightning effect." There was no forage for the horses, and they were close to giving out before feed was reached. None of this improved the disposition of the troopers and officers toward the prisoners, to whom it was freely conveyed that they deserved to hang.

After a grueling march on Wednesday the exhausted marchers reached the headquarters of Irvine's big Ogalalla ranch, sixty miles north of Douglas. Here the prisoner became host. The invaders were all invited to spend the night in the ranch house, and permission was granted, though a heavy guard was maintained. But when Major Fechet was invited to dinner he crisply declined, much to the annoyance of the quondam regulators.

Friday, the march was resumed. By now the weather had cleared and the sun was out. The plains which in summer were baked brown and speckled with sagebrush had become an endless sea of white which stretched away without a single relief for the eye. All along the road were enormous drifts. "The defiles were choked with snow, and from the castellated buttes overhead the sparkling billows hung so insecurely that they fell from time to time on the floundering soldiers and horses." It was beautiful, but the blinding glare of sun on snow added fresh torments for the riders, who were soon burned to a crisp. With the exception of the few who had dark glasses eyes were inflamed, and some of the men were close to snow blindness when the haven of Brown's Springs, thirty-five miles from journey's end, was reached that night.[3]

What had become of the "murderous rustlers" who were so bent on vengeance that they "might" attack the soldiers in order to seize and lynch the captives? What had happened to the "freely predicted" attacks, and where were Sheriff Angus and his "big posse of avengers"? Neither hide nor hair of them was seen. During the exchange of official telegrams over the transfer, Governor Barber had wired General Brooke: RELIABLE CITIZEN OF DOUGLAS TELEGRAPHS THAT ESCORT OF WOLCOTT PARTY SHOULD BE CAUTIONED AGAINST SHARPSHOOTERS, THAT BODIES OF ARMED MEN ARE GOING NORTH," and so on.[4] The "reliable citizen" was talking through his hat, but these thousand armed phantoms continued to haunt the march through the seven days it lasted, and like their ghostly prototypes in the song they never came down to earth.

Rough-looking cowboy types were seen at frequent intervals along the way but they had come to stare, not to demonstrate. Not a shot was fired. As the couriers were leaving Irvine's Ogalalla ranch on Friday morning there was a chorus of loud yells in the neighborhood of the ranch, where sixty cowboys had gathered to give vent to their feelings. But while they were loaded down with weapons they showed no disposition to use them. One of them walked up and shook hands with one of the regulators he recognized, probably as a former employer. Again there were no shots.[5]

In contrast to the near-hysteria which gripped the state capital was the air of calm which pervaded the command itself. Officers and men professed no fear of an attack, nor had they any complaints except about the weather. Some of them declared that there was no possibility of a fight nor even of a gun being fired unless the prisoners tried to escape.[6] "In that event," reported one of the first couriers to reach Douglas in advance of the party, "the cavalrymen will bring them to with a volley from their carbines."

Something about the tone of the comment suggested that the cavalrymen would not have minded the opportunity in the least. It was well known that the feeling among the soldiers and their families at McKinney was strongly on the side of the so-called rustlers, and even the children these days were playing a game of "rustlers and whitecaps," with the whitecaps always getting the worst of it.

As days passed with no word from Clover his office in Chicago became alarmed for the safety of its star reporter. Fearing that he might be held prisoner by the rustlers or even dead, it sent out a relief expedition composed of another *Herald* star named Seymour to find out what had happened to him. Seymour reached Douglas on Thursday, the twenty-first.[7]

This was the day everything happened; the day the "lost" command turned up at the Ogalalla ranch; the day the telegraph line was restored and the first couriers bringing news of the party reached Douglas.

As word spread that the whitecaps were being brought in, the town started filling up with cowboys and small ranchers from half Wyoming. They had come for a look at the enemy, and a good many were planning to ride out of town and give him a suitable reception, but right now they were staging the celebration of a lifetime. With the well-known western capacity for making whoop-de-do out of any special occasion large or small, from a spike-driving to a wake, the little metropolis on the North Platte, known as rather a dead place lately, proceeded to put on a blast the like of which had not been seen since the railroad came through six years earlier. Men whose trousers sagged with the weight of the weapons they carried filled the saloons and spilled over onto the board sidewalks, while at the post office little groups of ranchers and townspeople collected to discuss in solemn tones what all this trouble portended for the future of Wyoming. The crowd, "representing the curiosity of half a dozen counties," according to the correspondent from Chicago, kept growing every hour. One of the out-of-town visitors was Long Tom Bird, six feet seven inches tall, who had heard that his name was on the death list. Armed with two six-shooters, a long knife, and of course a bottle of whiskey, he said he wanted to see the men who had him marked for death. Before morning he had lost one of his six-shooters in a poker game and somebody had stolen his knife, and he was using the second six-shooter to defend the bottle of whiskey which a bartender was playfully trying to take away from him.

Seymour had settled down—if such it can be called—in Douglas to await the coming of the prisoners and Sam Clover, and while so doing he looked around him. The Chicagoan came to Wyoming as an intelligent stranger to whom everything he saw was new and who saw just about everything, and in his columns of sensitive reporting the life of a little western town long gone with the snows of yesteryear lives again for a day. Seymour lost no time in going native himself, as evidenced by this word picture of Douglas as it awaited the cattlemen:

All night long the saloons were ablaze with light, and men in shirtsleeves pounded the pianos for the men who stood against the bar. It was the biggest night known in this camp since the days when there were 1300 people and men fought to get a seat at a monte table. There are no monte games now, but a man may play poker until he gets black in the face. The rattling of chips sounded like a castanet accompaniment to the music of the fiddlers and pianos. Before morning the saloons were filled with men in all stages of collapse.

The blue-coated soldiers from Fort Russell were in it with the best of them, and those who took on too much joy juice were locked up in a boxcar in lieu of the guardhouse. Yet despite the staggering weight of armaments displayed the wild night saw only one casualty; a man from the Sweetwater country who was foolish enough to take sides with the cattlemen had his head split open with a neck-yoke.

When morning came with a burst of sunshine that polished every crystal on the Laramie range [the *Herald* scribe continues] the red-eyed vigil came to an end. A bugler standing leggins deep in sagebrush sounded reveille, a staggering crowd came out upon the sidewalks and preparations began to be made to receive the outfit now on its way from Mc-Kinney.[8]

In addition to the local entertainment resources a series of wild rumors and odd happenings kept the crowd occupied. Buffalo had heard that a new party of a hundred or more invaders were coming by wagon from Gillette. The sound of shooting near Buffalo had occasioned another alarm, but it turned out to be the cowboys at Bob Foote's ranch holding target practice—"a not uncommon thing lately." "Hard Winter" Davis was said to be trying to flee the state disguised in female attire.

The reader may recall that H. W. Davis was a prominent stockman who had planned to join the invasion, but on the night at Tisdales' when the fateful decision was made to proceed at once to wipe out the rustlers at the KC, his horse became suddenly fatigued and he could go no farther. Since he took no part in the killings he could hardly have been charged with anything serious, but he was taking no chances, and it was subsequently reported that he had lit out for Nebraska in such hot haste that he hit only the tops of the highest hills en route, and had not been seen since. Meanwhile the sheriff of Converse County was warned of his attempted escape in feminine raiment, plus a tip that he would be on a train coming through Douglas on a certain date. The law boarded the train and searched the cars until he found a hefty, masculine-looking female who seemed to fit the description. He was proceeding to drag her off when up rose a brawny farmer, saying: "She might look like a hard winter to you, but she's my wife."

The sheriff disappeared.

It was a curiously peaceable crowd. In the bars as the redeye did its work some wild and threatening talk was heard about what ought to be done to the whitecaps, but it wore off with next morning's hangover. During the whole three days of drinking and excitement not a shot was heard. The *Herald*'s own correspondent stated flatly: "There are no threats of trouble here."

Eight miles northwest of Douglas stood the crumbling remains of Fort Fetterman, once one of the chain of forts along the "Bloody Bozeman" trail. On Saturday the pitch of expectancy in Douglas was tightened; everyone knew that Major Fechet and his party would reach Fetterman sometime that afternoon. Seymour rode out to meet them. At three-thirty a lone horseman came galloping over the brow of a hill near the abandoned fort and dismounted when he reached the Platte River crossing. Seymour rode up to him. It was the indestructible Clover, burned to a blister by the sun and riding at the head of the troops as usual. The two fell on each other's necks.

Ten minutes later the command appeared. At the camping ground of the old post they dismounted, broke out the cooking equipment, and had dinner. They were not going into Douglas after all. Major Fechet, who thought of everything and deserved a medal, had decided to outwit the reception committee, besides saving the eight miles additional march into Douglas, by entraining the prisoners at Fetterman. At five o'clock the special train with the infantry on board pulled into the old fort and Major Egbert of the 17th plodded through cactus and sand to shake hands with his opposite number of the 6th Cavalry. By this time quite a crowd had gathered, composed in more or less equal parts of hostile local elements and the friends of the prisoners. Handshaking and back-slapping were freely permitted by indulgence of the ever-watchful major, but the guard was doubled, and a detachment of cavalry was sent to the top of a high butte nearby, where the landscape could be overlooked for miles around and any signs of approaching trouble detected. There were none.

The train went on to Douglas, with a company of troops in a car at either end of the car holding the prisoners. The onlookers gaping on the station platform reminded one observer of a crowd at the zoo which had come to stare at the animals.[9] The cattlemen were to be taken to Fort Russell, the Army post on the outskirts of Cheyenne, to be detained there for the next few weeks while arrangements for the transfer back to the civil authorities were perfected. The original plan had been to take them through to Fort Russell the same night, but a report had been received of a plot to wreck the train in the Platte River canyon, and Major Egbert wisely decided that it would be foolhardy to go through the canyon at night.

Friendly visitors had provided a supply of elixir to raise the spirits of the prisoners, and their car was soon a gay place, with song and boasting. Major Wolcott was in fine fettle. He would be eating sirloin steak and mushrooms in Chicago within two weeks. The rustlers were a pack of cowards. Just imagine—the scoundrels, to the number of hundreds, had surrounded a little party of fifty men without even the chivalry of offering their intended victims a chance to surrender! Next time a party, several parties, of over a hundred men each would attend to these blackguards, roving the state and purging it of its impurities.

Several correspondents en route back to civilization were on the train, including the two *Herald* men. During the overnight stop in Douglas the latter had filed a joint three-column opus covering the arrival of the prisoners and Clover's account of the difficult march. With that done they proceeded to polish off their assignment in best Chicago style; they torpedoed the correspondent of a rival paper by taking the telegrapher out and getting him drunk. They did not complete the trip to Cheyenne, but got off the train with the prisoners at Fort Russell, just before the capital was reached.

In his book *On Special Assignment* Clover tells a yarn of getting off the train early because he had learned of "a plot by the rustlers to kidnap him at Cheyenne and hold him as a witness against the cattlemen." This was nonsense on its face, since Cheyenne was Fortress Big Stockman and no rustler had a toehold there. In fact, as his private correspondence at the time reveals, Clover was terrified of the stockmen and convinced that in their ugly and desperate mood they would stop at nothing to keep him from testifying against them, which he could have been compelled to do. At Fort Russell he and Seymour descended to terra firma and changed to a carriage which had been thoughtfully provided for them by former Attorney General Hugo Donzelman who, along with all the rest of the highest-priced legal talent in the state, had been retained to defend the invaders.[10]

Once in the carriage the two reporters fell asleep as soon as they touched the cushions. They drove to the nearest point where they could pick up an eastbound train and so get across the line into Nebraska.

At Sidney they detrained. Clover had one last story to send. He had been fairly busy in the ten days since the surrender took place; and all this, be it remembered, was before the day of the portable typewriter. It was Sunday, and the telegrapher was in church with his best girl, but Seymour got him out with the proffer of a five-dollar bill. The story was sent under a faked Cheyenne dateline. Seymour then returned to Cheyenne to wind up the paper's business there while Clover caught the night express for Chicago. Back safely at last in the bosom of the *Herald* family, the Rover boy found himself a hero. The staff thumped him on the back, admired his tan, and told him they had had the headlines all set up telling of his death. They had also planned to quote his dying words to the effect that he hoped the story of his demise would be an exclusive for his paper.

Sic transit Clover from the Wyoming scene. He went on to a varied and successful publishing career, died in 1929 in Los Angeles.

The invaders were disappointed in their expectation of a speedy release. From the end of April the months ground on into January while money was poured out like water to save them and Johnson County went slowly bankrupt in the hopeless fight; but there could be only one outcome. As Seymour wrote of the eminent prisoners in the *Herald* for April 23:

They ... are backed not only by the Republican machine from President Harrison down to the state organization, but by at least $25,000,000 of invested capital. . . . They have the President, the governor, the United States senators, the legislature, the state organization, the courts and the army at their back.

It was enough.

6

Aftermath

The aftermath of a small civil war in Wyoming proved just as ugly and unedifying as the aftermath of a big civil war a generation earlier. In view of the way the dice were loaded no one really expected that the invaders would pay for their crime, but some of the methods by which they attempted to get themselves off the hook were just as self-willed and brutal, and just as unscrupulous, as the invasion plot had been in the first place. The kidnaping of two innocent witnesses and the conspiracy to impose a reign of bloodshed and terror on Johnson County do not make pleasant reading.

But neither does what happened in Johnson County. The term *reconstruction*, used of a postwar period, is a piece of unconscious doubletalk, since what it refers to all too often is not rebuilding but breakdown. Johnson County suffered a civic breakdown. While the county was defending itself against attack it won public sympathy; but then it turned around and destroyed its own image by committing a particularly wanton and evil murder—and condoning it.

Yet peace came sooner than anyone would have dared hope. Perhaps it was the climate. But in the high and glorious Wyoming air blood ceased to flow and wounds healed with wonderful completeness; leaving a few scars, it is true, like the marks of trenches on an old battlefield.

THIRTY-THREE

The Case of the
Innocent Bystanders

WITH THE cattlemen safely shut up in Fort Russell where no rustlers could get at them, the next order of business was getting rid of the witnesses. It was accomplished by means of one of the ugliest, most unscrupulous, most shameful cases of bulldozing and oppression in the history of the late nineteenth century—which is saying something.

After all, the railroading of witnesses was nothing new to this crowd. They had done it in the Cattle Kate case.

Bill Walker and Ben Jones, the two out-of-work roundup hands who got caught in the middle at the KC fight, were going into camp the night before at a spring just outside Nolan's old ranch house when Nate Champion saw them and invited them in for the night. What happened after that has been told. At the end of that terrible day they were set free by Wolcott and Irvine, and were told to head south and keep going. They obeyed with alacrity, so frightened by what they had seen that they stayed out in the hills for a week, until hunger and cold drove them into Casper. There they kept mum until they found out the state of public sentiment about recent events. It was violent.

Then they spilled everything. They told the whole story of the death of Champion and Ray and the firing of the cabin, and finding themselves heroes they told it some more. Naturally all this reached the newspapers. It became apparent that these two men were important witnesses. The idea struck both sides of the controversy at once—forcibly.

After these guileless characters had basked in the limelight a while Sheriff O. L. Rice of Natrona County noticed two hard-looking strangers hanging around, learned that they had been sent from Cheyenne to dispose of the witnesses in one way if not another. He notified Angus to come and look after them, but Angus knew he could not hold them and wired the sheriff of Converse County to take charge.[1]

Enter now E. H. Kimball, editor of that feisty little Democratic-Populist sheet, the Douglas *Graphic*, and a prolific correspondent of the *Rocky Mountain News* and other big-city dailies. Kimball was at times a noisy propagandist and at times a remarkably facile and lucid reporter. In addition he was undersheriff of Converse County, and at present acting sheriff, since the regular wearer of the badge was away on business in Washington. Kimball went to Casper and got the trappers and took them to Douglas and gave them a room in the sheriff's office and revolvers to protect themselves with. He warned them to stay inside after dark. About that time he was called to a neighboring town. It was very soon suspected that the call had been a ruse to get him out of the way. This was Wednesday, May 4. When he returned next day, the pair were gone.

It turned out that they had ignored his instructions and left the jail. Walker got very drunk. Jones, uncertain, went along. They were walking back and forth in front of the sheriff's office when they were approached by a livery-stable keeper named O. P. Witt, wearing the toothy smile of Little Red Riding Hood's grandmother, who inveigled them to his livery stable. There they were confronted by seven or eight armed men, described as "well-known cattlemen," and were ordered at gunpoint to get on two horses which were saddled and waiting, and get out of town. They left through an alley about 1 A.M., escorted by Witt. They took the revolvers with them.

Kimball had no authority to hold them. He could not subpoena them as witnesses because—a nice legal point—the cattlemen were still in the custody of the United States military; the Johnson County authorities had never been allowed to come near them; they had never been arrested and were under no charges; hence no subpoena power. He suspected that the witnesses had been hustled across the Nebraska line to the nearest rail point, so he got out warrants against them for theft of the revolvers and wired City Marshal Morrison at Crawford, Nebraska, to arrest them. Or rather he tried to wire, but it turned out that the telegraph line had been cut—the old familiar story—so no message could be got through until that afternoon, Thursday the fifth.

Thereafter a running fight raged for five days clear across Nebraska, with yelling mob scenes, near-riots, fist fights, legal shenanigans; a battle of warrants against warrants—Wyoming warrants, Nebraska warrants, federal warrants, habeas corpus, and headlines across the nation; the innocent bones of contention being the two terrified "trappers" or "freighters" who wanted nothing except Out.

That night and all next day the three men rode across the sandhill country of western Nebraska headed for the little tank station of Harrison, where they were to take the eastbound train, a matter of some hundred miles. During the night Witt dismounted, evidently acting under orders, threw his rope over the telegraph line and dragged it down, then took a pair of wire-cutters from his pocket and cut it in several places. Later he dismounted again and started lighting matches. Convinced that this was a signal to gunmen in the vicinity to come and kill them, his two prisoners pulled their guns on him and asked him what he was doing; he had been unaware that they were armed. He said he was lost and was lighting matches to look at his compass. They ordered him to get back on the road. When searched later he had no compass. At a ranch house where they stopped for breakfast a woman asked them whether they had seen a party of men riding through the country.

Jones, suspicious all along that the plan was to kill them, balked frequently and showed fight, but Walker went along like a lamb to the slaughter. While they were still in Wyoming Witt's horse gave out, and he told them to go on into Harrison while he made his way on foot to a nearer rail point. Right then and there was their chance to get away and get back to their friends if they had wished; Jones wanted to seize it and strike out across country, but Walker insisted on keeping on into Harrison. Witt had told them that, just before they reached town, they were to hide their saddles in a gulch and shoot the horses (to keep the brands from being seen and recognized). They hid the saddles but turned the horses loose.

When they got on the train, they were paralyzed to see that, in addition to the cattlemen's lawyer Fred Harvey and their friend Witt, a gang of six or seven armed men were on board. Arriving at Crawford after dark, they were pushed rudely off the train and the gang tried to hustle them across to the Burlington train which was waiting at another station two hundred yards away, bound east. Jones, now convinced that they were going to be killed, drew his gun and started yelling for help. Said lawyer Harvey soothingly, "This poor old man is my uncle and he is crazy and we are taking him east to an asylum." At this point here came City Marshal Morrison of Crawford with Kimball's warrants for theft of the revolvers—the only way he could hold the two men—and a free-for-all developed. It was now Thursday night, May 5, not twenty-four hours since the victims had been spirited out of Douglas.

During the fuss over Jones one of Harvey's henchmen had nabbed Bill Walker and was rushing him off to the B. M. train, now on the point of departure, but a deputy city marshal broke that up. Jones and Walker were locked up for safekeeping—still on those warrants—and Witt was jailed too, on general principles. But next day, Friday, Harvey wired the county judge at Chadron, twenty-six miles to the east, and obtained a writ of habeas corpus. The scrappy city marshal refused to give up his prisoners. Harvey got on the wires again, and soon a special train of engine and caboose came flying down the track from Chadron, with a squad of special deputies on board—and a warrant for the arrest of Morrison!

By this time the town of Crawford was worked up to such a pitch of indignation over the outrageous proceedings that it was ready to riot on behalf of its marshal and his prisoners, but the marshal wisely discouraged that and went along to Chadron on the special train—which he barred to Harvey and company. As for Kimball, who had been absent through all this, he got in on the regular train that night after the special had left.

What developed during those days of turmoil and shame was the familiar contest between money and influence on one side and the popular will on the other. Every sheriff and town marshal from Casper to Omaha was backing Kimball and in favor of Wyoming holding its witnesses, and the angry but helpless crowds made their feelings plain. The witnesses themselves were too terrified to go back even when they had the chance. They were simple men of no very high IQ and they had no wish to be heroes. Repeatedly during their ordeal these two poor bewildered fellows showed more fear of the sheriffs and the Nebraska citizens who were trying to rescue them from their kidnapers than they did of the smooth-talking lawyers and silent, menacing gunmen on the cattlemen's side. They did not want to go back to Wyoming to testify. In contrast to the redoubtable George Dunning, who had convictions and the courage of them, all they asked was to get out of this with a whole skin.

The habeas corpus case was heard in the county court at Chadron on the morning of Monday, May 9. As expected, the judge released the prisoners. At once there was pandemonium in the courtroom, with the spectators jumping on chairs and tables and everyone shouting at once. There was no doubt as to where the crowd stood. J. C. Dahlman, the famous sheriff who later became mayor of Omaha, tried to rearrest them on behalf of the Converse County officers. But the cattlemen had another ace up their sleeve—the power of the federal court and the United States Marshal. Two deputy United States marshals from Omaha were in the courtroom, armed with a federal warrant charging Walker and Jones with selling whiskey to Indians. It was an arrant fake, sworn out by O. P. Witt, the livery-stable Judas, who had never seen the men till

a week before, and in that time they could not have been near an Indian.
As soon as the judge had spoken—"Owing to lack of jurisdiction I will
have to order their release"—the deputies clapped irons on them.

Recalled an eyewitness in the courtroom that morning: "I shall never
forget the terror-stricken look in the eyes of the old trapper Jones as the
handcuffs and leg irons were fastened on his limbs. . . ."

Amid the uproar Sheriff Dahlman and his deputies had produced
their warrants and were demanding the prisoners, but Harvey and his
crowd were too fast for them. It was strongarm work pure and simple.
They simply hustled the prisoners out the door and to the railroad station, where another special train was waiting—with steam up. "The
whole thing was done so violently and speedily," Kimball wrote, "that
the spectators did not know what had occurred until it was too late."

The same courtroom spectator remembered: "That May morning
picture in Nebraska—the two innocent unoffending trappers with glittering steel shackles on their wrists and ankles, the U.S. marshal and
his assistants hurrying them along, the successful lawyers for the million-
aire murderers accompanying and the indignant, irresolute crowd that
followed after, will never be erased from my mind." [2]

Witt, incidentally, was by now in the same boat, having been arrested
on complaint of the Western Union agent for cutting the wires. Besides,
he knew too much by this time himself.

The last act in the kidnaping took place in Omaha the next day; as
related by Undersheriff Kimball, who had lost his witnesses but was still
functioning as a reporter, this is the way it was:

"Three bedraggled, unkempt and altogether rough-looking men, two
of them handcuffed together, and all of them with terror depicted on every
feature, huddled in a bunch at the heels of United States Deputy Hepfin-
ger about 5:30 last evening. . . . None of the prisoners gave evidence of
having enjoyed a moment's rest in many a day. They were gaunt and hol-
low-eyed, and glanced suspiciously at everyone and into every corner.

"Their arrival disturbed the siesta of United States Judge Dundy
who, although it was long past his usual hour for leaving the building,
had stretched himself on the lounge in Marshal Slaughter's office as if
he had an appointment and fully meant to keep it."

The arraignment was brief. The bond of the trapper witnesses was
fixed at $800 each, on their own recognizance. About eight-thirty in the
evening they entered a carriage with a leading attorney for the cattlemen
and were whirled away to the railroad station, where they boarded a
night express, eastbound.

The attorney in question, the slippery Hugo Donzelman, personally
escorted them all the way to their destination on the eastern seaboard;

New York state according to one version, Rhode Island according to another. They had been the recipient of frequent promises that they would be paid a handsome sum, something like $2500 apiece—when the troubles in Wyoming had simmered down. Checks in this amount were deposited in a bank at the place where they were staying—post-dated. When the agreed time arrived for them to cash their checks, they tried it.

They had been paid off in bad checks.[3]

Mad Dog Murder

WHILE THE western press was still in a furor over the body-snatching of the trappers, public opinion was shocked by another murder in Johnson County. On May 10, 1892, a pleasant and promising young man named George Wellman, newly appointed foreman of Henry A. Blair's Hoe ranch on Powder River, was shot and killed from ambush—a wanton act with no more sense or motivation than that of a mad dog which bites a passer-by.

After the invasion, law and order in Johnson County fell to an all-time low. Northern Wyoming, hourly expecting a bigger and bloodier invasion, was in a state of panic. Angus, who had acquitted himself nobly up to the time the cattlemen were transferred from Fort McKinney, now seemed to have lost his grip entirely. The worst criminal element boiled up to the surface like scum and took over. They threatened, looted, and terrorized, but their attentions were by no means confined to parties suspected of sympathizing with the recent invaders. Living in part by stealing cattle—and no one seems to know what else they lived by—they stole impartially from whitecap outfits and from loyal and respected Johnson County citizens who had defended the county against armed attack.[1]

Some were newcomers, wanted in other states, who had been attracted to Johnson County by the smell of trouble the way coyotes are attracted by carrion. But others were well known locally. A gang of fifteen or twenty of them took to riding into town, flourishing six-shooters and rifles and threatening to kill merchants who had sided with the invaders if the latter refused to hand over some item like a pearl-handled six-shooter which took their fancy. A pair of them offered to kill the city marshal but he stood his ground and disarmed them.

They looted ranches without any effort on the part of the county authorities to stop them, but with Johnson County so burned up over the invasion outrage it is hard to see what else could have been expected. At the Hesse ranch house they destroyed or removed furniture and shot the piano to pieces for good measure; and the character called One-Eyed Tex was seen strutting around Buffalo wearing a storebought suit recognized as belonging to Fred Hesse. Unfortunately there were low minds which found this funny, and people not ordinarily lawless were heard to declare that after what old Fred had done, the loss of a suit of clothes was the least he had coming to him.

The troublemakers were called the Red Sash gang, because they affected the then-popular cowboy style of a red sash around the waist as a badge of membership.* Their leader was Charles Taylor, who had drifted into the area recently from nearby Crook County bringing a bad reputation with him, including a record in Colorado. Taylor would have been comical if he had not been lethal—a shoddy, bucktoothed braggart whose favorite expression was "I'm a man of a few words. If it don't suit you I'll kill you."

One of his followers was a vicious nonentity called Ed Starr, who never even amounted to enough as a rustler to have his name entered on any of the "known rustler" lists. His place of origin and length of residence in Johnson County are not known, but he was a killer for killing's sake.[2]

Another member of the gang was "Black Henry" Smith, who was no newcomer and no nonentity. He was well known in the Powder River country, having been there at least six years, working for big outfits—Frewen's, the EK, and the Bar C. He was a tall, dark man with a big mustache, remembered as a brilliant talker and possessed of immense personal charm. He had good connections in Texas, who bailed him out when he tangled with the law; and he was known for his knack of impressing the rich upper crust in the cattle business with his easy flow of conversation, his picturesque appearance, and of course his travels—for he had conned one Bar C manager into borrowing money and taking him on an extensive tour of New York, South America, and Europe.

In the summer of 1891 he also impressed Owen Wister: "... the only unabridged 'bad man' I have ever had a chance to know," Wister wrote his mother.

... A tall, long-nosed dark fellow, with a shock of straight black hair on end, all over his head ... eyes ... of a mottled yellow, like agate or

---

* Red sashes had long been worn by dress-conscious cowboys. Charlie Russell wore one in Montana during the nineties, and to the end of his life. Twenty years earlier Wild Bill Hickok wore one in Abilene.

half-clear amber, large and piercing, at times burning with light. They are the very worst eyes I have ever looked at. Perfectly fearless and shrewd, and treacherous. . . . He is not a halfway man. . . . He is just bad through and through, without a scruple and without an affection. His face is entirely cruel, and you hear cruelty in his voice. . . . When I come to my Castle in Spain—my book about Wyoming—I shall strain my muscles to catch Smith.

With his novelist's intuition, Owen Wister had called the turn.[3]

About a week after George Wellman's death three of the Red Sash crew, including Charlie Taylor and Henry Smith, were arrested for trying to burn down the barracks at Fort McKinney. They tried twice, throwing kerosene on the buildings when a strong wind was blowing, but there was not enough evidence to hold them for trial. Their motive seems to have been simply objection to the presence of the troops, which they felt threatened their own activities.

When George Wellman was named foreman of the Hoe ranch he was thirty-two years old and had been a Hoe cowboy for a number of years. He was good-looking, likable, dependable, and several cuts above the average cowhand in ability. Although generally known as a whitecap sympathizer, he had been out of the country during the heat of the invasion troubles, and the only overt act ever charged against him was helping "a distressed newspaper correspondent," as the press put it (evidently poor Ed Towse) to get out of the state. In April he had gone east to Wisconsin to get married, planning to bring his wife to Wyoming later.

On his return he stopped off for a few days in Cheyenne, where on May 4 he was appointed a special deputy United States marshal to serve injunction papers to halt the rustlers' roundup, announced just prior to the invasion. The roundup injunctions were a farce. They were issued May 3 by the federal court on a tissue-paper pretext of jurisdiction, since the law proposed to be violated was a state law. By this time the rustlers' roundup had been called off anyway. But during the month of May all except one of the thirty-three writs were solemnly served, with no resistance or fuss. And that was all there was to that.

After leaving Cheyenne by rail on 5 May Wellman stopped off in Gillette to discuss certain new economy moves in the Hoe ranch operations with Blair's top man in Wyoming. They also talked about the roundup injunctions, in a bar, and the news of Wellman's appointment as a U.S. deputy spread fast and far. He reached the ranch on the afternoon of Monday, May 9.

Also on Monday afternoon nine members of the Red Sash gang, drinking, loud-mouthed, and quarrelsome, were congregated at Kid

Donnelly's place at Powder River crossing. Also present were two Hoe cowboys, one of them named Tom Hathaway, from whom the gang learned of Wellman's intended trip to Buffalo next morning. Also in the crowd, but not of it, before the night was out was the long-memoried Tommy Carr, now a mail carrier, who had just come in after a fifty-mile horseback ride with his saddlebags stuffed with mail from the tiny post offices of Riverside and Blue Creek, up in the canyon country where the headwaters of Powder River flow out of the mountains. Very early in the morning Carr was awakened when three of the gang got up and went out. Two of them were Ed Starr and Black Henry Smith.[4]

Wellman and Hathaway were both at the Hoe ranch by suppertime on the ninth, when Wellman announced the economy moves—including the discharge of four men. Next morning, Tuesday, May 10, he and Hathaway left together to go to Buffalo, where Wellman was to meet United States Marshal Joseph P. Rankin in the matter of those roundup injunctions. Since Hathaway was leaving for good he had all his belongings packed on a second horse which Wellman was leading for him because Hathaway's mount was nervous; or as the cowboy put it, "his horse had a more sociable disposition than mine." It was snowing again. Twelve miles out from the ranch they passed a low hill covered by tall sagebrush on the left. Shots rang out, and George Wellman fell dead from his saddle.

The story Hathaway told at the inquest went like this: "I and Mr. Wellman was riding along side by side on the road; he was leading the horse that had my bed packed on it, and we was riding along talking, when we heard a couple of shots close together; it made my horse jump and also Wellman's; then two more shots were fired. It started my horse on the run. The horse bucked me off but I got back on and rode down over the hill, but while I was standing there the two horses that Wellman had, the one he was riding and the one he was leading, run by me and the pack was turned on the pack horse. I looked back and noticed that Mr. Wellman was laying on the ground. I got on my horse and started down over the hill, I could not tell where the shooting was coming from and I run right down over the hill. . . . His horses went on and I run onto them and stopped them. . . . I was satisfied that Mr. Wellman was killed as he did not make a move." Hathaway did not go near the body.

He was clearly in a panic. Reaching Buffalo at four in the afternoon he told his story a number of times, changing it with each telling and showing all the marks of nervousness and guilt. He was watched; and that night the city marshal arrested him in the establishment of a "Widow Brown," charged with the murder of Wellman.

There followed a chapter of bungling, cowardice, and dirty politicking which has been equaled but never surpassed. Angus was in no hurry about leaving for the murder scene. Next day when he finally reached the spot where George Wellman's body was still lying in the road, thirty miles southeast of Buffalo, he made a hasty examination. He saw footprints but jumped to the conclusion that Hathaway had made them and went back to Buffalo, where he reported that Hathaway was guilty.

Charles H. Burritt, the garrulous, letter-writing mayor of Buffalo who was on a secret retainer as attorney for the stockmen in Cheyenne, was not satisfied that Angus would do anything, so he sent out three men of his own to investigate. Their findings were quite different. They followed the footprints to a gulch a short distance behind the hill where a man, out of sight of the road, had been holding three horses. They then followed the tracks of the three horses ten or twelve miles in a southwesterly direction toward the place where Powder River comes out of the mountains. Then they too gave up and returned to Buffalo, pleading lack of food and fresh horses.

Angus was scared to death. He had been warned by letter and telegram of probable attempts on his life. But the brave men of Burritt's faction were no better. They had no inclination to leave the safety of the town limits for the sagebrush where they stood a good chance of being dry-gulched like George Wellman. Even the permanent U.S. deputy marshal from Cheyenne, who was in Buffalo on the injunction matter and was generally respected as a brave officer, refused to stir out of town. Only one man had nerve enough to volunteer, and he was somewhat ungratefully referred to by Burritt as "a notorious thief"—typical of the stockmen's unwholesome habit of referring to anyone who had differed with them as a thief. Nobody ever followed the murderer's tracks.

George Wellman had been instantly killed by a rifle bullet through the back of the neck. The body had been robbed of his watch, ring, and six-shooter.[5]

Johnson County apologists maintained for as long as possible that "the rustlers" had nothing to do with the murder of George Wellman. They covered up for the killer gang and protected them, by official inaction, journalistic falsehood, and at times by the presence of fifty or more armed citizens.

Best of all was the canard launched by some Johnson County genius to the effect that the cattlemen themselves had murdered the innocent young man in order to throw the blame on the rustlers and gain sympathy for themselves. This whopper was repeated by A. S. Mercer, author of *The Banditti of the Plains,* who was an experienced journalist and knew better. But Mercer was writing a tract.[6]

Hathaway was released after the inquest. He continued to act very queerly, however, still hanging around Buffalo as though he had something on his mind, talking of going to Canada but not going, and holding long confabs with Mayor Burritt. He kept repeating his protestations of entire ignorance regarding the murder, saying he had told all he knew, but Burritt didn't believe him. Burritt, the long-winded attorney, was honest and no fool, and he was the only man in Wyoming at the time who was really trying to solve the Wellman case. At the end of June Hathaway was picked up by a federal officer and taken to Cheyenne, his arrest being a matter of protective custody since otherwise his life would have been worth nothing. He arrived on the twenty-eighth, and within a day or two he had told everything to the United States attorney. It was plenty.

After hearing the shots which killed Wellman he had seen a man with a gun in his hand but with no smoke coming out of it. The man was Clayton Cruse, one of the lesser Red Sashes. Afterward he saw Henry Smith and Ed Starr, both on foot, with Starr stooping over the body. He testified to all this under oath at a hearing on August 23. But the hearing was only on a federal conspiracy charge; not on the charge of murder.[7]

So the Wellman case was solved. But there is no consolation in the fact for lovers of justice, since the killers lived happily ever after.

Johnson County did nothing about the prosecution, though Red Angus and the city marshal did make some headway at tracing the real killers. In Cheyenne the quondam regulators showed no immediate interest in catching the murderers of their man Wellman; they were too busy concocting a scheme to promote civil strife in Johnson County and get the President to declare martial law. In Cheyenne the United States authorities were restricted to the cumbersome and roundabout process of federal law which did not cover the crime of murder. All they could charge was "conspiracy" to injure United States citizens for attempting to enforce their rights, et cetera, in the course of which conspiracy George Wellman was killed.

By the end of June Charlie Taylor, Henry Smith, and company, who had doubtless smelled a rat in connection with Hathaway's departure, had given up terrorizing the community and had fortified themselves on Crazy Woman Creek, where they were surrounded by fifty sympathizers. After incredible delays, United States Marshal Joseph P. Rankin managed to scrape up a posse of ten men, and at the end of July three of them tried to arrest Ed Starr and another member of the gang, but they got away after a fight. Otherwise the posse lazed around Buffalo until nearly the end of August, drinking and playing cards and explaining that they couldn't go out and make those arrests just yet because their horses had been stolen—the classic western excuse.

The only reason any arrests were ever made in this masterpiece of bungling and corruption was that the United States attorney in Wyoming, backed by the attorney general, kept at it. At the beginning of 1893 they hired a Pinkerton detective. His duties required him to go to New Mexico; that is all we know, except that at the end of March or thereabouts Henry Smith and Clayton Cruse were in custody.[8] Starr was never caught.

When Smith was tried in November 1893, Justice fell through a jurisdictional crack and bumped herself and broke her scales.

Since the case was a federal one, the issue was "conspiracy," not murder. But did Smith conspire? Did he know of the injunction suit; did he know that Wellman was a deputy United States marshal appointed for the purpose of serving the injunction writ and was so engaged at the time he was killed? It couldn't be proved.

When Tom Hathaway took the stand he was not allowed to tell what he saw on the road that fatal morning. The judge ruled that since the charge of murder was incidental to the charge of conspiracy, testimony on the murder could not be heard unless the conspiracy had been proved, which it had not. He directed the jury to acquit Henry Smith. The *Leader*'s reporter, captivated by Smith's well-known plausible charm, wrote a flattering column-length interview with this handsome young typical westerner; the *Leader* editorially, hewing to its pro-rustler line, cried shame that the poor young man had been held in jail so long in the alleged absence of any case against him.[9]

Black Henry, who had been supported by a battery of expensive counsel, went back to Johnson County eventually. So said the local yarn-spinners, who unlike the press had no illusions about him and whose reminiscences proved to be so remarkably accurate. They went on that he got mixed up later in a deal stealing government cattle in North Dakota. They said he got away with that too.

With Smith set free there was no point in trying Clate Cruse, and we hear of him no more. Also vanished from the record is Tom Hathaway, who at least tried to do the right thing, at the cost of great personal inconvenience and risk to his life. Hathaway's guilt feelings are understandable if he heard the murder plot discussed. He probably did.

For those who may question whether Hathaway was telling the truth there is a postscript to the story. A few miles north of Kaycee a rim of sand rocks with three pointed buttes stands above the low prairie, a landmark in the monotonous sage. In 1897 a man named Potts was looking after some cattle north of Kaycee, and up in the sand rocks he saw the top of a baking-powder can sticking up out of the ground. He took it out and found a gun inside, wrapped in a newspaper. He had no idea whose gun it was or how it got there, but it was of unusual design and well preserved, so he took it home. After his death his son kept it.

In 1935 Billy Hill, formerly a well-known rustler, came back from Canada where he had long since been living respectably, for a visit to his old haunts. He and some other old-timers drove out on the Kaycee road and after a while he said: "Stop here a minute." They walked over to the sand rocks and he said: "George Wellman's gun ought to be right there under that rock, down in the sand." Of course it wasn't there. But then he told the story. Hill, who was too friendly with the Red Sash gang for good reputation's sake, had run into Ed Starr a few days after the murder. With a killer's conceit Starr boasted of his deed and told of taking the gun off the blood-soaked body. Then he led Hill to the place under the sand rocks, dug in the sand and produced a five-pound baking-powder can. In it was George Wellman's gun.

The three old residents of Buffalo who heard Hill tell the story forty-three years later then recalled the mysterious gun the elder Potts had found in the same spot. Hill examined it and pronounced it positively the one Starr had shown him.[10] And so in this posthumous fashion was forged the final link in the chain of evidence wrapping up a murder.

Starr was definitely on the run for a while, and "they" say that he ended up in Montana, Canada, or somewhere away—the accounts differ. There is even a tale that he married a wife who was a churchgoer and henpecked him. At any rate the story of his ending, while apocryphal, has a certain sweet appropriateness. According to the story he fell into a dispute with a man who through some trickery got at Starr's six-shooter when the latter had gone out, unarmed, and removed the cartridges, substituting blanks. Then he provoked Starr into going for his gun.

THIRTY-FIVE

The Plot That Failed

IF THE prisoners relaxing in their nominal confinement were not particularly interested at first in following up the murder of George Wellman, it was because they had something bigger and better in mind—martial law.

Smarting after their recent failure and suffering from a martyr complex, they were determined to accomplish the ends of the invasion and punish what they called "the infected district"—northern Wyoming—by one means if not by another. They and their friends in Cheyenne were talking martial law before the train carrying them southward had even reached Fort Russell, combined with threats of a second invasion and much more manpower—"we'll get all these people yet."

Major Wolcott, the bloodthirsty little rooster, was obsessed with the idea of a bloodbath in Wyoming and was doing his best to bring it about. Said he: "The bloodshed is not yet begun." Around the first of June he was excused from Fort Russell by the amiable commandant of the post, who had often been a guest in the homes of his prominent prisoners, to make a trip to Omaha in order to put the case for declaration of martial law to Senator Manderson of Nebraska. The idea was to apply pressure on President Harrison.[1]

Federal martial law is equivalent to putting the affected area under military occupation like a conquered enemy country. Civil rights are suspended, including the writ of habeas corpus, civil trials and of course all civil administration, in favor of trial and administration by the military. It is so drastic that it has never been invoked in the face of a domestic peacetime crisis, but Wolcott and Irvine were confident that they had the federal establishment in their pocket and could get what they wanted. They were backed at every step by Senator Francis E. Warren and the chief counsel for the Wyoming Stock Growers' Association, Judge Willis O. VanDevanter. The methods of these two gentlemen were subtler, their language suaver, and their knowledge of law considerably greater than that of Messrs. Wolcott and Irvine, but the object was the same: revenge on Johnson county. However, there was some lingering prejudice in Washington in favor of legality and the plotters were turned down, much to their wrath.[2]

To appease his friends President Harrison ordered additional Army units to Wyoming. Six troops of the 9th cavalry were transferred from Fort Robinson, Nebraska, to Suggs, on lower Powder River; another six troops from Fort Niobrara went into camp between old Fort Fetterman and Casper, about six hundred men in all. This was on June 6.

In certain circumstances, including an appeal from the governor, the President could order the troops to move in to "suppress an insurrection." This was a step short of martial law but it was the next best thing —if not, in some ways, better. Now the only thing lacking was the insurrection.

The second stage of the scheme was more complex than the first. Rankin, the United States marshal, was to create an army of deputies, march into Johnson County, and serve a large number of warrants based on the familiar conspiracy charges. The murder of George Wellman, in which the cattlemen suddenly started to take an interest after the failure of the martial-law scheme, would provide an additional pretext. Service of the warrants would naturally be resisted, not only by the servees but in all likelihood by the population generally.

There was every reason to count on resistance. So bitter were the people over the invasion that one man said if his own brother had been among the whitecaps he would have "thrown down" on him. Constant rumors kept the population churned up in a state of excitement; Frank Canton was supposed to be at the KC with two hundred Texans; a hurriedly organized home guard kept lookouts on the hills and sent runners galloping into town at every fresh alarm. Since the warrants were returnable in Cheyenne instead of in Johnson or any of the other northern counties, Angus and others concluded that the point was to take them all to Cheyenne and kill them, either there or on the way. They said they would die before they would be arrested.

Thus a fight seemed certain, providing an excuse for calling on the President to "suppress an insurrection." Those showing resistance would thereupon be gunned down by federal troops, and the aim of the invasion would yet be accomplished.

It was an ingenious plan, but it ran into an unexpected obstacle in the person of Marshal Rankin, who had previously been in the cattlemen's camp, as had almost every other official in Cheyenne. However, he became quite well aware that his own role was that of a pawn whose life was to be sacrificed at the first move in the game if necessary. He was not enthusiastic. Second, he could not raise that authorized army of deputies. Men simply could not be found who were willing to stick their heads into the hornets' nest of Johnson County. Seven were all he could ever get, plus three in Buffalo.

Third, he balked at serving worthless conspiracy warrants. There were twenty-some warrants issued by a U.S. Commissioner in Cheyenne who habitually licked the boots of his masters. More than half of them had been issued on insufficient evidence and were voided later.[3]

On July 30 President Harrison issued a proclamation commanding all persons engaged in resisting "the laws and the process of the courts of the United States" to disperse and retire to their homes. Oddly enough the proclamation had some effect, and Johnson County began to quiet down. It looked as though the bloodshed were not going to come off after all.

Raging, Wolcott and Irvine bombarded Washington with letters demanding Rankin's scalp. Warren backed them as usual, and on September 11 the President himself sent a peremptory telegram to the attorney general demanding Rankin's removal.

But something strange was going on in that complex capital, for the Department of Justice failed to fire Rankin, President or no President. Instead it sent a special examiner out to Wyoming to investigate the charges. The examiner not only gave Rankin a ringing exoneration but issued two reports in which he denounced the conspiracy and the conspirators in blistering terms, throwing in a blast at the bootlicking U.S. Commissioner and his phony warrants for good measure. These are a few of examiner Frank B. Crossthwaite's remarks:

As one of the results of my invesigation, I am forced to the conclusion that it was not so much the intention to have the men arrested as it was to have them driven out of the country or killed.

Another reason for concluding that the arrest of the men was not desired nor expected is the fact that no substantial evidence was laid before the commissioner with the complaints.... Commissioner Churchill has exposed himself to criticism, in my opinion, for having issued the warrants for the arrest of those men without having first submitted them to the examination of the United States attorney.

It appears that nearly everyone in authority, or in official life, was doing just about what the representatives of the cattle owners told them to do.

Mr. Irvine told me in person that he "hoped and expected" that, when Marshal Rankin attempted to serve the warrants for the arrest of the rustlers in Johnson County, he would meet with the resistance threatened, namely that they would die in their tracks before they would allow service to be made, thereby placing the marshal, if he lived, in a position to call for the assistance of the United States troops.

I am also forced to the conclusion that a point was stretched to bring this matter within federal jurisdiction for the purpose of utilizing and securing to the cattle owners the strong arm of the federal government, with a view to accomplishing thereby what had been attempted by the unlawful invasion, but which proved such a miserable failure.[4]

In the meanwhile the mills of due process had been grinding slowly along. On July 5 the invader prisoners were turned over to the Johnson County authorities in the person of Undersheriff Howard Roles, who arrived with the warrants for their arrest on a charge of murder. The transfer of authority did not require their bodily removal to Johnson County. Therefore they made a short trip from Fort Russell, on the outskirts of Cheyenne, under an impressive escort which had more the aspect of a guard of honor than a police guard, to the state penitentiary at Laramie, where they were quartered in an unused wing, Judge J. W. Blake having assured the governor that these distinguished prisoners "will not under any circumstances come in contact with any of the convicts confined in another part of the building." [5]

Then began the arguments for a change of venue. To the surprise of no one at all, the judge ordered on July 19 that the trial be held in Laramie County—in the prisoners' own stronghold, Cheyenne—the only county in the state, he maintained, where there was no bias or prejudice in the case. The defendants were then returned to their own bailiwick, where they were nominally confined in Keefe Hall, a large auditorium. But they scarcely occupied Keefe Hall. The many prisoners who lived in Cheyenne slept at home. They came and went as they pleased, visiting saloons and carrying weapons. Frank Canton dropped his gun and shot himself in the foot and had to be carried into court one day on a stretcher. Several of the prisoners went on a junket to Denver. The guards and the hall hire were costing Johnson County a hundred dollars a day, but the guards had nothing to do except keep peace among the Texans, who were strangers in a strange land and relieved the monotony by getting into brawls with each other. One day two of them got into a fight on the stage, with considerable damage to the scenery.

The question of letting the prisoners out on bail came up with only the most formal objections from Johnson County, which was not merely going broke; it was broke. After some legal quibbling the judge found an excuse to give the defense what it wanted, and the defendants were admitted to bail on their own recognizance, a kind of legal honor system under which no hard money is put down, and if the bailees choose to skip out no one is out of pocket. This was on August 10. The Texans were paid off and headed for Fort Worth, promising to come back for the trial, set for August 22, though as things turned out not held until January. They never came back and nobody wanted them, not even the prosecution. Curiously enough, Johnson County held no grudge against these young strangers, regarding them as honest gunmen who had hired out through misunderstanding for a fight which was not their own.

THIRTY-SIX

George Dunning:
An Angry Man

On October 15, 1892, with the election only three weeks away, the misnamed "confession" of George Dunning burst with shattering effect upon the Wyoming scene in the columns of Asa Mercer's *Northwestern Livestock Journal*. The hireling whom Ijams had recruited in Idaho had spilled the beans, telling all about the invasion, the plans and the planners. Mercer was denounced as the instigator if not the author of it, and George Dunning as nothing but a renegade who had turned his coat to save his skin. The truth about the Dunning mystery, as best we have been able to learn it from Idaho sources follows.[1]

Ijams' ill-chosen recruit was regarded in certain quarters as a tough character; and he is still remembered locally as "a remarkable gunman" and "a crack shot," who practised his marksmanship continually. He was also a loner and a rebel. Through new evidence the main parts of his hotly disputed story now stand verified, which lends credence to the whole.

The tough part of his reputation rested on a single incident; in the course of acting as a special deputy sheriff to serve a warrant he killed two men. A bully named Vickers had roped a Chinaman and dragged him behind his horse until he was dead—"just to amuse himself," we are told. Vickers was in the house when George entered to make the arrest; George told him to come out, he reached for his gun, and Dunning shot him in the head. A young boy who had been on the lookout to protect Vickers now started shooting and—again quoting a local informant—"George told him if he didn't quit he'd have to shoot him. He didn't and George killed him."

Otherwise he is recalled by nieces and nephews as "interested in

horses—very quiet and soft-spoken—shy, and liked to be left alone."
He never married.

He came of a family well known and respected in Owyhee County,
and well educated. The father, Josiah W. Dunning, attended the University of Michigan medical school for a year, and George's brother,
Dow Dunning, attended the Literature School of the university in 1877–
1878.[2] He served in the state legislature at one time and had a large
cattle ranch. There is no record of George's ever having been to college,
but the original manuscript of the "confession" contains no misspellings,
and only rarely does he lapse into such western localisms as "I come"
for "I came." (Mercer allowed these to stand.) He was in his thirties at
the time of the invasion.

In his own state Dunning had been up to his neck in cattle troubles
similar to those of Wyoming, and as usual there is contradiction and
controversy. According to a fairly general local report, "he was in the
habit of always having lots of fresh beef on hand, although he owned
no cattle," and "at least once a year he was known to sell a large number
of hides to a buyer from Boise." He states himself that he was once
under two indictments for branding cattle, but was acquitted. The rest
of his version tells of his running series of battles with the Owyhee
County Stock Association, which was more or less a counterpart of the
Wyoming Stock Growers' Association, and then with his curious flat-
footed candor he goes on to say: "I and my friends in Idaho are about
the only ones that ever had any trouble with the stock association in
Owyhee county." And they had, or made, plenty. He accused the association of lying and blackmail. In return, "I and my friends took a very
active part in dealing the institution misery." Part of the "misery" according to Dunning consisted in forming a rival association of small stockmen
and "trying to bring to justice some of the perjurers and assassins whom
we claim were in the employ of the stock association."

Just how a man of this background came to be recruited by H. B.
Ijams to go to Wyoming and shoot rustlers—or, if you prefer, small
stockmen—mystifies a modern reader of the "confession" as much as it
mystified Dunning himself; except that Ijams seems to have been an
egregious ass. The go-between in the affair was Mayor John E. Stearns
of Nampa.

Dunning was introduced to Ijams in the mayor's office and listened
in amazement as the polite pretense about "a reliable man to run a cow
outfit" was dropped, and the Wyoming official proceeded with chilling
matter-of-factness to detail the make-up of the proposed armed force and
the plans. Ijams said that "he intended to divide the mob up after the first
month's work [the first objective, the liquidation of the sheriff and deputies

and other persons in and around Buffalo] and have five men in each squad, and have them ride over the country for several months and kill the thieves wherever they run on them. Mr. Ijams said the mob would probably kill off about 30 men in Johnson County while on their raid," visiting other counties afterwards.

Dunning could hardly believe his ears. "I thought the matter over a good deal. Ijams was perfectly sober at the time of our interview ... did not seem to get mad or excited during our conversation, but seemed to talk about the matter of murdering 30 or more men in much the same manner that many people would talk about taking a picnic excursion. I could not think for some time that Ijams was in earnest." He continued to ponder. "I could not conceive how Ijams could imagine that I and my friends were composed of the right material for a mob"; talked the matter over with one of the friends, a rancher named Henry Dement, and came to the conclusion that Ijams' proposal was "a fake."

The interview had taken place on the seventh of March. Within a week came the first of the letters which Ijams had promised to write him.[3] After the second one came, Dunning began taking Ijams' proposition seriously. He decided to accept it.

But before he left he took the precaution of leaving the three telltale letters from Ijams with Henry Dement, "so that if the mob came into Johnson county or were captured on the way they could not make any bull story stick in regard to their coming to Johnson county with peaceable intentions." George Dunning would not have made a bad lawyer.

He made several attempts to get a warning through to Johnson County about the coming invasion but failed in all of them. His account of invasion events squares almost perfectly with the others we have cited, and is often better because he gives more detail. In view of the established truth of so much of his story there is no reason to doubt what he tells of his last-ditch efforts to warn the doomed men at the KC. On the evening of the eighth, when four men were detailed to ride over and see whether the intended victims were still there, "I managed to get one of the Texans ... to let me go in his place," Dunning wrote. "I had caught my horse and started to saddle up, when Wolcott came down from the house and said I could not go along ... that us fellows would have to learn to obey orders and ask less questions. If I had gone along with the party of four ... I intended when we got in sight of the KC ranch to get off my horse and empty my Winchester at the rest of the gang and then go down to the house and inform the parties who were living there as to the state of affairs in their part of the country."

Next morning when the well-concealed invading army had the KC house surrounded and had already captured the first of the innocent bystanders, Dunning tried to attract the attention of the next men to appear. "I kept dodging up so they could see me, and the larger of the two [this must be a reference to Nick Ray] went in the house in a rush." But while the occupants had evidently become suspicious, nothing could have saved them, and Dunning proved to be mightier with the pen than with the Winchester.

By the time he had spent a few days in the Buffalo jail Sheriff Angus had found an opportunity to talk with him, for on April 19 Angus wrote a series of letters to persons living in Idaho, whose names had evidently been supplied by the prisoner as references.

For the most part the replies consisted of rather rosy character endorsements: "George Dunning ... has always had the reputation of being a very quiet and orderly man and a good cowboy ... reliable in every way ... never known as a man who was looking for trouble." (That was the mayor, who was playing it innocent and had never heard of the coming invasion.) "You ask me what kind of a man he is. I have known him for about six years would say he is a quiet man always tended to his own business [*sic*] never known of him having any trouble with any one during that time." ... "When George Dunning applied for insurance I made inquiries concerning him. All I learned then and since is that he is a good straight fellow." The exception was the Ada County sheriff, who gave him a rather tough character and referred to the two men he had killed when serving a warrant.

By far the most important answers were those of Henry Dement: "you spoke of some letters left in my charge by the man spoken of he did. I received a letter from him today asking me to send them to you hear they are." "Hear" they were indeed, dated March 13, 16, and 17, and written on the letterhead of the Board of Livestock Commissioners. The purport of all three letters was substantially the same, reiteration of the request for a party of five men, and the promise to advance money for travel expenses.

When July came Angus was still on the job, evidently determined to satisfy himself that Dunning was on the level; for another letter arrived from Henry Dement, postmarked July 4. Dement was not a very literate man, but his second misspelled scrawl told enough to clinch Dunning's story. Dunning had let his friend know that "he was going to notify the party known as the Rustlers."

In the meanwhile Governor Barber had been guilty of an oversight. You will remember that one lone stockman prisoner, Richard M. Allen, had been in Angus' custody ever since he was captured while trying to escape from Buffalo, and that the governor, with the backing of United States authorities, had demanded that he be turned over to the troops.

But the governor and everybody else either forgot or ignored the supposed cowardly deserter who had hidden out at the TA ranch and then walked into Buffalo. No one had any desire to rescue this apparent coward from the toils of the Johnson County authorities. So Dunning was not requisitioned along with Allen. Too late, the governor and his friends woke up to the fact that a hanging witness was still at large.

For before the end of April Dunning had talked too much, and the whole county now knew that he had been hired by the secretary of the state livestock commission and a good deal else besides. During the first week in May, while the Wyoming Stock Growers' Association and its lawyers were hounding the luckless trappers into oblivion, they were already eager to get their hands on Dunning, but their henchman in Buffalo, Charles Burritt, was unable to get past Angus' guard. And on May 7 Dunning was spirited out of the Buffalo jail with his willing consent. The doors were opened between midnight and 2 A.M. and Dunning was taken out by the back door of the courthouse, where horses and an escort were waiting, the latter including Tom Gardner and one of the teamsters. The party rode to Tom Gardner's ranch north of town; later the prisoner was transferred to another ranch, still guarded by the rifles of his friends; and it was weeks before the cattlemen's agents could even learn where he was.[4]

For the next five months Dunning and his importance to the case, despite some early leaks, were kept so thoroughly under wraps that on July 6 the heatedly pro-cattlemen Cheyenne *Sun* felt able to boast that with the trappers out of the country the case against the prisoners would collapse for want of evidence. It was even reported that Dunning had been hanged. But in October he turned up very much alive.

On the sixth of October he emerged from his hiding place and swore to the following affidavit at the county courthouse:

Personally appeared before me, T. P. Hill, clerk of the District court in and for Johnson county, state of Wyoming, George Dunning, who is personally known to me as the person who signed the foregoing statement [the "confession"], and deposes upon oath, duly administered to him, that the foregoing statement by him signed and comprising 44 pages, numbered in red ink from 1 to 44 inclusive, was written by him, is made without solicitation, fear or threats from any party or parties whatsoever, and that all the matters and things contained therein are true to his own knowledge and belief.

GEORGE DUNNING

Subscribed in my presence and sworn to before me this 6th day of October, 1892.

T. P. Hill
Clerk District Court.

In the summer of 1960 the writer was privileged to examine the original manuscript of the "confession," which had been kept hidden for sixty-eight years. Its forty-four pages and the red ink numbering are as described in the affidavit. Written in ink in a firm determined hand, without erasures or corrections, it shows no signs of inserts or substitutions or other editorial tampering except for a few very minor corrections in a different handwriting which were presumably made by Mercer when he prepared the manuscript for publication. The corrections consist mainly of spelling out such words as *governor* and *county* which Dunning abbreviated; also when the wrathful and repetitious author used the expression *the mob* (for the invaders) as many as seven times in one short paragraph, the editor substituted words like *they* or *the leaders*.

Certainly Dunning wrote it himself, and there is more than the physical appearance of the manuscript to confirm this. It is repetitious, overemphatic, and short on paragraphing and punctuation; the work of a man who had no thought of being a writer, but only of having something to say, and of dinning it in to the point of reader exhaustion if necessary. The idea that a fluent and experienced journalist like either Mercer or Jack Flagg would have composed such a naïve document is absurd on its face.

George Dunning stayed in Wyoming under heavy guard until late January 1893, prepared to testify at the trial which never took place. Early in January he was seen on the streets of Cheyenne on his way to the district courtroom, wearing two six-shooters, attended by an officer and looking pale from his long confinement. He had grown a full beard. That was the last contemporary report of him.

From thenceforth his trail vanished into thin air until only recently, when we were able to learn what became of him.

He got back safely to Idaho and spent the rest of his life in Owyhee County where, unlike his prominent brother Dow Dunning, he is remembered as something of a mystery—an introvert in an extraverted age. He lived alone, leading the self-sufficient yet lonely life of the aging bachelor in the West; spent several winters in the early teens of this century "baching" on a ranch on the middle fork of the Owyhee River and trapping all winter.

All lives come to an end, and all ends are sad. Came the bitterly cold winter of 1919, and the temperature went to thirty below. It was twenty-seven years since his adventure in Wyoming; George Dunning, getting up in years now, was staying alone at another ranch in some such capacity as caretaker. When a neighbor couple came over to see how he was getting along they found him confined to his bed, unable to get up and build a fire, with his whiskers frozen to the bedclothes. The wife stayed to look after him and the husband went for a doctor, but in a few days George Dunning was dead.

He is buried in Jordan Valley, Oregon, almost on the Idaho line. The marker has been removed from his grave.

However, he has another memorial. The laborious, determined hand-written document which he penned during his confinement near Buffalo that summer has come down to posterity in the form of an appendix to Mercer's polemic *The Banditti of the Plains.*

The Author of "The Banditti"

OF THOSE who in writing this particular piece of history, as we have said, "became part of it themselves," * the chief is Asa Shinn Mercer. He was a journalist who for most of his eight years in Wyoming had supported the cattlemen. His sincerity when he changed sides and launched his attack against *The Cattlemen's Invasion of Wyoming in 1892* has been questioned, but there is no question of the zeal with which they persecuted him and tried to suppress his book. In the long run they only made him famous. Even the term "invasion" was of Mercer's coinage. Without Mercer and his opponents' blundering persecution the "war" in Johnson County would have been a half forgotten local incident. Instead, largely because of him, it became immortalized in iniquity.

Mercer's little book with its denunciation of "The Crowning Infamy of the Ages" has made him a hero to a great many good people ever since its appearance in 1894. He has been praised as a "cow-country Zola," "whose sincerity of purpose and compassion for the underdog were never doubted," as "the advocate of the settlers, nesters and rustlers who annoyed or preyed upon the cattle barons." He has been pictured as a knight in shining armor who espoused the cause of the good settlers against the wicked cattle barons from the purest and noblest of motives.

Alas for a lovely legend. He never espoused their cause at all until midsummer of 1892, on the eve of an election in which he had decided suddenly to take the Democratic side.

On the contrary, the *Northwestern Livestock Journal*, which he had edited for eight years, had been a willing mouthpiece of the Wyoming

* See Foreword p. ix.

Stock Growers' Association, subsisting on their members' advertising and echoing their viewpoint. The *Journal* never uttered a peep against the invasion until three months after it was over. Until that time Mercer's voice had been as loud as any in denouncing the rustlers, whom he termed "human wolves"—he did not start calling them "settlers" until later. He upheld the Sweetwater hangmen in 1889 in terms almost past belief:

There is but one remedy and that is the freer use of the hanging noose. Cattle owners should organize and not disband until a hundred rustlers were left ornamenting the trees or telegraph poles of the territory. The hanging of two culprits merely acts as a stimulus to the thieves. Hang a hundred and the balance will reform or quit the country. Let the good work go on and lose no time about it.[1]

For this defense of a revolting crime, which certainly sounded like a clarion call for the coming invasion, he was denounced in the prosettler press as far away as Montana in such terms as "conscienceless advocate of mob law," one who "dances in the shadow of a strangled woman," and other typical editorial epithets. His future ally, E. H. Kimball of the Douglas *Graphic*, "roasted" him, and so did the influential liberal Laramie *Boomerang*. There is no question at all about his record in this hanging matter. Why then did he change sides so violently in the summer of 1892?

Critics have theorized that he deserted the cattlemen because running a livestock journal was no longer profitable, because the Democrats had offered him financial inducements to "come on over and join us," or both. But there is no evidence. However, he had attended a Cleveland rally in June, and an unmistakable odor of politics hovers over his dramatic switch soon after.[2]

The occasion was the arrest of E. H. Kimball of the Douglas *Graphic* on a charge of criminal libel. Kimball had been giving the cattlemen trouble all along, and on May 31 he reported in the *Rocky Mountain News* that a cow outfit with seventeen armed men from Texas were en route for Johnson County, ostensibly to work on the roundup, but actually to launch a second invasion and another massacre. He also reported that a price of $5000 each had been placed on the heads of Angus, Flagg, and himself.

The effect was as explosive as the most ambitious news correspondent could have wished. The prisoners and their friends were busy hatching their martial-law plot, which was not going too well, and rumor-torn, panic-ridden Johnson County was wild in expectation of another armed assault. Since the outfit referred to was George Baxter's, Baxter decided he had been criminally libeled, and Kimball was arrested, brought to Cheyenne, and jailed. A complaisant justice fixed his bail at the exorbitant figure of $2500, later reduced to $500 by order of the district judge. But this took a month and in the meanwhile Kimball remained behind bars, unable to raise such a sum. Around July 1 he was bailed out but was at once rearrested on another libel charge, and by now some twenty informations had been filed against him. It was plain that this cat-and-mouse game could go on forever. Nevertheless there were further offers to provide bail, and Mercer was one of those who came forward.

It was a strange move, since he and Kimball had up to now been editorial enemies of the most abusive sort. Mercer himself said he made the offer "out of sympathy for a brother quill driver," and so forth— but it is more likely that he did it as a gesture of support toward his newfound backers, the Democratic party of the state. No matter. His offer of bail was not accepted, but the day after it was made nearly every stockman ordered his advertising out of Mercer's paper.

In his next issue, July 7, the bellicose editor came out for the first time with a denunciation of the invasion as murder and of his former patrons the stockmen as murderers; and more—much more; Mercer was never at a loss for words. The war was on.[3]

What is one to make of a man who had written only three years before: "Cattle owners should organize and not disband until a hundred rustlers were left ornamenting the trees or telegraph poles of the territory," and now wrote this? Was his violent change of front a matter of calculation, of believing that his fortunes would be improved by aligning with the other party; or was it a sudden conversion, like getting religion after a life of sin?

Once committed he never paused. In his issue of August 18 he launched an attack on John Clay, Jr., in answer to something Clay had written in his Chicago market report for August 12; this sort of editorial broadsword-brandishing went on all the time. Calling Clay "this bulldozing foreigner," he continued: "The anarchy that exists" ("in fair young Wyoming") "is the direct result of the work of John Clay Jr. and his boon companions.... Too great a coward himself to shoulder a musket and fight, he sent one of his hired men and contributed to the extermination fund in cheap talk if not in shining shekels.... What cared he for the lives of his fellow men if by murder and arson more grass could be secured and more returns máde to his foreign shareholders ... ?" And so forth.

To even a modern reader who has outgrown the era of fisticuffs in society and canings on the floor of the United States Senate, such language does appear something of a bid for a poke in the nose. At any rate it led to one. C. A. Campbell, Clay's "hired man," walked into the *Live-stock Journal* office a few days later with several companions, under pretext of buying a paper. After an initial handshake he started an argument and then came back of the railing and struck Mercer, breaking the latter's eyeglasses and causing a cut on his face. Mercer fell. Others broke up the fight.

The assault caused considerable indignation because Campbell was a younger and bigger man than the slightly built editor. However, he was never charged with assault, merely fined for disturbing the peace.[4]

Mercer lost the battles but he won the war.

His next battle, in which he won the first round handily, was the publication of George Dunning's "confession" just before the election. The Republican party, identified with the invasion party, was on the run in the state and also in the nation. Dunning's *I Accuse*, appearing in such timely fashion, was promptly interpreted on prima facie grounds as having been cooked up or in some way inspired by Mercer. Just what did happen, just how and when he and the man from Idaho were brought together, is another mystery which will probably never be solved. But we do know that Mercer was in Buffalo on a campaign speaking trip on September twenty-fourth.

The publication of Dunning's statement caused a first-class political uproar. As parties to the invasion planning he named Governor Barber, Judge Blake, U.S. Marshal Rankin, Senators Carey and Warren, and the state attorney general. He said Ijams told him all this. The anguished denials filled column after column in the *Sun*, and some of those who denied perjured themselves mightily. Judge Willis O. VanDevanter prepared the cattlemen's answer to the charges for the editorial page, his approach being to undermine the credibility of Dunning as an assassin who had hired out to kill the very class of men whose friend he professed to be. His argument was suave and lawyerlike; very different from the *Sun's* ranting editorial tone. But it was also specious, since Dunning had hired out, according to his own statement, to warn the rustlers if possible and if not to bear witness against the invaders.

On Sunday, October 16, the regular edition of the *Journal* carrying the "confession" had already gone out to some 1400 subscribers and Mercer, apparently satisfied that all was going well, had left for Chicago, where he was to serve as commissioner for Wyoming at the World's Fair. At 11 A.M. the pressman had almost finished running off a large special edition for the Democratic state committee when a deputy sheriff descended, the doors were closed, the employees ousted, and another officer was given charge of the building. The occasion was an execution of judgment in favor of the St. Louis Type Foundry Company for a sum of some $1500 which Mercer was said to owe on a disputed bill for a printing press which had been wrecked in transit. The matter had dragged on since 1891, and everyone speculated as to why there was suddenly so much haste that the paper had to be seized on a Sunday. Through a not-so-queer coincidence the law firm of the state attorney general, identified by Dunning as privy to the invasion plot, represented the foundry company in the seizure action. But in the long run the attachment was frustrated because Mercer, like many a wise man, had put a part of his property in his wife's name; the hoped-for auction of assets could not take place, and he was soon able to resume publication of the *Journal*.[5]

While some of these things were going on the harassed editor, in Chicago, was arrested twice on libel charges preferred by John Clay. Both were based on Mercer's anti-Clay editorial of the preceding August, but since that was two months earlier it was clear that the Dunning publication was the real cause. He was first arrested for criminal libel but released at once on bond; he was arrested again in a civil action which alleged that he had damaged Mr. Clay's character to the tune of $150,000. This time bail was fixed at $5000, and Mr. Mercer did not even have time to take off his crimson World's Fair commissioner's badge before he was hustled off to jail. This one-two punch evidently aroused some sympathy and indignation among his fellow World's Fair commissioners, since no fewer than nine prominent gentlemen, representing six states and many millions of dollars, offered to go on his bond. Due to legal restrictions on out-of-state bondsmen, however, two citizens of Illinois came to his rescue again, and he was released after a little over twenty-four hours.[6]

What became of the Dunning confession after the plant was seized? According to Mercer's own statement, a part of the printing had already gone out when the Cheyenne postmaster held up the remaining copies on the ground that they were "obscene literature" and should not go through the mails. The ruling was appealed to the Postmaster General in Washington, who released the copies—after the election. In the meanwhile news of the plant seizure and the suppression had produced the usual results; the edition was soon selling for a dollar a copy, and ranchmen were reported to be riding twenty miles to get a look at it.[7]

The Wyoming Bourbons of 1892, blood kindred of the royal house whose members never forgot and never learned, simply could not divorce themselves from the notion that they could break the press if it ventured to oppose them. They made five separate tries at it in 1892. Every one was a failure.

They began with their advertising boycott of the *Leader* in March.

The boycott turned into a publicity triumph for the editor, John Carroll. That failed to teach them anything, so at the beginning of June they tried to put E. H. Kimball and the Douglas *Graphic* out of business by arresting him for libel. That didn't work, either, and it only brought Mercer into the open against them. Next they tried a boycott against Mercer followed by physical assault, which only earned him increasing fame and the headline title of "Mercer the Martyr." In the meanwhile, in the middle of June, they had tried another tack against the *Leader*, in the shape of a stockholders' suit brought by George Baxter of their group, to force the paper into receivership after which—with the court appointment of a suitable receiver—they could hope to control the editorial policy of the paper. This failed, too, and the complaint was withdrawn. For their next move they went after Mercer again.

It is an awe-inspiring thought that if these willful men had simply kept their hands off the press—more specifically if they had refrained from attacking Kimball and Mercer—*The Banditti of the Plains* would never have been written.

As to the question of Mercer's sincerity, the following would seem to be a safe general observation: By the time a man has been boycotted, beaten up, jailed, and had his property seized, he has probably begun to get mad in earnest.

Posterity, remembering Mercer's vitriolic pen, has all but forgotten that his personal political activities during these years occupied just as much of his time. In 1892 the Democrats swept the board both in the state, where the invasion was a big issue, and nationally, where the cattlemen's friend President Benjamin Harrison went out and Grover Cleveland came back in. In Wyoming the victorious Democrats went to scratching faces and pulling hair among themselves to such an extent that the heavily Democratic majority in the legislature was unable to agree on a successor to the seat of Republican Senator Francis E. Warren, which thereupon went vacant until Warren recaptured it in 1894. Mercer of course lined up with one of the factions. He got a job as state statistical agent for the Department of Agriculture—a post irreverently dubbed that of "pumpkin editor"—and since there was no further percentage for him in running a livestock journal he changed the name of his paper in February to the *Wyoming Democrat*. It ceased publication in July 1893.[8]

After spending the summer of 1893 in Chicago at the World's Fair, he returned to Wyoming in time to start writing his history of the invasion late in 1893, calling it *The Banditti of the Plains*, a title borrowed from a best-seller of a few years back, *The Banditti of the Prairies*. It was finished in time for the preface to be datelined "Cheyenne, Wyoming February 20th, 1894."

Thereafter the plot thickens. There are so many gaps in the turbulent history of this book that a whole jungle of folklore has grown up to fill them. It has been said that the book "was immediately suppressed by a court injunction in the course of a lawsuit instituted in Wyoming." But there is no mention of such a lawsuit or injunction in either the contemporary press or the court records of Laramie County from August to November 1894. It has been said that Mercer's printing plant was burned to the ground—but when? There is no evidence, and two of his children denied the story in a latter-day interview, though they said the plant was considerably damaged at some point—but again, when? It has been said that the book was repeatedly stolen from library shelves, even to the disappearance of the copyright copies from the Library of Congress. But despite the copyright notice appearing at the front of the rare original edition, the Library of Congress says the copies were never deposited, and that ought to be that.[9]

Yet after one has discounted every rumor, tracked down every false report, and waded through junkpiles of garbling without end, there is no getting away from the conclusion that something untoward happened to Mercer's book. It was suppressed, but no one can say with certainty how or when—the last and biggest Mercer mystery.

To begin with what is known: it was published in Denver.[10] It came out around the middle of August 1894, soon after the Republican state convention, and received a heavy barrage of sarcastic notice in the Republican Cheyenne press and elsewhere through September. Talk of a "conspiracy of silence" to douse Mercer's glim is, up to this point, nonsense. The Democrats evidently intended to use it for political purposes in the coming campaign, and around the first of September the Republican Douglas *Budget* advised readers interested in "Mercer's fairy tale": "You can get a copy for 50 cents now or wait a few weeks and get one for nothing from the Democratic state committee, who have published it as a campaign document."

After the eleventh of October and a last mention in the Buffalo *Bulletin*—which had, believe it or not, turned Republican—the book simply ceased to exist so far as the press was concerned, and in the thicket of rumor and hearsay which soon started to grow up around it there is more than a suggestion that the cattlemen had called out their old familiar goon squads once again. Apparently the Democratic committee never gave out a copy.

According to the reported recollection of Mercer's daughter, Mrs. Lou Webb, who was still living in the fifties, a first run of a thousand copies was printed in the *Times-Sun* office in Denver. This was the first and only shipment. It was a slim little book, inexpensively printed and bound in plain black cloth, selling for a dollar; somehow a few unbound copies also got into circulation. Mercer sold a few around Cheyenne, and in September he and his boys, Asa and Ralph, went on a tour of central Wyoming to promote the book, and Ralph has said that he personally sold a hundred fifty or two hundred copies from door to door. A shipment of five hundred copies was said to have been sent to Sheridan, in northern Wyoming, to be sold there, but the salesman was stopped in Buffalo and told to get out of the country, and the bundle of five hundred copies remained in the Burlington railroad station in Sheridan until 1909, when they were turned over to a local stationer and presumably sold. Between this shipment and the Mercer boys' selling trip, that first printing is pretty well accounted for.[11]

And there never was another. A second and larger printing of several thousand was ordered from the plant in Denver but it never reached Mercer's office. Either it was destroyed by a well-timed fire in the newspaper office, or it was seized and burned en route, according to the family's recollections.[12] Did this hijacking foil the plans to have it distributed by the Democratic state committee?

How thickly the legends multiplied—the "Mrs. X told me that Mr. Y told her fifty years ago," sort of thing—all quite worthless and impossible to trace, except for the curious insistence on certain themes: a cache of these "hot" books somewhere—in the basement of a building in Cheyenne, or of a private house in Cheyenne, or in the attic of the customs house in Denver, where the deputy collector of customs was said somehow to have come into possession of them, but an agent of the cattlemen, R. S. Van Tassell, destroyed them. The name at least is specific. And through all the hearsay, the persistent smell of burning.

Yes, Mercer lost all the battles. His book was a failure as a campaign document, and would have been even if distributed; the swing back to Republicanism—in the typical American pattern of violent alternating tides—was too strong. The invasion was dead as an issue. Statewide and nationwide, the Republicans came back in 1894, sweeping everything before them.

According to the vague recollections as reported from interviews with A. S. Mercer's family, he was hounded out of Cheyenne, but again, early in 1895 the family took up residence on a homestead on the western slope of the Big Horns at Hyattsville. Mercer never told the story about the campaign against his book; he only did a little writing in his later years on such innocuous projects as a local guidebook entitled *Big Horn Country*. He died in 1917, not knowing that he would come out the winner; and so great was the power of the willful men in Wyoming at that late date that while his obituary in a local paper did make mention of the *Banditti*, it did not mention the Johnson County war.[13]

Yet under the forced draft of suppression the fame of the violent little book smoldered along. In 1923 and in 1930 two privately printed editions appeared, one issued by John Mercer Boots in Los Angeles, the second by Ida McPherren in Sheridan, Wyoming. In 1935 a regular edition was published by the Grabhorn Press of San Francisco with a foreword by James M. Clark, son of one of the invaders. All three were small editions, quickly sold out. For years ranch people who had never seen the book knew it by reputation and spoke of it in tones of awe. In 1954 it was finally and permanently restored to every library shelf by the University of Oklahoma Press. Today the original edition is one of the highest-priced rarities in the western field. In 1961 the largest West Coast dealer in rare western books offered a copy for sale at $350. He found three takers at that price.[14]

The worst criticism of the Mercer book is his falsification of the Wellman case. The facts of that wretched affair had all been in print by the time he started writing, and of course he knew them; yet he harped on the fictitious theme that Wellman had been done to death by the cattlemen themselves.

With that discreditable exception his book has stood the test of time and the perspective of history remarkably well. Many of his most angrily disputed charges have been justified. The book stands as a strange mixture of diatribe and distortion with solid historical fact. But it stands.

Epilogue

On the second of January 1893, the mock trial of the invaders got under way in the First District court at Cheyenne. Forty-four men had been indicted, but of these one of the Texans had died of wounds and Fred O. deBillier of the Harvard team of Teschemacher and deBillier had suffered a nervous breakdown while at Laramie and had been allowed to go to his home in New York. The Texans had gone back to Texas for good, and another bond was forfeited as Teschemacher had been called to Switzerland by the sudden death of his brother. He never came back to Wyoming. Twenty-three defendants were left.

The effort to get a jury took up the next two and a half weeks, while the press yawned—as did everyone in the courtroom—and turned to other affairs. The defense was allowed twelve peremptory challenges for each defendant, in addition to normal exemptions, making 276 in all; and the prosecution six for each, or 138, a total of 414. By January twenty-first, 1064 veniremen had been examined, and only eleven bored and weary jurors sat in the box. Every eligible citizen of Cheyenne had been examined and most found wanting, and in order to get additional talesmen it would be necessary to go to the outlying ranch country at additional expense. Then came the surprise ending. Johnson County was sick of the expense and County Prosecutor Alvin Bennett moved to dismiss the case. Judge VanDevanter for the defense objected, on the grounds that a *nolle prosequi* would leave his clients open to further prosecution at some future date. Since there had been no trial, the constitutional ban against double jeopardy could not be invoked.

The opposing counsel then put their heads together and arrived at a solution. Looking around the courtroom, they saw among the spectators a blankly unoffending face. The individual was led to the vacant seat in the jury box and sworn. Neither side asked him a question. There were now twelve jurors and the so-called trial could proceed. Judge VanDe-vanter asked for a directed acquittal from the bench, which was denied. It was all hideously dull. Again County Prosecutor Bennett moved for a dismissal and again Judge VanDevanter for the defense entered his routine objection, which was overruled; and the cases were dismissed. But it made no difference because under the law a case which had once been tried under a change of venue—and with the twelfth juror sworn in this was technically a trial—could not be tried again. So the defendants were immune to further prosecution anyway, and went back to their business rejoicing.[1]

Wyoming was too exhausted and too sick of the whole business to care. Its sense of outrage over the invasion had spent itself over the past nine months, as one community after another had held meetings and passed resolutions condemning the invaders; it had gradually adjusted itself to the knowledge that they would never pay for their crime—and their friends had been swept out of office in the recent election. Wyoming, too, was ready to get back to business.

Nobody won the Johnson County war. The invaders lost it in the field, but since they outwitted the ends of justice by means of legal maneuvering, overpowering influence, and unlimited money, the outcome was a standoff. Johnson County had the moral victory within its grasp but threw it away when it failed to take action against the murderers of George Wellman.

But if nobody won, yet there was a victory after all. Time won, as it always does; and time and change and the blessing of new things to think about brought peace and the healing of wounds, like the ivy mantling old battle-scarred ruins and the green grass growing on old battlefields. Most remarkable was the fact that the chain reaction of killing, so often and direly predicted as a sequel to Wyoming's troubles, never materi-alized at all. Whether it was due to the cold climate or the absence of chile in the diet or what, we don't know, but such interminable feuds as the Hatfields and the McCoys, or the Horrell–Higgins feud in Texas, never got started, as people instinctively chose to patch things up and go forward together.

In May 1893 Dudley Champion, a brother of Nate, was shot and killed by Mike Shonsey. It was claimed by Shonsey that Champion drew first and he was released on grounds of self-defense, but there were doubts about this. A Texan in charge of a herd being held nearby talked to the dying Champion who gasped: "I can't cock it, I can't cock it." His gun was jammed by dirt in the cyclinder, which does not sound like a man deliberating a killing. Shonsey meanwhile had left the country. This was the last death to stem directly from the invasion.[2]

There were Montague–Capulet romances. A son of the murdered John A. Tisdale married a daughter of the hard-luck not-quite invader "Hard Winter" Davis. A daughter of the lively rustler Lee Moore, who later reformed and became a highly respectable stockman and pillar of the Wyoming Stock Growers' Association, married a son of W. C. Irvine.

And there was some evidence of guilt feeling on both sides in the shape of a wholesome impulse to make restitution for past misdeeds.

Johnson County, panicked by the threat of martial law and a second invasion, had defaulted on the prosecution of the Wellman murderers while they were still in the country and could be caught, but from midsummer onward it started showing a strong inclination to go after cattle thieves. Charles Burritt, the gossipy stockman mayor, was full of praise for Angus, with whom he was now working hand in glove, and that fall four men were convicted of killing a steer belonging to Dr. Harris of Laramie, owner of the TA ranch, whose foreman Charles Ford had been among the invaders. And now, in January, we learn that Dr. Harris is trying to get the thieves' sentences reduced! Truly no row of exclamation points could be long enough to do justice to this.[3]

After all the excitement over the roundup injunctions in May 1892, the regular authorized roundup went forward peaceably a month later, with the members of the Northern Wyoming Farmers' and Stockgrowers' Association—the blackballed men—on hand calmly gathering their cattle and sorting them out of the herd side by side with their former blood enemies. In a word, the roundup boycott had been buried with the dead. The *Leader* correspondent had a pleasant country vacation of several weeks visiting ranches and riding with the roundup at the head of the Middle Fork and along the red-walled valley of Buffalo creek—not yet, be it noted, referred to as the Hole in the Wall. Two wagons were on the roundup, that of the old EK and a "rustler" wagon. Al Allison and Lou Webb were working side by side with the official appointees of the Wyoming Stock Growers' Association. It would seem that the age of miracles had come.[4]

It did not arrive all at once, but at the next spring meeting of the Association it was proposed that the Association undertake to recover some of the good will it had lost by extending inspection privileges to nonmembers on payment of a fee. There were at the time only ninety-six members of the Association in Wyoming, and fifteen hundred livestock owners. The idea of such democratization was bitterly fought, but in the long run the principle of inspection for all was adopted, to become a mighty landmark in the progress of the state.

For some human postscripts datelined Johnson County, the writer is indebted, as for much else, to Fred W. Hesse, son of Fred G. S. Hesse, who was vastly generous with time and information to one with whom he disagreed vehemently and often. Fred Hesse, Senior, returned to Johnson County in 1894 and went back to ranching as usual on the 28 ranch south of Buffalo, his personal successor to the 76. Although the old dividing lines still showed and relations were often strained, the point is that nothing worse happened and everybody knows that in a small, thinly settled community where you rub elbows with your neighbors you must either get along with them or shoot them on sight. Johnson County decided to get along.

Here are some aftermath stories told by Fred W. Hesse. It seems that a couple of unreconstructed rustlers were still talking about how they were going to get old Fred Hesse; now, in the West killing talk filled the air around every campfire, and if there had been as much shooting as there was talking, there would have been more corpses than population. Anyway, Fred Hesse, Senior, was out one day hunting a horse and he happened to ride into the camp of these two who had been planning to kill him. Instead of turning tail he rode up to the campfire and said: "Gentlemen, have you seen a black horse?" Deponent forgot what their answer was, but afterward they were twitted by their friends.

"Well, you always said you were going to get him. Why didn't you do it when you had the chance?"

"B-b-but— he called us 'gentlemen,'" they replied.

And then there was the aftermath of Eat-'Em-Up-Jake, Ed Tway, known as a leading rustler, who was to have been co-foreman of that rustlers' roundup which never took place. In his declining years he wound up as a lowly foot-plodding irrigator on the ranch of his former enemy; and Fred W. Hesse, then a young boy, recalls that he spent a great deal of time reading the Bible, trying to figure out whether he could be forgiven for a murder he had once committed. One is sure that he was.

Yes, time won. There is a picture taken in 1897 of the Big Piney "pool" roundup. Big Piney—the next creek north of Clear Creek— was the home range of one of the big outfits involved in the invasion fracas. But now there was a "pool outfit" on Big Piney. A "pool outfit" is an association of little ranchers who combine their manpower—themselves—and their horses and their money and go on the roundup with their own wagon, just as big as the big ones. Montana had these pool outfits of small owners from the eighties. After much reading and inquiry, I have never tracked down such an association of small owners in Wyoming before this 1897 photograph.

So everything indicates that time did win, and won handily and soon enough so that Wyoming became a state of small independent ranchers before the slashing changes of the last industrial revolution drove the old-time cow business out of the picture, except for a few traditions. Time won and the small independent rancher won. And the latter, after all, is what the shooting was really about.

NOTES

The Setting: THE POWDER RIVER COUNTRY

[1] The origins of Johnson County, including the founding of Buffalo, are summarized in I. S. Bartlett, *History of Wyoming*, p. 522, and in Frances Birkhead Beard, *Wyoming from Territorial Days to the Present*, Vol. I, p. 288.

A graphic account of dawn on a frontier appears in the reminiscences of John R. Smith of Buffalo, *"My Tracks and Trails: When Wyoming Was Young,"* published serially in the Buffalo *Bulletin*, December 30, 1956, to May 30, 1957. Details on the founding of Buffalo in *The Old Occidental* by Howard B. Lott in *Annals of Wyoming*, Vol. VII, No. 1.

Chapter 1 THE BEEF BONANZA

[1] The classic source on this extravaganza of fun, folly, and disaster is John Clay's *My Life on the Range*, from which all subsequent writers including this one have borrowed heavily. First privately printed in 1924, it has been republished recently with chapter headings and an index by the Oklahoma University Press. Page references given here are to the old edition.

John Clay (p. 116) is the source of the never-too-oft-told tale of Luke Murrin's epigram; Clay is likewise the source of most business facts herein.

The Day of the Cattleman by Ernest Staples Osgood has never been superseded as the first and best history of cattle-raising on the northern plains. *Seventy Years* by Agnes Wright Spring, an official history of the Wyoming Stock Growers' Association (1942), is a carefully documented study of the early years of that body and its influential personalities. She, with John Clay, tells about all that is left to remember of the Cheyenne Club (pp. 65–69).

[2] The story of Gus Trabing's store on the road to Fort McKinney is from local sources and also from Burns, Gillespie, and Richardson, *Wyoming's Pioneer Ranches*, p. 602. The story of Moreton Frewen's dramatic arrival after crossing the Big Horns in the dead of winter is told in his *Melton Mowbray and Other Memories*, pp. 158, 165–67, 172–73. Frewen does not mention Trabing's by name, but it was the only store on Crazy Woman at that time.

[3] The verified incident is described in Harold E. Briggs, *Frontiers of the Northwest*, p. 203. A government trader, E. S. Newman, was bound for Utah with a wagon train of supplies. Caught in November 1864 by bad weather on the Laramie plains—than which there is no worse—he turned his oxen out to die, found them in the spring alive and healthy.

[4] John R. Craig, *Ranching with Lords and Commons*, p. 89.

[5] Robert G. Athearn, in *Westward the Briton*. The anecdote about the Englishman who asked the cowboy if his "master" was at home is on p. 80; the one about the Scottish duke who rode the cowcatcher of a locomotive is on p. 89; and on p. 110 he traces the origin of the famous "cow servant" expression to New Mexico.

[6] The beverage statistics are from Charles A. Guernsey, *Wyoming Cowboy Days*, p. 74. The best general source on the Cheyenne Club is Agnes Wright Spring, *Seventy Years;* and of course there are many references in Clay.

[7] Clay, p. 35.

Chapter 2 THE CASTLE BUILT ON SAND

The most colorful source on Moreton Frewen is himself in *Melton Mowbray and Other Memories*. In addition, the writer is much indebted for business details of his Powder River operations and for some personal details to Herbert O. Brayer's *The Great 76 Ranch on Powder River* in the December 1950 Chicago *Brand Book*.

Intimate details of his relationship with Horace Plunkett, of Plunkett's assumption of the American management of the Powder River Cattle Company, and the bitter quarrel which ensued are mentioned in Plunkett's diaries for 1886 and 1887. We have omitted much of this. (See Chapter 17.)

The description of the big Powder River roundups is from Jack Flagg, May 5, 1892.

[1] Courtship and marriage from Brayer, *op. cit.*, and from *Melton Mowbray*, pp. 178–80, 196–99, 204.

[2] Descriptions of the log "castle" on Powder River from Brayer and also from a local amateur of history, Howard Lott, a longtime resident of Buffalo, Wyoming, who edited the *Diary of Major Wise* in *Annals of Wyoming*, April 1940. Major Wise was a British Nimrod who visited the West to go hunting, and Lott's footnotes are a lively source on the Frewen mansion.

[3] Letter in the Frewen papers, Manuscript Division, Library of Congress.

[4] *Melton Mowbray*, p. 212; Brayer, *op. cit.*, p. 77.

[5] *Ibid.*, pp. 224–25. The same two pages contain his story of the death of the old buffalo bull and the friend's visit to the site twenty years later.

[6] Lott, *Diary of Major Wise*, note 6, p. 90.

[7] Cheyenne *Daily Sun*, Nov. 3, 1887.

Chapter 3 SEEDS OF TROUBLE I

[1] Osgood, *Day of the Cattleman*, pp. 241–43, and Agnes Wright Spring, "Carey Story Is a Wyoming Saga," in the *Hereford Journal*, July 15, 1938.

[2] Agricultural statistics from the 1880 census: *Census Office: Report on the Productions of Agriculture, Tenth Census;* Number of farms in the U.S. and by state, with analysis of farm products, pp. 3–8.

For 1890: *U.S. Census Office 1890, Vol. V, Statistics of Agriculture.* Total number of farms in U.S. and breakdown by states, Table I, p. 74. Breakdown by states and counties, Table 6, p. 235. Breakdown of crops in Wyoming for 1890, pp. 355, 421.

The figures on irrigated land occur in a separate report at the end of the same volume entitled "Report on Agriculture by Irrigation in the Western Part of the United States at the Eleventh Census; 1890." The Wyoming breakdown is on p. 248.

Population figures for both 1880 and 1890: *Census Reports: Eleventh Census, 1890, Vol. I: Statistics of Population,* pp. 2, 6.

Chapter 4 SEEDS OF TROUBLE II

[1] The story of the rise and development of the Wyoming Stock Growers' Association is given in most histories of the cattle boom on the northern plains. I have followed Osgood (pp. 119–21), but mainly Agnes Wright Spring, who in *Seventy Years* tells of the rise of the organization in detail, including dates and personalities.

[2] Clay, p. 245.

[3] Charles Lindsay in *The Big Horn Basin*, p. 116, quoting the WSGA executive minutes for April 9 and November 9, 1883.

[4] William Timmons, *Twilight on the Range*, pp. 27, 56.

[5] Brock papers: letter from George P. Webster to Elmer Brock. Charles Lindsay, *op. cit.*

[6] Abbott and Smith, *We Pointed Them North* (1939 ed.), p. 152; Fletcher, *Free Grass to Fences*, p. 78.

Chapter 5 HARD TIMES AND HARD FEELINGS

[1] Flagg, May 12, 1892.
[2] Prices from Pelzer, *The Cattlemen's Frontier*, p. 142.
[3] Osgood, p. 218.
[4] Plunkett letters, August 17, 1885; diary, October 26.
[5] References to the wage cut which caused the strike appear in Jack Flagg, May 19, 1892; the Cheyenne *Daily Sun*, April 4, 1886, and in a cutting from an unidentified newspaper dated March 29 of the same year.

John Clay (p. 123) speaks of a cowboy strike for higher wages at the headwaters of Powder River which was led by Jack Flagg in 1884, but he must be mistaken as to the date. There is no mention anywhere of any such strike in Wyoming other than the one in 1886.

In the Texas Panhandle near Tascosa there was a widespread walkout of cowboys in the spring of 1883 in protest against the miserably low wages of $25 a month. At least four big ranches were affected. The strike was lost. But on the whole the cowboys' situation was judged to have been improved, as a number of them, we are told, started up on their own hook afterwards, not hesitating to brand a few mavericks. The incident is described in *Lost Trails of the Cimarron* by Harry E. Chrisman.

[6] The provincial press of the Territory, most of which was heartily opposed to the Wyoming Stock Growers' Association, had a merry time over the strike. The two quotations here are from the *Rawlins Journal* (sic—the *Carbon County Journal* of Rawlins is obviously the paper meant) of June 8, as quoted in *Bill Barlow's Budget* of Fetterman, Wyoming, on June 16.
[7] Sturgis to F. P. Voorhees, Carey's manager, June 15, 1886.
[8] Secretary Sturgis was in the East this summer and Thomas B. Adams, later his successor, was acting secretary. There are numerous references in both the correspondence and the executive minutes to the "mutiny" and the blacklist question, including the difference with Peters, as follows:

W.S.G.A. correspondence: Adams to R. B. Connor, #892, June 16, 1886; Adams to Voorhees, #695, same date. Adams to Connor, #920, June 21; Plunkett to Sturgis, approving punishment of strikers, June 21; Sturgis to Adams, July 7; ibid, July 21; Adams to Clay, July 24; Adams to Connor, July 29; Sturgis to Adams, August 1; Adams to Clay, August 2.

Executive minutes; July 20 and August 2, 1886.

Chapter 6 THE WINTER OF DEATH

[1] The quotations on the drought in Wyoming are from Clay, pp. 176, 178, 181.

The dearth of literature on the hard winter in Wyoming, referred to later in the text, is such a strange phenomenon that it has led some writers to the conclusion (which this one does not share) that for inexplicable reasons the winter which shrouded the entire western plains area was noticeably milder in Wyoming. We don't think so; even though nobody mentioned it with the exceptions of John Clay and Jack Flagg.

On the other hand, there is an impressive literature on the subject of the terrible winter in Montana and the Dakotas. Eloquent chapters and much specific information are to be found in Granville Stuart's *Forty Years on the Frontier*, Abbott and Smith, *We Pointed Them North*, Joseph Kinsey Howard, *Montana, High, Wide and Handsome*, and a paper by Robert S. Fletcher—not to be confused with Robert H. Fletcher—which is cited in the bibliography.

Osgood, in *Day of the Cattleman*, supplied additional picturesque and horrible details obtained through his research in the Montana press.

As to the Dakotas, Hagedorn in his *Badlands* biography of Roosevelt, based on innumerable local interviews, and Lincoln Lang in *Ranching With Roosevelt* give evidence that the dreadful weather conditions were indeed, as John Clay stated, no local affair, but extended over a whole region.

Our own indebtedness to Professor T. A. Larson's research on the winter in Wyoming is noted in the text. All Wyoming weather and public opinion details are from Larson except where otherwise stated.

³ Drought details in Montana from Stuart, *Forty Years*, pp. 232–33; R. S. Fletcher, p. 124; Osgood, pp. 218–19. From the Dakotas Lang in *Ranching with Roosevelt* tells of grasshoppers and prairie fires; so does R. S. Fletcher; and Frances B. Beard's official history of Wyoming confirms the fact that prairie fires were a problem in Wyoming, p. 401.

³ Clay, p. 178.

⁴ Flagg in Buffalo *Bulletin*, May 19, 1892.

⁵ Osgood (p. 220) and Hagedorn (p. 435) are among the authors who mentioned the invasion of towns by starving cattle in their search for something to eat.

⁶ Quotation and additional details from Abbott, *We Pointed Them North*, pp. 205, 207, and Howard, pp. 158–59.

⁷ *Weekly Boomerang*, Jan. 5, 1888.

⁸ Chicago *Tribune*, March 21, 1887.

⁹ The "Ananias" in Fort Keogh enjoyed frequent references in the press of the region, among them the Cheyenne *Leader* of March 3 and 31; the Miles City (Montana) *Yellowstone Journal*, February 26, and many other papers, since these stories were picked up and widely reprinted. The most sensational of the Fort Keogh stories was front-paged in the New York *World*, February 14.

There is additional confirmation of the grotesque and incredible details of the winter's sufferings in both Hagedorn (p. 435) and Lang (p. 246).

¹⁰ The literature of the hard winter is so tremendous and its sources so scattered that the writer is in danger of overpowering the reader with an avalanche of footnotes.

Lincoln Lang told his story of the spring breakup twice, once in an interview extensively quoted by Hermann Hagedorn, later in his own book. I have combined the two versions; the page references are Hagedorn p. 437 and Lang p. 250.

¹¹ Clay's statistics given here are from p. 179. Larson's about the Crook County outfit are on p. 13 of his article, quoted from the Buffalo *Echo*. Robert H. Fletcher of Montana (*Free Grass to Fences*) was one of the leading cynics who pointed to an additional reason for the big writeoff, which certainly has to be taken into account.

¹² There are many details of Mr. Sturgis' career in *The National Cyclopedia of American Biography* XXX (1943), pp. 326–27.

Chapter 7 LONG ROPES AND RUNNING IRONS

¹ Sources on rustling are plentiful and colorful. Among the best are J. Evetts Haley, who discourses on the subject with his usual scholarship and humor in *Charles Goodnight: Cowman and Plainsman*, chap. vii; J. Frank Dobie in *The Longhorns*, chap. iii; Granville Stuart in *Forty Years on the Frontier*, pp. 195–209. And W. S. James, the cowboy turned preacher, gives a particularly astute and rollicking account of the "elastic conscience" in *Cowboy Life in Texas, or Forty Years a Maverick* [sic], especially p. 100 and most of chap. ix.

Apart from these sources the material for this chapter was gathered from here, there, and everywhere, including countless fireside sessions over years spent visiting in the West.

² From Robert H. Fletcher, *Free Grass to Fences*, pp. 98–99.

³ Stuart, *Forty Years*, II, 195.

Chapter 8 THE CASE OF WILLIAM MAVERICK

[1] *Forty Years,* II, 167.

[2] Hagedorn, *Roosevelt in the Badlands,* p. 256. Lindsay, in *The Big Horn Basin,* tells of the silent connivance of many employers (p. 120).

[3] Session Laws of Wyoming Territory, 1884. Chapter 87, Secs. 2, 6, 7, 8, 9.

[4] The *Weekly Boomerang's* comments were held in reserve for four years, until the maverick law came up for revision in the tenth legislative assembly. Jan. 19, 1888.

[5] Laramie *Daily Boomerang,* Jan. 28, Feb. 26 and Feb. 5, 1884.

[6] Session Laws, 1884. Chapter 88, Sec. 1.

[7] W. Turrentine Jackson, "The Wyoming Stock Growers' Association: Political Power in Wyoming Territory, 1873–1890," in *The Mississippi Valley Historical Review* (March 1947), pp. 580–81.

[8] *Boomerang,* Feb. 23 and Mar. 8, 1884.

[9] File 16 of the Legislative Council, reproduced in entirety in *Boomerang,* Jan. 26, 1884. Wyoming Session Laws of 1888, Chapter 28, Sec. 27.

[10] Flagg, May 5, 1892.

[11] Colorado livestock legislation is quoted in "Colorado Stock Laws," Denver, 1883, and "Colorado Stock Laws," Denver, 1892, both booklets publications of the Colorado Cattle Growers Association. They are in the collection of the Colorado State Historical Society in Denver.

Montana stock laws and practices are fully detailed in Robert H. Fletcher's *Free Grass to Fences.*

In addition the writer received clarifying letters from Mr. Fletcher and from Ralph Miracle, the present secretary of the Montana Stockgrowers' Association.

Chapter 9 WHO IS A CATTLE THIEF? I

[1] Executive Minutes, June 27 and September 5, 1883.

[2] There was great activity in the blacklist during the latter half of 1885, with threats of discipline against members for a variety of causes on August 25 and October 24, 1885.

[3] Executive Minutes, August 25, September 1, 7, and 14; letters, Sturgis to Jackson and Sturgis to Butler, September 1, 1885.

[4] The decision was reported in both the *Carbon County Journal* and the Laramie *Daily Boomerang* for October 23, 1886. On the same date the attorney for the two cowhands wrote a letter to the Association's legal firm proposing terms of a settlement which included removal of Cooper's name from the blacklist.

On December 3 a memo by Thomas Sturgis notes acceptance of the terms proposed, and on the same date there is a receipt for $750 in full settlement signed by Hugo Donzelman, attorney for the two men. Letters asking for reinstatement were signed by both Cooper and Lineberger on December 10, 1886. The required notice appeared in the *Northwestern Livestock Journal,* January 21, 1887.

[5] The fluctuating fortunes of Tom Collins may be followed in the official correspondence, including a letter of Sturgis to Collins, March 1, 1886, and in the *Carbon County Journal,* May 28, 1887. Jack Cooper continued to occupy a disproportionate amount of the committee's and secretary's time and attention until the late fall of 1887. There are references in the executive minutes for May 26, 1887, and in the correspondence for September 26 and 29, November 15 and 17.

[6] Dixon to Adams and/or Adams to Dixon, September 26 and 29, November 15 and 17, 1887.

Despite Cooper's vindication in court and the absence of any further charges against him, the Cheyenne-inspired press continued to refer to him as "the notorious cattle thief."

Chapter 10   WHO IS A CATTLE THIEF? II

[1] Horace Plunkett to Sturgis, June 27, 1886. "There is a feeling growing up among the cowboys that the Association 'don't amount to much,' that the maverick law is unconstitutional, and that the good old times of high wages for good rustlers are coming round again."

[2] Frank Canton wrote repeatedly of mavericking in his area: on October 30 and November 4, 1886; March 17, 26; May 8, 31; June 10; August 2 and 16, 1887. In this correspondence there is as yet no mention of illegal butchering of beeves or of changing brands; only of branding mavericks.

[3] Expressions of doubt as to the validity of the maverick law occur in various places, among them letters of Connor to Sturgis, August 16, 1887; Canton to Adams, March 26, 1887; executive minutes, October 24, 1885.

[4] Executive minutes, February 11, 1885; April 3, 24, 30, and June 15, 1886.

[5] W.S.G.A. correspondence; May 12, 13, and October 2, 1885; May 21, 1886; July 25, 1887.

[6] John Clay, pp. 249–50. Mr. Reel's remark about "the rustlers" and the maverick law was quoted in the *Cheyenne Daily Leader*, January 20, 1888.

[7] Adams to R. B. Connor, July 18, 1887.

[8] Adams to Dixon, May 19; executive minutes May 26, 1887. Smith himself had been accused of undue friendliness with Tom Collins.

[9] Circular letter from Adams, March 25, 1887. The dissension within Association ranks and its connection with Corlett and Reel is discussed in part by W. Turrentine Jackson, *The Wyoming Stock Growers' Association: Its Years of Temporary Decline*," p. 261

[10] Quoted by Jackson from a letter in the W.S.G.A. files.

[11] Connor to Adams, July 16, 1887.

[12] Adams to Reel, July 25, 1887.

Chapter 11   "YOU CAN'T GET A CONVICTION"

[1] Cox, p. 61. See also W. C. Holden, "The Problem of Stealing on the Spur Ranch." Holden's account is based on the letters to the management written by a succession of unusually articulate foreman. While the Spur Ranch suffered from thefts by settlers well up into the twentieth century, Holden points out that it never had any trouble with dishonesty on the part of employees. Moreover, those responsible for ranch policy fought a clean fight. They never descended to fighting lawlessness with lawlessness.

[2] The story is told in *Cattle*, by William McLeod Raines and Will C. Barnes, p. 241.

[3] R. H. Hall to Sturgis, July 14, 1887.

[4] The *Carbon County Journal* editorial which aroused Secretary Adams to action was reprinted in the July 29, 1887, issue of the *Northwestern Livestock Journal* with the Secretary's answer.

[5] Cheyenne *Weekly Leader*, September 1, and reports of trials.

[6] The account of the trials here given is from the Cheyenne *Daily Leader* for December 4, 6, 10, 11, 22, and 23, 1887.

[7] Laramie *Daily Boomerang*, December 23.

[8] The judge's charge is in the *Leader* for December 6; the grand jury's report, December 11.

[9] Pasche testimony was reported December 22 in the *Leader*.

[10] *Leader*, December 23.

[11] Laramie *Boomerang*, December 23.

Chapter 12 BILL MAVERICK AGAIN

[1] Adams to Harrison, August 23, 1887.

[2] Laramie *Daily Boomerang,* December 7, 9, and 12, 1887. Cheyenne *Sun* quoted in the *Boomerang,* December 8.

[3] Cheyenne *Daily Leader,* December 6 and 24, 1887; January 8, 1888.

[4] Sec. 4143 of the Revised Statutes of Wyoming, 1887; and Sec. 1081, repealed Feb. 10, 1888. Session Laws of 1888, Chapter 10.

[5] *Weekly Boomerang,* February 9, 1888.

[6] *Seven Vetoes by Thomas Moonlight, Governor, Wyoming Territory,* Tenth Legislative Assembly. Cheyenne, 1888.

[7] Chapter 28, "Session Laws of Wyoming Territory Passed by the Tenth Legislative Assembly." Cheyenne, 1888.

[8] Jackson, *WSGA Political Power,* pp. 575, 577.

[9] Session Laws of Eleventh Territorial Legislature, 1890, Chapter 53, Sec. 2.

[10] *Ibid.,* Chapter 53, Sec. 52.

[11] 1888 Session Laws, Chapter 28, has the provision for sale at the capital in Sec. 25; $2000 bonding provision in Sec. 27. See also Chapter 53, Session Laws of Eleventh Territorial Legislature in 1890, for re-enactment of these provisions.

[12] Instances of restriction on would-be maverick purchasers are, in order, from the Elmer Brock papers, from a letter in private hands, and from W.S.G.A. correspondence, Connor to Adams, July 28, 1886.

Chapter 14 THE CATTLEMEN COME—AND SO DO THE SETTLERS

[1] The estimates of early cattle numbers are by two pioneers in the area: John R. Smith in the Buffalo *Bulletin,* May 9, 1957, and Flagg, May 12, 1892.

[2] Frewen's remarks are found in the correspondence which has been microfilmed as part of Plunkett's American letters.

[3] Frank M. Ganton in *Frontier Trails;* William Gardner Bell, "Frontier Lawman," in *The American West* (Summer 1964); Laramie *Boomerang,* February 19, 1884.

Chapter 15 NEVER THE TWAIN SHALL MEET

[1] Virtually the entire contents of this chapter are from the diaries and American letters of Horace Plunkett, made available on microfilm through the courtesy of the Horace Plunkett Foundation in London (see bibliography). An earlier and very valuable source is the biography *Horace Plunkett; an Anglo-American Irishman* by Margaret Digby, executive director of the foundation.

Chapter 16 IF YOU CALL A MAN A THIEF

[1] Jack Flagg's series in the Buffalo *Bulletin* is a major source on the changes in Johnson County after 1885, especially under dates of May 26, June 2, 16, and 23, 1892.

Flagg's statements as to the terms of sale of the 76 cattle to Wibaux is confirmed by R. S. Fletcher in his article on the hard winter, pp. 128–29, and by Donald H. Welsh in "Pierre Wibaux, Cattle King," in *North Dakota History* (Jan. 1953), p. 13.

For biographical facts on Fred G. S. Hesse I am indebted to Fred W. Hesse of Buffalo.

[2] Cowboy layoffs and the innovation of charging for meals are reported by Flagg, May 12 and May 19.

The action of the Montana Stockgrowers Association in regard to grubline riding, and Roosevelt's influence on it, is from Ray H. Mattison, "Roosevelt and the Stockmen's Association," *North Dakota History* (July 1950), pp. 45–46.

294 *Notes*

² Flagg in Buffalo *Bulletin*, May 26, 1892; comments on Flagg are from W.S.G.A. correspondence, March 11 and March 17, 1887.

Flagg himself was less than candid in the matter of his being blackballed. Although he speaks of the cowboy strike in 1886, he avoids mention of his own part as a leader of it and writes as though he had left cowpunching voluntarily. It is probable that he took a homestead after he was blackballed instead of the other way around.

⁴ Omaha *Bee*, December 11, 1891. On December 17 and December 24, 1891, the Buffalo *Bulletin* dated "the system of blackballing which was put into effect in this county" from 1885, and added: "When a man who had been working in one of their outfits had the audacity to take up land for himself, the big fellows blackballed him. But the little fellow hung on; he was thereupon branded a rustler."

The *Bulletin* was so violently partisan as to be taken with a grain of salt, but the *Bee* was far enough away to maintain an objective attitude.

⁵ *Bulletin*, May 19, 1892.

Chapter 17 THE HAT OUTFIT

¹ J. Elmer Brock was president of the Wyoming Stock Growers' Association (1930–1932) and a son of Albert Brock, Johnson County pioneer. He was also an indefatigable local historian. Some of his papers are locked up in the University of Wyoming archives, not to be opened until 1973, but others, not restricted, were made available to the writer by Mrs. Brock. They are one source on the Hat outfit; another is a manuscript history compiled by Anita Webb Deininger, daughter of Lou Webb.

² The sources of the statements, so far as we have been able to trace them, are: Two hundred cases, A. J. Mokler *History of Natrona County*, pp. 264–65; about three hundred indictments, J. Elmer Brock, "Who Dry-Gulched the Hoe Ranch Foreman?" in Denver *Westerners' Brand Book*, Vol. IX (1953); several hundred indictments, Cheyenne *Daily Sun*, July 3, 1892; one hundred eighty indictments in four weeks with only one conviction, quoted by R. B. David in *Malcolm Campbell*, p. 135, but appeared originally in the Chicago *Herald* for April 13, 1892, and repeated April 25; seventy-five cases nolle prossed at one time, letters of W. C. Irvine to Dr. Penrose, December 6, 1913.

³ *Bulletin*, June 23, 1892.

⁴ Flagg, loc. cit. Shonsey's name was probably Shaughnessy, but it is usually spelled as given except by Jack Flagg. We have followed the prevailing usage.

⁵ *Bulletin*, June 23, 1892.

⁶ Incoming correspondence of W.S.G.A., 1886 through 1888; Canton to secretary.

⁷ Information on John A. Tisdale is from his son, the late "Johnny" Tisdale; the Brock papers; and on the Tisdale-Canton feud, from Maurice Frink, *Cow Country Cavalcade*, p. 139.

Chapter 18 THE CRIME ON THE SWEETWATER

¹ The best known source on the Sweetwater hangings is a chapter in Alfred J. Mokler's *History of Natrona County*. Mr. Mokler was a Casper newspaper publisher who made extensive use of the local press and evidently had access to local personal sources who are no longer available. The tone of his work is sober and factual.

Other sources used by the present writer, some as to the facts of the lynching and some as to the myths, are: Wyoming papers: *Carbon County Journal*, Casper *Weekly Mail*, Cheyenne *Daily Leader*, Cheyenne *Daily Sun*, Cheyenne *Weekly Sun*, Laramie *Daily Boomerang*.

Denver papers: Denver *Republican*, Denver *Times*, *Rocky Mountain News*.

Other papers: Chicago *Interocean*, New York *World*, Omaha *Bee*.

² The facts about Ella Watson as stated were assembled from scattered references in the contemporary press, but *not* the press of Cheyenne.

³ Dates of homestead filings: Mokler, p. 271.

⁴ Letter from John De Corey in the Casper *Mail*, August 30.

⁵ The interviews with Gene Crowder and Frank Buchanan were published in the Casper *Weekly Mail* for July 26, 1889. They were used extensively by the historian Mokler, and the issue is not in the files. However, the article was reprinted in the *Carbon County Journal* for August 3. The statement by John De Corey is from the letter cited in Note 4.

⁶ The alleged member of the lynching party quoted by Mokler was R. B. Connor (p. 268).

⁷ The *Carbon County Journal* of July 27 quoted a telegram from Douglas to the Cheyenne *Sun*, dated July 24. This first report was almost surely the work of E. H. Kimball, who had recently purchased the Douglas *Graphic* and was to achieve fame or notoriety—depending on the political point of view—in the troubled years to come. This writer has tentatively assumed that most of the dispatches on the hanging datelined Douglas were Kimball's work. They are marked by internal evidence including characteristic tricks of style—and a significant symptom—the correct spelling of the name Averell. The misspelling *Averill* was one earmark of the propaganda ground out by the Cheyenne machine.

⁸ Names in *Carbon County Journal*, July 27, and *Boomerang*, July 24; also Mokler, p. 266.

⁹ Snatches of the Cattle Kate fiction were published widely, but the two most detailed versions appeared in the New York *World* for July 24, datelined Cheyenne the twenty-third, and in the Laramie *Boomerang*, July 27. The *World* topped the record for silliness on the latter date with a remarkable editorial which proves that even as early as 1889 the myth of the pure cowboy who never kissed anybody but his horse had gained a firm foothold in the East. "The cowboys of Wyoming did not like Kate Maxwell's style, so they lynched her. . . . It wasn't a very gallant thing for 'the boys' to do, but Kate's methods of getting cattle were not such as to popularize her on the plains. Her social life, too, was a trifle shady, and cowboys are particular."

¹⁰ The posse: from Douglas dispatch July 24 appearing in *Carbon County Journal*, July 27.

¹¹ The "farcical" aspect of the hearing was described in *ibid.*, the *Boomerang*, July 27, and the Casper *Weekly Mail*, August 2 and September 13.

¹² P. 91. 1936. Guernsey called Averell a civil engineer, thus upgrading him a notch or two above surveyor, but this confirms the impression that the victim had not only opinions but a troublesome degree of know-how in land matters.

¹³ August 2.

¹⁴ Penrose manuscript. Dr. Charles Bingham Penrose took part in the invasion a few years later.

¹⁵ Mercer, p. 19; Mokler, p. 271. Mokler was off on his timing, since Cole did not leave Averell's ranch after the hanging; he testified at the inquest. Nevertheless, the story as a whole appears to hold water, especially in view of Clay's admission as to Henderson's "indirect connection."

Chapter 19 "Caught on the Market"

¹ J. W. Hammond of Cheyenne and Charles Hecht of Laramie were the executive-committee members. William C. Irvine, though not on the executive board at this time, was a permanent power in the Wyoming Stock Growers' Association.

² Osgood, p. 246.

³ Operation of the seizure practice was described in detail in the Cheyenne *Leader*, March 27, 1892.

⁴ Interview in the *Leader*, December 25, 1891.

⁵ Petition to livestock board: *Bulletin*, February 11 and March 3; *Leader*, February 24.

⁶ Cheyenne *Leader*, March 22 *et seq.*

Chapter 20 JOE DEBARTHE'S BUFFALO

[1] The available personal facts on Joe DeBarthe are to be found, strangely enough in a biographical sketch of his wife, from whom he was later divorced, in *Women of Wyoming* by Mrs. Alfred H. Beach (Cora Beach.) He died in 1928.

At the same time he was editor and part-owner–publisher of the Buffalo *Bulletin*, he was also publisher of the weekly *Wyoming Commonwealth*, official organ of the state board of mines, of which the prolific journalist-historian C. G. Coutant was editor.

The taciturn Grouard had been approached time and again by writers who wanted to tell the story of his life and had turned them all down, but eventually yielded to the urgings of DeBarthe and gave the story to him. It was published in St. Joseph, Missouri, in 1894. New edition: Oklahoma University Press, 1958.

[2] The total value of Wyoming farm products in 1889—the year the 1890 census was taken—was $2,241,590 compared to a valuation on cattle of $31,431,495. From *Compendium of the Eleventh Census of the United States, 1890*, Part III, pp. 433ff.

The county-by-county report on Wyoming agriculture in the same document contained such phrases as "farming poor," "water supply inadequate for agriculture," "stock growing the most important industry," "small crops sometimes successful," many of the last, it added, produced for local consumption.

[3] The *Leader* ran a number of editorials attacking the cattle thieves and coming to the defense of the cattlemen from the end of July on through August. The *Bulletin's* reply appeared in that paper on August 13.

[4] *Bulletin*, July 23, from Trabing under dateline July 20.

[5] The story of the runaway was told in the *Bulletin*, July 2, 1891.

Chapter 21 THE WEATHER BREEDER

[1] There are any number of secondary sources on the Waggoner hanging, but the only primary sources are the contemporary press: the Buffalo *Bulletin* for June 25, quoting the Newcastle *Journal;* the Cheyenne *Daily Sun*, special from Newcastle, June 20 and June 24; and the Rawlins *Republican*, June 25, quoting the *Sun Dance Gazette*.

[2] Reported in the Cheyenne *Daily Leader*, November 17, 1892.

[3] Letter of Fred Hesse to Major Frank Wolcott, January 25, 1893; W. C. Irvine letter to Dr. Charles B. Penrose, December 6, 1913.

[4] Virginia Cole Trenholm, *"Last of the Invaders,"* in *True West* (February 1962). Her material is based on an interview some years ago with the late Mike Shonsey and on an unpublished paper by W. E. Guthrie, one of the invaders and Shonsey's longtime employer.

The Flagg material is from the Buffalo *Bulletin*, June 30, 1962.

[5] David, p. 128.

[6] A who's who of rustlers running to two columns in length and listing twenty-three names appeared in the Chicago *Herald* for April 19, 1892. The context indicates that it was taken from cattleman sources but its general accuracy as shown by numerous crosschecks is remarkable in view of the passions of the time. The column pinpoints the man Charlie Taylor, and says of Nate Champion that he was "called honest till lately."

[7] Those two polar opposites, Horace Plunkett and Jack Flagg, are in agreement as to the essential facts. Plunkett diary, August 4, 1888, and Flagg, June 2, 1892.

[8] Clay, p. 276.

Chapter 22 BLOOD ON A TARPAULIN

[1] I was piloted over the site on an unforgettable summer day in 1960 by the late Johnny Tisdale and other friends from Buffalo.

[2] The story of the attack is combined from several sources: an interview with Nate Champion published in the Buffalo *Bulletin* for December 17, 1891; Jack Flagg's account, July 7, 1892; a personal interview with Johnny Tisdale; and an interview given by Tommy Carr to J. Elmer Brock, February 2, 1936, in the University of Wyoming archives (see Note 3).

[3] Tommy Carr was T. F. Carr, not to be confused with T. Jefferson Carr, who was a deputy U.S. marshal in Cheyenne at the time.

[4] All versions of the affair have John Tisdale tangled up in a confrontation which may well have led to his death. Tommy Carr's version had Tisdale cornering Shonsey and forcing him to talk, and the Cheyenne *Sun*, December 4, 1891, just after the murder of Tisdale, had some story about Tisdale waylaying "a cowboy."

[5] Another Tommy Carr recollection, related to the writer by Oliver Grey Norval, an old-time resident of Buffalo.

[6] Maurice Frink, p. 140. Frink had access to the papers of J. Elmer Brock—first-rate grass-roots research—and this detail is identifiable on its face as Brock material.

[7] The organization meeting is described by Flagg, July 7, 1892; and there was considerable news about the new body in the Buffalo *Bulletin* from December 17 onwards.

Chapter 23 THE READER IS THE JURY I

[1] All reports of the evidence in the case of the killing of John Tisdale, as they appear in this chapter, are taken from accounts of the hearing in the Frank Canton case in the Buffalo *Bulletin*, December 10, 1891, seven and a half columns, and from the Buffalo *Echo*, December 12, 1891, eleven columns, except where otherwise indicated.

[2] Information on Ranger Jones' background and on his murder is from Jack Flagg's series in the *Bulletin*, May 26 and July 14, 1892. There is a note on his last trip to town in the Cheyenne *Daily Sun*, December 5, 1891.

[3] Tommy Carr to Anita Webb Deininger, personal interview, sometime in the 1930s.

[4] Cheyenne *Daily Leader*, December 4, 1891.

[5] Flagg, *Bulletin*, July 14, 1892.

Chapter 24 THE READER IS THE JURY II

[1] The peculiar behavior of the members of the cattlemen's club while Tisdale and Jones were in town were recalled by Tommy Carr in the interview with Anita Webb Deininger, already quoted.

[2] Canton interview in Cheyenne *Daily Sun*, December 25.

[3] Buffalo *Bulletin*, March 17 and 24.

[4] The principal source for the hearings in chambers is Mercer, but with corroboration in the press.

Chapter 25 BANQUO'S GHOST AND OTHER OMENS

[1] Cheyenne *Leader*, July 29, August 1, 2, 8, and 18, 1891; Omaha *Bee*, December 5.

[2] South Dakota convictions, Omaha *Bee*, December 2, 1891; shooting of thieves near Deadwood, Cheyenne *Sun*, December 12. The quotation about improved conditions in Texas is from the sprightly cowboy preacher, W. S. James, p. 37

[3] Threatened exodus of herds: Omaha *Bee*, December 5, 1891, Cheyenne *Sun*, December 9 and *Leader* of previous August 8.

[4] Penrose, from his manuscript in University of Wyoming archives. Guthrie, in a statement in the Western Range Cattle Industry Study, Colorado State Historical Society, Denver.

[5] Clay, p. 273. The trial of Tregoning was reported in the Cheyenne *Leader* August 9, 11, 13, and 15, with three columns of testimony on the eleventh. A. J. Mokler, the Natrona County historian, also describes the quarrel between the two men and subsequent shooting in some detail.

[6] The Buffalo *Bulletin* reported the activities of the Northern Wyoming Farmers' and Stockgrowers' Association in a number of articles, including March 17 and March 31, 1892. It also printed a letter from the New England-born coroner, Dr. Watkins, indignantly refuting the charges in the *Bee*.

Chapter 26 THE WILLFUL MEN

[1] Agnes Wright Spring lists all the early members of the Wyoming Stock Growers' Association and its preceding Laramie County association in the appendix of *Seventy Years' Cow Country*, as well as all members of the executive committee from the start of the organization.

The eight invaders who came to Wyoming in 1879 or earlier were Irvine, Wolcott, the Harvard partners, Teschemacher and deBillier, E. W. Whitcomb, W. E. Guthrie; and, from Johnson County, Frank Canton and Fred Hesse. The latter two were not men of influence in the same sense as the first six.

[2] The Penrose papers in the archives of the University of Wyoming consist of letters from Dr. Charles B. Penrose to his brother Boies Penrose, later Senator Penrose of Pennsylvania, written in April 1892, just after he had left the expedition and been confined briefly in the Douglas jail; a narrative based on these letters and written by Dr. Penrose in later years; and a series of long letters from W. C. Irvine to Dr. Penrose written at the end of 1912 and beginning of 1913. The papers were made the subject of an M.A. thesis by Lois Van Valkenburgh, with introduction and notes, in 1939. The narrative of Dr. Penrose was published in Douglas, Wyoming, a few years ago under the title *The Rustler Business*, but the other portions remain unpublished.

[3] The several sources of the recruitment of gunmen in Texas are in substantial agreement: Irvine to Penrose, December 6, 1913; Mercer; and Dunning, pp. 159 and 169. The story of George Dunning's recruitment by Ijams is told in a later chapter of this book. Irvine's negotiations with the railroads, same letter.

[4] Mercer, p. 40, gives the text of the order from the adjutant general. It was of course kept secret at the time.

[5] Penrose ms., pp. 33–35. Judge VanDevanter was chief counsel for the Wyoming Stock Growers' Association at this time. Lewis L. Gould, who is an unquestioned authority on both VanDevanter and Senator Warren, denies positively that either one of them had any foreknowledge of the invasion, stating that there is no evidence to that effect in either the Warren or VanDevanter papers and some negative evidence to the contrary.

In view of their position in Cheyenne, however, it is hard to see how they could have avoided knowing what so many others in their circle knew unless they were deaf and blind. At the same time one must agree with Mr. Gould that both men were far too shrewd to have countenanced such a mad illegal venture which they must have seen was foredoomed to failure.

Francis E. Warren, incidentally, despite his prominence as a stockgrower, governor, and United States Senator, cannot be considered on the record as a full-fledged member of the so-called Cheyenne ring. Although one of the early comers admitted to membership in the Wyoming Stock Growers' Association in 1877, he was not particularly active in its affairs as shown by the fact that he never served as an officer or member of the executive committee.

[6] Irvine letter, November 2, 1913. George Dunning's account of the plans to kill the sheriff and deputies in Buffalo and then send smaller bands roving through other counties to hang rustlers tallies very closely with that of Robert B. David—see below; he details the plan on pp. 159–60, 171–72, 178, and 188–89.

The letter about the list alleged to have been found in Frank Canton's suitcase was written by Miss Mary S. Watkins and was published in the Laramie *Boomerang* of April 18, 1892. There is no further trace of the list.

[7] David, pp. 151–52.

[8] P. 305. The invaders were bitter at the failure of their friends to come to their aid.

[9] Mercer, pp. 35–37, 39. The fear expressed that the rustlers would escape to the mountains appeared in print several times, among other places the Cheyenne *Leader*, April 23, 1892.

Chapter 27   THE SECRET SPECIAL

[1] The count of heads in the invaders' party varies slightly according to different sources. It also varies at different stages of the expedition as some members were added and others dropped out, through death or desertion.

After careful checking this writer arrived at the figure of fifty-two on the train. This agrees with the figure given by George Dunning, p. 177 of Mercer's *Banditti*.

Sam Clover wrote a thinly fictionized account of his adventures, published in the guise of a book for boys entitled *On Special Assignment* in 1903. While his own and some other names are changed, many real names are used, and the book may be taken with caution as a source.

Clover's visit to Sitting Bull is confirmed in Stanley Vestal's book, p. 281.

[2] Clover, George Dunning, Dr. Penrose, and W. C. Irvine all left firsthand accounts of the invasion in one form or another. Inevitably there are discrepancies of detail, especially in view of the lapse of years before Penrose and Irvine set down their recollections, and the bitter animosities in the group. I have selected what seem to be the likeliest among conflicting accounts. David added some interesting details.

[3] The story of the captives and of the German sheepherder did not reach the papers until April 10, when it appeared simultaneously in the Cheyenne *Sun* and *Leader* and in the Omaha *Bee*. David tells it well, pp. 175–77; and Struthers Burt's graphic sidelight is on p. 300.

[4] Cheyenne *Daily Leader* and *Sun;* Omaha *Daily Bee;* Denver *Rocky Mountain News;* Chicago *Herald;* April 9 through 14.

Chapter 28   THE DEATH OF NATE CHAMPION

[1] The firsthand sources on the march to Tisdales' are the same as those cited in the foregoing chapter: W. C. Irvine's letters to Dr. Penrose, the latter's account, and George Dunning's "confession."

On the KC siege itself, Sam Clover's story in the Chicago *Herald* for April 16, 1892 is the all-time classic which has furnished the basis for nearly everything written since, but Robert David's *Malcolm Campbell, Sheriff* still stands as the fullest account. While obviously relying on Clover for the main outlines of his KC chapter, he has embellished it with many details possibly obtained from his private sources.

[2] Mike Shonsey's report of fourteen rustlers at the KC is in the Irvine letter of November 2, 1913.

According to David, however, the number of rustlers at the KC the night of the seventh and eighth was not fourteen but five, and he names the three visitors as Billy Hill, Ed Star (*sic*), and Jack Long. Local residents cast doubt on David's story that Mike Shonsey spent the night at the cabin at all, since he would hardly have been welcome in view of the blood feud between him and Nate Champion. Still less is it likely that the rustlers, as stated, "had been careless with their conversation in his presence, talking boldly before him of . . . their scheme of taking a bunch of stolen cattle over to the graders' camp of the Burlington and Missouri extension near Gillette the day after tomorrow." The rustlers did not then know that Shonsey was a paid spy, but they did know of his part in the attempt to kill Nate Champion. Had Champion in fact been minded to move stolen cattle "the day after tomorrow," Mike Shonsey was scarcely the man before whom he would have discussed such plans, or discussed anything.

³ The quarreling at Tisdale's was reported by Sam Clover in a savage letter to his sponsor, Henry A. Blair, dated May 15, 1892, published in the Chicago *Westerners Brand Book* for February 1953 and copyrighted by Herbert O. Brayer.

The untruth that warrants were to be served, told by Frank Canton in his autobiography *Frontier Trails* and by invasion apologists at the time, is exploded by the Clover letter as well as by the plain facts of the KC murders.

⁴ Penrose ms., pp. 51, 71.

⁵ *Rocky Mountain News,* April 15, 16, 17. Chicago *Herald* and Cheyenne *Leader,* same dates.

⁶ Clover in Chicago *Herald,* April 16, 1892; George Dunning "confession," p. 181.

⁷ Clover in Chicago *Herald,* April 16.

⁸ Flagg's own version (Buffalo *Bulletin,* July 14, 1892) agrees with that of William C. Irvine (letter of November 2, 1913) in that Flagg was almost on top of the gunman before he was recognized, and that Charles Ford was the first to recognize him and fire.

⁹ Irvine letter, November 2, 1913.

¹⁰ Clover himself in *On Special Assignment* does not acknowledge writing the sign, stating that it was writen by Major Wolcott, who handed it to him to pin on. However, both Irvine (letter of February 22, 1914) and Dunning (p. 187) say that Clover wrote it himself.

¹¹ *On Special Assignment,* p. 269, and letter to Henry Blair, May 15, 1892.

Despite Irvine's corroboration of the diary's being found, there may still be skeptics who will question its genuineness, since Clover, never notorious for his dedication to the truth, might have faked the contents. This is unlikely, however, since a summary of the text, agreeing substantially with Clover's full-length version, appeared in the Cheyenne *Leader* for April 14, two days before the *Herald* story came out. The *Leader* man undoubtedly heard about it from one of the captured teamsters.

Chapter 29 A SURPRISE FOR THE REGULATORS

¹ Mainly from Flagg's story in the Buffalo *Bulletin,* July 14, 1892.

² Irvine to Penrose, November 2, 1913.

³ The story of Jim Dudley's tragic mishap is taken largely from Sam Clover's story in the *Herald,* May 9, with some variant details from Irvine's letter, cited above.

Clover is the sole authority for the statement that the purpose of the first stop at the TA was to let Charlie Ford see his wife, which the writer questions as altogether too ridiculous for even such a mismanaged expedition as this. Clover never hesitated to improve on the truth in order to beef up a paragraph, besides following the current newspaper dictum *when lacking facts, invent them.* A more probable reason for the stop is that suggested by the less imaginative Dunning, who states that it was made in order to obtain a change of horses for the suffering Dudley (p. 187).

The unfortunate man went into the Fort McKinney hospital under the alias of Gus Green. His full name was James Augustus Greenberry Dudley.

A touching and much misspelled letter from a brother-in-law in Paris, Texas, to the coroner in Buffalo was reprinted in Jack Flagg's newspaper, *The People's Voice,* May 28, 1892. It asked whether "there is annything Due him or His family from these cattlemen"; also whether the respondent would be "Cind enough to Give me the Name and address of His nurse;" and "Do you no whether Dudley taken an accidental policy or Not."

The people of Johnson County, then and thereafter, exonerated the Texans from any share of blame in the tragic events of that season. They felt that these young southerners had simply been misled.

⁴ Letter to Penrose, November 2.

⁵ This Clover version is from his May 9 story in the *Herald*. Irvine (November 2) agrees with Dunning (p. 190) in timing the arrival of DuFran and Sutherland.

⁶ Clover's story of his trip into town and his rescue by Major Fechet is from *On Special Assignment*, pp. 268–69. He also mentions the rescue in his April 16 newspaper story, without, however, admitting that he had been with the "regulators."

⁷ All accounts of the excitement in Buffalo and the manning of the outposts around the TA ranch are from newspapers, but the Buffalo *Bulletin* for April 14 —which appeared late due to recent events—appears the most trustworthy because it was local. Mercer's *Banditti* does some elaborating but relies on the same sources.

⁸ The Cheyenne *Leader*, April 13 and 24, is the most complete source on scenes and persons at the Covington ranch headquarters of the besiegers. News of the influx of recruits was carried repeatedly in all the papers.

⁹ The picture of the teamsters is a mosaic pieced together from many sources, mainly the newspapers which have been cited constantly throughout this chapter. It was the Cheyenne *Leader* of April 23 which referred to the teamsters' warm reception in Buffalo.

¹⁰ The fortifications were described in detail in the Cheyenne *Leader* for April 13, the Chicago *Herald*, April 16 and 25; and by Flagg in the Buffalo *Bulletin*, July 14.

Chapter 30 "I WILL SURRENDER TO YOU—"

¹ The ups and downs of the telegraph line were compiled by the writer from reference after reference scattered through a dozen different newspapers in many columns of fine print.

One notation will suffice for almost the entire story of the TA siege and the stockmen's surrender, including the timing of the innumerable telegrams which finally brought about the rescue of the latter by the troops. It is covered in great detail in the Cheyenne *Leader* for April 13, 14, 15, and 24; also in the Chicago *Herald* for April 13 to 19, inclusive, and April 25; and in the Buffalo *Bulletin*, April 14 and July 14, the latter date containing Jack Flagg's account.

A few additional but minor details, not in the papers, are from A. S. Mercer's *Banditti of the Plains* and Robert B. David's *Malcolm Campbell, Sheriff*.

Details and comments supplied by W. C. Irvine are from his letters to Penrose of November 2 and December 6, 1913.

² The uncertain moves made by the Governor in Cheyenne in response to the telegram from Mayor Hogerson are from the Cheyenne *Sun* and the *Leader*, both April 12.

³ Report of Colonel J. J. Van Horn in U.S. Army Archives, Fort McKinney, Post Letters Sent. April 14, 1892.

In going out of his way to pay this tribute to the behavior of the local population, the colonel contradicts a story of Clover's, apparently invented by the latter, that the "rustlers" made a move as if to rush the prisoners and troops.

Chapter 31 HOW BUFFALO LOST THE RAILROAD

¹ Chicago *Herald*, April 22.

² The death of Dr. Watkins and the account of the three funerals are from the Buffalo *Bulletin*, April 14 (the issue was several days late) and the *Leader*, April 16.

³ Mercer, p. 89, and *Herald*, April 22.

Chapter 32 AND MARCHED THEM DOWN AGAIN

[1] Description from the Cheyenne *Daily Leader* for April 23.

[2] *Leader,* April 20.

[3] The mass of minutiae, scattered through column after column of fine print on successive days of at least two newspapers, would make precise documentation extremely tedious if attempted. Details of the march are from the Chicago *Herald* of April 22, 23, and 24, especially the last.

Next to Major Fechet the ranking officers were Captain Stanton, C Troop; Captain Scott, D Troop; and Captain Wallace, H Troop.

[4] David, p. 290.

[5] Chicago *Herald,* April 22.

[6] *Ibid.*

[7] Seymour's stories in the *Herald,* like Clover's, were unsigned, but they are easy to identify. The "second expedition" and anxiety over Clover were referred to in his story of April 24, page 1. His name was revealed in the Cheyenne *Leader* for April 26, which has the following: "Sam Clover, who went north with the expedition, returned (to Cheyenne) on Sunday with the party. He and Mr. Seymour, another reporter of the same paper"—and so on. Seymour also appears in Clover's *On Special Assignment* under the name of Saybrooke.

The arrival of the "second expedition" in Douglas on the twenty-first is marked by the abrupt change in character of the dispatches.

[8] The quotation is taken with some very minor changes from the *Herald* of April 23. Nearly the whole picture of Douglas as given here is from the same paper, with a few details from the issues of the twenty-second and twenty-fourth.

[9] From the Cheyenne *Leader,* April 26. The remaining description of the train's departure, including the boasting conversation of the prisoners, is from the *Herald,* April 24.

[10] The account of the departure of the two Chicago correspondents is from *On Special Assignment,* pp. 292 ff., with the name of Hugo Donzelman added from the *Leader,* April 26.

Chapter 33 THE CASE OF THE INNOCENT BYSTANDERS

[1] The number-one source on the trappers' ordeal is to be found in the dispatches of the fiery E. H. Kimball to the *Rocky Mountains News* of Denver, May 6 through 11. Many of these dispatches were repeated identically in other papers. I have references to the Omaha *Daily Bee,* which cannot be rechecked, since the Library of Congress has thrown out these files—and to the San Francisco *Chronicle,* besides the Cheyenne *Leader.* The final dispatch from Omaha May 10 (newspapers May 11) is quoted fully in Mercer, pp. 103–5.

The Longest Rope by D. F. Baber (Caldwell, Idaho: Caxton Printers, 1947), while so heavily fictionized and loaded with errors as to be ineligible as a source for the most part, follows Kimball in the main on the railroading of the trappers. But Mrs. Baber makes additional points, probably from Bill Walker himself (whom she interviewed in his old age), notably regarding the reluctance of these bewildered men to go back to Wyoming.

Except for this one point, I have followed Kimball's dispatches.

The Chicago *Herald* carried a number of stories independently, confirming Kimball, from May 8 through 10 or 11.

[2] An undated clipping from the Scotts Bluff *Daily Star-Herald* which was sent to the writer. It was stated, however, that the author of the clipping was A. E. Sheldon, who at the time of the trappers' incident was editor of a newspaper in Chadron and later secretary of the Nebraska State Historical Society.

[2] Mrs. Baber says they were taken to Rhode Island; W. C. Irvine that it was New York state. Both informants, Walker and Irvine, were elderly men speaking long after.

The payoff in bad checks, cited by Mrs. Baber on pp. 287–88, is such a low double-cross that it might sound incredible, were it not confirmed by W. C. Irvine in his letter to Penrose of December 6, 1913.

Chapter 34   MAD DOG MURDER

The main sources are found in the letters of attorney Charles H. Burritt, mayor of Buffalo, Wyoming, in 1892, published by the Buffalo *Bulletin*, January 26–June 22, 1961; the Rankin papers (Joseph P. Rankin, United States Marshal for the District of Wyoming, 1892) in the Department of Justice archives, National Archives, Washington, D.C.; and of course the Cheyenne press, the *Leader* and the *Sun*, whose name-calling and heavy sarcasm, especially in an election year, become exceedingly wearisome to the researcher, but they do yield some facts.

Also the Wellman inquest in the Brock papers; and J. Elmer Brock, "Who Dry-Gulched the Hoe Ranch Foreman?" in the Denver *Westerners' Brand Book*, IX (1953); and other sources.

[1] The disorders in Johnson county are described in the Burritt letters running from May 6 through May 26, 1892. Outside origin of some of the troublemakers, mentioned by Burritt, July 8, 1892; also in appeal of stockmen to the governor for martial law, Mercer, pp. 108–11; Rankin papers.

[2] Charlie Taylor: Burritt letters; Chicago *Herald*, April 19 and 25, 1892; *Leader*, July 31, 1892.

Ed Starr: Brock papers; frequent references in the Rankin papers, especially during the latter part of 1892; Cheyenne *Sun*, July 26, 1892.

[3] Henry Smith: Thelma Condit in *Annals of Wyoming* (April 1958) and to author; Owen Wister letters and diaries in *Owen Wister Out West*, pp. 117–18; and Cheyenne *Leader*, November 23, 1893.

[4] The gathering at Powder River Crossing was famous, because it was the basis of the federal conspiracy charges which later came to nothing. There are numerous references to it in the Rankin papers and also in the Cheyenne press, especially August 1892. Also Thelma Condit manuscript.

[5] The story of the events immediately following Wellman's death is told at great length in Burritt's letters of May 14 and 15.

[6] Burritt to W. R. Stoll, May 22, 1892, quoting the Denver *Rocky Mountain News*, May 19; also Burritt, May 14; Buffalo *Bulletin*, May 26; Mercer's *Banditti*, p. 112. On the congregations of armed men there is much in the Rankin reports.

[7] Rankin papers: Senator Carey to Attorney General, July 1, 1892, and U.S. Attorney Benjamin F. Fowler to Attorney General, September 16, describing Hathaway's removal and confession. The hearing in Cheyenne at which he testified to the identity of the three killers was in the case of one Frank Smith, a sad-sack fringe member of the Red Sash gang who couldn't afford to buy a red sash, at worst a very minor accomplice in the Wellman killing and proved guilty of nothing but some foolish talk. But he was kept in jail for five months, being unable to furnish bail, on one after another of the innumerable conspiracy charges.

Hathaway's testimony is in the *Leader*, August 24.

[8] Department of Justice correspondence, letters from B. F. Fowler, January 11 through April 12, 1893.

[9] Henry Smith trial, *Leader*, November 22, 1893; November 23, with editorial and interview; Cheyenne *Sun*, November 18, 20, and 22.

[10] Tape recording of Martin A. Tisdale interview, December 1952, courtesy Mrs. Frank T. Hinckley. Buffalo *Bulletin*, May 18, 1961. The gun is in the Buffalo museum today.

Chapter 35 THE PLOT THAT FAILED

The almost incredible plot to foist martial law on northern Wyoming or, if that failed, some other form of intervention by federal troops, with resultant bloodshed, was participated in by some of the state's leading citizens, including United States Senator Francis E. Warren and Judge Willis O. VanDevanter. It was discussed in the Cheyenne press off and on from early June through September; with the Republican Cheyenne *Sun* predictably beating the tom-toms for martial law and the *Leader* just as predictably denouncing the conspiracy.

But the real issues remain unclarified until one resorts to the Rankin papers in the National Archives. Rankin was selected as the "goat" in the plot that failed; he balked, and the subsequent struggle between those who wanted him fired and those who stood up for him can only be followed in the records of the Department of Justice.

[1] Wolcott's trip East: *Leader,* June 4 and 5, 1892.

[2] Failure of Washington to agree to the martial-law scheme; Lewis L. Gould to author, June 7, 1965, and Senator Warren to W. C. Irvine, July 2, 1892. For the movement of additional federal troops into Wyoming, *Leader,* July 7.

[3] All this was spelled out in scorching detail in the reports of Frank B. Crossthwaite, special examiner for the Department of Justice, who was ordered to Wyoming on September 24, 1892, to investigate the charges against Rankin. Efforts of Warren and Carey to have Rankin removed are also in the archives, September 3, 1892, seconded by the President, September 11. Also discussed in the *Leader* through September, especially on September 18, 21, 22, and 24.

[4] Remarks quoted from Crossthwaite report No. 1, November 2.

His second report is dated December 22.

[5] These events are detailed in the Cheyenne press from July 6 through August 11, the *Leader* generally being more specific. It should be unnecessary to point out that an event which took place on a given day usually appears in the paper the following day, except sometimes in the case of an afternoon paper.

Roamings of the nominal prisoners: *Leader* for August 3, 5, and 11 (the last an editorial).

Judge Blake's letter to Governor Barber is quoted by both David (p. 336) and Mercer (pp. 122–23). I did not succeed in finding it in the newspapers.

Chapter 36 GEORGE DUNNING: AN ANGRY MAN

[1] I am deeply indebted to Mr. Oliver Gray Norval of Buffalo, Wyoming, who in 1960 revealed the existence of certain letters and papers concerning George Dunning, which had been bequeathed to him by Sheriff W. G. Angus of Buffalo and which confirm the most important features of the Dunning story.

I am also indebted to Mr. Jerry E. Stanke of Nampa, Idaho, president of the Owyhee County Historical Society and a mountain climber and chess player besides, who went to great effort on my behalf to assemble previously unpublished facts on George Dunning's family and his personal background.

These two sources go a long way toward filling out the gaps in our knowledge of George Dunning.

[2] Information supplied by the University of Michigan to Jerry Stanke.

[3] In describing his conversation with Ijams Dunning wrote (p. 162): "Ijams said it would be necessary for him to return immediately to Cheyenne and confer with two other men who were officers in the stock association," etc.

The text of Ijams' first letter follows:

Office of
BOARD OF LIVE STOCK COMMISSIONERS
Of Wyoming

Cheyenne March 13 92

Geo. Dunning
Silver City Idaho
Dear Sir:

I find on arrival here that both of the men whom I should consult are out of town. But I take the responsibility of saying to you that we will want you and the other man of whom you spoke to come. I wish you could get three more men that you will be willing to work with to come with you, making five all told in your party. I believe this would be best as it is possible that after the first part of the work is accomplished, that it may be necessary to divide your work. Then if there were five of you in your party you could take your men and take a part of the work with your own party. So if you can at once get three more men that will satisfy you get them. I will write you again so it will arrive in Silver City on the evening of the 19th, telling you just when to come and when the money will be with Montie B. Gwinn at Caldwell to defray all expenses.

Yours truly
H. B. Ijams

The reiterated insistence on a party of five men, in each of Ijams' three letters to Dunning, and the references to "the first part of the work," and "dividing the work," go far to confirm Dunning's statement that the plan was, after the attack on Buffalo, to break up into smaller hanging parties of five men each and so proceed through the country.

[4] The removal of George Dunning from the Buffalo jail and the vain efforts of Charles Burritt to locate him are told in the Burritt letters, May 4 and June 15 and 18, 1892.

Chapter 37 THE AUTHOR OF "THE BANDITTI"

Lewis L. Gould has dispelled some of the myths about Mercer and brought out little-known facts in "A. S. Mercer and the Johnson County War: A Reappraisal," appearing in *Arizona and the West* (Spring 1965).

N. Orwin Rush studied Mercer's career in two publications, both of which missed several aspects. "Mercer's Banditti of the Plains," a short monograph, was published by the library of Florida State University in 1961. An article with the same title had previously appeared in *The Westerners' New York Posse Brand Book* (New York, 1960), Vol. VII, No. 3.

The two publications will be referred to as Rush, monograph, and Rush, brand book.

[1] One of the Mercer mysteries concerns the disappearance of the files of the *Northwestern Livestock Journal*, with the exception of one bound volume for 1887, and scattered issues in the Bancroft Library. His prohanging editorial was reprinted in the Laramie *Daily Boomerang* for August 31, 1889.

[2] Lewis L. Gould in *Arizona and the West* (Spring 1965), 10–12.

[3] While the original of Mercer's editorial is lost along with the rest of the 1892 files, it was reprinted almost verbatim in the *Leader* of July 8. The story of Kimball's arrest and incarceration is told in the *Leader* for June 8 and 9 and July 3.

[4] The assault was reported in the *Leader* August 23 in an interview with Mercer. But the text of his editorial attack on John Clay, which provoked it, is found in the Chicago *Herald* two months later when Clay decided to sue for libel. See below.

[5] The story of the seizure appears in both the *Leader* and the *Sun* for October 18. Judge VanDevanter's editorial was unsigned, but Lewis Gould is authority for the statement that he was the author.

⁶ The double-barreled libel action against Mercer was detailed in a column story on an inside page of the Chicago *Herald*, October 27, which also quotes his editorial. The case was put over to November 6, but a minute item on p. 5, that date, reveals that it was again continued, after which it virtually disappeared from the Chicago paper, but it is clear from other sources that both of Clay's suits were dropped or dismissed.

⁷ The charge that the Dunning edition of the *Livestock Journal* was held up by the post office rests on Mercer's own statement, p. 151. Since there is no confirmation, its veracity has been questioned. However, it accords with the known methods of the cattlemen and their influence. Ranchmen riding twenty miles; *Leader* editorial, October 27.

⁸ Gould, p. 18.

⁹ No record of court action: Gould, p. 19, footnote. Family says printing plant never burned: Rush brand book, p. 63, col. 2.

¹⁰ Printed in Denver: Rush monograph, pp. 10–11. There were also references in the contemporary press.

¹¹ First and only printing 1000 copies: Rush monograph, p. 25, quoting Mercer children Mrs. Lou Webb and Ralph Mercer. The selling trip of Mercer and his boys, or at least of the boys, is well authenticated, as the late Ralph Mercer told both Rush and this writer about it. It was also referred to in the local press; Gould, p. 19. The story of a shipment of 500 copies to Sheridan occurs in the Rush monograph, p. 25. It passes this writer's test of reasonable credibility in that it is specific as to name, place, and date—"Burlington railroad station—Mr. J. C. Jackson of the Mills Stationery Store—1909"—and the exact disposal price.

¹² Both versions of the mishap to the second printing are supplied by Rush, based on interviews with the Mercer family. Rush, however, gives two different versions of what they told him in his two publications appearing a year apart; in the monograph, p. 10; and the Brand Book article, p. 63, col. 2.

¹³ Move to Hyattsville, Ralph Mercer to writer in 1962. Failure to mention the Johnson County war, Gould, p. 20, footnote.

¹⁴ Dick Mohr of International Bookfinders, Beverly Hills, California, was able to scare up two additional copies to satisfy these requests. He has had only four copies for sale in ten years.

EPILOGUE

¹ *Leader*, January 3 through 22; *Sun*, January 22.

² Mercer, pp. 140–41, and a statement by Dr. William A. Hendricks of Douglas, Wyoming, in the Wyoming University archives.

By 1897 the red-walled valley of Buffalo creek, tributary to Powder River and now known as the Hole in the Wall, had become the headquarters of a gang of bank and train robbers famed as the "Wild Bunch." A few local boys had the bad judgment to "throw in" with some members of this gang so far as stealing cattle was concerned, and they preyed on the herds of Judge Carey's CY outfit, south on the Platte. In midsummer of 1897 Bob Divine, the CY foreman—bearded and past fifty, one of the best cow foremen who ever lived—rode into the Hole in the Wall at the head of a group of men to bring back stolen CY cattle. A young rustler died—the victim of youthful bravado, and a sad story it was too—see the writer's "The Truth About the Hole in the Wall Fight," in *Montana* magazine (Summer 1961). But this was five years after the invasion and had nothing to do with it.

³ The sudden change in the attitude toward cattle-stealing is reflected in the letters of lawyer Burritt, the cow-country Boswell, for July 3, July 8, November 2, and December 2, 1892, and January 10, 1893. Burritt's tributes to Angus during this period—which had started earlier—should be enough to settle the question of Angus' reputation for honesty.

⁴ *Leader*, June 29, 1892.

BIBLIOGRAPHY

I. Books

Abbott, E. C. and Helena Huntington Smith. *We Pointed Them North.* Farrar and Rinehart, 1939; Oklahoma University Press, 1955.

Athearn, Robert G. *High Country Empire.* McGraw-Hill Book Company, 1960.

————. *Westward the Briton.* Charles Scribner's Sons, 1953.

Atherton, Lewis. *The Cattle Kings.* Indiana University Press, 1961.

Baillie-Grohman, William A. *Camps in the Rockies.* Charles Scribner's Sons, 1884.

Bartlett, I. S. *History of Wyoming.* The S. J. Clarke Publishing Company (Chicago), 1918.

Beach, Mrs. Alfred H. (Cora M.). *Women of Wyoming.* S. E. Boyer and Company (Casper, Wyoming).

Beard, Frances Birkhead. *Wyoming from Territorial Days to the Present.* American Historical Society, Inc. (Chicago and New York), 1933.

Billington, Ray Allen. *Westward Expansion.* The Macmillan Company, 1949.

Bratt, John. *Trails of Yesterday.* University Publishing Company, 1921.

Briggs, Harold E. *Frontiers of the Northwest.* D. Appleton-Century, 1940.

Brisbin, Gen. James S., USA. *The Beef Bonanza, or How to Get Rich on the Plains.* J. B. Lippincott and Company, 1881.

Burns, Robert Homer, Andrew Springs Gillespie and Willing Gay Richardson. *Wyoming's Pioneer Ranches.* Top-of-the-World Press (Laramie, Wyoming), 1955.

Burt, Struthers. *Powder River.* Farrar and Rinehart, 1938.

Canton, Frank M. *Frontier Trails,* edited by Edward Everett Dale. Houghton Mifflin Company, 1930.

Chatterton, Fenimore. *Yesterday's Wyoming.* Powder River Publishers and Booksellers (Aurora, Colorado), 1957.

Chrisman, Harry. *The Ladder of Rivers.* Sage Books (Denver), 1962.

————. *Lost Trails of the Cimarron.* Sage Books (Denver), 1961.

Clay, John. *My Life on the Range.* Privately printed, Chicago, 1924. Later edition, with index, University of Oklahoma Press, 1962. (The page references given in this book are to the early edition.)

Clover, Sam T. *On Special Assignment.* Lothrop Publishing Company (Boston), 1903.

Cox, James. *Historical and Biographical Record of the Cattle Industry and the Cattlemen of Texas and Adjacent Territory.* Woodward and Tiernan Printing Company (St. Louis), 1895.

Craig, John R. *Ranching with Lords and Commons.* William Briggs (Toronto), 1903.

Cunningham, Eugene. *Triggernometry.* The Press of the Pioneers (New York), 1934.

Dale, Edward Everett. *The Range Cattle Industry.* University of Oklahoma Press, 1930.

David, Robert B. *Malcolm Campbell, Sheriff.* Wyomingana, Inc. (Casper), 1932.

Dick, Everett. *The Sod House Frontier.* D. Appleton-Century, 1937.

————. *The Story of the Frontier.* D. Appleton-Century, 1941.

Digby, Margaret. *Horace Plunkett; an Anglo-American Irishman.* Basil Blackwell (Oxford), 1949.

Flagg, O. H. *A Review of the Cattle Business in Johnson County, Wyoming since 1882, and the Causes That Led to the Recent Invasion.* Serialized in the Buffalo (Wyoming) *Bulletin,* May 5–July 14, 1892.

Fletcher, Robert H. *Free Grass to Fences.* University Publishers (New York), 1960.

Frewen, Moreton. *Melton Mowbray and Other Memories.* H. Jenkins Ltd. (London), 1924.

Frink, Maurice. *Cow Country Cavalcade: Eighty Years of the Wyoming Stock Growers' Association.* Old West Publishing Company (Denver), 1954.

————. *When Grass Was King,* in collaboration with W. Turrentine Jackson and Agnes Wright Spring. University of Colorado Press, 1956.

Gard, Wayne. *Frontier Justice.* University of Oklahoma Press, 1949.

Guernsey, Charles Arthur. *Wyoming Cowboy Days.* G. P. Putnam's Sons, 1936.

Hagedorn, Hermann. *Roosevelt in the Badlands.* Houghton Mifflin Company, 1921.

Haley, J. Evetts. *Charles Goodnight.* Houghton Mifflin Company, 1936.

Hebard, Grace Raymond and E. A. Brininstool. *The Bozeman Trail.* The Arthur H. Clark Company (Glendale, California), 1922.

Hibbard, Benjamin Horace. *A History of the Public Land Policies.* The Macmillan Company, 1924.

Howard, Joseph Kinsey. *Montana, High, Wide and Handsome.* Yale University Press, 1943.

James, W. S. *Cowboy Life in Texas; or 27 Years a Mavrick* [sic] Donahue, Henneberry and Company (New York), 1893.

Lang, Lincoln A. *Ranching with Roosevelt.* J. B. Lippincott Company, 1926.

LeFors, Joe. *Wyoming Peace Officer.* Laramie Printers, Inc. (Laramie, Wyoming), 1953.

Mercer, A[sa] S[hinn]. *The Banditti of the Plains; or the Cattlemen's Invasion of Wyoming in 1892 (The Crowning Infamy of the Ages).* Cheyenne, Wyoming, 1894. Privately printed.

————. *The Banditti of the Plains ...,* with a foreword by James M. Clarke. Grabhorn Press (San Francisco), 1935.

————. *The Banditti of the Plains ...,* foreword by William H. Kittrell. Oklahoma University Press, 1954. Page references in this book are to the Oklahoma edition.

Mokler, Alfred James. *History of Natrona County, Wyoming, 1888–1922.* The Lakeside Press (Chicago), 1923.

Osgood, Ernest Staples. *The Day of the Cattleman.* University of Minnesota Press, 1929.

Paxson, Frederic L. *The Last American Frontier.* The Macmillan Company, 1910.

Pelzer, Louis. *The Cattlemen's Frontier*. The Arthur H. Clark Company (Glendale, California), 1936.

Raine, William McLeod. *Famous Sheriffs and Western Outlaws*. The New Home Library (New York), 1944.

———— and Will C. Barnes. *Cattle*. Doubleday, Doran, and Co., 1930.

Richthofen, Walter, Baron von. *Cattle-Raising on the Plains of North America*. D. Appleton and Co., 1885.

Roosevelt, Theodore. *An Autobiography*. Charles Scribner's Sons, 1913.

————. *Cowboys and Kings: Three Great Letters by Theodore Roosevelt*. Harvard University Press, 1954.

————. *The Wilderness Hunter*. G. P. Putnam's Sons, 1893.

Rush, N. Orwin. *Mercer's Banditti of the Plains*. Florida State University Library (Tallahassee), 1961.

Sandoz, Mari. *The Cattlemen*. Hastings House, 1958.

Siringo, Charles. *Two Evil Isms*. Published by author, Chicago, 1915.

Spring, Agnes Wright. *Seventy Years: a Panoramic History of the Wyoming Stock Growers' Association*. Cheyenne, 1942.

Strahorn, Robert E. *Handbook of Wyoming and Guide to the Black Hills and Big Horn Regions*. Cheyenne, 1877.

Stuart, Granville. *Forty Years on the Frontier*. Arthur H. Clarke Co. (Cleveland), 1925.

Timmons, William. *Twilight on the Range*. University of Texas Press, 1962.

Webb, Walter Prescott. *The Great Plains*. Ginn & Co., 1921.

II. SHORT PUBLICATIONS

Baker, E. D. "A Rustler's Account of the Johnson County War," in the *Westerners' Brand Book, 1945–46*, Chicago Posse, 1947.

Brayer, Herbert O. "New Light on the Johnson County War," in the *Westerners' Brand Book*, Chicago, February 1953.

————. "Range Country Troubles, 1885," in *The Westerners' Brand Book*, Denver, March 1952.

————. "The 76 Ranch on the Powder River," in *The Westerners' Brand Book*, Chicago, December, 1950.

————. "When Dukes Went West," in the *1948 Brand Book*, The Westerners, Denver. (This was an annual edition.)

Brock, J. Elmer. "A Timely Arrival," in *Annals of Wyoming* (January 1943), 63.

————. "Who Dry-Gulched the Hoe Ranch Foreman?", in *The Denver Westerners' Brand Book*, IX (1953), The Denver Westerners, 1954.

Condit, Thelma Gatchell. "The Hole in the Wall," in *Annals of Wyoming*, (October 1955 and April 1957).

Ellis, Olive Herman. "Robert Foote," in *Annals of Wyoming* (January 1943).

Fletcher, Robert S. "That Hard Winter in Montana," in *Agricultural History* (October 1930), 123.

Gould, Lewis L. "A. S. Mercer and the Johnson County War: a Reappraisal" in *Arizona and the West* (Spring 1965).

Hebard, Grace R. "Teaching Wyoming History by Counties," State of Wyoming, Department of Education, 1926.

Holden, W. C. "The Problem of Stealing on the Spur Ranch," in *West Texas Historical Association Yearbook* (June 1932).

Jackson, W. Turrentine. "The Administration of Thomas Moonlight, 1887–1889," in *Annals of Wyoming* (July 1946).

———. "The Wyoming Stock Growers' Association; Political Power in Wyoming Territory, 1873–90," in the *Mississippi Valley Historical Review* (March 1947).

———. "The Wyoming Stock Growers' Association; Its Years of Temporary Decline, 1886–1890," in *Agricultural History* (October 1948).

Larson, Alfred (T.A.). "The Winter of 1886–87 in Wyoming," in *Annals of Wyoming* (January 1942).

———. "Wyoming," in *Encyclopedia Americana*, 1961 edition.

Lindsay, Charles. "The Big Horn Basin," in *Nebraska University Studies* (1928–29).

Lott, Howard B. "Diary of Major Wise, Hunting Trip in Powder River Country in 1880," in *Annals of Wyoming* (April 1940).

———. "The Old Occidental," in *Annals of Wyoming* (April 1955).

Mattison, Ray H. "Roosevelt and the Stockmen's Association," in *North Dakota History* (April and July 1950).

Paxson, Frederic L. "The Cow Country," in *American Historical Review* (October 1916).

Rush, N. Orwin. "The Banditti of the Plains," in *The Westerners' New York Posse Brand Book*, New York, 1961.

Spring, Agnes Wright. "Carey Story Is a Wyoming Saga," in *The Hereford Journal* (July 15, 1938).

III. LETTERS, MANUSCRIPT COLLECTIONS, THESES

Angus, W. G., Papers, in the hands of Oliver G. Norval of Buffalo, Wyoming.

Brock, J. Elmer. Papers in private hands and in the custody of the Western History Research Center, University of Wyoming, Laramie. A portion of the Brock papers are in a sealed envelope marked *Not to be opened until 1973*.

Burritt, Charles H., Letters. Originals in the Johnson County Museum, Buffalo, Wyoming; transcripts in the Western History Research Center at Laramie.

Frewen, Moreton. Papers in Manuscript Division, Library of Congress, Washington, D.C.

Penrose, Dr. Charles B. Correspondence and memoir at the Western History Research Center, Laramie, Wyoming.

Van Valkenburgh, Lois. "The Papers of Dr. Charles Bingham Penrose in the Library of the University of Wyoming"; MA thesis, 1939.

Wyoming Stock Growers' Association. Papers at the Western History Research Center.

IV. NEWSPAPERS

(Published in Wyoming except where otherwise indicated; dates indicated in text or footnotes.)

Buffalo *Bulletin*
Buffalo *Echo*
Carbon County Journal (Rawlins)
Casper *Weekly Mail*
Cheyenne *Daily Leader* and *Weekly Leader*
Cheyenne *Daily Sun* and *Weekly Sun*
Chicago *Herald* (Illinois)
Denver *Republican* (Colorado)
Denver *Times* (Colorado)
Laramie *Daily Boomerang* and *Weekly Boomerang*
New York *World* (New York)
Northwestern Livestock Journal
Omaha *Daily Bee* (Nebraska)
People's Voice, later the Buffalo *Voice*
Rocky Mountain News (Denver, Colorado) later the Denver *Daily News*

v. Public Documents and Records

Wyoming:

Compiled Laws of Wyoming 1876
Revised Statutes of Wyoming in Force January 1, 1887
Session Laws of Wyoming Territory, 8th Legislative Assembly, 1884
Session Laws of Wyoming Territory, 10th Legislative Assembly, 1888
Session Laws of Wyoming Territory, 11th Legislative Assembly, 1890
Session Laws of the State of Wyoming, First State Legislature, 1890–91
Wyoming (Territory) Governor, Reports to the Secretary of the Interior, 1885–90

Federal:

House Executive Document # 232, 50th Congress, First Session (1886–87)
Report of the Commissioner of the General Land Office (Andrew Jackson Sparks), 1885, 1886
United States Census Office: Reports: 11th Census, 1890
United States Department of Agriculture, *1941 Yearbook of Agriculture*, "Climate and Man"

About the Author

Helena Huntington Smith was born in Peekskill, New York, of New England ancestry and went to Smith College. Possibly because of the contrast with this highly proper background, a trip to Glacier Park, Montana, at the age of twenty-one revolutionized her life. A lucky chance eventually led to her meeting with E. C. Abbott, known to many a real-life cowboy fan as "Teddy Blue," with whom she wrote *We Pointed Them North: Recollections of a Cowpuncher*. Later she co-authored the reminiscences of another pioneer of the rip-roaring early '80's, Nannie Tiffany Alderson, in *A Bride Goes West*. Between Western trips she had two children, both now grown, and accumulated much magazine writing experience, including war correspondence for Crowell-Collier in 1944–45.

Her official residence is Alexandria, Virginia—across the Potomac from Washington, D.C.

Veterans of Foreign Wars
Roy Eaton Post and
Auxiliary # 1560.
Bulletin #7.   758 Broadway
                        Sheridan
B.E. Chastain Publisher Wyo
227 E College.
Sheridan, Wyo 82801